Eighth
Edition

THE MANAGER'S BOOKSHELF

A Mosaic of Contemporary Views

RELEASED

Jon L. Pierce

University of Minnesota Duluth

John W. Newstrom

University of Minnesota Duluth

PEARSON
Prentice
Hall

UPPER SADDLE RIVER, NJ 07458

Library of Congress Cataloging-in-Publication Data

The manager's bookshelf : a mosaic of contemporary views / [collected by]
Jon L. Pierce, John W. Newstrom.—8th Ed.

    p. cm.

Includes bibliographical references and index.

ISBN 978-0-13-230165-7 (pbk. : alk. paper)

1. Management literature—United States. I. Pierce, Jon L. (Jon Lepley)
II. Newstrom, John W.

HD70.U5M32 2007

658—ßdc22

2007018320

Editor-in-Chief: David Parker
Acquisitions Editor: Michael Ablassmeir
Product Development Manager: Ashley Santora
Project Manager, Editorial: Keri Molinari
Editorial Assistant: Kristen Varina
Marketing Manager: Jodi Bassett
Marketing Assistant: Susan Osterlitz
Managing Editor: Renata Butera
Project Manager, Production: Angela Pica
Permissions Project Manager: Charles Morris
Senior Operations Supervisor: Arnold Vila
Operations Specialist: Michelle Klein
Central Publishing Creative Director: Jayne Conte
Cover Design: Bruce Kenselaar
Cover Illustration/Photo: Adam Jones/Photodisc Red/Getty Images, Inc.
Composition: Laserwords
Full-Service Project Management: BookMasters, Inc.
Printer/Binder: RR Donnelley–Harrisonburg
Typeface: 10/12 Times Ten

Credits and acknowledgments borrowed from other sources and reproduced, with
permission, in this textbook appear on the appropriate page within the text.

Pearson Education LTD.
Pearson Education Singapore, Pte. Ltd
Pearson Education, Canada, Ltd
Pearson Education–Japan

Pearson Education Australia PTY, Limited
Pearson Education North Asia Ltd
Pearson Educación de Mexico, S.A. de C.V.
Pearson Education Malaysia, Pte. Ltd.

10 9 8 7 6 5 4 3 2 1
ISBN-13: 978-0-13-230165-7
ISBN-10: 0-13-230165-2

We dedicate this book to our beloved grandchildren—Madison, Peter, Eric, Sawyer, William, and Ruth Lillian—who give us great hope for the future.

Brief Contents

Contents

Preface

The last three decades were marked by a proliferation of books published on topics in management, leadership, and various organizational issues. This explosion of products reflects an intense and continuing fascination by managers, future managers, and the general public with the inner workings of organizations and their managers, work teams and their leaders, and employees. Bookstores around the country and distribution sources on the Internet continue to offer a large number of management books, and many of these books have appeared on various "best-seller" lists—some remaining there for months and years at a time. Clearly, managers and others (including business school students at both graduate and undergraduate levels, as well as liberal arts students who are headed for a career in business or public organizations) remain intrigued by, and are searching for insights and answers in, the popular business literature.

We prepared *The Manager's Bookshelf: A Mosaic of Contemporary Views* to serve the needs of both managers and management students. A significant number of individuals in both of these groups do not have sufficient time to read widely, yet many find themselves involved in conversations where someone else refers to ideas such as vision, self-directed work teams, ethics, "flow," organizational politics, civility, or cultural intelligence. We believe that a laudable and critical goal for managers, as well as all students of management, is to remain current in their understanding of the views being expressed about organizational and management practices. To help you become a better-informed organizational citizen, we prepared *The Manager's Bookshelf,* which introduces you to more than 50 popular management books—both recent and "classic."

The Manager's Bookshelf, as a book of concise **summaries**, does not express the views of just one individual on the management of organizations, nor does it attempt to integrate the views of several dozen authors. Instead, *this book is a collage*—a composite portrait constructed from a variety of sources. It provides you with insights into many aspects of organizational management from the perspectives of a diverse and sometimes provocative group of management writers, including some highly regarded authors such as Peter Drucker, James Collins, Thomas Friedman, Edward Lawler III, Malcolm Gladwell, Chris Argyris, Stephen Covey, Douglas McGregor, Clayton Christensen, Spencer Johnson, Thomas Peters, Michael Porter, and Peter Senge. Through this collection we will introduce you to the thoughts, philosophies, views, and experiences of a number of authors whose works have caught the attention of today's management community—and often captivated them in the process.

This book contains a rich array of pieces. From a topical perspective, its inclusions focus on motivation, ethics, global perspectives, environmental trends, inclusiveness, corporate strategy, leadership styles, and other key concerns of managers. This collection includes the views from a variety of individuals, including practitioners (e.g., Bill George), philosophers (e.g., Peter Drucker), management consultants (e.g., Tom Peters and Marcus Buckingham), and organizational scholars (e.g., Karl Weick and Alfred Marcus). The selections reflect a wide variety in terms of their tone and tenor, as well as the diverse bases for their conclusions. Indeed, critics have praised some of the authors' works as passionate, invaluable, stimulating, and insightful, whereas other business books have been attacked as being overly academic, superficial, redundant, glib, or unrealistic.

The nature and source of the ideas expressed in this collection are diverse. Some inclusions are prescriptive in nature, whereas others are more dispassionately descriptive; some are thoughtful and philosophical, whereas others limit themselves to reporting directly on their personal or organizational experiences; some of these works represent armchair speculation, whereas others are based on empirical study. Finally, the selections take a variety of forms. Some of the readings are excerpts extracted from the original book, some are articles written by the book's author in which part of their overall perspective on management is revealed, while the majority of the inclusions are objective summaries of popular books that have been specially prepared for inclusion in *The Manager's Bookshelf.*

This mosaic of readings can provide you with useful insights, evoke your own reflective thinking, and spark stimulating dialogue with your colleagues about the management of today's organizations. We expect that these readings will prompt you to raise questions of yourself and your peers about the viability of many of the ideas expressed by these authors regarding the practice of organizational management. We hope and predict that these readings will prompt you to read the full text of many of the authors' works; these books often contain rich anecdotes, compelling stories, provocative assertions, and detailed data that are not possible to include in our summaries. Finally, we hope that these summaries will encourage you to continue your managerial self-development through a variety of avenues, including ongoing reading of both the popular and scientific (research-based) literature. If these goals are met, our purpose for assembling this collection will be realized.

Acknowledgments

We would like to express our sincere and very warm appreciation to several colleagues who played key roles in the preparation of this edition of *The Manager's Bookshelf: A Mosaic of Contemporary Views.* Their commitment and dedication to students of organizations and management, coupled with their efforts, made this improved and updated edition possible.

We would also like to single out our late friend and colleague Larry L. Cummings (Carlson School of Management at the University of Minnesota and "The Institute") for his "reflections on the best-sellers" contained in the introduction to our book. We thank Larry for taking the time to reflect on this part of the organization and management literature and to offer his insightful observations on this genre of books. He will always be remembered and valued for his intellectual contributions and for his friendship. We also value the additional comments provided on managerial "best-sellers" offered by Brad Jackson and Anne Cummings, which greatly enrich the discussion in that section.

CONTRIBUTORS TO THIS EDITION

We would like to express our appreciation to a number of individuals who provided us with a great deal of assistance and support for the preparation of this book. Many of our management colleagues, former students, and professional managerial associates took the time and effort—always under tight time pressures—to contribute to this book by carefully reading and preparing a summary of one of the selected books. Many of these individuals wanted to offer their personal opinion, add their endorsements or criticisms, and surface elements of their own management philosophies, but at our urging they stuck to their task. To them we express our thanks for their time, energy, and commitment to furthering management education.

The following individuals prepared book summaries for this edition of *The Manager's Bookshelf:*

Introduction

Kelly Nelson, AK Steel—Argyris's *Flawed Advice and the Management Trap*

Best-Seller "Classics"

John D. Stavig and Shaker A. Zahra, University of Minnesota—Drucker's *The Practice of Management*

William B. Gartner, Georgetown University, and **M. James Naughton**, Expert-Knowledge Systems, Inc.—Deming's *Out of the Crisis*
Gayle Porter, Rutgers University—McGregor's *The Human Side of Enterprise*
Dorothy Marcic, Vanderbilt University—Senge's *The Fifth Discipline*
Sara A. Morris, Old Dominion University—Porter's *Competitive Advantage*

High-Performing Organizations

Kristie J. Loescher, University of Texas at Austin—Buckingham's *The One Thing You Need to Know About Great Managing, Great Leading, and Sustained Individual Success*
Allen Harmon, University of Minnesota Duluth and WDSE-TV—Marcus'
Big Winners and Big Losers
Christopher R. Steele, formerly with Best Buy Co.—Weick and Sutcliffe's *Managing the Unexpected*
Stephen Rubenfeld, University of Minnesota Duluth—Cascio's *Responsible Restructuring*

Organizational Strategy and Execution

Sanjay Goel, University of Minnesota Duluth—Kaplan and Porter's *The Strategy-Focused Organization*
Christian F. Edwardson—Bossidy, Charan, and Burck's *Execution*
Allen Harmon, University of Minnesota Duluth and WDSE-TV—Joyce, Nohria, and Roberson's *What (Really) Works*

Focusing on The Human Dimension

Danielle DuBois Kerr, Uponor, Inc.—Lawler's *Treat People Right!*
Jannifer David, University of Minnesota Duluth—Ventrice's *Make Their Day!*
Kelly Nelson, AK Steel—Csikszentmihalyi's *Good Business*
Gary Stark, Northern Michigan University—Lawrence and Nohria's *Driven*

Motivation

Shelley Ovrom, City of Azusa—Sirota, Mischkind, and Meltzer's *The Enthusiastic Employee*
Shannon Studden, North Shore Mining Company—Thomas' *Intrinsic Motivation at Work*
AnneMarie Kaul, American Red Cross—Katzenbach's *Why Pride Matters More than Money*

Teams and Teamwork

Shannon Studden, North Shore Mining Company—LaFasto and Carlson's *When Teams Work Best*
Katherine A. Karl, Marshall University—Hackman's *Leading Teams*
David L. Beal, formerly with Consolidated Papers, Inc.—Beyerlein, Freedman, McGee, and Moran's *Beyond Teams*

Leadership

John Kratz, University of Minnesota Duluth—Goleman, Boyatzis, and McKee's *Primal Leadership*
Rebecca M. Carlson, Piper Jaffray—Dean's *Leadership for Everyone*
Warren Candy, Allete/Minnesota Power—Kellerman's *Bad Leadership*

Thinking Inclusively and Acting Civilly

Kristina Bourne, University of Wisconsin at Eau Claire—Miller and Katz' *The Inclusion Breakthrough*
Linda Hefferin, Elgin Community College—Winfeld's *Straight Talk about Gays in the Workplace*
Kelly Nelson, AK Steel—Forni's *Choosing Civility*

Organizational Change

Peter Stark, University of Minnesota Duluth—Quinn's *Building the Bridge as You Walk On It*
Warren Candy, Allete/Minnesota Power—Christensen, Raynor, and Anthony's *The Innovator's Solution*
Martha Golden, University of Minnesota Duluth/Wintergreen Northern Wear—Lawler & Worley's *Built to Change*

Intra-Organizational Dynamics

Cathy Hanson, City of Azusa—Kleiner's *Who Really Matters*
AnneMarie Kaul, American Red Cross—Reardon's *It's All Politics*

Managerial Decision Making

Paul C. Nutt, The Ohio State University—Nutt's *Why Decisions Fail*
Linda Rochford, University of Minnesota Duluth—Murnighan and Mowen's *The Art of High-Stakes Decision-Making*
Cheri Stine, Stampin' Up!—Gladwell's *Blink!*

Ethics and Values

Adam Surma, Target Corporation—Lennick and Kiel's *Moral Intelligence*
Gary P. Olson, Center for Alcohol and Drug Treatment—Batstone's *Saving the Corporate Soul & (Who Knows?) Maybe Your Own*
Stephen B. Castleberry, University of Minnesota Duluth—Bennis and Thomas' *Geeks & Geezers*
Randy Skalberg, University of Minnesota Duluth—George's *Authentic Leadership*

Emotions at Work

Beverly Frahm, Frahm Consulting—Boyatzis and McKee's *Resonant Leadership*
Gary J. Colpaert, Milwaukee's Eye Institute—Frost's *Toxic Emotions at Work*

Cathy A. Hanson, City of Azusa—Seligman's *Authentic Happiness*
Gary P. Olson, Center for Alcohol and Drug Treatment—Pattakos' *Prisoners of Our Thoughts*

Emerging Dimensions of Organizational Environments

Stephen Rubenfeld, University of Minnesota Duluth—Friedman's *The World is Flat*
Robert Stine, University of Minnesota College of Natural Resources—Robbins' *Greening The Corporation*
Sanjay Goel, University of Minnesota Duluth—Thomas and Inkson's *Cultural Intelligence*

Management Fables and Lessons for Personal Success

Charles C. Manz, University of Massachusetts, Amherst—Blanchard and Johnson's *The One Minute Manager*
Gary Stark, Northern Michigan University—Johnson's *Who Moved My Cheese?*
David L. Beal, formerly with Consolidated Papers, Inc.—Covey's *The 8th Habit*

In addition to those who provided constructive feedback on previous editions, we appreciate the recommendations for inclusions in this eighth edition made by several reviewers, adopters, and friends. To Connie Johnson, who provided always-patient administrative support, we want to say "Thank you" for helping us complete this project in a timely fashion. We appreciate the supportive environment provided by Dean Kjell Knudsen and our colleagues in the Department of Management Studies here at the University of Minnesota Duluth. We especially appreciate the continued project commitment from Jeff Shelstad and the editorial support and assistance that we have received from Melissa Pellerano and Keri Molinari, all at Prentice Hall.

Jon L. Pierce
John W. Newstrom

About the Editors

Jon L. Pierce is a Morse-Alumni Distinguished Teaching Professor of Management and Organization in the Labovitz School of Business and Economics at the University of Minnesota Duluth (UMD). He received his Ph.D. in management and organizational studies at the University of Wisconsin-Madison. He is the author of more than 60 papers that have been published or presented at various professional conferences. His publications have appeared in the *Academy of Management Journal, Academy of Management Review, Journal of Management, Journal of Organizational Behavior, Journal of Applied Behavioral Science, Journal of Social Psychology, Journal of Occupational and Organizational Psychology, Organizational Dynamics, Organizational Behavior and Human Decision Processes, Personnel Psychology*, and *Review of General Psychology*. His research interests include sources of psychological ownership, employee ownership systems, and organization-based self-esteem. He has served on the editorial review board for the *Academy of Management Journal, Personnel Psychology, Journal of Management*, and the *Scandinavian Management Journal*. He is the co-author of six other books—*Management, Managing, Management and Organizational Behavior: An Integrated Perspective*, and along with John W. Newstrom, *Alternative Work Schedules, Windows into Management*, and *Leaders and the Leadership Process* (now in its fifth edition). In 2000 he was inducted into the Academy of Management Journals' Hall of Fame; in 2005 he received UMD's prestigious Chancellor's Award for Distinguished Research. Dr. Pierce may be contacted at jpierce@d.umn.edu.

John W. Newstrom is a Morse-Alumni Distinguished Teaching Professor Emeritus of Management in the Labovitz School of Business and Economics at the University of Minnesota Duluth, where he taught for 28 years. Prior to that, he completed his doctoral degree in management and industrial relations at the University of Minnesota and then taught at Arizona State University for several years. His work has appeared in publications such as *Academy of Management Executive, Personnel Psychology, California Management Review, Journal of Management, Academy of Management Journal, Business Horizons*, and the *Journal of Management Development*. He has served as an editorial reviewer for the *Academy of Management Review, Academy of Management Journal, Academy of Management Executive, Human Resource Development Quarterly, Advanced Management Journal*, and the *Journal of Management Development*. He is the author or co-author of 39 books in various editions, including *Organizational Behavior: Human Behavior at Work* (twelfth edition), *Supervision* (ninth edition), *Transfer of Training* (with Mary Broad), *Leading With a Laugh* (with Robert C. Ford), and *The Big Book of Teambuilding Games* (with Ed Scannell). He is a member of the University of Minnesota's Academy of Distinguished Teachers, and has served on the Boards of Directors for several non-profit organizations. He has also actively served as a seminar leader for leadership development programs around the country, and as a consultant to many other organizations. One of his current interests lies in helping managers create and sustain a fun work environment for their employees. Dr. Newstrom may be contacted at jnewstro@d.umn.edu.

PART

I

INTRODUCTION

Part I contains three readings. The first, *Understanding and Using the Best-Sellers*, prepared by the editors of *The Manager's Bookshelf*, provides insight into why such a large number of management-oriented books have found themselves in the downtown bookstores, on coffee tables in homes, and on the bookshelves of those who manage today's organizations. Pierce and Newstrom discuss the rationale for this mosaic of contemporary views on organizations and management, and they provide you with insight into the nature and character of *The Manager's Bookshelf*. They challenge you to read and reflect upon this collection of thoughts and experiences. They invite you to debate the ideas and philosophies that are presented here. They encourage you to let these contemporary management books stimulate your thinking, to motivate you to look more systematically into the science of organizations and management, and to provide you with the fun of learning something new.

As a result of their concern that these contemporary books will be seen as "quick and dirty" cures for organizational woes, Pierce and Newstrom encourage you to read books such as Ralph H. Kilmann's *Beyond the Quick Fix: Managing Five Tracks to Organizational Success*. In it, the author provides a valuable message, one that should serve as the backdrop to your consumption and assessment of all of the purported "one minute" cures for organizational problems and for the management of today's complex organizations. Kilmann encourages managers to stop perpetuating the myth of organizational and management simplicity and to develop a more complete and integrated approach to the management of today's complex organizations.

Many other writers have echoed these thoughts and cautions. For example:

- Jeffrey Pfeffer and Robert I. Sutton (*Harvard Business Review*, January 2006, p. 63) assert that "Executives routinely dose their organizations with strategic snake oil: discredited nostrums, partial remedies, or untested management miracle cures."
- Robert J. David and David Strand (*Academy of Management Journal*, 2006, 49:2, p. 215) assert that "Management fashions are a striking feature of contemporary organizational life (but) . . . enthusiasm soon wanes, skepticism mounts, and yesterday's panacea becomes today's run-of-the-mill application."
- Eric W. Ford and colleagues (*Academy of Management Executive*, 2005, 19:4, p. 24) contend that "rather than being interested in systematic and

long-term solutions, managers are generally infatuated with the latest fads and fashions in their search for quick fixes."

- Geoffrey Colvin (*Fortune*, June 28, 2004, p. 166), in "A Concise History of Management Hooey," suggests that "Idea-starved managers . . . were so hungry they created an entirely new phenomenon in publishing, the business bestseller."
- Danny Miller and associates (*Business Horizons*, July–August 2004, p. 7) begin their condemnation of management fads by getting right to the point: "Many popular administrative ideas are epitomized by a search for the quick fix—a simple solution that all organizations can embrace to make employees more productive, customers happier, or profits greater."
- Michael Harvey (*SAM Advanced Management Journal*, Autumn 2001, p. 37) concludes that "there is an immense wrong-headedness or slipperiness in most normative approaches" to management as portrayed in various management best-sellers.
- Eric Abrahamson (*Academy of Management Review*, January 1998, p. 263) concludes that management fashions are "cultural commodities deliberately produced by fashion setters in order to be marketed to fashion followers."
- Shari Caudron (*TD*, June 2002, p. 40) notes that the fads presented in management best-sellers are taken up with great enthusiasm for a short while and then quickly discarded. This, she suggests, is done because "the tools were sold into companies by charlatans who didn't understand the concepts but knew the right buzzwords."
- Kristine Ellis (*Training*, April 2001, p. 41) concludes that the worst of the best-sellers are promoted as "magic bullets" to solve organizational problems but often become little more than the prevailing "flavor of the month."
- Business columnist Dale Dauten (*The Arizona Republic*, February 19, 2004, p. D3) suggests that there are three types of business books on the market to avoid: the Obvious (compilations of clichéd truths), the Envious (stories of successful businesspeople), and the Obnoxious (books that insult your intelligence).
- Eileen Shapiro, author of *Fad Surfing in the Boardroom* (*Across the Board*, January 2000, p. 23), hints that most leadership books "ought to be stocked among the romance novels" of bookstores.
- Paula Phillips Carson et al. (*Academy of Management Journal*, 2000, p. 1154) conclude that the life spans of current management fashions have decreased. A rising wave of genuine concern over the quality of the content in popular business books has clearly emerged.
- Danny Miller and Jon Hartwick (*Harvard Business Review*, October 2002, p. 26) note that management fads usually have short life cycles and are quickly replaced by new ones. Typical fads, according to Miller and Hartwick, are simple, prescriptive, falsely encouraging, broadly generic, overly simplistic, closely matched to contemporary business problems, novel and fresh-appearing, and achieve their legitimacy through the status and prestige of gurus (as opposed to the merits of empirical evidence).

- Jeffrey Pfeffer (*Harvard Business Review*, February 2005, p. 54) surveyed the 30,000-plus business books in print and concluded that "Much of this advice is, at best, a waste of time. At worst, it can—if followed—create more problems than it solves."
- Another cautionary perspective is provided in *The Witch Doctors*. After systematically and objectively reviewing a wide array of popular management books, authors John Micklethwait and Adrian Wooldridge conclude that managers must become critical consumers of these products. Being critical means being suspicious of the faddish contentions, remaining unconvinced by simplistic argumentation by the authors, being selective about which theory might work for you, and becoming broadly informed about the merits and deficiencies of each proposal.

Readers interested in more comprehensive and critical portraits of the management best-seller literature are encouraged to read "Management Fads: Emergence, Evolution, and Implications for Managers" by Jane Whitney Gibson and Dana V. Tesone (*Academy of Management Executive*, 2001, 15:4, pp. 122–133) and the reviews of four books on management fads in "Resource Reviews" (*Academy of Management Learning and Education*, 2003, 2:3, pp. 313–321).

In an explicit attempt to provoke your critical thinking about management fads, we have included (as Reading 2) a summary of *Flawed Advice and the Management Trap*. Harvard professor Chris Argyris presents two models of behavior. He voices a cautionary note when it comes to the managerial advice that is presented through the "popular management" press. Much of these prescriptions, such as those presented in Stephen R. Covey's *The Seven Habits of Highly Effective People* (see Reading 4 in Part XVI) are presented as though they are sound and valid principles of management, when in fact these prescriptions cannot be tested and therefore proven correct (workable). In order to avoid the management trap that stems from the adoption of "flawed advice," Argyris offers an alternative through Model II behavior.

Argyris has received numerous awards and is the recipient of 11 honorary degrees from universities around the world. He is the James Bryant Conant Professor Emeritus of Education and Organizational Behavior at Harvard's Graduate School of Business. He has written more than 400 articles and 30 books across a 45-year career, including *The Next Challenge for Leadership: Learning, Change, and Commitment* and (with Donald Schon) *Organizational Learning: A Theory of Action Perspective*. Interested readers may wish to read the "retrospective" comments on his career by Argyris and others in the *Academy of Management Executive* (2003, 17:2, pp. 37–55).

Currently two types of voices create "messages" relevant to management education. One is the organizational scholar (e.g., Karl Weick, Edward E. Lawler III, Lyman Porter, J. Richard Hackman), who offers us rich theories of management and organization and rigorous empirical observations of organizations in action. The other source includes management consultants and management practitioners (e.g., Bill George, Daniel Goleman, Jack Welch, Tom Peters, Stephen Covey, Bill Gates), who offer us perspectives from their lives on or near the "organizational firing line."

Traditional academics—students of tight theory and rigorous empirical study of organizational behavior—often find a large disparity between these two perspectives on management and organization. Confronted with the increasing popularity of the "best-sellers," the editors of *The Manager's Bookshelf* began to ask a number of questions about this nontraditional management literature. For example:

- Is this material "intellectual pornography," as some have claimed?
- Do we want college and university students to read this material?
- Should managers of today's organizations be encouraged to read this material and to take it seriously?
- What contributions to management education and development come from this array of management books?
- What are the major deficiencies or limitations of these books?

For answers to these questions we turned to three colleagues—Professors Larry L. Cummings, Brad Jackson, and Anne Cummings. We asked each of them to reflect upon the current and continued popularity of this literature. The questions we asked them (and their responses) are intended to help you frame, and therefore critically and cautiously consume, this literature. Their reflections on the role of the popular books in management education are presented as Reading 3 in Part I.

1

UNDERSTANDING AND USING THE BEST-SELLERS

JON L. PIERCE AND JOHN W. NEWSTROM

For several decades now, a large number of books have focused on various aspects of management. These books have been in high demand at local bookstores and on the Internet. Several individuals have authored books that have sold millions of copies, among them Peter Drucker (*The Practice of Management*), Tom Peters and Bob Waterman (*In Search of Excellence*), Spencer Johnson (*Who Moved My Cheese?*), Jim Collins (*Good to Great*), Lee Iacocca (*Iacocca: An Autobiography*), Stephen Covey (*The Seven Habits of Highly Effective People*), Kenneth Blanchard and Spencer Johnson (*The One Minute Manager*), and Thomas Friedman (*The World Is Flat*).

Some of these books have stayed on "best-seller" lists for many weeks, months, and even years. What are the reasons for their popularity? Why have business books continued to catch the public's attention through both good economic times and bad?

We have all heard newspaper stories about (and many have felt the shock waves and personal impact of) downsizing, pension fund losses, restructuring, corporate ethical scandals, outsourcing of jobs, globalization, and excessive executive compensation and benefits. We have all read stories about the success of foreign organizations—especially in the automotive and electronics industries. We have continued to watch bigger and bigger portions of our markets being dominated by foreign-owned and foreign-controlled organizations. We have witnessed foreign interests purchase certain segments of America, while more and more jobs have been moved offshore. Perhaps in response to these trends, a tremendous thirst for American success stories and a desire to learn what would prevent some of these negative phenomena have arisen. In essence, the public is receptive and the timing is right for the writing, publication, and sale of popular management books.

A second reason for the upsurge in management books stems from another form of competition. Many management consultants, fighting for visibility and a way to differentiate their services, have written books they hope will become best-sellers. Through the printed word they hope to provide a unique take-home product for their clients, communicate their management philosophies, gain wide exposure for themselves or their firms, and profit handsomely.

Third, the best-sellers also provide an optimistic message to a receptive market. In difficult economic times or under conditions of extreme pressure to produce short-term results, managers may be as eager to swallow easy formulas for business success as sick patients are to consume their prescribed medicines. Sensing this propensity, the authors of the best-sellers (and of many other books with lesser records) often claim, at least implicitly, to present managers with an easy cure for their organizational woes, or with an easy path to personal success. In a world characterized by chaos, environmental turbulence, and intense global competition, managers are driven to search for the ideas provided by others that might be turned into a competitive advantage.

Fourth, we are witnessing an increased belief in and commitment to proactive organizational change and a search for differentiating one's approach. An increasing number of managers are rejecting the notion that "if it ain't broke, don't fix it," and instead are adopting what Peters and Waterman portrayed as a bias toward action. These managers are seriously looking for and experimenting with different approaches toward organizational management. Many of the popular books provide managers with insights into new and different ways of managing. At a minimum, readers are engaging in the process of benchmarking their competition and adopting "best practices" that have worked for others; hopefully, they are using the established practices of others as a springboard to developing even better ideas themselves.

In their search for the "quick fix," generations of risk-taking American managers have adopted a series of organizational management concepts, such as management by objectives, job enlargement, job enrichment, sensitivity training, flextime, and a variety of labor-management participative schemes, such as quality circles, total-quality management, and quality of work-life programs. Each has experienced its own life cycle, often going through the stages of market discovery, wild acceptance by passionate believers, careful questioning of it by serious critics, broad disillusionment with its shortcomings, and sometimes later being abandoned and replaced by another emerging management technique (while a few advocates remain staunchly supportive of the fad).[1]

As a consequence of this managerial tendency to embrace ideas and then soon discard them, many viable managerial techniques have received a tarnished image. For example, many of the Japanese participative management systems that were copied by American managers found their way into the garbage cans of an earlier generation of American managers. The continuing demand for quick fixes stimulates a ready market for new, reborn, and revitalized management ideas. We encourage you to read and seriously reflect on the questionable probability of finding a legitimate quick fix. The search for solutions to major organizational problems in terms of "one-minute" answers reflects a Band-Aid® approach to management—one that is destined to ultimately fail, and one that we condemn as a poor way to enrich the body of management knowledge and practice.

We alert you to this managerial tendency to look for "new" solutions to current organizational problems. The rush to resolve problems and take advantage of opportunities frequently leads to the search for simple remedies for complex organizational problems. Yet few of today's organizational problems can be solved with any single approach. The high-involvement management, the learning organization, and the compassionate corporate culture advocated in today's generation of popular management books may also join the list of tried-and-abandoned solutions to organizational woes if implemented without a broader context and deeper understanding. We especially hope that the quick-fix approach to organizational problem solving that characterizes the management style of many will not be promoted as a result of this mosaic (i.e., *The Manager's Bookshelf*) of today's popular business books.

RATIONALE FOR THIS BOOK

The business world has been buzzing with terms like vision, alignment, flow, pride, authenticity, innovation, credibility, narcissism, paradigms, stewardship, the learning organization, the spirit of work, the soul of business, transformational and charismatic leaders, knowledge management, high-involvement management and organizations, and corporate cultures. On the negative side, these terms feed the management world's preoccupation with quick fixes and the perpetuation of management fads. On the positive side, many of these concepts serve as catalysts to the further development of sound management philosophies and practices.

In earlier decades a few books occasionally entered the limelight (e.g., *Parkinson's Law, The Peter Principle, The Effective Executive, My Years with General Motors*), but for the most part they did not generate the widespread and prolonged popularity of the current generation of business books. Then, too, many were not written in the readable style that makes most contemporary books so easy to consume.

Managers find the current wave of books not only interesting, but enjoyable and entertaining to read. A small survey conducted by the Center for Creative Leadership found that a significant number of managers who participated in a study of their all-around reading selections chose one or more management books as their favorite.[2] In essence, many of the popular management books are being read by managers—probably because the books are often supportive of their present management philosophies! Many managers report that these books are insightful, easily readable, interestingly presented, and seemingly practical. Whether the prescriptions in these books have had (or ever will have) a real and lasting impact on the effective management of organizations remains to be determined.

Despite the overall popularity of many business best-sellers, some managers do not read any current management books, and many others have read only a limited number or small parts of a few.* Similarly, many university students studying management have heard about some of these books, but have not read them. *The Manager's Bookshelf* presents perspectives from (but not a criticism of) a number of those popular management books. *The Manager's Bookshelf* is designed for managers who are interested in the best-sellers but do not have time to read all of them in their entirety, and for students of management who want to be well informed as they prepare to enter the work world. Reading about the views expressed in many of the best-sellers will expand the knowledge and business vocabulary of both groups and enable them to engage in more meaningful conversations with their managerial colleagues.

Although reading the 55 summaries provided here can serve as a useful introduction to this literature, they should not be viewed as a substitute for immersion in the original material, nor do they remove the need for further reading of the more

---

*For a discussion on incorporating these types of management books into management training programs, see J. W. Newstrom and J. L. Pierce, "The Potential Role of Popular Business Books in Management Development Programs," *Journal of Management Development*, 8 (2, 1989).

substantive management books and professional journals. The good news is that the popularity of these books suggests that millions of managers are reading them and they are exhibiting an interest in learning about what has worked for other managers and firms. This step is important toward the development of an open system paradigm for themselves and for their organizations.

We strongly advocate that both managers and students be informed organizational citizens. Therefore, we believe it is important for you to know and understand what is being written about organizations and management. We also believe that it is important for you to know what is being read by the managers who surround you, some of which is contained in best-sellers, much of which is contained in more traditional management books, as well as in professional and scientific journals.[3]

CONTENTS OF THE BEST-SELLERS

What topics do these best-selling books cover, what is their form, and what is their merit? Although many authors cover a wide range of topics and others do not have a clear focus, most of these books fall into one of several categories. Some attempt to describe the more effective and ineffective companies and identify what made them successes or failures. Others focus on "micro" issues in leadership, motivation, or ethics. One group of authors focuses their attention on broad questions of corporate strategy and competitive tactics for implementing strategy. Some focus on pressing issues facing the contemporary organization such as social responsibility, globalism, the natural environment, workforce diversity, and the virtual workplace.

In terms of form, many contain apparently simple answers and trite prescriptions. Others are built around literally hundreds of spellbinding anecdotes and stories. Some have used interviews of executives as their source of information; others have adopted the parable format for getting their point across. As a group their presentation style is rich in diversity. As editors of this mosaic, we have necessarily had to exclude thousands of books while attempting to provide you with a rich exposure to an array of perspectives. For the most part, we have not included books that focus on a single executive's career success (e.g., Jack Welch or Steve Jobs), a single successful firm (e.g., Wal-Mart or Southwest Airlines) or failed organization (e.g., Enron), or a historical reinterpretation of a key person's practices (e.g., *Leadership Secrets of Sitting Bull* [or Sir Ernest Shackleton, Sun Tzu, General George Patton, William Shakespeare, or the Sopranos!]).

Judging the merits of best-sellers is a difficult task (and one that we will leave for readers and management critics to engage in). Some critics have taken the extreme position of calling these books "intellectual wallpaper" and "business pornography." Certainly labels like these, justified or not, should caution readers. A better perspective is provided by an assessment of the sources, often anecdotal, of many of the books. In other words, much of the information in business best-sellers stems from the experiences and observations of a single individual and is often infused with the subjective opinions of that writer. Unlike the more traditional academic literature, these books do not all share a sound scientific foundation. Requirements pertaining to objectivity, reproducibility of observations, and tests for reliability and validity have not guided the creation of much of the material. As a consequence, the authors are at liberty to say whatever they want (and often with as much passion as they desire).

Unlike authors who publish research-based knowledge, authors of management best-sellers do not need to submit their work to a panel of reviewers who then critically evaluate the ideas, logic, and data. The authors of these popular management books are able to proclaim as sound management principles virtually anything that is intuitively acceptable to their publisher and readers. Therefore, readers need to be cautious consumers who are vigilant about being misled. The ideas presented in these books need to be critically compared with the well-established thoughts from more traditional sources of managerial wisdom.

CRITIQUING THESE POPULAR BOOKS

Although the notion of one-minute management is seductive, we may safely conclude that there are no fast-acting cures to deep and complex business problems. Recognizing that simple solutions are not likely to be found in 200 pages of anecdotal stories and that the best-sellers frequently present (or appear to present) quick fixes and simple solutions, we strongly encourage you to read these popular books, looking less for simple solutions and more toward using them to stimulate your thinking and challenge the way you go about doing your business. We encourage you not only to achieve comprehension and understanding, but ultimately to arrive at the level of critique and synthesis—far more useful long-term skills.

To help you approach these works more critically, we encourage you to use the following questions to guide your evaluation:[4]

- **Author credentials:** How do the authors' background and personal characteristics uniquely qualify them to write this book? What relevant experience do they have? What unique access or perspective do they have? What prior writing experience do they have, and how was it accepted in the marketplace? What is their research background (capacity to design, conduct, and interpret the results of their observations)?
- **Rationale:** Why did the authors write the book? Is their self-proclaimed reason legitimate?
- **Face validity:** On initial examination of the book's major characteristics and themes (but before reading the entire book and actually examining the evidence provided), do you react positively or negatively? Are you inclined to accept or reject the authors' conclusions? Are the major contentions believable? Does it fit with your prior experience and expectations, or does it rock them to the core?
- **Target audience:** For whom is this book uniquely written? What level of manager in the organizational hierarchy would most benefit from reading the book and why? Is it for *you*?
- **Integration of existing knowledge:** A field of inquiry can best move forward only if it draws upon and then extends existing knowledge. Was this book written in isolation of existing knowledge? Do the authors demonstrate an awareness of and build upon existing knowledge, while giving appropriate credit to other sources of ideas?
- **Readability/interest:** Do the authors engage your mind? Are relevant, practical illustrations provided that indicate how the ideas have been or could be applied? Are the language and format used appealing to you?

- **Internal validity:** To what degree do the authors provide substantive evidence that the phenomenon, practice, or ideas presented actually and directly produce a valued result? Does an internally consistent presentation of ideas demonstrate the processes through which the causes for their observations are understood?
- **Reliability/consistency:** To what degree do the authors' conclusions converge with other sources of information available to you, or with the product of other methods of data collection? Do the authors stay consistent in their "pitch" from beginning to end of the book?
- **Distinctiveness:** Is the material presented new, creative, and distinctive (providing you with "value added"), or is it merely a presentation of "old wine in new bottles"?
- **Objectivity:** To what extent do the authors have a self-serving or political agenda, or have the authors presented information that was systematically gathered and objectively evaluated? Have the authors offered both the pros and cons of their views?
- **External validity:** Are the ideas likely to work in your unique situation, or are they bound to the narrow context within which the authors operated? What are the similarities that give you confidence that the recommendations made can be safely and effectively applied to your context?
- **Practicality:** Are the ideas adaptable? Do the authors provide concrete suggestions for application? Are the ideas readily transferable to the workplace in such a way that the typical reader could be expected to know what to do with them a few days later at work? Is it possible to produce an action plan directly from the material that you have read?

These are only some of the questions that should be asked as you read and evaluate any popular management book.

NATURE OF THIS BOOK

This is the eighth edition of *The Manager's Bookshelf*. The first edition was published in 1988. Recent language editions have also appeared in Italian, Spanish, and Chinese, pointing to the international popularity of these books. The current edition includes many books that were not previously summarized, representing a substantial revision. *The Manager's Bookshelf* provides a comprehensive introduction to many of the major best-sellers in the management field during recent years.

Some authors have achieved such a level of market success with their first book that they have been driven to follow up their earlier success with one or more additional books. In response to this trend, this edition of *The Manager's Bookshelf* includes summaries of subsequent books written by authors whose work appeared in an earlier edition of *The Manager's Bookshelf*. Examples of "repeat" authors in this edition include Warren Bennis, Edward E. Lawler III, Spencer Johnson, Jon Katzenbach, Stephen Covey, and Malcolm Gladwell.

The selections contained in this book are of two types: excerpts of original material and summaries prepared by a panel of reviewers. In some cases, we provide the reader with not only the main ideas presented by the author of a best-seller, but also the flavor (style or nature) of the author's literary approach. For some selections, we obtained permission to excerpt directly a chapter from the original book—particularly chapters that are the keystone presentation of the author's major theme. In other cases, the author's original thoughts and words were captured by selecting an article (representing part of the book) that the author had written for publication in a professional journal. Here again, the reader will see the author's ideas directly, though only sampled or much condensed from the original source.

The major format chosen for inclusion is a comprehensive, but brief and readable summary of the best-seller prepared by persons selected for their relevant expertise, interest, and familiarity. These summaries are primarily descriptive, designed to provide readers with an overall understanding of the book. These summaries are not judgmental in nature, nor are they necessarily a complete or precise reflection of the book author's management philosophy.

Determining what constituted a management best-seller worthy of inclusion was easy in some cases and more difficult in others. From the thousands of books available for selection, the ones included here rated highly on one or more of these criteria:

1. *Market acceptance:* Several books have achieved national notoriety by selling hundreds of thousands, and occasionally millions, of copies.
2. *Provocativeness:* Some books present thought-provoking viewpoints that run counter to "traditional" management thought.
3. *Distinctiveness:* A wide variety of topical themes of interest to organizational managers and students of management is presented.
4. *Representativeness:* In an attempt to avoid duplication from books with similar content within a topical area, many popular books were necessarily excluded.
5. *Author reputation:* Some authors (e.g., Warren Bennis, Edward E. Lawler III) have a strong reputation for the quality of their thinking and the insights they have generated; therefore, some of their newer products were included.

AUTHORS OF THE BEST-SELLERS

It is appropriate for a reader to examine a management best-seller and inquire, "Who is the author of this book?" Certainly the authors come from varied backgrounds, which can be both a strength and weakness for the best-sellers as a whole. Their diversity of experience and perspective is rich, yet it is possible that some authors are ill qualified to speak and portray themselves as experts.

Some of the authors have been critically described as self-serving egotists who have little to say constructively about management, but who say it with a flair and passion such that reading their books may appear to be very exciting. Some books are seemingly the product of armchair humorists who set out to entertain their readers with tongue in cheek. Other books on the best-seller lists have been written with the aid of a ghost writer (i.e., by someone who takes information that has been provided by another and then converts it into the lead author's story) or with the assistance of a professional writer who helps a busy executive organize and present his or her thoughts. Other books are the product of a CEO's reflection on his or her career or heartfelt positions on contemporary issues in organizations (e.g., authors Bill George and Larry Bossidy). A rather new and refreshing change has been the emergence in the best-seller literature of books prepared by respected academic professionals who have capably applied the best of their substantive research to pressing management problems and subsequently integrated their thoughts into book form. (Examples in this edition of such academics include Edward E. Lawler III, J. Richard Hackman, Karl Weick, Wayne Cascio, Alfred Marcus, and Paul Lawrence.) In summary, it may be fascinating to read the "inside story" or delve into a series of exciting anecdotes and "war stories," but the reader still has the opportunity and obligation to challenge the author's credentials for making broad generalizations from that experience base.

Conclusions

We encourage you to read and reflect on this collection of thoughts from the authors of today's generation of management books. We invite you to expand and enrich your insights into management as a result of learning from this set of popular books. We challenge you to question and debate the pros and cons of the ideas and philosophies that are presented by these authors. We hope you will ask when, where, how, and why these ideas are applicable. Examine the set of readings provided here, let them stimulate your thinking, and, in the process, learn something new. You'll find that learning—and especially critical thinking—can be both fun and addictive!

Notes

1. See, for example, B. Ettore, "What's the Next Business Buzzword?" *Management Review*, 1997, 86:8, 33–35; "Business Fads: What's In— and Out," *Business Week*, January 20, 1986; W. W. Armstrong, "The Boss Has Read Another New Book!" *Management Review*, June 1994, 61–64.
2. Frank Freeman, "Books That Mean Business: The Management Best Sellers," *Academy of Management Review*, 1985, 345–350.
3. See, for example, a report on executive reading preferences by Marilyn Wellemeyer in "Books Bosses Read," *Fortune*, April 27, 1987.
4. See John W. Newstrom and Jon L. Pierce, "An Analytic Framework for Assessing Popular Business Books," *Journal of Management Development*, 1993, 12:4, 20–28.

2

FLAWED ADVICE AND THE MANAGEMENT TRAP

CHRIS ARGYRIS

SUMMARY PREPARED BY KELLY NELSON

Kelly Nelson *is a 1991 graduate of the University of Minnesota Duluth. Since graduation, she has served in various operating management and human resource positions in the steel industry. She is currently working as a General Manager, Human Resources at AK Steel in Ohio. She is committed to dispensing "unflawed" advice as often as possible, particularly when dispensing parenting knowledge to her son John.*

Many individuals receive and accept advice that is fundamentally flawed, which leads to counterproductive consequences. The acceptance of flawed advice stems from Model I behaviors that strive to protect oneself, while unilaterally treating all others the same (i.e., not dealing specifically and directly with behaviors in order to effect change). Model II behaviors, on the other hand, provide organizations the opportunity to share information, act cooperatively, and deal directly and firmly with behaviors in order to effect change. Organizations that adopt Model II behaviors also provide themselves the opportunity to analyze advice to ensure it is not flawed, thereby avoiding the "management trap."

INCONSISTENT AND UNACTIONABLE ADVICE

Stephen Covey's *The Seven Habits of Highly Effective People* (1989) is based upon a set of principles that direct individuals to effectiveness through *inside-out management,* one that begins with a focus on one's self. The goal is to develop a positive attitude through developing trust, generating positive energy, and sidestepping negative energy. Covey's strategy suggests suppressing negative feelings and putting on a "false face" of positive feedback. However, the premise of this suppression flies in the face of Covey's basic principles (i.e., to develop trust). Furthermore, the "theory" espoused by Covey cannot be tested; therefore, it cannot be proven.

This inconsistent and unactionable advice is also demonstrated by Doyle and Strauss (*How to Make Meetings Work,* 1982), management consultants who advise groups on

Chris Argyris. *Flawed Advice and the Management Trap: How Managers Can Know When They're Getting Good Advice and When They're Not.* New York: Oxford University Press, 2000.

actions to produce effective meetings. According to Doyle and Strauss, if a group is having difficulty deciding where to begin and how, it is best to wait until the group is convinced it needs the consultant (or leader). The group will then ask for assistance and the consultant can take control and give direction to the group. In any group, this tactic may become a self-fulfilling prophecy. Further, Doyle and Strauss do not give specific guidelines on the point at which the consultant should intervene. Also, the actual behaviors of the consultant are not detailed. Similar to Covey's theory, Doyle and Strauss's theory cannot be tested; therefore, it cannot be proven.

As demonstrated by the examples of Covey and Doyle and Strauss, popular management advice is published as valid and actionable and is widely adopted. However, the advice reveals a pattern of gaps and inconsistencies, leading to unintended consequences and an inability to systematically correct the deficiencies.

ORGANIZATIONAL CONSEQUENCES OF USING INCONSISTENT ADVICE

The most common advice for designing and implementing programs for organizational change and improvement involves the following four elements:

1. Define a vision.
2. Define a competitive strategy that is consistent with the vision.
3. Define organizational work processes that, when carried out, will implement the strategy.
4. Define individual job requirements so that employees can produce the processes effectively.

The elements are sound and understandable. However, they lead to inconsistencies when the vision, strategy, work processes, and job requirements are developed to support contradictory goals. For example, a 1996 study concluded that a vast majority of companies held only a superficial commitment to internal participative decision making. Eighty-three percent of the middle managers responding favored more involvement; yet, their supervisors did not know it. Top managers were not committed to the strategy, nor were they aware of the lack of credibility they were demonstrating.

For the four elements to succeed and to lead to consistent improvement, *internal commitment* of every employee (gained through intrinsic motivation) is needed. However, most organizations attempt to develop the elements' *external commitment* (top-down policies). This inherent inconsistency lays the groundwork for failure. The failure is demonstrated through the organization's failure to improve performance, increase profits, and develop cooperative behaviors.

WHY FLAWED ADVICE EXISTS

If so much professional advice, even if implemented correctly, leads to counterproductive consequences, why have so many users found that advice to be helpful? Because people hold two different "theories of action" about effective behavior—one they *espouse* and one they actually *use* (i.e., *Model I*). While using Model I, people strive to satisfy their actions when they:

- Define goals and try to achieve them. (They don't try to develop, with others, a mutual definition of shared purpose.)
- Maximize winning and minimize losing. (They treat any change in goals, once they are decided on, as a sign of weakness.)
- Minimize the generation or expression of negative feelings. (They fear this would be interpreted as showing ineptness, incompetence, or lack of diplomacy.)
- Be rational. (They want to remain objective and intellectual, and suppress their feelings.)

To accomplish these ends, under Model I, people will seek to:

- Design and manage the environment unilaterally, that is, plan actions secretly and persuade or cajole others to agree with one's definition of the situation.
- Own and control the task.
- Unilaterally protect themselves, that is, keep from being vulnerable by speaking in abstractions, avoiding reference to directly observed events, and withholding underlying thoughts and feelings.
- Unilaterally protect others from being hurt, in particular, by withholding important information, telling white lies, suppressing feelings, and offering false sympathy. Moreover, they do not test the assumption that the other person needs to be protected or that the strategy of protection should be kept secret.

Following Model I behavior leads to a self-sealing loop in which the individual treats others unilaterally while protecting him- or herself. As individuals follow Model I behavior, they become skilled and their actions will appear to have "worked" in that they achieve their intended objectives while appearing spontaneous and effortless. Model I behaviors are not only performed by individuals but also by groups. This provides an organization-wide network of Model I behavior in which all members are protecting themselves (whether individually or as a group). Furthermore, the Model I behaviors are enforced and perpetuated by Human Resource Department individuals who also practice Model I behaviors.

On the other hand, *Model II* behaviors involve sharing power with anyone who has competence and is relevant to deciding about implementing the action in question. Defining and assigning tasks are shared by all decision makers. In the Model II method, decision-making networks are developed with the goal of maximizing the contribution of each member.

Model I behaviors allow individuals to remain within their comfort zones and encourage all to place responsibility on problems "out there" instead of on the systematic faults of the advice being used. Hence, it is attractive and still widely used. Model II behavior forces individual behavioral change and accepts all participants as equals in the process. While pulling individuals out of their comfort zones, it requires individuals to face up to their own commitments and reflect upon their own assumptions, biases, and reasoning.

VALIDITY AND ACTIONABILITY LIMITS TO MODEL I

The four main reasons Model I behavior produces unskilled awareness and incompetence are:

1. The advice represents *espoused* theories of effectiveness.
2. The advice, as crafted, contains evaluations and attributions that are neither tested nor testable.
3. The advice is based on self-referential logic that produces limited knowledge about what is going on.
4. The advice does not specify causal processes.

Critiquing Advice

How can managers determine if the advice they are receiving is Model I–based advice? It is important that individuals focus on reducing inconsistencies, closing knowledge gaps, and addressing personal fear. Instead of judging others as defensive, wrong, and/or unjust, the individual must request illustrations of evaluations and attributions, and craft tests of their validity. Instead of judging others as naïve, complainers, or crybabies, one should request illustrations and tests, then inquire about how others responded to test attempts. One must also illustrate how the gaps and inconsistencies in the reasoning process are likely to backfire. Finally, evaluations and attributions about counterproductive actions must be illustrated and testing encouraged.

If most of the advice is abstract and does not specify the theory required to implement it, Model I behaviors will result. Some may espouse Model II behavior, but they will be unaware of and unable to explain the gaps. Finally, Model II behavior is more direct and is much tougher on holding people responsible for true changed behaviors.

Model I is often integrated in performance review systems. Often performance appraisals are "eased into" by the appraiser in order to save the recipient's feelings. Also, negative feedback is given in general terms, and quickly followed by positive reinforcement (often given only to get away from the negative portion of the review). Performance evaluations such as these are classic Model I examples, with inconsistencies, information gaps, and behavior not changed as a result.

On the other hand, performance evaluations based in Model II are specific, direct, and produce discussion about tough, productive reasoning that results in compelling decisions. It also facilitates change of the organization to generating internal commitment to organization values.

Generating Internal Commitment to Values to Produce Desired Outcomes

In order for an organization's values to become internal commitments on an individual level, Model II behavior needs to be practiced at all levels of the organization. Nondefensive information sharing and decision making, along with individual awareness of their own gaps and inconsistencies, provide the culture in which value commitment becomes internal to the individual.

The organization's values lead to strategic choices. High-quality choices possess four key attributes:

1. They are genuine.
2. They are sound.
3. They are actionable.
4. They are compelling.

Obstacles to high-quality strategic choices include politics, bad analyses, turbulent markets and, most commonly, flawed processes. In flawed processes, choices either do not get framed, do not get made, appear to get made but fall apart, are made but are not sound, or choices get made but the subsequent action is not timely.

To ensure strategic choices are high quality and meet the internal commitment to values adopted by individuals, a *choice-structuring process* is necessary. The goal of a choice-structuring process is to produce sound strategic choices that lead to successful action.

The strategic choice-structuring process has five steps:

1. Frame the choice.
2. Brainstorm possible options.
3. Specify conditions necessary to validate each option.
4. Prioritize the conditions that create the greatest barrier to choice.
5. Design valid tests for the key barrier conditions.

Summary

Model I behaviors prohibit strategic choice-structuring because protectionism and defensiveness are the bases for the behavior. In Model II environments, successful strategic choice structuring is possible because the advice adopted is not flawed. The advice adopted stipulates that (1) the theories in use should specify the sequence of behavior required to produce the intended consequences or goals; (2) the theories in use should be crafted in ways that make the causality transparent; (3) the causalities embedded in the theories in use are testable robustly in the context of everyday life; and (4) actionable knowledge must specify the values that underlie and govern the designs in use.

Model II behaviors provide organizations with the opportunity to analyze advice directly to ensure advice adopted by the organization is not flawed.

3

REFLECTIONS
ON THE BEST-SELLERS

JON L. PIERCE AND JOHN W. NEWSTROM,

WITH LARRY L. CUMMINGS, BRAD JACKSON, AND ANNE
CUMMINGS

Dr. Larry L. Cummings *was the Carlson Professor of Management in the Carlson School of Management at the University of Minnesota. He previously taught at Columbia University, Indiana University, the University of British Columbia, the University of Wisconsin in Madison, and Northwestern University. Dr. Cummings published more than 80 journal articles and 16 books. He served as the editor of the* Academy of Management Journal, *as a member of the Academy's Board of Governors, and President of the same association. Dr. Cummings was a consultant for many corporations, including Dow Chemical, Cummins Engine, Eli Lilly, Prudential, Samsonite, Touche-Ross, and Moore Business Forms.*

Dr. Brad Jackson *is Head of School at the Victoria Management School at Victoria University of Wellington in New Zealand. Dr. Jackson taught previously at Denmark's Copenhagen Business School in Denmark and at the University of Calgary in Canada. Jackson's research interests include the changing role of the CEO, the global management fashion industry, and organizational political processes associated with managing change. He has taught courses in Organizational Behavior, Change Management, Intercultural Management, Organizational Communication, and Management Learning. Jackson has published three books—*Management Gurus and Management Fashions, The Hero Manager, *and* Organisational Behaviour in New Zealand.

Dr. Anne Cummings *taught General Management, Organizational Behavior, Teams, Negotiations, and Leadership for undergraduate, MBA, Ph.D., and Executive Education audiences at the University of Pennsylvania's Wharton School, and is now on the Management Studies faculty at the University of Minnesota Duluth. Dr. Cummings won the David W. Hauck teaching award at Wharton in recognition of her outstanding ability to lead, stimulate, and challenge students. She holds a Ph.D. in Organizational Behavior from the*

University of Illinois at Urbana-Champaign, and her research has appeared in the Academy of Management Journal, Journal of Applied Psychology, California Management Review, *and* Leadership Quarterly.

This opening section provides our reflections upon management (both the body of knowledge and its practice), as well as upon the wave of management books that has almost become an institutionalized part of the popular press. We hope it will provide some helpful perspectives and point you in some new directions.

One of the world's premier management gurus, the late Peter F. Drucker, suggested that managing is a "liberal art." It is "liberal" because it deals not only with fundamental knowledge, but also self-knowledge, wisdom, and leadership; it is an "art" because it is also concerned with practice and application. According to Drucker, "managers draw on all the knowledge and insights of the humanities and the social sciences—on psychology and philosophy, on economics and history, on ethics—as well as on the physical sciences."* Building on this, we note that management can be defined as the skillful application of a body of knowledge to a particular organizational situation. This definition suggests that management is an art form as well as a science. That is, there is a body of knowledge that has to be applied with the fine touch and instinctive sense of the master artist. Peter Drucker reminds us that the fundamental task of management is to "make people capable of joint performance through common goals, common values, the right structure, and the training and development they need to perform and to respond to change" (p. 4). Consequently, execution of the management role and performance of the managerial functions are more complex than the simple application of a few management concepts. The development of effective management, therefore, requires the development of an in-depth understanding of organizational and management concepts, careful sensitivity to individuals and groups, and the capacity to grasp when and how to apply this knowledge.

The organizational arena presents today's manager with a number of challenges. The past few decades have been marked by a rapid growth of knowledge about organizations and management systems. As a consequence of this growth in management information, we strongly believe that it is important for today's manager to engage in lifelong learning by continually remaining a student of management. It is also clear to us that our understanding of organizations and management systems is still in the early stages of development. That is, there remain many unanswered questions that pertain to the effective management of organizations.

Many observers of the perils facing today's organizations have charged that the crises facing American organizations today are largely a function of "bad management"—the failure, in large part, to recognize that management is about human beings. It is the ability, according to Drucker, "to make people capable of joint performance, (and) to make their strengths effective and their weaknesses irrelevant. This is what organization is all about, and it is the reason that management is the critical, determining force" (p. 10). Similarly, Tom Peters and Bob Waterman have observed that the growth of our society during the twentieth century was so rapid that almost any management approach appeared to work and work well. The real test of effective management systems did not appear until recent decades, when competitive, economic, political, and social pressures

---

*Page references are to Peter F. Drucker, "Management as a social function and liberal art," *The Essential Drucker: The Best of Sixty Years of Peter Drucker's Essential Writings on Management.* Harper Business, 2003.

created a form of environmental turbulence that pushed existing managerial tactics beyond their limits. Not only are students of management challenged to learn about effective management principles, but they are also confronted with the need to develop the skills and intuitive sense to apply that management knowledge.

Fortunately, there are many organizations in our society from which they can learn, and there is a wealth of knowledge that has been created that focuses on effective organizational management. There are at least two literatures that provide rich opportunities for regular reading. First, there is the traditional management literature found in management and organization textbooks and academic journals (e.g., *Academy of Management Journal, Administrative Science Quarterly, Harvard Business Review, Managerial Psychology, Research in Organizational Behavior*, and *California Management Review*). Second, the past few decades have seen the emergence of a nontraditional management literature written by management gurus, management practitioners, and management consultants who describe their organizational experiences and provide a number of other management themes. Knowledge about effective and ineffective management systems can be gleaned by listening to the management scholar, philosopher, and practitioner.

Since not all that is published in the academic journals or in the popular press meets combined tests of scientific rigor and practicality, it is important that motivated readers immerse themselves in both of these literatures. Yet neither source should be approached and subsequently consumed without engaging in critical thinking.

CRITICAL THINKING AND CAUTIOUS CONSUMPTION

We believe that the ideas promoted in these best-sellers should not be integrated blindly into any organization. Each should be subjected to careful scrutiny in order to identify its inherent strengths and weaknesses; each should be examined within the context of the unique organizational setting in which it may be implemented; and modifications and fine-tuning of the technique may be required in order to tailor it to a specific organizational setting and management philosophy. In addition, we strongly encourage juxtaposing the concepts, ideas, and management practices presented in these books with the scientific management literature. To what extent have these "popular press" ideas been subjected to investigation following the canons of the scientific method? Have they been supported? Are they endorsed by other respected management philosophers and practitioners? If these ideas or similar ones have not been rigorously examined scientifically, it would be prudent to ask the important question "Why not?" If these ideas have not been endorsed by others, we should once again raise the question "Why not?" before blindly entering them into our storehouse of knowledge and "bag of management practices." Finally, the process that is used to implement the management technique may be as important to its success as the technique itself, as good ideas (techniques, programs) may still fail if the processes employed to implement them are seriously flawed.

This is an era of an information-knowledge explosion. We would like to remind consumers of information of the relevance of the saying *caveat emptor* (let the buyer beware) from the product domain, because there are both good and questionable informational products on the best-seller market. Fortunately, advisory services like Consumer Reports exist to advise us on the consumption of consumer goods. There is, however, no similar guide for our consumption of information in the popular management press. Just because a book has been published or even become a best-seller does not mean that the information contained therein is worthy of direct consumption. It may be a best-seller because it presents an optimistic message, it is enjoyable reading, it contains simple solutions that appeal to those searching for easy answers, the author is a recognized figure, or because it has been successfully marketed to the public.

The information in all management literature should be approached with caution; it should be examined and questioned. We suggest that a more appropriate guide for readers might be *caveat lector, sapeat lector* (which loosely translates to "Let the reader beware, but first let the reader be informed"). The pop-management literature should not be substituted for more scientific-based knowledge about effective management. In addition, this knowledge should be compared and contrasted with what we know about organizations and management systems from other sources—the opinions of other experts, the academic management literature, and our own prior organizational experiences.

We invite you to question this best-seller literature. In the process there are many questions that should be asked. For example: What are the author's credentials, and are they relevant to the book? Has the author remained an objective observer of the reported events? Why did the author write this book? What kind of information is being presented (e.g., opinion, values, facts)? Does this information make sense when it is placed into previously developed theories? Could I take this information and apply it to another situation at a different point in time and in a different place, or was it unique to the author's experience? These and similar questions should be part of the information screening process.

INTERVIEWS WITH THREE ORGANIZATIONAL SCHOLARS

As we became increasingly familiar with the best-sellers through our roles as editors, we began asking a number of questions about this type of literature. We then sought and talked with three distinguished management scholars—Professors L. L. Cummings, Brad Jackson, and Anne Cummings. Following are excerpts from those interviews.

Exploring the Contributions of Best-Sellers

We have witnessed an explosion in the number and type of books that have been written on management and organizations for the trade market. Many of these books have found themselves on various "best-seller" lists. What, in your opinion, has been the impact of these publications? What is the nature of their contribution?

Larry Cummings's Perspective

Quite frankly, I think these books have made a number of subtle contributions, most of which have not been labeled or identified by either the business press or the academic press. In addition, many of their contributions have been inappropriately or inaccurately labeled.

Permit me to elaborate. I think it is generally true that a number of these very popular "best-seller list" books, as you put it, have been thought to be reasonably accurate translations or interpretations of successful organizational practice. Although this is not the way that these books have been reviewed in the academic press, my interactions with managers, business practitioners, and MBA students reveal that many of these books are viewed as describing organizational structure, practices, and cultures that are thought to contribute to excellence.

On the other hand, when I evaluate the books myself and when I pay careful attention to the reviews by respected, well-trained, balanced academicians, it is my opinion that these books offer very little, if anything, in the way of generalizable knowledge about successful organizational practice. As organizational case studies, they are the most dangerous of the lot, in that the data (information) presented has not been systematically, carefully, and cautiously collected and interpreted. Of course, that criticism is common for case studies. Cases were never meant to be contributions to scientific knowledge. Even the best ones are primarily pedagogical aids, or the basis for subsequent theory construction.

The reason I describe the cases presented in books like *In Search of Excellence* as frequently among the most dangerous is because they are so well done (i.e., in a marketing and journalistic sense), and therefore, they are easily read and so believable. They are likely to influence the naive, those who consume them without critically evaluating their content. They epitomize the glamour and the action orientation, and even the machoism of American management practice; that is, they represent the epitome of competition, control, and order as dominant interpersonal and organizational values.

Rather, I think the contributions of these books, in general, have been to provide an apology, a rationale, or a positioning, if you like, of American management as something that is not just on the defensive with regard to other world competitors. Instead, they have highlighted American management as having many good things to offer: a sense of spirit, a sense of identification, and a sense of clear caricature. This has served to fill a very important need. In American management thought there has emerged a lack of self-confidence and a lack of belief that what we are doing is proactive, effective, and correct. From this perspective these books have served a useful role in trying to present an upbeat, optimistic characterization.

Brad Jackson's Perspective

It is very difficult to assess the true nature of the impact that the best-sellers have on management practice. We might infer from the huge number of books that are sold each year that their impact might be quite substantial. Corporations and consulting firms purchase many business best-sellers on a bulk basis. It is difficult to ascertain how many of these are actually distributed and received. The next question to consider, of course, is the extent to which these books are actually read. Anecdotal evidence (as well as personal experience!) suggests that, even with the best intentions, most readers manage to peruse the book jacket, the testimonials, the preface, and, at best, the introductory chapter. Few find the time to read the book's entire contents.

Most crucially, however, we should try to understand the nature of the impact that the reading of a best-seller, even if it is very partial, has on how the individual manager perceives the world and how she or he acts on that world as a result of being exposed to the ideas expressed in this genre of books. This is a task that is fraught with difficulty, as managers are exposed to so many different influences and are shaped and constrained by a wide range of organizational environments. In my book, *Management Gurus and Management Fashions* (Jackson, 2001), I suggest that business best-sellers not only make an intellectual contribution, they also provide quite important psychological and emotional support to managers. It is no accident that we can observe the swelling of the personal growth section of the business book section during times of widespread turbulence.

During the 1990s, organizations across all sectors embraced new management ideas (management fashions) that were promoted by management gurus in business best-sellers. Organizational improvement programs such as Total Quality Management, Business Process Reengineering, The Balanced Scorecard, and Knowledge Management were seized upon as the panacea for organizations desperate to retain their competitive edge or merely survive. Vestiges of these and older programs can still be traced in the language, systems, and structures of these organizations, but their influence and attention are well past their peak. We have very little to go on in terms of understanding how these management fashions are adapted and institutionalized, but a few studies have shown that these ideas tend to be only selectively adopted or they are reworked or even actively resisted by managers and employees. The bottom line is that it is very difficult to accurately trace the impact of best-sellers. However, we should be prepared to accept that the final impact is likely to be quite different than what the best-selling author originally intended!

Anne Cummings's Perspective

These best-selling business books have offered my teaching a variety of important contributions:

- They offer powerful corporate examples that I use for illustrating conceptual points in class. I often find the examples of what didn't work (and the ensuing discussion about why) as useful (if not more useful!) than the examples of what did work.
- They update me on the newest terminology and techniques that managers are reading about, which helps me to communicate efficiently and effectively with them, using their vocabulary.
- They stimulate interesting conversations with Executive Education participants, who often question the value of the latest fads and want to explore how these new ideas compare to their managerial experience and to the conceptual foundations about management that they learned a decade earlier.
- Some of the books offer basic frameworks for viewing problems and issues, and this encourages students to begin thinking conceptually. I can then nudge students toward thinking further about cause-effect relationships, contingencies, and the utility of academic research.
- Some of the books offer important insights into environmental trends, shifting managerial pressures, and even new ways of thinking about things—sometimes long before academics explore these areas.

Possible Concerns about Best-Sellers

In addition to a large volume of sales, surveys reveal that many of these books have been purchased and presumably read by those who are managing today's organizations. Does this trouble you? More specifically, are there any concerns that you have, given the extreme popularity of these types of books?

Larry Cummings's Perspective

I am of two minds with regard to this question. First, I think that the sales of these books are not an accurate reflection of the degree, the extent, or the carefulness with which they have been read. Nor do I believe that the sales volumes tell us anything about the pervasiveness of their impact. Like many popular items (fads), many of these books have been purchased for desktop dressing. In many cases, the preface, the introduction, and the conclusion (maybe the summary on the dust jacket) have been read such that the essence of the book is picked up and it can become a part of managerial and social conversation.

Obviously, this characterization does not accurately describe everyone in significant positions of management who has purchased these books. There are many managers who make sincere attempts to follow the management literature thoroughly and to evaluate it critically. I think that most of the people with whom I come in contact in management circles, both in training for management and in actual management positions, who have carefully read the books are not deceived by them. They are able to put them in the perspective of representations or characterizations of a fairly dramatic sort. As a consequence, I am not too concerned about the books being overly persuasive in some dangerous, Machiavellian, or subterranean sense.

On the other hand, I do have a concern of a different nature regarding these books. That concern focuses upon the possibility that the experiences they describe will be taken as legitimate bases or legitimate directions for the study of management processes. These books represent discourse by the method of emphasizing the extremes, in particular the extremes of success. I think a much more fruitful approach to studying and developing prescriptions for management thought and management action is to use the method of differences rather than the method of extremes.

The method of differences would require us to study the conditions that gave rise to success at Chrysler, or McDonald's, or which currently gives rise to success at Merck or any of the other best-managed companies. However, through this method we would also contrast these companies with firms in the same industries that are not as successful. The method of contrast (differences) is likely to lead to empirical results that are much less dramatic, much less exciting, much less subject to journalistic account (i.e., they're likely to be more boring to read), but it is much more likely to lead to observations that are more generalizable across managerial situations, as well as being generative in terms of ideas for further management research.

Thus, the issue is based on the fundamental method that underlies these characterizations. My concern is not only from a methodological perspective. It also centers on our ethical and professional obligations to make sure that the knowledge we transmit does not lead people to overgeneralize. Rather, it should provide them with information that is diagnostic rather than purely prescriptive.

The method of extremes does not lead to a diagnostic frame of mind. It does not lead to a frame of mind that questions why something happened, under what conditions it happened, or under what conditions it would not happen. The method of differences is much more likely to lead to the discovery of the conditional nature of knowledge and the conditional nature of prescriptions.

Brad Jackson's Perspective

I tend to be less concerned about the large volume of business best-sellers than a lot of my academic colleagues. While I wish that there were bigger public appetites for more academically oriented management books, I am generally encouraged by the widespread interest in business and management. It's important for managers to take an interest in what is going on beyond their immediate work environment and to ask questions about why things are being done in a certain way and what could be done differently. Best-sellers typically challenge the status quo in provocative and dramatic ways that readily engage managers' attentions. Subsequently, many managers wish to learn more and sign up for some form of formal management education. It is in this forum that they can become exposed to alternative and more rigorously researched accounts of management theory and practice that challenge some of the assumptions made in the best-sellers. I have found that encouraging managers to take a more critical reading of the business best-sellers can be highly instructive for both them and me, especially when they are presented alongside academically oriented texts which they find to be slightly less accessible, but ultimately more rewarding.

Anne Cummings's Perspective

My greatest concern with these books is that many readers do not have the time, motivation, or managerial experience to appropriately apply the contents. Unfortunately, a few students seem to be mostly interested in "speaking the language" with bravado just to demonstrate how up-to-date they are. Others seem to want to simply imitate the successful examples that they have read about, as though these reports of alleged best practices represent a "cookbook" approach that can be easily applied elsewhere. Most managers consider their time an extremely valuable resource, and consider this reading a "luxury"; they tell me they therefore approach these readings looking for "take-aways" from each one—short lists of guiding principles, practical procedures they can implement immediately, or a simple diagram or model to organize a project or change they are leading. All students of management can benefit from remembering that the process of building solid theories and best practices from isolated case examples (i.e., inductive learning) is a complex one; some discipline and patience are required to avoid premature generalizing before valid evidence is available and well understood. The challenge is for readers to expend some real effort and apply critical thinking to these products—to analyze when and why the practices might be successful. Demanding conversations with colleagues, mentors, and competitors; comparisons of apparent discrepancies; and asking tough "why" and "how" questions are all useful techniques to achieve this discipline.

Recent Changes in Best-Sellers

The modern era of business best-seller popularity now spans roughly a quarter-century. Have you witnessed any changes or evolution in the nature of these best-seller books over the past decade or so?

Brad Jackson's Perspective

Looking back, I characterize the 1990s as the "guru decade." This was the era in which a few highly influential management gurus such as Michael Hammer, Tom Peters, Michael Porter, Peter Senge, and Stephen Covey reigned supreme among the best-sellers. Their larger-than-life presences helped to spawn a few very powerful management ideas that drove a lot of conventional management thinking in North America and beyond. I do not see the same concentration of interest in either management gurus or management fashions in the current business book market. Instead I see a lot of niche-based ideas that are being promoted by specific consulting firms. None of these seem to have had the same pervasive influence that the gurus previously held. On the other hand, I see a lot of interest in biographical accounts of what I call "hero managers" such as Jack Welch, Richard Branson, and Lou Gerstner. Most of these are inspirational self-celebratory accounts but, of course, there has also been a lot more interest in exposing some of the darker sides of corporate life in the wake of the Enron and other corporate scandals.

Words of Advice

Do you have any insights or reflections or words of advice to offer readers of business best-sellers?

Brad Jackson's Perspective

I like to share the advice that Micklethwait and Wooldridge (*The Witch Doctors*, 1996) give at the end of their excellent exposé on the management theory industry. They argue that because management theory is comparatively immature and underdeveloped, it is vital that managers become selective and critical consumers of the products and services offered by the management theory industry. In particular, they suggest that managers should bear in mind the following advice when making book purchase decisions:

1. Anything that you suspect is bunk almost certainly is.
2. Beware of authors who aggrandize themselves more than their work.
3. Beware of authors who argue almost exclusively by analogy.
4. Be selective. No one management theory will cure all ills.
5. Bear in mind that the cure can sometimes be worse than the disease.
6. Supplement these books with reactions from academic reviewers to get an informed and critical perspective on the value of new management theories and their proponents.

All I would add to this succinct list is to encourage managers to read more widely and to look to other disciplines such as philosophy, history, psychology, and art for supplemental insights into management practice and organizational life. I'm always surprised by how much I learn when I browse through books in the other sections of the library or bookstore.

Conclusion

We hope that you have enjoyed reading the views of these management scholars (Professors Larry Cummings, Brad Jackson, and Anne Cummings) on the role of popular management books. In addition, we hope that the readings contained in the eighth edition of *The Manager's Bookshelf* will stimulate your thinking about effective and ineffective practices of management. We reiterate that there is no single universally applicable practice of management, for management is the skillful application of a body of knowledge to a particular situation. We invite you to continue expanding your understanding of new and developing management concepts. In a friendly sort of way, we challenge you to develop the skills to know when and how to apply this knowledge in the practice of management.

PART

II

BEST-SELLER "CLASSICS"

Many of those books that found their way into earlier editions of *The Manager's Bookshelf* as a part of our mosaic of contemporary views continue to have a message that many managers reference frequently and still want to study. As a result, for the eighth edition of *The Manager's Bookshelf* we have included summaries of selected books published in earlier years that continue to be popular references for managers today.

Peter F. Drucker—a writer, consultant, and teacher—was the Marie Rankin Clarke Professor of Social Sciences and Management at Claremont Graduate University, and previously taught at New York University. He received his doctorate from Germany's University of Frankfurt in 1931. Having awed the world with his writings across a half century until his death at age 95 in 2005, Drucker was variously described as "the man who invented management," "the patron saint of socially aware executives," a "prolific and profound management thinker," and "the world's foremost pioneer of management theory." He was the author of 40 books and an astounding 35 articles that appeared in the prestigious *Harvard Business Review* journal. In 2002, he was awarded the Presidential Medal of Freedom, the nation's highest civilian award.

In *The Practice of Management*, Drucker suggests that executives ask several penetrating questions, such as What is our business? Who is our customer? What does our customer value most? He argues that management is a distinct (but previously underappreciated) function that is practice-oriented and can be improved through education. He emphasizes the importance of the external environment, pursuing multiple goals, accenting innovation and knowledge workers, acting with integrity, following a systematic decision-making process, and viewing the firm as a social institution. He also pioneered the concept of Management by Objectives (MBO).

Quality, customer service, total quality management, and continuous improvement have been organizational buzzwords for the past several years. One of the leaders in developing strategies for building quality into manufacturing processes was the late W. Edwards Deming. During the 1950s, Deming went to Japan to teach statistical control, where his ideas received a very warm reception. The Japanese built on Deming's ideas and moved the responsibility for quality from the ranks of middle management down to the shop floor level.

Deming's ideas on quality control soon became an integral feature in Japanese management. Deming has been called by his admirers both the "prophet of quality" and the "man of the century." He certainly demonstrated a powerful force of personality and singular focus.

Total quality control (TQC) means that responsibility for quality is a part of every employee's job. Deming's *Out of the Crisis* calls for long-term organizational transformation through the implementation of a 14-step plan of action focusing on leadership, constant innovation, and removal of barriers to performance. Interested readers may also wish to examine other works about Deming and his influence in *The World of W. Edwards Deming, The Deming Dimension, Thinking About Quality*, and Deming's *Road to Continual Improvement*.

A true classic in the management literature is Douglas McGregor's *The Human Side of Enterprise*, first published in 1960. Because of the book's popularity, its timeless theme, and genuine relevance for organizations in the twenty-first century, McGregor's seminal work continues to be valuable reading.

McGregor explores alternative assumptions that managers might hold and that drive different approaches to the management of organizations and their employees. Through the presentation of two sets of assumptions—labeled Theory X and Theory Y—McGregor urges managers to see employees as capable of innovation, creativity, commitment, high levels of sustained effort, and the exercise of self-direction and self-control.

Douglas McGregor received his doctorate at Harvard University. Before his death in 1964, he served on the faculties of Harvard University and the Massachusetts Institute of Technology and was president of Antioch College. McGregor is also the author of *The Professional Manager*.

A contemporary of McGregor's, Abraham Maslow, has sometimes been called the "greatest psychologist since Freud," and a "significant contributor to the humanistic psychology movement." He is well-known to psychology students for his books *Toward a Psychology of Being* and *The Psychology of Science*. However, he is equally well known to most business students for his highly popularized and defining work on postulating a hierarchy of human needs beginning at the physiological level and proceeding up through safety, social, esteem, and self-actualizing levels, and suggesting that any need level, when fully satisfied, can no longer be a powerful motivator. Maslow also published *Eupsychian Management* (which received little acclaim in the 1960s), which has been republished (with additional material from a variety of admirers) as *Maslow on Management*. In this book, Maslow lays out the underlying assumptions for a eupsychian organization. Maslow taught at Brooklyn College and Brandeis University and, while writing his final book, was an in-depth observer of worker behaviors at the Non-Linear Systems plant in Del Mar, California.

Peter M. Senge is the Director of the Systems Thinking and Organizational Learning Program at MIT's Sloan School of Management. His book *The Fifth Discipline* emphasizes the importance of organizations developing the capacity to engage in effective learning. Senge identifies and discusses a set of disabilities that are fatal to organizations, especially those operating in rapidly changing environments. The fifth discipline—systems thinking—is presented as the cornerstone for the learning organization. Personal mastery, mental models, shared vision, and team learning are presented as the core disciplines and the focus for building the learning organization. Senge has also published *The Fifth Discipline Fieldbook* and *The Dance of Change*.

Michael E. Porter, a Harvard Business School faculty member and holder of the Bishop Lawrence University Professorship, continues to make contributions to our understanding of organizations and their competitive strategies. He received the 1986 George R. Terry book award for his book *Competitive Advantage*, which was published in 1985. *Competitive Advantage* was a follow-up to his earlier book *Competitive Strategy*. Porter is also the author of *Competitive Advantage of Nations*. He has argued that firms can achieve above-average profits by synthesizing and applying their unique strengths effectively within their industry. They can do this either through creating a cost advantage, or by differentiating a product or service from that of their competitors. The key, which some firms seemingly ignore, is to link strategy formulation successfully with strategy implementation. Porter encouraged managers to study their industry in depth, to select a course of competitive advantage, to develop a set of strategies that adapt the firm to its external environment, and to draw on their executive leadership talents.

In *Competitive Advantage*, Porter provides insight into the complexity of industry competition by identifying five underlying forces. Low cost, differentiation, and focus are presented as generic strategies for the strategic positioning of a firm within its industry. The popularity of this book is revealed by its widespread adoption by managers and academics, as it has undergone its sixtieth printing in English and translation into 17 languages. Interested readers might wish to explore "An Interview with Michael Porter" by Nicholas Argyres and Anita M. McGahan in the *Academy of Management Executive*, 2002, 16:2, pp. 43–52.

1 THE PRACTICE OF MANAGEMENT

PETER F. DRUCKER

SUMMARY PREPARED BY JOHN D. STAVIG AND SHAKER
A. ZAHRA

John D. Stavig is the Professional Director of the Center for Entrepreneurial Studies at the Carlson School of Management, University of Minnesota. He holds a BSB from the Carlson School and an MBA from the Wharton School. John has over 15 years of experience in management consulting, private equity, and industry. As a founding principal of a $100 million private equity fund, he sourced and managed investments in numerous early-stage communications firms. John also served as CEO, CFO, and board member for several start-up and early-stage technology firms, and led numerous investments, acquisitions, and divestitures. As a Principal at Gemini Consulting and Arthur Andersen, he provided strategic and financial consulting services to senior executives in Fortune 1000 firms throughout the world. John has also taught in the MBA program at the University of St. Thomas.

Shaker A. Zahra is the Robert E. Buuck Chair of Entrepreneurship and Professor of Strategy at the Carlson School of Management at the University of Minnesota. He is also the Co-Director of the Center for Entrepreneurial Studies and Co-Director of the Integrative Leadership Center. His research has appeared in leading journals. He has also published or edited 10 books. His research has received several major awards. He is the Chair for the Entrepreneurship Division of the Academy of Management. His teaching, research, and service activities have received several awards.

Management is the brain of an enterprise and the primary source of long-term differentiation between firms. It is the disciplined and integrated practice of managing business, managers, workers, and work. It is also the creative process that drives **innovation** (the process of transforming discoveries into products, goods, and services) and entrepreneurship in a company. Management is entrusted with

---

Peter F. Drucker, *The Practice of Management*, New York: Harper & Row Publishers, Inc., 1954.

the responsibility for directing resources for the attainment of profits and the betterment of society.

Management is a practice, rather than an exact science or profession. As such, it requires judgment. *Management represents a systematic and fluid process of establishing and pursuing shared objectives for the enterprise, managers, and workers.* The role of management is to create a customer and organize the firm's resources toward the attainment of shared objectives. Managers must live in both the present and the future by balancing often-conflicting objectives. They need also to develop and maintain the logical linkages among strategy, objectives, and incentives throughout the enterprise.

The quality and performance of management are the only sustainable advantages for a business. A business is a social institution, created and managed by people. Rather than adapting to external conditions, management is creative and forward looking. It is the proactive creator of economic growth by deliberate action. Managing a business must always be entrepreneurial, focusing on creating customers through innovation and marketing. Management drives continued improvements and avoids inertia.

A CONCEPT OF THE FIRM

Organizations—and their managers—should be:

- Outward looking – both influenced by and shaping their external environment.
- A social institution – created by people; contributing to society.
- Pursuing multiple goals – both financial and nonfinancial.
- Innovative – emphasizing creativity, innovation, and entrepreneurship.
- Focused – answering and aligning resources to the question What is our primary business?
- Spirited – creating self-controlled and motivated managers.

Management has important economic and social responsibilities. Though economic performance is the first priority and management must make a profit to cover its risk premium, it must also consider the impact of its policies and decisions on society.

Advances in technology and automation will challenge managerial capabilities. These advances will lead to a more highly skilled workforce, the growth of **knowledge workers** (employees with high levels of education, skills, and competencies), and create demand for managers with better capabilities to lead these employees. Rank-and-file jobs will become increasingly managerial, resulting in a displacement of jobs, rather than replacement. Properly executed, the application and management of automation will drive productivity and wealth creation.

THE JOBS OF MANAGEMENT

Determining the Business and Purpose

Management's first responsibility is to answer the question *What is our business?* This is a challenging question that requires deliberate analysis based upon a thorough understanding of who the customers are, what they're actually buying, and what they value. Customers must be the foundation of the business, based upon the value they receive. Forward-looking companies seek to assess market potential and structure and introduce innovations that deliver value to customers, a process that determines what the business should be long term. Therefore, a company's entrepreneurial functions of innovation and marketing must cut across the entire business in order to satisfy customer needs. Customer satisfaction should be a company's primary goal. Profit is not the purpose of business, but rather a test of the validity of the business. *A firm's objective cannot simply be profit maximization.*

Setting and Measuring Progress Against the Objectives of a Business

Fundamental to the management of the business is the development of shared objectives. This must be derived from a creative and fluid process of deliberate goal setting. Objectives are required in every area of the business where performance impacts the survival and success of the business. Objectives determine what action to take today to obtain results tomorrow. Objectives must be forward looking and management should anticipate the future and be prepared to respond. Deliberate emphasis on innovation in setting objectives can be most valuable in areas where it appears less obvious. Management must implement regular, systematic, and unbiased measurements against set objectives, ideally based on feedback from the customer. Objectives should include areas of manager performance and development, worker performance and attitudes, and social responsibility. **Social responsibility** is simply the contribution a firm makes to its society. To some, this means making a profit, while others expect the firm to do more than this by ameliorating social problems. Setting objectives to improve worker performance and attitudes is one of the greatest challenges for management.

Balancing objectives across the different parts of a business is a critical role of management and requires judgment. Objectives can be changing, conflicting, intangible, and of differing duration. Objectives must be balanced based on organizational priorities and timing. A balanced set of objectives can serve as the "instrument panel" for piloting business.

Managing Managers by Objectives

Managers are the basic resource of business. They depreciate the fastest and require the greatest nourishment. **Management by Objectives (MBO)** is the process where employees set goals, justify them, determine resources needed to accomplish them, and establish timetables for their completion. These goals reflect the overall objectives of the organization. MBO develops individual responsibility toward a common direction. For an enterprise to grow beyond a single leader, there is a need for an organized and integrated team that focuses on shared objectives. Also required is the regular, systematic, and unbiased measurement of performance and the results against established objectives.

Being a manager means sharing in the responsibility for the enterprise. Every manager should responsibly participate in the development of the objectives to the unit he or she works for. Objectives must be clear and specific. They should be balanced and incorporate short- and long-term, tangible and intangible objectives. Objectives must be measurable—clear, simple, rational, relevant, reliable, and understandable.

Using MBO, emphasis on teamwork and shared goals should occur at every level of management. To ensure cooperation, individual managers should be measured on the following: performance from the individual unit, contribution to help other units achieve their objectives, and contribution expected from other units. MBO fosters self-control and motivation. This requires managers to convert objectives into personal goals, enabling them to direct, measure, and motivate themselves. To be in control and motivated, a manager's job should have the following characteristics: clear and measurable contribution to the success of the enterprise; directed and controlled by objectives, rather than the boss; broad scope and authority—decisions pushed down as far as possible; and duty to assist subordinates and peer managers to attain their objectives.

Productively Utilizing All Resources

Management is responsible for the productive utilization of all resources to meet their overall objectives. It should create a desired balance between all factors of production that will give the greatest output for the smallest effort. Productivity must incorporate both direct labor and managerial talent, because management is the scarcest and most expensive resource in the organization. Management should be the creative driver of increased productivity, rather than parasitical overhead. Companies should focus on increasing contributed value and the proportion of this value retained as profit.

Management should also understand company capabilities and consider outsourcing certain activities, even if potentially profitable. By evaluating this process mix, management will focus its resources on the activities that the company is best at performing, enabling it to create the most value for its customers.

Fostering a Positive Spirit

The spirit of the organization determines the motivation of its managers. It must be built on integrity and demonstrated by the actions of its leaders. Excellence and continuous improvement of the performance of the whole group must be encouraged, recognized, and rewarded. Managerial focus should underscore strengths, not weaknesses. Recognition, promotion, and financial incentives need to be tied to objectives and team performance. A positive spirit prepares for leadership, enabling the execution of objectives and the attainment of superior results.

Developing Managers

Managers are the firm's scarcest and most expensive resource. Management must challenge employees at all levels to pursue self-development to meet future managerial requirements. While management should encourage and direct the development of employees, the responsibility for development must remain with the subordinate manager. This development should place a large number of individuals in positions with general management responsibility across the business, rather than in a rotational program that promotes functional specialization for a select few. It is imperative that management creates the opportunities and tests the ability of its future managers to run and lead a whole business long before they reach the top.

Management of the Worker and Work

A key role for management is to define the nature of work, create a stimulating work environment, set standards, and train employees to assume progressively higher and more challenging responsibilities. Work should be rewarding—both financially and psychologically—in order to improve productivity.

Structure of Management

The **management structure** of an organization—the way managers divide, share, coordinate, and evaluate the work they do in planning and organizing the firm's overall operations—must facilitate the achievement of its objectives. *Structure does not always create good performance, but it can certainly inhibit results.* The structure should be flat, simple, and focused on performance. In determining the appropriate structure, management should consider the following: What activities are needed to achieve objectives? What decisions, and at what level, are necessary to achieve objectives? To what degree are activities and decisions interdependent?

Management structure should focus on business performance and results, contain the least possible number of levels, and enable the training and testing of future managers. When possible, autonomous product businesses are superior in meeting these requirements. A functional organization, even when decentralized, encourages specialization at the expense of company-wide perspective, adds unnecessary levels of management, and limits the development of future general managers.

2 | OUT OF THE CRISIS

W. Edwards Deming

Summary Prepared by William B. Gartner and
M. James Naughton

William B. Gartner *is a Professor at Georgetown University.*

M. James Naughton *is the owner of Expert-Knowledge Systems, Inc.*

Deming provides an ambitious objective for his book when he begins by saying:

> The aim of this book is transformation of the style of American management.
> Transformation of American style of management is not a job of reconstruc-
> tion, nor is it revision. It requires a whole new structure, from foundation
> upward. *Mutation* might be the word, except that *mutation* implies unordered
> spontaneity. Transformation must take place with directed effort.

Few individuals have had as much positive impact on the world economy as Dr. W. Edwards Deming. With the broadcast of the NBC white paper, "If Japan Can, Why Can't We?" on June 24, 1980, Dr. Deming gained national exposure as the man responsible for the managerial theory that has governed Japan's transformation into a nation of world leaders in the production of high-quality goods. This transformation did not happen overnight. Since 1950, when Dr. Deming first spoke to Japan's top managers on the improvement of quality, Japanese organizations have pioneered in the adaptation of Dr. Deming's ideas.

As a result of his seminars, Japan has had an annual national competition for quality improvement (the Deming Prize) since 1951. Japan has numerous journals and books devoted to exploring and furthering the implications of Deming's theory. However, it has only been within the last few years that a number of books have been published in the United States on "the Deming Theory of Management." An overview of the ideas that underlie Deming's theory, which cut across all major topical areas in management, will be provided here.

W. Edwards Deming, *Out of the Crisis.* Cambridge, MA: MIT Press, 1986.

DISEASES AND OBSTACLES

Deming's book is not merely about productivity and quality control; it is a broad vision of the nature of organizations and how organizations should be changed. Deming identifies a set of chronic ailments that can plague any organization and limit its success. These, which he calls "deadly diseases," include an overemphasis on short-term profits, human resource practices that encourage both managers and employees to be mobile and not organizationally loyal, merit ratings and review systems that are based on fear of one's supervisor, an absence of a single driving purpose, and management that is based on visible figures alone.

The reason that managers are not as effective as they could be is that they are the prisoners of some structural characteristics and personal assumptions that prevent their success. Among the obstacles that Deming discusses are the insulation of top management from the other employees in the organization, lack of adequate technical knowledge, a long history of total reliance on final inspection as a way of ensuring a quality product, the managerial belief that all problems originate within the workforce, a reliance on meeting specifications, and the failure to synthesize human operators with computer systems for control.

THE CONCEPT OF VARIABILITY

The basis for Deming's theory is the observation that variability exists everywhere in everything. *Only through the study and analysis of variability, using statistics, can a phenomenon be understood well enough to manipulate and change it.* In many respects, using statistics is not very radical. Statistics are fundamental to nearly all academic research. But Deming asks that the right kind of statistics (analytical) be applied to our everyday lives as well. And that is the rub. To recognize the pervasiveness of variability and to function so that the sources of this variability can be defined and measured are radical. In Deming's world, the use of statistical thinking is not an academic game; it is a way of life.

The concept of variability is to management theory and practice what the concept of the germ theory of disease was to the development of modern medicine. Medicine had been "successfully" practiced without the knowledge of germs. In a pre-germ theory paradigm, some patients got better, some got worse, and some stayed the same; in each case, some rationale could be used to explain the outcome. With the emergence of germ theory, all medical phenomena took on new meanings. Medical procedures thought to be good practice, such as physicians attending women in birth, turned out to be causes of disease because of the septic condition of the physicians' hands. Instead of rendering improved health care, the physicians' germ-laden hands achieved the opposite result. One can imagine the first proponents of the germ theory telling their colleagues who were still ignorant of the theory to wash their hands between patients. The pioneers must have sounded crazy. In the same vein, managers and academics who do not have a thorough understanding of variability will fail to grasp the radical change in thought that Deming envisions. Deming's propositions may seem as simplistic as "wash your hands!" rather than an entirely new paradigm of profound challenges to present-day managerial thinking and behaviors.

An illustration of variability that is widely cited in the books on Deming's theory is the "red bead experiment." Dr. Deming, at his four-day seminar, asks for 10 volunteers from the attendees. Six of the students become workers, two become inspectors of the workers' production, one becomes the inspector of the inspectors' work, and one becomes the recorder. Dr. Deming mixes together 3,000 white beads and 750 red beads in a large box. He instructs the workers to scoop out beads from the box with a beveled paddle that scoops out 50 beads at a time. Each scoop of the paddle is treated as a day's production. Only white beads are acceptable. Red beads are defects. After each worker scoops a paddle of beads from the box, the two inspectors count the defects, the inspector of the inspectors inspects the inspectors' count, and the recorder writes down the inspectors' agreed-upon number of defects. Invariably, each worker's scoop contains some red beads. Deming plays the role of the manager by exhorting the workers to produce no defects. When a worker scoops few red beads he may be praised. Scooping many red beads brings criticism and an exhortation to do better, otherwise "we will go out of business." The manager reacts to each scoop of beads as if it had meaning in itself rather than as part of a pattern. Figure 2–1 shows the number of defective beads each worker produced for four days of work.

Dr. Deming's statistical analysis of the workers' production indicates that the process of producing white beads is in statistical control; that is, the variability of this production system is stable. The near-term prediction about the *pattern,* but not the

---

FIGURE 1   Number of Defective Items by Operator, by Day

			Day		
Name	1	2	3	4	All 4
Neil	3	13	8	9	33
Tace	6	9	8	10	33
Tim	13	12	7	10	42
Mike	11	8	10	15	44
Tony	9	13	8	11	41
Richard	12	11	7	15	45
All 6	54	66	48	70	238
Cum $\bar{x}$	9.0	10.0	9.3	9.92	9.92

$$\bar{x} = \frac{238}{6 \times 4} = 9.92$$

$$\bar{p} = \frac{238}{6 \times 4 \times 50} = .198$$

$$\left.\begin{matrix} \text{UCL} \\ \text{LCL} \end{matrix}\right\} = x \pm 3\sqrt{\bar{x}(1-\bar{p})} = 9.9 \pm 3\sqrt{9.9 \times .802}$$

$$= \begin{cases} 18 \\ 1 \end{cases}$$

Source: Adapted from Deming, p. 347.

individual draws, of the system's performance can be made. Near-future draws will yield an average, over many experiments, of 9.4 red beads. Any one draw may range between 1 and 18 red beads. In other words, the actual number of red beads scooped by each worker is out of that worker's control. The worker, as Dr. Deming says, "is only delivering the defects." Management, which controls the system, has caused the defects through design of the system. There are a number of insights people draw from this experiment. Walton lists the following:

- Variation is part of any process.
- Planning requires prediction of how things and people will perform. Tests and experiments of past performance can be useful, but not definitive.
- Workers work within a system that—try as they might—is beyond their control. It is the system, not their individual skills, that determines how they perform.
- Only management can change the system.
- Some workers will always be above average, some below.[1]

The red bead experiment illustrates the behavior of systems of stable variability. In Deming's theory, a system is all of the aspects of the organization and environment—employees, managers, equipment, facilities, government, customers, suppliers, shareholders, and so forth—fitted together, with the aim of producing some type of output. Stability implies that the output has regularity to it, so that predictions regarding the output of the system can be made. But many of these systems are inherently unstable. Bringing a system into stability is one of the fundamental managerial activities in the Deming theory.

In Deming's theory, a stable system, that is, a system that shows signs of being in statistical control, behaves in a manner similar to the red bead experiment. In systems, a single datum point is of little use in understanding the causes that influenced the production of that point. It is necessary to withhold judgment about changes in the output of the system until sufficient evidence (additional data points) becomes available to suggest whether or not the system being examined is stable. Statistical theory provides tools to help evaluate the stability of systems. Once a system is stable, its productive capability can be determined; that is, the average output of the system and the spread of variability around that average can be described. This can be used to predict the near-term future behavior of the system.

The inefficiencies inherent in "not knowing what we are doing," that is, in working with systems not in statistical control, might not seem to be that great a competitive penalty if all organizations are similarly out of control. Yet we are beginning to realize that the quality of outputs from organizations that are managed using Deming's theory are many magnitudes beyond what non-Deming organizations have been producing. The differences in quality and productivity can be mind-boggling.

For example, both Scherkenbach[2] and Walton[3] reported that when the Ford Motor Company began using transmissions produced by the Japanese automobile manufacturer, Mazda, Ford found that customers overwhelmingly preferred cars with Mazda transmissions to cars with Ford-manufactured transmissions—because the warranty repairs were 10 times lower, and the cars were quieter and shifted more smoothly. When Ford engineers compared their transmissions to the Mazda transmissions, they found that the piece-to-piece variation in the Mazda transmissions was nearly three times less than in the Ford pieces. Both Ford and Mazda conformed to the engineering standards specified by Ford, but Mazda transmissions were far more uniform. More uniform products also cost less to manufacture. With less variability there is less rework and less need for inspection. Only systems in statistical control can begin to reduce variability and thereby improve the quality and quantity of their output. Both authors reported that after Ford began to implement Deming's theory over the last five years, warranty repair frequencies dropped by 45 percent and "things gone wrong" reports from customers dropped by 50 percent.

FOURTEEN STEPS MANAGEMENT MUST TAKE

The task of transformation of an entire organization to use the Deming theory becomes an enormous burden for management, and Deming frequently suggests that this process is likely to take a minimum of 10 years. The framework for transforming an organization is outlined in the 14 points (pp. 23–24):

1. Create constancy of purpose toward improvement of product and service, aiming to become competitive, to stay in business, and to provide jobs.
2. Adopt the new philosophy. We are in a new economic age. Western management must awaken to the challenge, must learn their responsibilities, and must take on leadership in order to bring about change.
3. Cease dependence on inspection to achieve quality. Eliminate the need for inspection on a mass basis by building quality into the product in the first place.
4. End the practice of awarding business on the basis of the price tag. Instead, minimize total cost. Move toward a single supplier for any one time and develop long-term relationships of loyalty and trust with that supplier.
5. Improve constantly and forever the systems of production and service in order to improve quality and productivity. Thus, one constantly decreases costs.
6. Institute training on the job.
7. Institute leadership. Supervisors should be able to help people to do a better job, and they should use machines and gadgets wisely. Supervision of management and supervision of production workers need to be overhauled.
8. Drive out fear, so that everyone may work effectively for the company.
9. Break down barriers between departments. People in research, design, sales, and production must work as a team. They should foresee production problems and problems that could be encountered when using the product or service.
10. Eliminate slogans, exhortations, and targets that demand zero defects and new levels of productivity. These only create adversarial relationships because the many causes of low quality and low productivity are due to the system, and not the workforce.
11. **a.** Eliminate work standards (quotas) on the factory floor. Substitute leadership.
    b. Eliminate management by objectives. Eliminate management by numbers or numerical goals. Substitute leadership.
12. **a.** Remove barriers that rob hourly workers of their right to pride of workmanship. The responsibility of supervisors must be changed from sheer numbers to quality.
    b. Remove barriers that rob people in management and in engineering of their right to pride of workmanship. This means, *inter alia,* abolishing the annual merit rating and management by objectives.

13. Institute a vigorous program of education and self-improvement.

14. Put everybody in the company to work to accomplish the transformation. The transformation is everybody's job.

As mentioned earlier, the 14 points should not be treated as a list of aphorisms, nor can each of the 14 points be treated separately without recognizing the interrelationships among them.

Conclusions

Out of the Crisis is full of examples and ideas, and Deming calls for a radical revision of American management practice. To his credit, Deming constantly recognizes ideas and examples from individuals practicing various aspects of his theory. This constant recognition of other individuals provides a subtle indication that a body of practitioners exists who have had successful experiences applying his 14 steps and other ideas.

A transformation in American management needs to occur; it can take place, and it has begun already in those firms applying Deming's theory. Deming offers a new paradigm for the practice of management that requires a dramatic rethinking and replacement of old methods by those trained in traditional management techniques. In conclusion, Deming recognizes that "it takes courage to admit that you have been doing something wrong, to admit that you have something to learn, that there is a better way" (Walton, 1986, p. 223).

Notes

1. William B. Gartner and M. James Naughton. "The Deming Theory of Management." *Academy of Management Review,* January 1988, pp. 138–142.

2. William W. Scherkenbach. *The Deming Route to Quality and Productivity: Roadmaps and Roadblocks.* Milwaukee, WI: ASQC, 1986.

3. Mary Walton. *The Deming Management Method.* New York: Dodd, Mead & Company, 1986.

3

THE HUMAN SIDE OF
ENTERPRISE

DOUGLAS MCGREGOR

SUMMARY PREPARED BY GAYLE PORTER

Gayle Porter obtained her doctorate from The Ohio State University in Organizational Behavior and Human Resource Management and is now at Rutgers University—Camden. Articles and ongoing research interests include the effects of dispositional differences in the workplace; group perceptions of efficacy and esteem; and the comparison of influence on employees through reward systems, leadership, and employee development efforts. Her prior experience includes positions as Director of Curriculum Development for a human resource management degree program; consultant on training programs, financial operations, and computer applications; financial manager for an oil and gas production company; and financial specialist for NCR Corporation.

*T*he Human Side of Enterprise was written during an ongoing comparative study of management development programs in several large companies. In McGregor's view, the making of managers has less to do with formal efforts in development than with how the task of management is understood within that organization. This fundamental understanding determines the policies and procedures within which the managers operate, and guides the selection of people identified as having the potential for management positions. During the late 1950s McGregor believed that major industrial advances of the next half century would occur on the human side of enterprise and he was intrigued by the inconsistent assumptions about what makes managers behave as they do. His criticism of the conventional assumptions, which he labels Theory X, is that they limit options. Theory Y provides an alternative set of assumptions that are much needed due to the extent of unrealized human potential in most organizations.

Douglas McGregor, *The Human Side of Enterprise.* New York: McGraw-Hill, 1960.

THE THEORETICAL ASSUMPTIONS OF MANAGEMENT

Regardless of the economic success of a firm, few managers are satisfied with their ability to predict and control the behavior of members of the organization. Effective prediction and control are central to the task of management, and there can be no prediction without some underlying theory. Therefore, *all managerial decisions and actions rest on a personally held theory, a set of assumptions about behavior.* The assumptions management holds about controlling its human resources determine the whole character of the enterprise.

In application, problems occur related to these assumptions. First, managers may not realize that they hold and apply conflicting ideas and that one may cancel out the other. For example, a manager may delegate based on the assumption that employees should have responsibility, but then nullify that action by close monitoring, which indicates the belief that employees can't handle the responsibility. Another problem is failure to view control as selective adaptation, when dealing with human behavior. People adjust to certain natural laws in other fields; for example, engineers don't dig channels and expect water to run uphill! With humans, however, there is a tendency to try to control in direct violation of human nature. Then, when they fail to achieve the desired results, they look for every other possible cause rather than examine the inappropriate choice of a method to control behavior.

Any influence is based on dependence, so the nature and degree of dependence are critical factors in determining what methods of control will be effective. Conventional organization theory is based on authority as a key premise. It is the central and indispensable means of managerial control and recognizes only upward dependence. In recent decades, workers have become less dependent on a single employer, and society has provided certain safeguards related to unemployment. This limits the upward dependence and, correspondingly, the ability to control by authority alone. In addition, employees have the ability to engage in countermeasures such as slowdowns, lowered standards of performance, or even sabotage to defeat authority they resent.

Organizations are more accurately represented as systems of *inter*dependence. Subordinates depend on managers to help them meet their needs, but managers also depend on subordinates to achieve their own and the organization's goals. While there is nothing inherently bad or wrong in the use of authority to control, in certain circumstances it fails to bring the desired results. Circumstances change even from hour to hour, and the role of the manager is to select the appropriate means of influence based on the situation at a given point in time. If employees exhibit lazy, indifferent behavior, the causes lie in management methods of organization and control.

Theory X is a term used to represent a set of assumptions. Principles found in traditional management literature could only have derived from assumptions such as the following, which have had a major impact on managerial strategy in organizations:

1. The average human being has an inherent dislike of work and will avoid it if possible.
2. Because of this human characteristic of dislike of work, most people must be coerced, controlled, directed, and threatened with punishment to get them to put forth adequate effort toward the achievement of organizational objectives.
3. The average human being prefers to be directed, wishes to avoid responsibility, has relatively little ambition, and wants security above all.

These assumptions are not without basis, or they would never have persisted as they have. They do explain some observed human behavior, but other observations are not consistent with this view. Theory X assumptions also encourage us to categorize certain behaviors as human nature, when they may actually be symptoms of a condition in which workers have been deprived of an opportunity to satisfy higher-order needs (social and egoistic needs).

A strong tradition exists of viewing employment as an employee's agreement to accept control by others in exchange for rewards that are only of value outside the workplace. For example, wages (except for status differences), vacation, medical benefits, stock purchase plans, and profit sharing are of little value during the actual time on the job. Work is the necessary evil to endure for rewards away from the job. In this conception of human resources we can never discover, let alone utilize, the potentialities of the average human being.

Many efforts to provide more equitable and generous treatment to employees and to provide a safe and pleasant work environment have been designed without any real change in strategy. Very often what is proposed as a new management strategy is nothing more than a different tactic within the old Theory X assumptions. Organizations have progressively made available the means to satisfy lower-order needs for subsistence and safety. As the nature of the dependency relationship changes, management has gradually deprived itself of the opportunity to use control based solely on assumptions of Theory X. A new strategy is needed.

Theory Y assumptions are dynamic, indicate the possibility of human growth and development, and stress the necessity for selective adaptation:

1. The expenditure of physical and mental effort in work is as natural as play or rest.
2. External control and the threat of punishment are not the only means for bringing about effort toward organizational objectives. People will exercise self-direction and self-control in the service of objectives to which they are committed.
3. Commitment to objectives is a function of the rewards associated with their achievement (*satisfaction of ego and self-actualization needs can be products of effort directed toward organizational objectives*).
4. The average human being learns, under proper conditions, not only to accept but to seek responsibility.
5. The capacity to exercise a relatively high degree of imagination, ingenuity, and creativity in the solution of organizational problems is widely, not narrowly, distributed in the population.
6. Under the conditions of modern industrial life, the intellectual potentialities of the average human being are only partially utilized.

The Theory Y assumptions challenge a number of deeply ingrained managerial habits of thought and action; they lead to a management philosophy of integration and self-control. Theory X assumes that the organization's requirements take precedence over the needs of the individual members, and that the worker must always adjust to needs of the organization as management perceives them. In contrast, the principle of *integration* proposes that conditions can be created such that individuals can best achieve their own goals by directing their efforts toward the success of the enterprise. Based on the premise that the assumptions of Theory Y are valid, the next logical question is whether, and to what extent, such conditions can be created. How will employees be convinced that applying their skills, knowledge, and ingenuity in support of the organization is a more attractive alternative than other ways to utilize their capacities?

THEORY IN PRACTICE

The essence of applying Theory Y assumptions is guiding the subordinates to develop themselves rather than developing the subordinates by telling them what they need to do. An important consideration is that the subordinates' acceptance of responsibility for self-developing (i.e., self-direction and self-control) has been shown to relate to their commitment to objectives. But the overall aim is to further the growth of the individual, and it must be approached as a managerial strategy rather than simply as a personnel technique. Forms and procedures are of little value. Once the concept is provided, managers who welcome the assumptions of Theory Y will create their own processes for implementation; managers with underlying Theory X assumptions cannot create the conditions for integration and self-control no matter what tools are provided.

The development process becomes one of role clarification and mutual agreement regarding the subordinate's job responsibilities. This requires the manager's willingness to accept some risk and allow mistakes as part of the growth process. It also is time-consuming in terms of discussions and allowing opportunity for self-discovery. However, it is not a new set of duties on top of the manager's existing load. It is a different way of fulfilling the existing responsibilities.

One procedure that violates Theory Y assumptions is the typical utilization of performance appraisals. Theory X leads quite naturally into this means of directing individual efforts toward organizational objectives. Through the performance appraisal process, management tells people what to do, monitors their activities, judges how well they have done, and rewards or punishes them accordingly. Since the appraisals are used for administrative purposes (e.g., pay, promotion, retention decisions), this is a demonstration of management's overall control strategy. Any consideration of personal goals is covered by the expectation that rewards of salary and position are enough. If the advancement available through this system is not a desired reward, the individuals are placed in a position of acting against their own objectives and advancing for the benefit of the organization only. The alternative (for example, turning down a promotion) may bring negative outcomes such as lack of future options or being identified as employees with no potential.

The principle of integration requires active and responsible participation of employees in decisions affecting them. One plan that demonstrates Theory Y assumptions is *The Scanlon Plan.* A central feature in this plan is the cost-reduction sharing that provides a meaningful cause-and-effect connection between employee behavior and the reward received. The reward is directly related to the success of the organization and it is distributed frequently. This provides a more effective learning reinforcement than the traditional performance appraisal methods. The second central feature of the Scanlon Plan is effective participation, a formal method through which members contribute brains and ingenuity as well as their physical efforts on the job. This provides a means for social and ego satisfaction, so employees have a stake in the success of the firm beyond the economic rewards. Implementation of the Scanlon Plan is not a program or set of procedures; it must be accepted as a way of life and can vary depending on the circumstances of the particular company. It is entirely consistent with Theory Y assumptions.

Theory X leads to emphasis on tactics of control, whereas Theory Y is more concerned with the nature of the relationship. Eliciting the desired response in a Theory Y context is a matter of creating an environment or set of conditions to enable self-direction.

The day-to-day behavior of an immediate supervisor or manager is perhaps the most critical factor in such an environment. Through sometimes subtle behaviors superiors demonstrate their attitudes and create what is referred to as the psychological "climate" of the relationship.

Management style does not seem to be important. Within many different styles, subordinates may or may not develop confidence in the manager's deeper integrity, based on other behavioral cues. Lack of confidence in the relationship causes anxiety and undesirable reactions from the employees. No ready formula is available to relay integrity. Insincere attempts to apply a technique or style—such as using participation only to manipulate subordinates into believing they have some input to decisions—are usually recognized as a gimmick and soon destroy confidence.

In addition to manager–subordinate relationships, problems connected to Theory X assumptions can be observed in other organizational associations such as staff-line relationships. Upper management may create working roles for staff groups to "police" line managers' activities, giving them an influence that equates psychologically to direct line authority. Top management with Theory X assumptions can delegate and still retain control. The staff function provides an opportunity to monitor indirectly, to set policy for limiting decisions and actions, and to obtain information on everything happening before a problem can occur.

Staff personnel often come from a very specialized education with little preparation for what their role should be in an organization. Will full confidence in their objective methods and training to find "the best answer," they often are unprepared for the resistance of line managers who don't share this confidence and don't trust the derived solutions. The staff may conclude that line managers are stupid, are unconcerned with the general welfare of the organization, and care only about their own authority and independence. They essentially adopt the Theory X assumptions and readily accept the opportunity to create a system of measurements for control of the line operations.

To utilize staff groups within the context of Theory Y, managers must emphasize the principle of self-control. As a resource to all parts and levels of the organization, staff reports and data should be supplied to all members who can use such information to control their own job—not subordinates' jobs. If summary data indicate something wrong within the manager's unit of responsibility, the manager would turn to subordinates, not to the staff, for more information. If the subordinates are practicing similar self-control using staff-provided information, they have most likely discovered the same problem and taken action before this inquiry occurs. There is no solution to the problem of staff-line relationships in authoritative terms that can address organizational objectives adequately. However, a manager operating by Theory Y assumptions will apply them similarly to all relationships—upward, downward, and peer level—including the staff-line associations.

THE DEVELOPMENT OF MANAGERIAL TALENT

Leadership is a relationship with four major variables: the characteristics of the leader; the attitudes, needs, and other personal characteristics of the followers; the characteristics of the organization, such as its purpose, structure, and the nature of its task; and the social, economic, and political environment in which the organization operates. Specifying which leader characteristics will result in effective performance depends on the other factors, so it is a complex relationship. Even if researchers were able to determine the universal characteristics of a good relationship between the leader and the other situational factors, there are still many ways to achieve the same thing. For example, mutual confidence seems important in the relationship, but there are a number of ways that confidence can be developed and maintained. Different personal characteristics could achieve the same desired relationship.

Also, because it is so difficult to predict the situational conditions an organization will face, future management needs are unpredictable. The major task, then, is to provide a heterogeneous supply of human resources from which individuals can be selected as appropriate at a future time. This requires attracting recruits from a variety of sources and with a variety of backgrounds, which complicates setting criteria for selection. Also, the management development programs in an organization should involve many people rather than a few with similar qualities and abilities. Finally, management's goal must be to develop the unique capacities of each individual, rather than common objectives for all participants. We must place high value on people in general—seek to enable them to develop to their fullest potential in whatever role they best can fill. Not everyone must pursue the top jobs; outstanding leadership is needed at every level.

Individuals must develop themselves and will do so optimally only in terms of what each of them sees as meaningful and valuable. What might be called a "manufacturing approach" to management development involves designing programs to build managers; this end product becomes a supply of managerial talent to be used as needed. A preferred alternative approach is to "grow talent" under the assumption that people will grow into what they are capable of becoming, if they are provided the right conditions for that growth. There is little relationship (possibly even a negative one) between the formal structure for management development and actual achievement of the organization, because programs and procedures do not *cause* management development.

Learning is fairly straightforward when the individual desires new knowledge or skill. Unfortunately, many development offerings soon become a scheduled assignment for entire categories of people. Learning is limited in these conditions, because the motivation is low. Further, negative attitudes develop toward training in general, which interferes with creating an overall climate conducive to growth. In many cases, managers may have a purpose in sending subordinates to training that is not shared with or understood by that individual. This creates anxiety or confusion, which also interferes with learning. It is best if attendance in training and development programs is the result of joint target-setting, wherein the individual expresses a need and it can be determined that a particular program will benefit both the individual and the organization.

Classroom learning can be valuable to satisfying needs of both parties. However, it can only be effective when there is an organizational climate conducive to growth. Learning is always an active process, whether related to motor skills or acquisition of knowledge; it cannot be injected into the learner, so motivation is critical. Practice and feedback are essential when behavior changes are involved. Classroom methods such as case analysis and role playing provide an opportunity to experiment with decisions and behaviors in a safe environment, to receive immediate feedback, and to go back and try other alternatives. Some applications of classroom learning may be observed directly on the job. In other cases, the application may be more subtle, in the form of increased understanding or challenging one's own preconceptions. Care must be taken so that pressures to evaluate the benefits of classroom learning don't result in application of inappropriate criteria for success while the true value of the experience is overlooked.

Separate attention is given to management groups or teams at various levels. Within Theory X assumptions, direction and control are jeopardized by effective group functioning. On the other hand, a manager who recognizes interdependencies in the organization—one who is less interested in personal power than in creating conditions so human resources will voluntarily achieve organization objectives—will seek to build strong management groups. Creating a managerial team requires unity of purpose among those individuals. If the group is nothing more than several individuals competing for power and recognition, it is not a team. Again, the climate of the relationships and the fundamental understanding of the role of managers in the organization will be critical. One day the hierarchical structure of reporting relationships will disappear from organizational charts and give way to a series of linked groups. This shift in patterns of relationships will be a slow transition, but will signify recognition of employee capacity to collaborate in joint efforts. Then we may begin to discover how seriously management has underestimated the true potential of the organization's human resources.

Conclusion

Theory X is not an evil set of assumptions, but rather a limiting one. Use of authority to influence has its place, even within the Theory Y assumptions, but it does not work in all circumstances. A number of societal changes suggest why Theory X increasingly may cause problems for organizations needing more innovation and flexibility in their operating philosophy. It is critically important for managers honestly to examine the assumptions that underlie their own behavior toward subordinates. To do so requires first accepting the two possibilities, Theory X and Theory Y, and then examining one's own actions in the context of that comparison. Fully understanding the implications on each side will help identify whether the observed choices of how to influence people are likely to bring about the desired results.

4

MASLOW ON MANAGEMENT

ABRAHAM H. MASLOW

It should be possible to implement an enlightened management policy into an organization, where employees can *self-actualize* (institute their own ideas, make decisions, learn from their mistakes, and grow in their capabilities) while creating *synergy* (attaining beneficial results simultaneously for the individual and the organization). Such a policy (and associated practices) would not necessarily apply to all people, because everyone is at a different level on the motivational hierarchy (from physiological to safety to love to esteem to self-actualization). Nevertheless, the assumptions that would need to be true in order to create an ideal (eupsychian) society can be identified and then explored. They include the following dimensions. People are:

- psychologically healthy;
- not fixated at the safety-need level;
- capable of growth, which occurs through delight and through boredom;
- able to grow to a high level of personal maturity;
- courageous, with the ability to conquer their fears and endure anxiety.

They have:

- the impulse to achieve;
- the capacity to be objective about themselves and about others;
- the capacity to be trusted to some degree;
- a strong will to grow, experiment, select their own friends, carry out their own ideas, and self-actualize;
- the ability to enjoy good teamwork, friendships, group spirit, group harmony, belongingness, and group love;
- the capacity to be improved to some degree;
- the ability to identify with a common objective and contribute to it;
- a conscience and feelings.

Abraham H. Maslow, *Maslow on Management.* New York: Wiley & Sons, Inc., 1998.

Everyone prefers:

- to love and to respect his or her boss;
- to be a prime mover rather than a passive helper;
- to use all their capacities;
- to work rather than being idle;
- to have meaningful work;
- to be justly and fairly appreciated, preferably in public;
- to feel important, needed, useful, successful, proud, and respected;
- to have responsibility;
- to have personhood, identity, and uniqueness as a person;
- to create rather than destroy;
- to be interested rather than bored;
- to improve things, make things right, and do things better.

Given this portrait of a certain type of individual described by these assumptions, we can conclude the following:

- Authoritarian managers are dysfunctional for them;
- People can benefit by being stretched, strained, and challenged once in a while;
- Everyone should be informed as completely as possible;
- These types of persons will do best at what they have chosen, based on what they like most;
- Everybody needs to be absolutely clear about the organization's goals, directions, and purposes.

In conclusion, *enlightened management is the wave of the future.* It will be seen more and more for a very simple reason that can be stated as a fundamental principle of human behavior: "Treating people well spoils them for being treated badly." In other words, once employees have experienced any aspect of enlightened management, they will never wish to return to an authoritarian environment. Further, as other workers hear about enlightened work organizations, they will either seek to work there or demand that their own workplaces become more enlightened.

5

THE FIFTH DISCIPLINE

PETER M. SENGE

SUMMARY PREPARED BY DOROTHY MARCIC

*Dorothy Marcic is an Adjunct Professor at Vanderbilt University's Owen Graduate School of Management. Previously, she served as Director of Graduate Programs in Human Resource Development at Peabody College and Fulbright Scholar at the University of Economics—Prague, and held academic appointments at Arizona State University and the University of Wisconsin—La Crosse. Dorothy's research and consulting interests include how to develop the kinds of structures, values, and systems that help create learning organizations that are uplifting to employees. Addressing that issue is one of the 10 books she has authored—*Managing With the Wisdom of Love: Uncovering Virtue in Organizations.

Learning disabilities can be fatal to organizations, causing them to have an average life span of only 40 years—half a human being's life. *Organizations need to be learners, and often they are not.* Somehow some survive, but never live up to their potential. What happens if what we term "excellence" is really no more than mediocrity? Only those firms that become learners will succeed in the increasingly turbulent, competitive global market.

LEARNING DISABILITIES

There are seven learning disabilities common to organizations.

Identification with One's Position

American workers are trained to see themselves as what they do, not who they are. Therefore, if laid off, they find it difficult, if not impossible, to find work doing something else. Worse for the organization, though, is the limited thinking this attitude creates. By claiming an identity related to the job, workers are cut off from seeing how their responsibility connects to other jobs. For example, one American car had three assembly bolts on one component. The similar Japanese make had only one bolt. Why? Because the Detroit manufacturer had three engineers for that component, while a similar Japanese manufacturer had only one.

Peter M. Senge, *The Fifth Discipline: The Art and Practice of the Learning Organization.* New York: Doubleday, 1990.

External Enemies

This belief is a result of the previously stated disability. *External enemies* refers to people focusing blame on anything but themselves or their unit. Fault is regularly blamed on factors like the economy, the weather, or the government. Marketing blames manufacturing, and manufacturing blames engineering. Such external fault-finding keeps the organization from seeing what the real problems are and prevents them from tackling the real issues head-on.

The Illusion of Taking Charge

Being proactive is seen as good management—doing something about "those problems." All too often, though, being proactive is a disguise for reactiveness against that awful enemy out there.

The Fixation on Events

Much attention in organizations is paid to events—last month's sales, the new product, who just got hired, and so on. Our society, too, is geared toward short-term thinking, which in turn stifles the type of generative learning that permits a look at the real threats—the slowly declining processes of quality, service, or design.

The Parable of the Boiled Frog

An experiment was once conducted by placing a frog in boiling water. Immediately the frog, sensing danger in the extreme heat, jumped out to safety. However, placing the frog in cool water and slowly turning up the heat resulted in the frog getting groggier and groggier and finally boiling to death. Why? Because the frog's survival mechanisms are programmed to look for sudden changes in the environment, not gradual changes. Similarly, during the 1960s, the U.S. auto industry saw no threat by Japan, which had only 4 percent of the market. Not until the 1980s when Japan had over 21 percent of the market did the Big Three begin to look at their core assumptions. Now with Japan holding about 30 percent share of the market, it is not certain if this frog (U.S. automakers) is capable of jumping out of the boiling water. Looking at gradual processes requires slowing down our frenetic pace and watching for the subtle cues.

The Delusion of Learning from Experience

Learning from experience is powerful. This is how we learn to walk and talk. However, we now live in a time when direct consequences of actions may take months or years to appear. Decisions in R&D may take up to a decade to bear fruit, and their actual consequences may be influenced by manufacturing and marketing along the way. Organizations often choose to deal with these complexities by breaking themselves up into smaller and smaller components, further reducing their ability to see problems in their entirety.

The Myth of the Management Team

Most large organizations have a group of bright, experienced leaders who are supposed to know all the answers. They were trained to believe there are answers to all problems and they should find them. People are rarely rewarded for bringing up difficult issues or for looking at parts of a problem that make them harder to grasp. Most teams end up operating below the lowest IQ of any member. What results are "skilled incompetents"—people who know all too well how to keep *from* learning.

SYSTEMS THINKING

There are five disciplines required for a learning organization: personal mastery, mental models, shared vision, team learning, and systems thinking. The fifth one, systems thinking, is the most important. Without systems thinking, the other disciplines do not have the same effect.

The Laws of the Fifth Discipline

Today's Problems Result from Yesterday's Solutions

A carpet merchant kept pushing down a bump in the rug, only to have it reappear elsewhere, until he lifted a corner and out slithered a snake. Sometimes fixing one part of the system only brings difficulties to other parts of the system. For example, solving an internal inventory problem may lead to angry customers who now get late shipments.

Push Hard and the System Pushes Back Even Harder

Systems theory calls this compensating feedback, which is a common way of reducing the effects of an intervention. Some cities, for example, build low-cost housing and set up jobs programs, only to have more poor people than ever. Why? Because many moved to the cities from neighboring areas so that they, too, could take advantage of the low-cost housing and job opportunities.

Behavior Gets Better Before It Gets Worse

Some decisions actually look good in the short term, but produce *compensating feedback* and crisis in the end. The really effective decisions often produce difficulties in the short run but create more health in the long term. This is why behaviors such as building a power base or working hard just to please the boss come back to haunt you.

The Best Way Out Is to Go Back In

We often choose familiar solutions, ones that feel comfortable and not scary. But the effective ways often mean going straight into what we are afraid of facing. What does *not* work is pushing harder on the same old solutions (also called the "what we need here is a bigger hammer" syndrome).

The Cure Can Be Worse than the Disease

The result of applying nonsystematic solutions to problems is the need for more and more of the same. It can become addictive. Someone begins mild drinking to alleviate work tension. The individual feels better and then takes on more work, creating more tension and a need for more alcohol, and the person finally becomes an alcoholic. Sometimes these types of solutions only result in shifting the burden. The government enters the scene by providing more welfare and leaves the host system weaker and less able to solve its own problems. This ultimately necessitates still more aid from the government. Companies can try to shift their burdens to consultants, but then become more and more dependent on them to solve their problems.

Faster Is Slower

Every system, whether ecological or organizational, has an optimal rate of growth. Faster and faster is not always better. (After all, the tortoise finally did win the race.) Complex human systems require new ways of thinking. Quickly jumping in and fixing what *looks* bad usually provides solutions for a problem's symptoms and not for the problem itself.

Cause and Effect Are Not Always Related Closely in Time and Space

Effects here mean the symptoms we see, such as drug abuse and unemployment, whereas *causes* mean the interactions of the underlying system which bring about these conditions. We often assume cause is near to effect. If there is a sales problem, then incentives for the sales force should fix it, or if there is inadequate housing, then build more houses. Unfortunately, this does not often work, for the real causes lie elsewhere.

Tiny Changes May Produce Big Results; Areas of Greatest Leverage Are Frequently the Least Obvious

System science teaches that the most obvious solutions usually do not work. While simple solutions frequently make short-run improvements, they commonly contribute to long-term deteriorations. The *non*obvious and *well-focused* solutions are more likely to provide leverage and bring positive change. For example, ships have a tiny trim tab on one edge of the rudder that has great influence on the movement of that ship, so small changes in the trim tab bring big shifts in the ship's course. However, there are no simple rules for applying leverage to organizations. It requires looking for the structure of what is going on rather than merely seeing the events.

You Can Have Your Cake and Eat It Too—But Not At the Same Time

Sometimes the most difficult problems come from "snapshot" rather than "process" thinking. For example, it was previously believed by American manufacturers that quality and low cost could not be achieve simultaneously. One had to be chosen over the other. What was missed, however, was the notion that improving quality may also mean eliminating waste and unnecessary time (both adding costs), which in the end would mean lower costs. Real leverage comes when it can be seen that seemingly opposing needs can be met over time.

Cutting the Elephant in Half Does Not Create Two Elephants

Some problems can be solved by looking at parts of the organization, whereas others require holistic thinking. What is needed is an understanding of the boundaries for each problem. Unfortunately, most organizations are designed to prevent people from seeing systemic problems, either by creating rigid structures or by leaving problems behind for others to clean up.

There Is No Blame

Systems thinking teaches that there are not outside causes to problems; instead, you and your "enemy" are part of the same system. Any cure requires understanding how that is seen.

THE OTHER DISCIPLINES

Personal Mastery

Organizations can learn only when the individuals involved learn. This requires personal mastery, which is the discipline of personal learning and growth, where people are continually expanding their ability to create the kind of life they want. From their quest comes the spirit of the learning organization.

Personal mastery involves seeing one's life as a creative work, being able to clarify what is really important, and learning to see current reality more clearly. The difference between what's important, what we want, and where we are now produces a "creative tension." Personal mastery means being able to generate and maintain creative tension.

Those who have high personal mastery have a vision, which is more like a calling, and they are in a continual learning mode. They never really "arrive." Filled with more commitment, they take initiative and greater responsibility in their work.

Previously, organizations supported an employee's development only if it would help the organization, which fits in with the traditional "contract" between employee and organization ("an honest day's pay in exchange for an honest day's work"). The new, and coming, way is to see it rather as a "covenant," which comes from a shared vision of goals, ideas, and management processes.

Working toward personal mastery requires living with emotional tension, not letting our goals get eroded. As Somerset Maugham said, "Only mediocre people are always at their best." One of the worst blocks to achieving personal mastery is the common belief that we cannot have what we want. Being committed to the truth is a powerful weapon against this, for it does not allow us to deceive ourselves. Another means of seeking personal mastery is to integrate our reason and intuition. We live in a society that values reason and devalues intuition. However, using both together is very powerful and may be one of the fundamental contributions to systems thinking.

Mental Models

Mental models are internal images of how the world works, and they can range from simple generalizations (people are lazy) to complex theories (assumptions about why my co-workers interact the way they do). For example, for decades the Detroit automakers believed people bought cars mainly for styling, not for quality or reliability. These beliefs, which were really unconscious assumptions, worked well for many years, but ran into trouble when competition from Japan began. It took a long time for Detroit even to begin to see the mistakes in their beliefs. One company that managed to change its mental model through incubating a business worldview was Shell.

Traditional hierarchical organizations have the dogma of organizing, managing, and controlling. In the new learning organization, though, the revised "dogma" will be values, vision, and mental models.

Hanover Insurance began changes in 1969 designed to overcome the "basic disease of the hierarchy." Three values espoused were

1. *Openness*—seen as an antidote to the dysfunctional interactions in face-to-face meetings.
2. *Merit,* or making decisions based on the good of the organization—seen as the antidote to decision making by organizational politics.
3. *Localness*—the antidote to doing the dirty stuff the boss does not want to do.

Chris Argyris and colleagues developed "action science" as a means for reflecting on the reasoning underlying our actions. This helps people change the defensive routines that lead them to skilled incompetence. Similarly, John Beckett created a course on the historical survey of main philosophies of thought, East and West, as a sort of "sandpaper on the brain." These ideas exposed managers to their own assumptions and mental models, and provided other ways to view the world.

Shared Vision

A shared vision is not an idea. Rather it is a force in people's hearts, a sense of purpose that provides energy and focus for learning. Visions are often exhilarating. Shared vision is important because it may be the beginning step to get people who mistrusted each other to start working together. Abraham Maslow studied high-performing teams and found that they had a shared vision. Shared visions can mobilize courage so naturally that people don't even know the extent of their strength. When John Kennedy created the shared vision in 1961 of putting a man on the moon by the end of the decade, only 15 percent of the technology had been created. Yet it led to numerous acts of daring and courage.

Learning organizations are not achievable without shared vision. Without that incredible pull toward the deeply felt goal, the forces of *status quo* will overwhelm the pursuit. As Robert Fritz once said, "In the presence of greatness, pettiness disappears." Conversely, in the absence of a great vision, pettiness is supreme.

Strategic planning often does not involve building a shared vision, but rather announcing the vision of top management, asking people, at best, to enroll, and, at worst, to comply. The critical step is gaining commitment from people. This is done by taking a personal vision and building it into a shared vision. In the traditional hierarchical organization, compliance is one of the desired outcomes. For learning organizations, commitment must be the key goal. Shared vision, though, is not possible without personal mastery, which is needed to foster continued commitment to a lofty goal.

Team Learning

Bill Russell of the Boston Celtics wrote about being on a team of specialists whose performance depended on one another's individual excellence and how well they worked together. Sometimes that created a feeling of magic. He is talking about *alignment,* where a group functions as a whole unit, rather than as individuals working at cross purposes. When a team is aligned, its energies are focused and harmonized. They do not need to sacrifice their own interests. Instead, alignment occurs when the shared vision becomes an extension of the personal vision. Alignment is a necessary condition to empower others and ultimately empower the team.

Never before today has there been greater need for mastering team learning, which requires mastering both dialogue and discussion. *Dialogue* involves a creative and free search of complex and even subtle issues, whereas *discussion* implies different views being presented and defended. Both skills are useful, but most teams cannot tell the difference between the two. The purpose of dialogue is to increase individual understanding. Here, assumptions are suspended and participants regard one another as on the same level. Discussion, on the other hand, comes from the same root word as *percussion* and *concussion* and involves a sort of verbal ping-pong game whose object is winning. Although this is a useful technique, it must be balanced with dialogue. A continued emphasis on winning is not compatible with the search for truth and coherence.

One of the major blocks to healthy dialogue and discussion is what Chris Argyris calls *defensive routines.* These are habitual styles of interacting that protect us from threat or embarrassment. These include the avoidance of conflict (smoothing over) and the feeling that one has to appear competent and to know the answers at all times.

Team learning, like any other skill, requires practice. Musicians and athletes understand this principle. Work teams need to learn that lesson as well.

OTHER ISSUES

Organizational politics is a perversion of truth, yet most people are so accustomed to it, they do not even notice it anymore. A learning organization is not possible in such an environment. In order to move past the politics, one thing needed is openness—both speaking openly and honestly about the real and important issues and being willing to challenge one's own way of thinking.

Localness, too, is essential to the learning organization, for decisions need to be pushed down the organizational hierarchy in order to unleash people's commitment. This gives them the freedom to act.

One thing lacking in many organizations is time to reflect and think. If someone is sitting quietly, we assume they are not busy and we feel free to interrupt. Many managers, however, are too busy to "just think." This should not be blamed on the tumultuous environment of many crises. Research suggests that, even when given ample time, managers still do not devote any of it to adequate reflection. Therefore, habits need to be changed, as well as how we structure our days.

6

COMPETITIVE ADVANTAGE

MICHAEL E. PORTER

SUMMARY PREPARED BY SARA A. MORRIS

Sara A. Morris received her Ph.D. in business policy and strategy from the University of Texas at Austin. Now on the faculty at Old Dominion University, she teaches capstone courses in strategic management and graduate seminars in competitive strategy. Her current research is in business ethics and social responsibility and concerns CEO misconduct and the use of unethical techniques for obtaining competitor information.

How can a firm obtain and maintain an advantage over its competitors? The answer lies in an understanding of industries, the five forces that drive competition in an industry, and three generic strategies that a firm can use to protect itself against these forces. An industry is a group of firms producing essentially the same products and/or services for the same customers. The profit potential of an industry is determined by the cumulative strength of five forces that affect competition in an industry.

1. Jockeying for position on the part of current competitors in the industry
2. Potential for new competitors to enter the industry
3. The threat of substitutes for the industry's products or services
4. The economic power of suppliers of raw materials to the industry
5. The bargaining power of the industry's customers

Three strategies that a firm can use to neutralize the power of these five forces are low costs, differentiation, and focus. Several specific action steps are required to execute each of these three generic strategies.

Michael E. Porter, *Competitive Advantage: Creating and Sustaining Superior Performance.* New York: Free Press, 1985.

PRINCIPLES OF COMPETITIVE ADVANTAGE

A firm creates a competitive advantage for itself by providing more value for customers than competitors provide. Customers value either (1) equivalent benefits at a lower price than competitors charge, or (2) greater benefits that more than compensate for a higher price than competitors charge. Thus, there are two possible competitive advantages, one based on costs and one based on differentiation (benefits). Each of these tactics will be discussed in detail, following an examination of the value chain.

THE VALUE CHAIN

The *value chain,* consisting of value-producing activities and margin, is a basic tool for analyzing the large number of discrete activities within a firm that are potential sources of competitive advantage. The inclusion of margin in the value chain is a reminder that, in order for a firm to profit from its competitive advantage, the value to customers must exceed the costs of generating it. Value-producing activities fall into nine categories—five categories of primary activities and four categories of support activities. Primary activities include inbound logistics, operations, outbound logistics, marketing/sales, and service. Support activities include procurement (of all of the inputs used everywhere in the value chain), technology development (for all of the myriad of technologies that are used in every primary and support activity), human resource management (of all types of personnel throughout the organization), and the firm infrastructure (general management, planning, finance, accounting, legal and government affairs, quality management, etc.).

Firms perform hundreds or thousands of discrete steps in transforming raw materials into finished products. The value chain decomposes the nine value-producing activities into numerous subactivities because each separate subactivity can contribute to the firm's relative cost position and create a basis for differentiation. In most subactivities, the firm is not significantly different from its rivals. The strategically relevant subactivities are those that currently or potentially distinguish the firm from competitors.

Value chain activities are not independent from one another, but interrelated. The cost or performance of one activity is linked to many other activities. For example, the amount of after-sale service needed depends on the quality of the raw materials procured, the degree of quality control in operations, the amount of training given to the sales force regarding matching customer sophistication and model attributes, and other factors. Competitive advantage can be created by linkages among activities as well as by individual activities. Two ways that firms can derive competitive advantage from linkages are through optimization of linkages and coordination of linkages.

The configuration and economics of the value chain are determined by the firm's *competitive scope.* By affecting the value chain, scope also affects competitive advantage. Four dimensions of scope are:

1. *Segment scope*—varieties of products made and buyers served
2. *Vertical scope*—the extent of activities performed internally rather than purchased from outside
3. *Geographic scope*—the range of locations served
4. *Industry scope*—the number of industries in which the firm competes

Broad-scope firms operate multiple value chains and attempt to exploit interrelationships among activities across the chains to gain competitive advantages. Narrow-scope firms use focus strategies to pursue competitive advantages; by concentrating on single value chains, they attempt to perfect the linkages within the value chain.

COMPETITIVE ADVANTAGE THROUGH LOW COST

The starting point for achieving a cost advantage is a thorough analysis of costs in the value chain. The analyst must be able to assign operating costs and assets (fixed and working capital) to each separate value chain activity. There are 10 major factors that are generally under the firm's control and which drive costs:

1. Economies (or diseconomies) of scale
2. Learning, which the firm can control by managing with the learning curve and keeping learning proprietary
3. Capacity utilization, which the firm can control by levelling throughput and/or reducing the penalty for throughput fluctuations
4. Linkages within the value chain, which the firm can control by recognizing and exploiting
5. Interrelationships between business units (in multi-industry firms), which the firm can control by sharing appropriate activities and/or transferring management know-how
6. The extent of vertical integration
7. Timing, which the firm can control by exploiting first-mover or late-mover advantages, and/or timing purchases over the business cycle
8. Discretionary policies (regarding products made, buyers served, human resources used, etc.)
9. Location
10. Institutional factors imposed by government and unions, which the firm can influence if not control outright

Moreover, costs are dynamic; they will change over time due to changes in industry growth rate, differential scale sensitivity, differential learning rates, changes in technology, aging, and the like. Each individual value chain activity must be analyzed separately for its cost drivers and cost dynamics.

By definition, the firm has a cost-based competitive advantage if the total costs of all its value chain activities are lower than any competitor's. A firm's cost position relative to competitors depends on the composition of its value chain compared to competitors' chains, and the firm's position relative to its competitors vis-à-vis the cost drivers of each value chain activity. Two ways that a firm can achieve a cost advantage, therefore, are (1) by controlling cost drivers, and (2) by reconfiguring the value chain through means such as changing the production process, the distribution channel, or the raw materials. A cost-based competitive advantage will be sustainable only if competitors cannot imitate it. The cost drivers that tend to be harder to imitate are economies of scale, interrelationships, linkages, proprietary learning, and new technologies that are brought about through discretionary policies.

COMPETITIVE ADVANTAGE THROUGH DIFFERENTIATION

Successful *differentiation* occurs when a firm creates something unique that is valuable to buyers and for which buyers are willing to pay a price premium in excess of the extra costs incurred by the producer. This statement begs two questions: (1) What makes something valuable to buyers, and (2) Why does the producer incur extra costs? With regard to the first question, a firm can create value for buyers by raising buyer performance, or by lowering buyer costs (in ways besides selling the product at a lower price). With regard to the second question, differentiation is usually inherently costly because uniqueness requires the producer to perform value chain activities better than competitors.

In order to achieve a differentiation advantage, strategists must be thoroughly familiar with the many discrete activities in their own value chain(s) and in the buyer's value chain, and must have a passing knowledge of the value chains of competitors. Each discrete activity in the firm's value chain represents an opportunity for differentiating. The firm's impact on the buyer's value chain determines the value the firm can create through raising buyer performance or lowering buyer costs. Since competitive advantages are by definition relative, a firm's value chain must be compared to those of its competitors.

For each separate activity in the firm's value chain, there are *uniqueness drivers* analogous to the cost drivers described previously. The most important uniqueness driver is probably the set of policy choices managers make (regarding product features, services provided, technologies employed, quality of the raw materials, and so forth). Other uniqueness drivers, in approximate order of importance, are linkages within the value chain and with suppliers and distribution channels, timing, location, interrelationships, learning, vertical integration, scale, and institutional factors.

Buyers use two types of purchasing criteria: (1) *use criteria,* which reflect real value, and (2) *signaling criteria,* which reflect perceived value in advance of purchase and verification. Use criteria include product characteristics, delivery time, ready availability, and other factors that affect buyer value through raising buyer performance or lowering buyer costs. Signaling criteria include the producing firm's reputation and advertising, the product's packaging and advertising, and other factors through which the buyer can infer the probable value of the product before the real value can be known. Differentiators must identify buyer purchasing criteria; the buyer's value chain is the place to start.

Armed with an understanding of multiple value chains, uniqueness drivers, and buyer purchasing criteria, managers can pursue differentiation. There are four basic routes to a differentiation-based competitive advantage. One route is to enhance the sources of uniqueness, by proliferating the sources of differentiation in the value chain, for example. A second route is to make the cost of differentiation an advantage by exploiting sources of differentiation that are not costly, minimizing differentiation costs by controlling cost drivers, and/or reducing costs in activities that do not affect buyer value. Another route is to change the rules to create uniqueness, such as discovering unrecognized purchase criteria. The fourth route is to reconfigure the value chain to be unique in entirely new ways.

A differentiation-based competitive advantage will be sustainable only if buyers' needs and perceptions remain stable and competitors cannot imitate the uniqueness.

The firm can strongly influence the buyer's perceptions by continuing to improve on use criteria and by reinforcing them with appropriate signals. The firm is, nevertheless, at risk that buyers' needs will shift, eliminating the value of a particular form of differentiation. The sustainability of differentiation against imitation by competitors depends on its sources, the drivers of uniqueness. The competitive advantage will be more sustainable if the uniqueness drivers involve barriers such as proprietary learning, linkages, interrelationships, and first-mover advantages; if the firm has low costs in differentiating; if there are multiple sources of differentiation; and/or if the firm can create switching costs for customers.

TECHNOLOGY AND COMPETITIVE ADVANTAGE

One of the most significant drivers of competition is technological change. Because technologies are embedded in every activity in the value chain as well as in the linkages among value chain activities, a firm can achieve and/or maintain low costs or differentiation through technology. The first step in using technology wisely is to identify the multitude of technologies in the value chain. Then, the astute manager must become aware of relevant technological improvements coming from competitors, other industries, and scientific breakthroughs.

A firm's technology strategy involves choices among new technologies, and choices about timing and licensing. Rather than pursuing technological improvements involving all value chain activities and linkages indiscriminately, managers should restrict their attention to technological changes that make a difference. New technologies are important if they can affect (1) the firm's particular competitive advantage, either directly or through its drivers, or (2) any of the five forces that drive competition in the industry. A firm's timing matters in technological changes because the technology leader will experience first-mover advantages (e.g., reputation as a pioneer, opportunity to define industry standards) as well as disadvantages (e.g., costs of educating buyers, demand uncertainty). Thus, the choice of whether to be a technology leader or follower should be made according to the sustainability of the technological lead. When a firm's competitive advantage rests on technology, licensing the technology to other firms is risky. Although there are conditions under which licensing may be warranted (to tap an otherwise inaccessible market, for example), often the firm inadvertently creates strong rivals and/or gives away a competitive advantage for a small royalty fee.

COMPETITOR SELECTION

A firm must be ever vigilant in pursuing and protecting its competitive advantage; however, there are dangers in relentlessly attacking all rivals. It is prudent to distinguish desirable competitors from undesirable ones. Desirable competitors may enable a firm to increase its competitive advantage (e.g., by absorbing demand fluctuations, or by providing a standard against which buyers compare costs or differentiation), or may improve industry structure (i.e., may weaken one or more of the five forces that collectively determine the intensity of competition in an industry). Characteristics of desirable competitors include realistic assumptions; clear, self-perceived weaknesses; enough credibility to be acceptable to customers; enough viability to deter new entrants; and enough strength to motivate the firm to continue to improve its competitive advantage. A smart industry leader will encourage some competitors and discourage others through tactics such as technology licensing and selective retaliation.

SCOPE AND COMPETITIVE ADVANTAGE

An industry consists of heterogeneous parts, or segments, due to differences in buyer behavior and differences in the economics of producing different products or services for these buyers. Therefore, the intensity of competition (i.e., the collective strength of the five competitive forces) varies among segments of the same industry. Moreover, because segments of the same industry have different value chains, the requirements for competitive advantage differ widely among industry segments. The existence of multiple industry segments forces a firm to decide on competitive scope, or where in the industry to compete. The attractiveness of any particular industry segment depends on the collective strength of the five competitive forces, the segment's size and growth rate, and the fit between a firm's abilities and the segment's needs. The firm may broadly target many segments or may use the generic strategy of focus to serve one or a few segments.

The competitive scope decision requires the manager to analyze all the current and potential industry segments. To identify product segments, all the product varieties in an industry must be examined for differences they can create in the five competitive forces and the value chain. The industry's products may differ in terms of features, technology or design, packaging, performance, services, and in many other ways. To identify buyer segments, all the different types of buyers in an industry must be examined for differences they can create in the five competitive forces and the value chain. Buyers can differ by type (e.g., several types of industrial buyers, several types of consumer buyers), by distribution channel, and by geographic location (according to weather zone, country stage of development, etc.).

When the value chains of different segments in the same industry are related at multiple points, a firm can share value-producing activities among segments. Such segment interrelationships encourage firms to use a broad-target strategy, unless the costs of coordination, compromise, and inflexibility in jointly accomplishing value-producing activities outweigh the benefits of sharing. Broad-target strategies often involve too many segments, thereby pushing coordination, compromise, and inflexibility costs too high and making the broadly targeted firm vulnerable to firms with good focus strategies.

Whereas broad-target strategies are based on similarities in the value chains among segments, focus strategies are based on differences between segments' value chains. A focuser can optimize the value chain for one or a few segments and achieve lower costs or better differentiation than broad-target firms because the focuser can avoid the costs of coordination, compromise, and inflexibility required for serving multiple segments. The sustainability of a focus strategy is determined by its sustainability against (1) broad-target competitors, (2) imitators, and (3) substitutes, the next topic of interest.

Both the industry's product or service and its substitutes perform the same generic function for the buyer (i.e., fill the same role in the buyer's value chain). The threat of substitution depends on (1) the relative value/price of the substitute compared to the industry's product, (2) the cost of switching to the substitute, and (3) the buyer's propensity to switch. The relative value/price compares the substitute to the industry's product in terms of usage rate, delivery and installation, direct and indirect costs of use, buyer performance, complementary products, uncertainty, etc. Switching costs include redesign costs, retraining costs, and risk of failure. Buyer propensity to substitute depends on resources available, risk profile, technological orientation, and the like. The threat of substitution often changes over time because of changes in relative price, relative value, switching costs, or propensity to substitute. To defend against substitutes, the focuser can reduce costs, improve the product, raise switching costs, improve complementary goods, etc.

CORPORATE STRATEGY AND COMPETITIVE ADVANTAGE

Whereas business-level strategy is concerned with the firm's course of actions within an individual industry, corporate-level strategy is generally concerned with the multi-industry firm's course of actions across industries. By exploiting interrelationships among its business units in distinct but related industries, the multi-industry corporation can increase its competitive advantage within one or more of those industries. Porter uses the term *horizontal strategy* to refer to a corporation's coordinated set of goals and policies that apply across its business units, and argues that horizontal strategy may be the most critical issue facing diversified firms today. It is through its horizontal strategy that a corporation achieves synergy.

There are three types of interrelationships among a multi-industry corporation's business units: tangible, intangible, and competitor-induced. *Tangible interrelationships* occur when different business units have common elements in their value chains, such as the same buyers, technologies, or purchased inputs. These common elements create opportunities to share value chain activities among related business units. Sharing activities may lower costs or increase differentiation, thereby adding to competitive advantage. However, the benefits of sharing do not always exceed the costs of sharing. One cost of sharing is the need for more coordination in the shared value chain activities. Another cost is the need for compromise in the way shared value chain activities are performed; the compromise must be acceptable to both business units, but may be optimal for neither. A third cost of sharing is greater inflexibility in responding to changing environmental conditions.

A second type of interrelationship, *intangible interrelationships*, occurs when different business units can transfer general management know-how even though they have no common elements in their value chains. It is possible, though less likely, for intangible interrelationships to lead to competitive advantage. A third type of interrelationship, *competitor-induced interrelationships*, occurs when two diversified corporations compete against each other in more than one business unit. Such multipoint competition between two corporations means that any action in one line of business can affect the entire range of jointly contested industries. Therefore, for multipoint competitors, a competitive advantage in one line of business will have implications for all the linked industries.

Any diversified corporation will face impediments to exploiting interrelationships: The managers of business units that receive fewer benefits than they contribute will resist sharing; managers of all business units will tend to protect their turf; incentive systems may not appropriately measure and reward a business unit's contributions to other units; and so forth. Therefore, corporate-level executives must articulate an explicit horizontal strategy and organize to facilitate horizontal relations. Examples of organizational practices and mechanisms that are particularly helpful are horizontal structures (e.g., groupings of business units, inter-unit task forces), horizontal systems (e.g., inter-unit strategic planning systems and capital budgeting systems), horizontal human resource practices (e.g., cross-business job rotation and management forums), and horizontal conflict resolution processes.

A special case of interrelationships occurs when the industry's product is used or purchased with complementary products. Because the sale of one promotes the sale of the other, complementary products have the opposite effect of substitutes. Three types of decisions that a corporation must make regarding complementary products concern whether to control these products internally (as opposed to letting other firms supply them), whether to bundle them (i.e., sell complementary products together as a package), and whether to cross-subsidize them (i.e., price complementary products based on their interrelationships instead of their individual costs). All three types of decisions have repercussions for competitive advantage.

IMPLICATIONS FOR OFFENSIVE AND DEFENSIVE COMPETITIVE STRATEGY

The *industry scenario* is a planning tool that may be used to guide the formulation of competitive strategy in the face of major uncertainties about the future. Constructing industry scenarios involves identifying uncertainties that may affect the industry, determining the causal factors, making a range of plausible assumptions about each important causal factor, combining assumptions into internally consistent scenarios, analyzing the industry structure that would prevail under each scenario, identifying competitive advantages under each scenario, and predicting the behavior of competitors under each scenario. Managers may then design competitive strategies based on the most probable scenario, the most attractive scenario, hedging (protecting the firm against the worst-case scenario), or preserving flexibility.

Defensive strategy is intended to lower the probability of attack from a new entrant into the industry or an existing competitor seeking to reposition itself. The preferred defensive strategy is deterrence. The old saying about "the best offense is a good defense" holds here; a firm with a competitive advantage that continues to lower its costs or improve its differentiation is very difficult to beat. Nevertheless, when deterrence fails, the firm must respond to an attack under way. When a firm's position is being challenged, defensive tactics include raising structural barriers (e.g., blocking distribution channels, raising buyer switching costs) and increasing expected retaliation.

Sometimes attacking an industry leader makes sense. The most important rule in offensive strategy is never to attack a leader head-on with an imitation strategy. In order to attack an industry leader successfully, the challenger must have a sustainable competitive advantage, must be close to the leader in costs and differentiation, and must have some means to thwart leader retaliation. There are three primary avenues to attack a leader: (1) change the way individual value-producing activities are performed, or reconfigure the entire value chain; (2) redefine the competitive scope compared to the leader; (3) pure spending on the part of the challenger. The leader is particularly vulnerable when the industry is undergoing significant changes, such as technological improvements, changes in the buyer's value chain, or the emergence of new distribution channels.

PART

III

HIGH-PERFORMING ORGANIZATIONS

Most organizations don't want merely to survive; they want to be effective, or even excellent, at what they do. To do so requires a prior definition of success, and defining success often encourages the managers of an organization to examine the actions of their best competitors for comparative models (benchmarks). The assumption is that if they can identify the organizational characteristics that allow others to succeed, perhaps these attributes can be transplanted (or adapted, or even improved upon) to facilitate their own success. Consequently, a wide variety of organizations and management groups has shown considerable interest in what "high-performing organizations" actually do and what the guiding principles are.

Marcus Buckingham is the author of *The One Thing You Need to Know*. In this book Buckingham focuses on several themes, each of which envisions organizational success (i.e., high performance) as that which is achieved through the "proper" management of people. The author notes that the chief responsibility assumed by great managers is to find what is unique about each person and capitalize on it instead of trying to remedy each individual's shortcomings. Turning the talents that a person brings to the organization into performance is more critical to organizational performance than trying to change (i.e., "fix") each employee. The chief responsibility of great leaders is to rally people to a better future.

Buckingham, a graduate of England's Cambridge University, worked for the Gallup organization for 17 years. During much of that time he conducted research focusing on the world's best managers, leaders, and workplaces. He is also the author of *First, Break all the Rules: What the World's Best Managers Do Differently*, and *Now, Discover Your Strengths*.

In *Big Winners and Big Losers*, Alfred A. Marcus reports on his findings from a detailed review of the performance of the 1,000 largest corporations in the United States. Marcus reports that there is a consistent pattern that distinguishes the big winners from the big losers. Ranjay Gulati from the Kellogg School of Management at Northwestern University writes, "This book provides an excellent synthesis of the strategies that differentiate successful firms from the rest of the world," and Michael Cuscumano from MIT's Sloan School of Management notes that a central theme in Marcus's book highlights the idea that "successful companies . . . balance complementary and at times contradictory skills—the agility to find the right markets, focus on discipline to succeed, and the agility again to re-focus and adapt as markets change."

Marcus received his Ph.D. from Harvard University and currently holds the Edson Spencer Chair of Strategic Management and Technological Leadership in the Carlson School of Management at the Minneapolis campus of the University of Minnesota. He is the author or co-editor of 11 books, and he has published numerous articles in such journals as the *Academy of Management Review*, *California Management Review*, and the *Strategic Management Journal*.

Managing the Unexpected uses the example of high-reliability organizations (e.g., aircraft carriers or nuclear power plants) to provide a model for twenty-first century organizations. The authors suggest that all organizations can and must learn to anticipate and respond to ambiguity, uncertainty, and unexpected challenges in their environments, and to do so with flexibility, consistency, and effectiveness. The primary key to this is through *mindfulness*, which encompasses a preoccupation with failure, a reluctance to simplify interpretations, a sensitivity to operations, a commitment to resilience, and a deference to expertise wherever it may reside.

Co-authors Karl E. Weick and Kathleen M. Sutcliffe are faculty members at the University of Michigan Business School. Weick is the Rensis Likert Distinguished University Professor of Organizational Behavior and Psychology and is well known for exploring unique concepts such as enactment, naive thinking, bricolage, sensemaking, organizational learning, and loose coupling. His other books include *Sensemaking in Organizations* and *The Social Psychology of Organizing*; the latter book was designated by *Inc.* magazine as one of the nine best business books ever written. He is the recipient of the Academy of Management's lifetime achievement award for Distinguished Scholarly Contributions. Sutcliffe received her Ph.D. from the University of Texas at Austin and has researched and published extensively on organizational performance, functionally diverse teams, and cognitive and experiential diversity.

Corporate downsizing, sometimes euphemistically referred to as "rightsizing," has cost hundreds of thousands of employees their jobs in the past decade while organizations sought to reduce their costs, redirect their resources, and improve their stock price. Wayne Cascio, in *Responsible Restructuring*, reports on the results of an eighteen-year study of major firms that destroys many common myths about downsizing's presumably positive effects. By contrast, Cascio found that downsizing has a negative impact not only on the morale and commitment of the survivors, but also on key indicators of productivity, profits, and quality. He presents an alternative to layoffs—a step-by-step blueprint that revolves around treating employees as assets to be developed, and demonstrates how responsible restructuring has worked effectively at Compaq, Cisco, Motorola, and Southwest Airlines.

Wayne Cascio is a professor of management at the University of Colorado–Denver, and also instructs in the Rotterdam School of Management. Cascio is a past chair of the Human Resources division of the Academy of Management and past president of the Society for Industrial and Organizational Psychology. A consultant and writer, he is the author of numerous other books, including *Applied Psychology in Human Resource Management*, *The Cost Factor*, *Costing Human Resources*, and *Managing Human Resources*.

1

THE ONE THING YOU NEED TO KNOW

Marcus Buckingham

Summary Prepared by Kristie J. Loescher

Kristie J. Loescher is a Lecturer in the Management Department of the McCombs School of Business at The University of Texas at Austin where she teaches management, leadership, and business communications. She has her doctorate in business administration from Nova Southeastern University, specializing in human resource management. Prior to her career in academia, Kristie worked in the health care industry for 15 years in the areas of quality assurance, utilization management, and clinical research. Her academic publications focus on ethical education, organizational ethics, change management, and diversity management.

What *controlling insight* explains great managing, great leading, and high levels of individual success? Research conducted to identify the best explanation for each of these is based on examining greatness in each area. Greatness is not accomplished by avoiding what causes failure, or by doing the opposite of what causes failure, but by following a distinct set of behaviors that specifically define greatness. To be called *the one thing*, a controlling insight had to pass three research tests:

1. Be present with greatness in a variety of situations
2. Act as a multiplier, leading to high levels of sustained success when applied
3. Describe behaviors or actions

These tests are applied to both great organizational success stories (through evaluation of great managers and great leaders) and great individual success stories to identify *the one thing* you can do to achieve success yourself.

GREAT ORGANIZATIONAL SUCCESS

This section presents behaviors that provide a foundation for both managerial and leadership success. Management and leadership are separate and distinct roles, and they require separate and distinct behaviors for success.

Marcus Buckingham, *The One Thing You Need to Know . . . About Great Managing, Great Leading, and Sustained Individual Success,* New York: Free Press, 2005.

Great Managing

The controlling insight for management is to *capitalize on uniqueness*. Successful management begins with the individual employee and focuses on knowing that employee's skills and abilities, and then pointing that person in the direction of organizational goals. You must make understanding and serving the individual employee your first priority as a manager, so employees will believe you sincerely care about them and are invested in their success.

To be successful and enjoy the job of management requires an instinct for coaching and the ability to identify people's unique talents. You must enjoy watching people grow and succeed. Managers must also be talented at identifying an individual's skills, abilities, personality, and goals and at understanding how best to utilize these attributes for the benefit of both the employee and the organization. In addition to these two main talents, the following four skills are critical to successfully "capitalize on uniqueness":

1. Select the right people. Know the skills, abilities, and personality traits you need in each of your employees to reach organizational goals. Then use structured interviewing techniques to identify candidates that meet these needs.
2. Define clear behavior expectations. Provide a clear focus for your employees, so they understand the factors that define excellence for their job.
3. Motivate and shape behavior with praise. Once you define behaviors critical to job success, reinforce employees who exhibit these behaviors with frequent and sincere praise. Other employees will watch what gets praised, so set the bar high for excellence and praise the steps toward it and reward those who reach it.
4. Demonstrate your care and concern. Create strong bonds of trust and respect between yourself and each employee—only then can you expect them to forge similar bonds with each other and with customers. An employees' trust in you is built on a foundation of feeling understood and believing that you care about and are invested in his or her success.

As stated in the fourth point above, to gain employees' trust you must demonstrate that you understand them and their goals. Since each person is different and unique, the majority of a manager's time must be spent in the pursuit of understanding what is unique in each employee and devising how to use it in pursuit of both organizational and employee goals. The manager is an *intermediary* between the individual and the organization, and this job must be performed one-on-one. To the extent there is dissonance or disagreement between an employee's goals and those of the organization, the successful manager remains focused on the employee, which may mean changing the way the company operates or even helping the employees find a way to reach their goals at a different company. There are three unique characteristics, or *levers*, that a successful manager must know about each employee to "capitalize on uniqueness," and these include strengths and weaknesses, motivators, and learning style.

Strengths and Weaknesses

Focusing people on their strengths provides more payoff than trying to get them to improve on their weaknesses. A successful manager helps employees identify their key talents and use them in the pursuit of the organization's goals. Managers must also help employees identify whether their weaknesses are a result of a lack of training or a lack of ability. A lack of training can be fixed, but a lack of ability requires you to change the employee's job or help the employee find success elsewhere.

Motivators

Identifying what motivates employees and keeps them performing at their highest level is a key competency for managers. These motivators may be extrinsic (praise, recognition, rewards), intrinsic (opportunities for learning, advancement, empowerment, autonomy), or a combination of both. You need to know what fuels each employee's desire to give their best.

Learning Style

Understanding the best way for an employee to build new skills and learn new processes helps a manager maximize the potential of each employee. Effective learning approaches vary among individuals. Some employees learn by analyzing, others by doing, and some by imitating. Therefore, you will provide written instructions for the analyzer, allow the doer to use trial and error, and set up on-the-job training for the imitator.

If employee-focused management is good for the employee and satisfying for the manager, can it also be good for the organization? Indeed, focusing on individual employee strengths and goals creates four advantages for the manager and the company:

- **Saves time.** By using the talents of each employee and not expecting employees to be capable at everything, you save time correcting and disciplining employees, while increasing your opportunities to praise them.
- **Increases employee accountability.** People improve most in areas where they are already talented, rather than in areas where they are weak. Therefore, by focusing employees on their areas of greatest skill and ability, you can challenge them to deliver higher levels of performance. Recognizing they are being asked to do what they do best, they will be more likely to accept and meet your challenge.
- **Builds stronger team cohesion.** By focusing employees on their strengths, you create more interdependence between employees. In an environment with high interdependence, employees will recognize how much they need each other and will value those who have skills in other areas required to complete job tasks.
- **Creates healthy disruption.** Meeting each employee's unique needs challenges you as the manager to think creatively and to change systems and processes. In meeting the needs of your employees, you must continuously improve the match between employee skills and abilities and the organization. By doing so, you have the opportunity to discover new, more effective and efficient methods for meeting the organization's goals. In addition, by focusing employees on their talents, you open yourself and the organization up to the potential for benefiting from their exploration and discoveries.

Great Leadership

Successful leadership begins with a vision (a vivid mental image of a potential future for an organization) and focuses on making that vision clear and compelling for people to follow. The controlling insight for leadership is to *capitalize on the universal*. Despite each individual's unique qualities and outlook, the leader's job is to make each of us see and believe in the leader's vision by tapping into the basic needs we all have in common:

1. Need for security, driven by our fear of death
2. Need for community, driven by our fear of the outsider

3. Need for clarity, driven by our fear of the future and the unknown
4. Need for authority, driven by our fear of chaos and need for order
5. Need for respect, driven by our fear of insignificance

By showing us how their vision for the future meets one or more of these five needs, leaders are able to motivate and encourage us to follow them. However, *the most important of these needs for an effective leader to focus on is the need for clarity to alleviate our fear of the future.* To be effective, leaders must be optimists with the ability not only to see, but also to clearly describe our bright prospects to us, thereby decreasing our fear and uncertainty about the future.

Providing goal clarity for followers, while allowing them room to design the path toward that goal, is the key balance point for effective leadership. Leaders must provide clarity in four areas:

- **Primary customers**—identifying who is the main audience
- **Focal asset**—specifying what they have/do that makes us special/different
- **Key measure**—clarifying how they know how well we're doing
- **Principal actions**—taking actions as a leader to reinforce their vision

Leaders maintain their ability to provide clarity and their creativity to provide direction through the disciplines of reflecting on the past and the future, selecting superior role models for themselves and their employees, and practicing the communication of their vision.

Primary characteristics of good leaders include *optimism* about the future, dissatisfaction with the *status quo*, and *self-assurance* in their ability to make their vision of the future a reality. Because these characteristics are so critical to successful leadership and tend to be wired into an individual's brain at birth, great leaders are, in essence, born rather than made.

SUSTAINED INDIVIDUAL SUCCESS

Maintaining *sustained success* means using your talents in work that you find rewarding and fulfilling over a long period of time. The controlling insight for sustained individual success, paradoxically, is "discover what you don't like doing and stop doing it." In researching highly successful, happy people, the main thing they have in common is the discipline to say no to activities that do not play to their strengths. They know their strengths in terms of their skills, abilities, and aptitudes, and they know their weaknesses. But instead of spending time improving their weaknesses, they spend their time focused on using and continuously growing their strengths. While you should always try new activities that utilize aptitudes you have not yet explored, pay attention to how you feel once you have learned the basics of any work activity or role. Stop doing those activities or roles that leave you feeling:

- **Bored**—that are acutely uninteresting to you
- **Unfulfilled**—that are inconsistent with your values and goals
- **Frustrated**—that inhibit your strengths and/or force you to use your weaker skills and abilities
- **Drained**—those profoundly disagreeable tasks that make you dread your work

By focusing on your strengths, you not only enjoy your work, you are able to perform at a higher level than you will ever achieve by focusing on your weaknesses. You will feel more confident and more enthusiastic about doing what you do well. The controlling insight speaks to what you should stop doing because the great challenge of sustained success occurs once you identify your strengths and begin to enjoy success. You will then tend to attract "opportunities" for promotion or for additional roles, and the discipline to say no to those offers that take you away from using your strengths or that force you to rely on your weaker skill sets will make the difference between achieving sustained success and hating your job. If you find yourself in a situation where you have accepted an opportunity that has begun to bore you, frustrate you, or leave you unfulfilled, you have three choices:

1. Quit the role
2. Change or refocus the role on your strengths
3. Find a partner who has strengths to complement your weaknesses to share the responsibilities

Conclusion

A key theme running through all three controlling insights is intentional imbalance. Great managers do not try to "do it all," but instead focus on their employees and what makes them unique contributors to the company. Likewise the great leader has an equally tight focus on communicating clarity and optimism about the future, while the individual looking for sustained success focuses on saying no to things that are not engaging their strengths. This type of focus requires discipline, commitment, and courage.

2 | BIG WINNERS AND BIG LOSERS

ALFRED A. MARCUS

SUMMARY PREPARED BY ALLEN HARMON

Allen Harmon is President and General Manager of WDSE-TV, the community-licensed PBS member station serving Northeastern Minnesota and Northwestern Wisconsin. He also currently serves as an adjunct instructor in the Labovitz School of Business and Economics at the University of Minnesota Duluth, where he teaches strategic management. Before joining WDSE, Mr. Harmon held a series of senior management positions in a regional investor-owned electric utility. He earned an MBA from Indiana University's Kelly School of Business and has completed the University of Minnesota Carlson School of Management Executive Development Program.

A natural parity prevails in most industries. Sustained competitive advantage is rare. Over the decade from 1992 to 2002, a scant 3 percent of the top 1,000 U.S. companies consistently delivered returns that bettered the average of their industry. Only 6 percent of the top 1,000 consistently underperformed industry averages. *What are the distinctive traits of the big winners that an organization should seek to emulate to reap the rewards of consistent winning? What traits should an organization eschew to avoid the punishment borne by the big losers?*

Winners occupy **sweet spots** in the market, which are attractive market positions characterized by a lack of direct competition that present incumbents with the opportunity to control the five classic industry forces. Winners move to those positions with agility, demonstrate the discipline to protect those positions by developing hard-to-imitate capabilities, and focus on fully exploiting the position's potential. Losers are disadvantaged by being positioned in industry **sour spots**, which are highly contested market positions affording incumbents little opportunity to control the five classic industry forces. Losers are hindered in moving from those positions by their own rigidity and are inept in developing the capabilities that would allow them to protect their positions. Losers' efforts to exploit desirable positions they might occupy are too diffuse to be effective.

Alfred A. Marcus, *Big Winners and Big Losers: The 4 Secrets of Long-Term Business Success and Failure.* Pennsylvania: Wharton School Publishing, 2006.

IDENTIFYING THE WINNERS AND LOSERS

Big winners and big losers were selected for study from the *Wall Street Journal*'s Scorecard on the basis of stock market returns over the period from 1992 to 2002. A final screen was applied to determine whether the selected companies' performance during the turbulent first half of 2002 was consistent with results over the preceding 10 years. The *Wall Street Journal*'s industry designations were used; pairs of winners and losers in nine industry sectors were selected for study.

A separate analysis of the Fortune 1000 list with consideration for minor differences in timing and composition affirmed the selections of big winners and big losers. Use of accounting data in lieu of market data was considered and rejected; market data was favored for being forward looking and less susceptible to company manipulation.

Winning company performance met the following benchmarks:

- As of January 1, 2002, ten-, five-, three- and one-year market returns exceeded their industry average.
- Five-year average market return was two or more times the industry average.
- Return for the period January 1, 2002, to June 1, 2002, exceeded the industry average.

Losing company performance was described by:

- As of January 1, 2002, ten-, five-, three-, and one-year market returns were less than the industry average.
- Five-year average market return was half or less than half the industry average.
- Return for the period January 1, 2002, to June 1, 2002, was less than half the industry average.

The screening process identified nine pairs of companies:

Industry Sector	Company	5-Year Average Annual Market Return (%)
Technology	Amphenol	34.0
	LSI Logic	3.4
Manufacturing/Appliance	SPX	28.8
	Snap-On	1.7
Software	FiServ	31.2
	Parametric	−21.2
Food	Dreyers	22.4
	Campbell Soup	−2.8
Drugs/Chemicals	Forest Labs	58.5
	IMC Global	−18.7
Manufacturing/Industrial	Ball	23.9
	Goodyear	−11.5
Financial	Brown & Brown	48.7
	Safeco	−1.0
Retail	Family Dollar	36.1
	Gap	9.8
Entertainment/Toys	Activision	24.1
	Hasbro	−0.1

THE ANALYSIS

Over 500 experienced managers, each trained and competent in strategic management, participated in the effort to identify what differentiated the big winners from the big losers. Five teams of five or six manager/analysts were assigned each industry pair and participated in an iterative process of analysis and peer review that sought to answer:

- What external challenges did the company face?
- How did the company's internal strengths and weaknesses relate to those challenges?
- What moves did the company make?
- Why were the moves of one company more successful than those of the company it was paired with?

As the analysis progressed, patterns began to emerge. Winners tended to be smaller than losers—on average, winners in the sample generated $3.49 billion in annual revenue and employed 14,000; losers on average generated $10.66 billion in annual revenue and employed 48,000. Winners tended to be less well known than losers. Winners tended to have a broad customer base; losers found their customers more concentrated.

SWEET SPOTS VS. SOUR SPOTS

Perhaps most significant, big winners were found in industry "sweet spots" where they faced virtually no direct competition. Because they had come to offer something rare, valuable, and non-substitutable to their customers, big winners had achieved control over the five classic industry forces. Winners bring a combination of low cost and differentiation to their customers in striking packages. The net result is exceptional value.

In contrast, big losers were found in industry "sour spots" where they faced multiple competitors offering similar or equally good products or services. As their products offered customers nothing special, the losers had little leverage with which to control industry forces. Losers often found themselves disadvantaged by prices too high for customers to afford, prices too low to be profitable, and/or processes too complex to be managed effectively.

GAINING THE SWEET SPOT

Winners found sweet spots in their industries by achieving significant alignment with their customers. By successfully providing unique solutions to complex customer needs and by embedding themselves in customer processes and operations, winners were in a position to identify and exploit unique opportunities. This accomplishment took various forms—for Ball, it was providing a process for producing specialty packaging meeting customer needs; for Dreyers, it was managing the grocer's difficult-to-manage freezer space; for Family Dollar, it was geographic, embedding stores in underserved urban neighborhoods. In each case, achieving significant alignment with customers opened opportunities for the winners in uncontested markets and allowed them to grow under their competitors' radar.

Three Traits of Winners

Knowledge of customer needs gave winners a place to go; three traits shared by the winners—agility, discipline, and focus—gave them the ability to get there.

Agility

Each of the big winners knew exactly where they wanted to go. They also displayed the agility to get there, and the capacity to regularly reinvent themselves. Whether through merger, acquisition, or internal growth, they added businesses that showed promise. They showed no reluctance to divest those businesses that did not show promise. Hallmarks of agility include:

- Responding quickly to changes in the market such as overcapacity and consolidations of competitors with new innovations
- Maintaining flexibility by controlling size, focusing on profitable growth, and building partnerships or outsourcing where others could contribute needed competencies
- Seeking growth in customers' changing needs, responding with products and services that become an intimate part of the customer's process
- Moving to markets that present specialized needs that only the company can satisfy, that are underserved, or that are perceived as unattractive and thus ignored by others
- Aggressively seeking acquisitions to exploit opportunities or to broaden and enhance product and service offerings
- Achieving sufficient diversification so that declines in one sector might be offset by improved performance in another

Discipline

Exercise of internal discipline allows big winners to protect their sweet spot positions by maintaining the scarce, hard-to-imitate capabilities that create best value propositions for customers. Evidence of organizational discipline is seen in:

- Effectively reducing costs and raising quality through applying technology, instituting process controls, achieving volume-driven efficiencies, and attaining best-in-class levels of service
- Controlling distribution through efforts ranging from employing aggressive globalization to serve new and existing markets efficiently and developing technology to track merchandise, to avoiding product deterioration in transit
- Smoothly integrating acquisitions; carefully selecting those targets that fit the organization's goals, quickly consolidating operations, and eliminating low- or no-profit components
- Creating a culture of employee involvement through selective hiring of skilled, aggressive individuals given the training, recognition, and respect that supports their ability to make a difference to the company
- Monitoring and influencing regulatory changes—winners willingly comply with regulations, have good environmental records, and promote ethical behavior and integrity

Focus

Big winners do more than just defend their sweet spot positions; they are actively committed to growth by broadening and deepening the sweet spot. Risk of failure was reduced by focus on core competencies. Big winners demonstrated focus in:

- Focusing on core strengths by spinning off non-core activities; avoiding activities with high risk of failure; allowing others to assume risks (such as R&D), consistent with their own competencies; and demonstrating total dedication to selected customer categories, developed brands, and related products
- Developing high-growth, application-specific products for growth markets, deepening relationships with customers to offer solutions driven by emerging customer needs rather than by a particular product or technology
- Extending reach globally, capitalizing on growth opportunities overseas through acquisition or internal development to extend the organization's global presence

While big winners demonstrated these three traits in a variety of ways, *all demonstrated consistent mastery of the one competence most difficult to replicate: balance*. A tension exists among the three key traits. In the extreme, focus and discipline can impair agility by closing off consideration of opportunities. The organization must at once defend and develop the space it holds while prospecting for new positions to occupy. Continual reinvention of the company produces stress between what the organization is and what it intends to become. The distinctive performance of the big winners is the result of achieving a unique balance of these attributes.

MIRED IN A SOUR SPOT

Losers found themselves competing in occupied sour spots in the market with products that were too expensive to be attractive to customers, products priced too low to be profitable, or business models that were too complex to execute effectively. They had, in short, lost contact with their customers and found themselves focused on products or internal processes rather than customer needs. Without the leverage provided by a unique value position, losers had little control over the classic industry forces.

Without the sense of direction that an intimate knowledge of their customers provided the big winners, when big losers moved (and they did), they moved in the wrong direction or at the wrong time. As a group, big losers demonstrated the traits of rigidity, ineptness, and diffuseness that prevented them from escaping their sour spots.

Rigidity—Like the big winners, losers sought movement. Their moves were often defensive and in reaction to a threat, however, rather than an offensive initiative to better align with customer needs. Their moves were characterized by a sense of rigidity that showed itself in:

- Exclusive reliance on expansion of core products for growth, sticking with the company's original business or current niche even as it lost potential, putting effort into expanding unprofitable businesses, and ignoring the prospects of non-core brands or holdings
- Reliance on commoditized products sold on the basis of price, or to concentrated buyers who because of that concentration hold pricing power

- Accumulating excess capacity at times of stagnant or declining demand; losers tended to expand too rapidly, buying weak or commodity businesses at inflated prices with debt that later became a burden
- Failing to mount a vigorous response such as new product development, capacity adjustments, or new market entrance to declines in the core business
- Failing to recognize and respond to changes in customer tastes or competitors' innovations
- Favoring size over agility and consequently becoming burdened with bureaucracy, losing the ability to anticipate and exploit changes in demand, profitable new niches, and competitors' blunders

Ineptness — Losers lacked the skills to create best-value propositions to offer their customers, finding themselves unable to defend what positions they did occupy from more adept competitors. Losers were unable to escape from the sour spots in part due to:

- Inability to provide best-in-class service or customized product offerings at low cost; losers exacerbated their disadvantages by failing to successfully correct even recognized inefficiencies or unwisely cutting the activities valued by customers in their efforts to reduce costs
- Failure to master their supply chain, alienating distributors and retailers of their products through ineffective performance and not developing the long-term relationships with customers that could be translated into leverage over suppliers
- Ineffective management of acquisition activities, resulting in overpayment, ineffective integration, and a failure to realize operational synergies
- Demoralizing employees by creating disarray and disruption when implementing new systems, developing an adversarial relationship with unions and ineffective (or nonexistent) incentive compensation plans
- Failure to maintain high ethical standards or to deal effectively with regulation, resulting in violations of environmental and accounting regulations.

Diffuseness — Without focus, losers activities were ineffective in building competitive advantage that might have liberated them from their sour spots. The losing companies failed to reinforce the positions they occupied against attack from more competent competitors, failed to integrate disparate acquisitions to achieve common goals, and invested in R&D that was never destined to serve their customers. Evidence of the diffuseness infecting the big losers included:

- Lack of clear strategic direction meant that activities of both existing and newly acquired business units failed to coalesce around common goals or to exploit synergies among them; acquisitions were executed without a long-term plan, operations became needlessly complex or duplicative, and poorly executed attempts at vertical integration took one loser into value chain functions where it lacked competence
- Focusing internally on products and marketing existing, diverse brands caused losers to ignore promising opportunities presented by the market; out of touch with customers and the market, they failed to identify growth opportunities, or to adequately support the rapidly growing product lines they did hold

- Looking to global markets as a fix for domestic problems only compounded losers' problems as they failed in the same ways in new markets: acquisitions failed, service levels fell short of customer requirements, local regulations were not dealt with effectively, and opportunities that did present themselves were not pursued aggressively

LOOKING FOR PATTERNS

Each of the big winners built competitive advantage through combinations of traits demonstrating agility, discipline, and focus; their performance resulted from building difficult-to-copy combinations of these contrasting traits. Multiple positive traits were interwoven to reinforce one another. In no case was success the product of a single positive trait.

Success, then, is not the result of building the strengths separately, but of combining strengths into a larger whole. Achieving that whole requires making nontrivial trade-offs in achieving a balance between agility and discipline and focus.

Conversely, the prolonged poor performance of the big losers was in no case the product of a single weakness. Multiple weaknesses in a pattern that reinforced each other condemned the losers to failure. Big losers had difficulty managing tension. Under stress, one negative trait simply piled on top of another negative trait.

TURNAROUNDS

Updating the selection process to include the most recent five-year period (1999–2004) shows that for the most part, big winners have continued to win and big losers have continued to lose. Of the 18 companies, only 2 have seen a reversal of fortunes.

Insurer Safeco went from loser to winner, beating the performance of the Dow Jones Industrial Average beginning in 2001. Safeco began its turnaround by embracing focus, cutting back on acquisitions while determining what kind of company it wanted to be and what it could do well. Divesting businesses that did not fit the new definition of the company reduced its size and increased its agility. Discipline—to increase accountability and aggressiveness, reduce costs, and raise quality—completed the groundwork for Safeco's turnaround.

Manufacturer SPX saw its performance deteriorate. While it did not fall behind big loser Snap-On during the period, the former winner did slide into mediocrity, barely besting the Dow Jones Industrial Average for the period. At the root of SPX's decline was diffuseness, as the company lost its strategic direction and spread itself too thin. Weakness then piled on weakness. Without clear strategic direction, diverse acquisitions quickly bloated the company and rigidity replaced agility. The unraveling continued as a loss of discipline led to inept ethical breaches in setting executive compensation.

The turnarounds at Safeco and SPX offer confirmation of the observation that *success results from building a reinforcing pattern of positive traits—agility, discipline, and focus—and managing the tensions inherent among them.* Failure is the product of a pattern of negative traits: diffuseness, rigidity, and ineptness.

3

MANAGING
THE UNEXPECTED

KARL E. WEICK
AND KATHLEEN M. SUTCLIFFE

SUMMARY PREPARED
BY CHRISTOPHER R. STEELE

Christopher R. Steele is a certified public accountant, certified internal auditor, and a 1980 graduate of the University of Minnesota Duluth. Steele's career has included roles on nuclear submarines and at Wells Fargo, Target Corporation, The Limited, and Best Buy. He retired from Best Buy, Inc., a $20 billion specialty retailer, in 2001 as Vice President—Financial Shared Services and Accounting Operations.

A fundamental skill of high-performance companies is their ability to deal effectively with unexpected challenges. In some organizations the unexpected is managed in ways that produce tragic outcomes, while in other organizations the unexpected is routinely managed successfully. There are several organizations that consistently operate under very dynamic conditions, commonly experience significant unexpected events, and yet reliably achieve their objectives. Examples of these **Highly Reliable Organizations** (HROs) include emergency rooms, hostage negotiation teams, nuclear power plants, aircraft carriers, and wilderness firefighting crews. Organizations such as these provide a template for those organizations that want to improve reliability.

THE OBJECTIVE

Surprises are events or outcomes different from the expected that arise from an action or inaction by someone inside or outside the organization. Those skilled in dealing with the unexpected manage surprises mindfully. **Mindful management** of the unexpected requires rapid recognition of the warning signs, containment, resolve, resilience, and swift restoration of system functioning. Identifying and applying the processes used by

Karl E. Weick and Kathleen M. Sutcliffe, *Managing the Unexpected: Assuring High Performance in an Age of Complexity.* San Francisco: Jossey-Bass, 2001.

HROs to improve the skills needed to mindfully manage the unexpected are useful objectives for organizations.

FIVE KEY ATTRIBUTES

Highly reliable organizations have a culture and operating style that allow them to consistently and successfully manage the unexpected. This operating style provides a road map useful for all organizations and levels within organizations.

While the flight deck of an aircraft carrier (or hostage negotiating team) is an organization different from all others, like all businesses there are input processes, outputs, resource constraints, teams, *and* surprises. What differentiates the flight deck from many businesses is the cultural commitment to the five attributes of mindful management:

1. *Preoccupation with failure:* HROs treat lapses, small or large, as symptoms of a system failure, a failure with potentially significant consequences. HROs recognize that a number of small lapses could occur simultaneously with grave results. Consequently, HROs create a culture that encourages the reporting of errors and near misses, and they extract the lessons that can be learned from these events. They are also aware of the complacency and compromises that can accompany success and are wary of the arrogance that success may bring.

2. *Reluctance to simplify interpretations:* HROs manage their complex worlds through developing a deep and detailed view of an operation that allows for a nuanced understanding. They avoid simplifications and position themselves to see and understand as much as possible. Mindful managers create an open environment where diverse points of view are shared and reconciled.

3. *Sensitivity to operations:* Surprises frequently originate where system vulnerabilities have been present for some time without any apparent business disruption. Unexpected events are prevented when these vulnerabilities or deficiencies are identified and addressed prior to a disruption. HROs have high situational awareness and relational understandings that allow for continuous adjustments that stop small errors from cascading into big events. Sensitivity to operations requires a common language and shared goals across the organization.

4. *Commitment to resilience:* HROs are not "zero defects" organizations. While they may strive to be perfect, they are not. When mistakes occur, HROs are not disabled by those errors. Their resilience is the result of addressing problems when they are small and developing "workarounds" (alternative scenarios of actions) to keep the system functioning. These two elements of resilience require deep knowledge of the system—people, process, technology and raw materials, experience, expertise, and training.

5. *Deference to expertise:* In an HRO, those with the most expertise make decisions at the front line. Top-down and decision-making authority, based on rank instead of expertise, result in high-level errors that predictably exacerbate errors made at lower levels.

UNMINDFUL MANAGEMENT OF THE UNEXPECTED

A few years ago the Union Pacific (UP) Railway merged with Southern Pacific (SP), and optimism for improved operations at the new Southern Pacific ran high. The expertise of UP was expected to turn around the deteriorating SP. Instead, surprises, followed by disappointment, were just ahead.

Following the merger, the railroad proved to be a more dangerous place than an aircraft carrier. Soon thereafter the UP experienced six major collisions and the deaths of five employees and two trespassers. In addition to this carnage, the accidents resulted in regulatory attention. Federal regulators began riding trains and found untrained employees, poor maintenance, and crews on duty working more hours than allowed by law.

Problems were not confined to compliance issues. Railroad customers found service levels deteriorating in the form of delayed deliveries, lost shipments, and untraceable shipments. The average speed of trains dropped from 19 to 12 MPH, equivalent to a loss of 1,800 locomotives or one-fourth of the fleet capacity. Gridlock from the Gulf Coast to Chicago existed and 550 trains could not move because of a lack of locomotives or crews.

The Union Pacific Culture

Union Pacific was a company focused on success, with management isolated from bad news. Slowdowns were underreported until problems were nearly irreversible. Management ranks were filled with like-minded railroaders. The homogeneity of management allowed executives to misinterpret or be blind to the early warning signs. Management defined sensitivity to operations as balance sheet improvement and cost controls. The bottom of the organization was sensitive to a railroad system grinding to a halt. The by-the-books culture at UP viewed workarounds and improvisation as insubordination. Consequently, when trains began backing up, no new actions were taken and the problems worsened. With top-down decisions made far from the yard that was at the center of the system meltdown, a deep, nuanced understanding of the problem was not possible.

Hubris and the disconnect between the Union Pacific growth strategy and its operational capabilities prevented the company from recognizing warning signs and taking early preventative measures. As problems cascaded, the rhetoric of competence and arrogance of isolated leaders proved unhelpful.

MINDFUL MANAGEMENT ON AN AIRCRAFT CARRIER'S FLIGHT DECK

An aircraft carrier's numbers are staggering:

- Six thousand people jammed into a 90,000-ton ship that is filled with nuclear weapons and jet fuel and powered by a nuclear reactor. The 1,100-foot-long ship operates in an unforgiving environment of fog, heavy seas, and hostile "competitors."
- Sixty-five-thousand-pound planes land in "controlled crashes" on a pitching, heaving deck that is blanketed in salt water and jet fuel. Landings at night are accomplished without the benefit of lights.
- Two-million horsepower steam-powered catapults allow jets to reach 150 miles per hour in three seconds. These catapults simultaneously launch jets from the bow as other approaching planes hook arresting wires and land on the stern.

The carrier's output is a plane in the air and the subsequent safe return of the plane and its crew. Jets become airborne (and land) through people, process, and technology.

Businesses have the same types of inputs to transform the materials that arrive at the dock door into sales and earnings.

The attributes in short supply at Union Pacific are deeply embedded in a carrier's culture. The crew understands that success cannot be banked. From this understanding comes a *preoccupation with failure*. Landings are graded, near misses are debriefed, incidences are reported, and small problems are viewed in the context of underlying issues such as communications breakdowns.

Flight crews assume nothing and are *reluctant to simplify*. Responsibilities are clear. Communication, confirmation, and verification are via voice, hand, and visual cues. The *sensitivity to operations* is evidenced by the continuous communications loops and the exchange of information about flight deck operations. The constant flow of communications exists to ensure that the unexpected is noticed and addressed before it becomes an incident. The opening credits sequence in the movie *Top Gun* provides a visual example of teamwork and the continuous flow of information in an HRO.

Deep, hands-on knowledge of the carrier's equipment, technologies, and crew and its capabilities enables the ship to react and improvise as necessary. The ability to creatively solve problems brings *resilience*. Finally, despite a clear chain of command and the hierarchical nature of military operations, lower-level staff can override superiors when conditions and circumstances dictate. This *deference to expertise* is necessary because systems operating in a dynamic environment must be refined as conditions warrant and expectations evolve.

BARRIERS TO MINDFULNESS

Mindful organizations are adept at both recognizing and containing the unexpected. Preoccupation with failure, reluctance to simplify, and sensitivity to operations lead to recognition while resilience and deference to expertise allow for containment.

The liabilities of success are understood by HROs. To counter the pull of pride and the resulting astigmatism that accompanies success, HROs are obsessed with failure and incident reviews. Incident reviews in HROs are both frequent and timely to prevent the rewriting of history to save face and protect images.

Non-HRO organizations see close calls as evidence of skill and success. In contrast, HROs see close calls as failures from which learnings can be extracted. Postmortems are most successful when diverse perspectives and information not held in common are allowed to surface.

When the unexpected arises, containment in its early stages is required. Coping skills, capacity, capabilities, flexibility, and an ability to act while thinking are enablers to rapid containment. A nonhierarchical leadership style that shifts decision making to the area or individual who currently has the expertise and answer is essential.

The planning process creates a barrier to both recognition and containment. Plans are developed in an environmental context and planners expect the future to unfold in a predictable, systematic manner. While operating within the plan, there is no place for events not contemplated by the plan. The plan and its assumptions cause people to limit what they see and how they interpret the things occurring in their midst. The tendency is to interpret anomalies in the context of the plan and not as something requiring attention and containment.

Furthermore, plans focus capabilities in a particular direction and are unaware of how capabilities can be reconfigured to address the unexpected. Finally, plans assume that repeatable processes will yield predictable results. Dealing with a surprise requires the ability to sense something novel and then act contrary to the plan. Sizable investments in plans reduce both sensing and innovation capabilities of individuals and organizations.

THE PATH FORWARD

A widely administered audit to assess organization mindfulness and mindfulness tendencies should be conducted across organizational boundaries, hierarchies, and specialties. If material improvement is needed, a culture and management style change is necessary.

Culture—what people think, feel, and do—is a by-product of management's beliefs, values, and actions. It reflects their communications, perceived values and philosophy, the reward system, and employee beliefs and attitudes.[1] HROs have a culture of mindfulness coupled with institutional practices. Cultural properties that influence mindfulness include safe practices, being informed, reporting systems, just practices, flexibility, and the valuation of continued learning.

Inattention to safe practices can lead to errors with unexpected consequences. Safety requires learning from small errors to prevent larger ones from occurring. If errors cannot be reported without fear of adverse consequences, mistakes will not see the light of day. Mistakes must be dealt with in a consistently just manner. Disciplinary action is appropriate for a few "across the line" errors, while most mistakes fall on the other side of the line. If disciplinary action is inconsistent or unjust, self-reporting of errors is unlikely. Flexible authority structures and nonhierarchical decision making permit information to flow freely to where the expertise resides. Openness, truth, and the reconciliation of divergent interpretations shared freely across boundaries increases the collective knowledge of the enterprise, and this knowledge can be leveraged with effective management to deal mindfully with the unexpected.

Effective managers in a mindful organization:

- Allocate resources to both production and protection,
- State not only goals to be accomplished but also errors that cannot occur,
- Create an error-friendly learning atmosphere,
- Are humble and aware of their vulnerabilities,
- Promote healthy debates by those with diverse views,
- Break down hierarchies and divisional barriers,
- Push decision making to where the expertise resides. The deep knowledge of experts is a by-product of a commitment to training, job rotation, feedback loops, and debriefing that accompanies the routine reporting of errors and organizational capacity.

---

[1] Edgar Schein said that culture has six properties: "(1) shared basic assumptions that are (2) invented, discovered or developed by a given group as it (3) learns to cope with its problem of external adaptation and internal integration in ways that (4) have worked well enough to be considered valid, and, therefore, (5) can be taught to new members of the group as the (6) correct way to perceive, think and feel in relation to those problems."

Conclusion

Plans, mental models, management styles, and company culture create blind spots that allow rich opportunities for learning to pass by undetected. When these opportunities go unnoticed, the chance to make small corrections to prevent a subsequent large surprise also passes. *The skills and culture of non-traditional organizations (HROs) that routinely manage the unexpected successfully are transportable to more traditional entities.* If these organizations wish to improve reliability and join the ranks of high-performance companies, they have an exciting opportunity to do so through mindful management.

4

RESPONSIBLE
RESTRUCTURING

WAYNE F. CASCIO

SUMMARY PREPARED BY STEPHEN RUBENFELD

Stephen Rubenfeld is Professor of Human Resource Management at the Labovitz School of Business and Economics at the University of Minnesota Duluth. He received his doctorate from the University of Wisconsin–Madison and was previously on the faculty of Texas Tech University. His professional publications and presentations have covered a wide range of human resource and labor relations topics, including job search behaviors, human resource policies and practices, job security, and staffing challenges. He has served as a consultant to private and public organizations and is a member of the Society for Human Resource Management, the Academy of Management, and the Industrial Relations Research Association.

Ahighly competitive business context carries with it both boundless opportunities and daunting challenges. On one hand, organizations are stimulated to become better at what they do by economizing, innovating, and honing their competitive advantage. But at the same time, the very existence of a business can be threatened by pricing pressures, declining profit margins, and burgeoning capital investment needs. This is not a situation that calls for "just getting by," mediocrity, or hoping that things will work themselves out. Intense competition is a call to action that tests the mettle of organizations and their leaders. It is a situation that demands thoughtful and aggressive actions. The pressures attributable to the global marketplace, pervasive technology, and more assertive consumers are not going to abate. Decisive steps are necessary to ensure that the critical elements of competitive success—price, quality, and customer service—are in place and fine-tuned to support continued organizational vitality.

The active pursuit of efficiencies, effective operations, and customer responsiveness are all subjects of much organizational rhetoric, but in practice it is the cost containment part of the equation that gets most of the attention. In fact, it is easier, faster, and more predictable to cut costs than it is to increase revenues or to fundamentally improve the

Wayne F. Cascio, *Responsible Restructuring: Creative and Profitable Alternatives to Layoffs.* San Francisco: Berrett-Koehler, 2003.

organization's product or service. Whether driven by a current financial crisis or the desire to avoid future problems, actions directed at cutting or controlling costs, rooting out inefficiencies, and keeping prices in check have become almost universal. Unlike earlier times, this self-imposed pressure to focus on cost containment is not limited to organizations swimming in red ink; it has become a benchmark of good business practice.

Because employment costs are the most visible and frequently an organization's largest variable cost, downsizing along with wage and benefit containment are at the heart of most efforts to enhance competitiveness. Often characterized euphemistically as organizational restructuring, the logic of these efforts to control expenses by having fewer employees is compelling: Reducing costs will increase profit margins, which will produce immediate bottom-line results and help ensure future success. But the promised benefits of cost containment through reducing headcount often are elusive. Whether couched in the verbiage of *downsizing, rightsizing,* or other emotionless synonyms for reducing the number of employees, the benefits tend to be fleeting. By themselves these methods rarely offer a sustainable solution to the barriers to competitiveness. Likewise, wage freezes and benefits cuts may have an immediate and visible bottom-line impact, but the true savings are often reduced by diminished productivity along with undesired turnover or other employee withdrawal behaviors.

The net effect is that *restructuring that is built primarily on downsizing or containment of compensation costs will not have a positive effect on the areas where real competitiveness is built: innovation, quality, and customer service.* In the end, this approach to restructuring does not achieve the forecasted cost savings and does not help to improve long-term competitive vitality of the organization. If downsizing is not the solution, how can an organization succeed in a competitive marketplace?

IS RESTRUCTURING BAD?

Restructuring can be constructive and even essential when a company is struggling to regain or achieve economic success. Similarly, evolving technologies, nonperforming assets, or even aggressive moves by competitors can be a powerful impetus to restructure. It is obvious that job losses, layoffs, and sometimes radical changes to the jobs that remain are integral to most restructurings, but as is often the case, the devil is in the details. The issue is *how* these employment changes are made. Experience carries with it the lesson that across-the-board layoffs and hiring freezes, or similar *slash and burn* downsizing strategies, rarely achieve the promised benefits. The hidden costs and secondary impacts may even worsen the competitive crisis.

Many of the costs of downsizing are obvious and calculable. The decision to restructure typically carries with it a recognition that costs associated with severance pay, accrued vacations, benefit costs, outplacement, and additional administrative expense will be incurred. In contrast, there are many indirect costs that may be ignored or not even recognized. Even where acknowledged as potential problem areas, their severity is often underestimated. Although it may be difficult to accurately estimate their future costs and impacts, these costs are real and can have a dramatic negative impact on competitiveness. Examples of such hidden costs include:

- Reduced morale
- Risk-averse behaviors by surviving employees
- Loss of trust

- Costs of retraining continuing employees
- Legal challenges
- Reduced productivity
- Loss of institutional competencies and memory
- Survivor burnout

While these problems and costs may impede competitiveness efforts, restructuring is not inherently bad. Many businesses have successfully downsized and restructured to improve their productivity and financial success, but downsizing is not a panacea. Research conducted over the past 25 years indicates that *downsizing strategies for most organizations do not result in long-term payoffs that are significantly greater than those where there are stable employment patterns.*

MYTHS ABOUT DOWNSIZING

When confronted by the need to reduce costs, many employers (who self-righteously proclaim that "employees are our greatest asset") turn to layoffs first when responding to a competitive dilemma. This may be fueled by a number of myths and misunderstandings about downsizing. For example, the following six myths are refuted by research and experience (facts):

Myth 1: Downsizing increases profits.
Fact 1: Profitability does not necessarily improve.

Myth 2: Downsizing boosts productivity.
Fact 2: Productivity results are mixed.

Myth 3: Downsizing doesn't negatively affect quality.
Fact 3: Quality does not improve and may go down.

Myth 4: Downsizing is a one-time event.
Fact 4: The best predictor of future downsizing is past downsizing.

Myth 5: Downsizing has few effects on remaining employees.
Fact 5: Negative impacts on morale, stress, and commitment are common.

Myth 6: Downsizing is unlikely to lead to sabotage or other vengeful acts.
Fact 6: Such behaviors are not rare and their consequences can be severe.

These findings should offer decision makers a note of caution about the potential consequences of restructuring efforts painted with a broad brush. An obvious conclusion is that restructuring should not be done blindly, and when restructuring does appear to be necessary, it should be approached strategically and responsibly.

RESPONSIBLE RESTRUCTURING

The approaches that employers take toward restructuring reflect significant differences in how they view their employees. Organizational decision makers can be thought of as falling into two camps concerning their view of employees—those that see employees as *costs to be cut,* and those that see employees as *assets to be developed.* The *cost cutters* consider employees to be the source of the problem. They think of employees as commodities. Through the lens of the balance sheet, they strive to achieve the minimum number of employees and the lowest possible labor expenditures needed to run the business successfully. In contrast, the *responsible restructurers* view employee expertise and contributions as central to any solution. They consider their employees as essential in fashioning and carrying forward sustainable answers to competitiveness challenges. The initial focus of the responsible restructurers is not on reducing headcount or shrinking the budget, but rather on enhancing effectiveness and empowering employees to overcome competitive challenges.

Responsible restructurers turn to broad-based layoffs and compensation cuts only as a last resort. Their initial and primary approach is to use a variety of developmental and effectiveness-oriented practices to achieve and maintain competitive viability. These organizations are likely to:

- Flatten their hierarchical structures.
- Create an empowered, team-oriented work environment.
- Seek labor-management partnerships.
- Share information.
- Make extensive use of training.
- Demonstrate a culture of continuous learning.
- Link compensation to performance and skills.

These employers do not advocate and use these responsible restructuring strategies primarily as acts of compassion or for other altruistic reasons. They truly believe that there are benefits that come from employment stability and that the best and most sustainable outcomes are achieved when employees are part of the solution.

These companies, which include in their ranks Southwest Airlines, SAS Institute, Cisco, Charles Schwab, Procter & Gamble, and 3M, share the following critical characteristics:

1. A clear vision of what they want to achieve and how to communicate this vision to stakeholders,
2. The ability to execute and develop employee-centered initiatives, and
3. Highly empowered employees who are committed to help the organization succeed.

These companies don't start with the premise that the minimal number of employees is the best number of employees. Rather, they ask how their employees can help them fashion a solution and meet the market challenge. They know that short-term downsizing does not solve long-term problems.

HOW DO WE MOVE FORWARD?

In addition to the basic elements of responsible restructuring already described, it is useful to keep these recommendations in mind as issues of competitiveness are confronted:

- Deal with the underlying competitive problem, not just the bottom line.
- Integrate staffing decisions with the strategic business plan and the drivers of success.

- Involve employees in shaping broad solutions as well as specific organizational responses.
- Consider the payoffs from employment stability.
- Communicate regularly, openly, effectively, and honestly.
- If layoffs are necessary, be logical, targeted, fair, and consistent.
- Give survivors a reason to stay and prospective employees a reason to join the organization.
- Empower survivors to succeed and encourage them to beware of burnout.

Conclusion

The ultimate payoff from successfully pursuing *responsible restructuring* rather than budget slashing in responding to competitive challenges is better and longer lasting solutions. The organization also is more likely to reap the rewards of higher customer satisfaction, have the ability to respond more quickly and more successfully to future challenges, maintain a recruiting and retention advantage over its labor market competitors, and have committed employees who are not unduly risk averse. Remove the barriers to effective competition and financial success will follow.

PART

IV

ORGANIZATIONAL STRATEGY AND EXECUTION

Many of the authors in this book suggest that organizations can benefit by defining their own standard of effectiveness, especially after examining other successful firms. An organization's external environment has a powerful influence on organizational success and needs to be monitored for significant trends and influential forces. In addition, effective executives need to recognize when internal changes are necessary to adapt to the external environment.

The three readings in this section are designed to stimulate thinking about management through a focus on the management and leadership of the organization from its very top. Taken collectively, these readings suggest that organizations can (and should) proactively take control of their destinies. One way of doing this is by articulating an engaging vision that can systematically guide them into the future. In effect, managers are urged to have a master plan that defines their mission, identifies their unique environmental niche, builds on their strengths, and adapts to changing needs. This overall vision is then converted into operational goals by applying several very specific management practices.

In their book *The Strategy-Focused Organization*, Robert S. Kaplan and David P. Norton focus their attention on performance measurement. Based upon their observations, many of today's organizations continue to function with management systems and tactics that were designed for yesterday's organization. They contend that too many organizations fail to execute strategy successfully. Addressing this issue, the authors identify five key factors that are required for building a "strategy-focused organization."

Robert S. Kaplan is the Marvin Bower Professor of Leadership at the Harvard Business School. His co-author, David P. Norton, is president of Balanced Scorecard Collaborative, Inc.

Execution: The Discipline of Getting Things Done by Larry Bossidy and Ram Charan, with Charles Burck, is the second reading in this section. Through numerous examples of success and failures the authors provide two themes. The first deals with "execution"—the process of moving from vision formulation to implementation. Second, the authors go to great length to provide insight into the mechanisms associated with making execution an organizational building block. In too many instances top management fails either because it tends to micromanage new organizational initiatives or because it remains aloof and too far removed. Bossidy and Charan, with Burck, argue that it is important to find the right balance between over- and under-involvement. To this end they highlight several essential leadership characteristics.

Larry Bossidy is the chairman and former CEO of Honeywell International. He had a long managerial career serving as vice chairman and COO at General Electric Capital, which was followed by several years as CEO of Allied Signal, assisting with its merger with Honeywell International. Ram Charan has taught at the Harvard School of Business and the Kellogg School at Northwestern University. He has also served as an advisor to CEOs and executive managers for over three decades.

William Joyce (professor of strategy and organization theory at Dartmouth's Amos Tuck School of Business), Nitin Nohria (business administration professor at the Harvard Business School), and Bruce Roberson (a partner with McKinsey & Company) combined to write *What (Really) Works*. A question driving this book asks "Why do some organizations consistently outperform their competitors? What do their managers know and do?"

To answer these two questions the authors analyzed data from the Evergreen Project, a major field study analyzing more than 10 years of data from 160 companies and more than 200 different management practices. In *What (Really) Works* the authors report their discovery of six specific management practices engaged in by all of the successful companies.

1

THE STRATEGY-FOCUSED ORGANIZATION

ROBERT S. KAPLAN AND DAVID P. NORTON

SUMMARY PREPARED BY SANJAY GOEL

Sanjay Goel (Ph.D., Arizona State University) is an Associate Professor of Management at the University of Minnesota Duluth. His research and teaching interests are primarily in the areas of strategic management, management of innovation and technology, and corporate governance. As a management consultant in the agribusiness sector, he was involved in new project appraisals and project monitoring.

No matter how thoughtful, creative, and detailed an organization's strategy is, it is worth nothing if it is not executed. Strategy execution has proven to be the Achilles' heel of most organizations. In fact, a 1999 *Fortune* story based on prominent CEO failures concluded that it is poor strategy execution, not strategy itself, that is the real problem behind corporate failure. The task of creating an organization that is focused on strategy execution is indeed critical to unleashing the real value trapped in an organization's strategy. Unfortunately, organizations seem to be slipping farther behind in linking strategy formulation and strategy execution. This has been due to a shift in real value within organizations from tangible to intangible assets, a shift in strategies from efficiency to knowledge-based, and a shift in decision focus from centralized to decentralized. Due to these developments, the metrics, controls, and structures used to measure strategy execution have become outdated and out of sync with the actual needs of organizations to monitor strategy execution. Five principles define a strategy-focused organization, which tighten the link between an organization's strategy and its execution.

THE PRINCIPLES

Principle 1. *Translate the strategy to operational terms.* This is the first step to enabling strategy execution, the premise being that unless a strategy can be elaborated in operational metrics, it does not communicate actionable steps to the rest of the organization.

Robert S. Kaplan and David P. Norton, *The Strategy-Focused Organization: How Balanced Scorecard Companies Thrive in the New Business Environment.* Cambridge, MA: Harvard Business School Press, 2001.

Strategy-focused organizations translate the strategy to operational terms by developing a *strategy map,* which then serves as a framework for building *balanced scorecards* for the organization.

> *Strategy maps:* A **strategy map** is a logical relationship diagram that defines a strategy by specifying the relationship among shareholders, customers, business processes, and an organization's competencies. The relationships establish cause-and-effect links between activities. These explicit linkages can then be communicated and incorporated in developing a balanced scorecard for the organization.
>
> *Balanced scorecard:* A balanced scorecard provides measurement and control metrics for an organization's strategy map along four key dimensions: financial, customer, internal business process, and learning and growth perspective. Thus it highlights not just the financial and nonfinancial outcomes of an organization's strategy, but also the lead indicators and processes that would need to be monitored to achieve the desired outcomes. In this manner, it provides a framework to describe and communicate strategy in a consistent way throughout the organization. Most importantly, it establishes accountability throughout the organization for strategy execution.

Principle 2. *Align the organization to the strategy.* Strategy cannot be implemented if organizations do not change to accommodate the needs of the planned strategy. Balanced scorecards in a strategy-focused organization are used to align the organization with its strategy in two ways: by creating business unit synergy, and by creating synergy across shared services.

> *Creating business unit synergy:* This involves clarifying the value created by common ownership of multiple businesses under a single corporation. Value could be created by any one of the four perspectives of the balanced scorecard. For instance, optimizing capital allocation could create financial synergies by increasing shareholder value. In addition, promoting cross selling could create customer synergies by increasing the share of the customer's total account.
>
> *Creating synergies through shared services:* Synergies can be created by aligning an organization's internal units that provide shared services. These support services frequently become bureaucratic and unresponsive to the demands of strategy execution of operating divisions. These shared services can be aligned to the strategic needs of operating divisions by adopting either of the following two models:
>
> - **The strategic partner model:** In this approach the shared service unit is a partner in the development of, and adherence to, the balanced scorecard of the operating business unit.
> - **The business-in-a-business model:** In this approach, the shared service unit must view itself as a business, and the operating business units as its customers. A shared service scorecard serves as a written, explicit definition of this relationship.

Principle 3. *Make strategy everyone's day job.* This principle has roots in the simple fact that strategy cannot be implemented by the CEO and senior leadership of an organization. Everyone in the organization must be involved in strategy execution by developing specific activities within their own sphere of influence. Strategy-focused organizations use the balanced scorecard in three ways to align their employees to the strategy:

- **Communicating and educating:** Strategy needs to be communicated to the entire organization in a holistic manner, so that everybody understands it and is able to implement it.
- **Developing personal and team objectives:** Managers must help employees set individual and team goals that are consistent with strategic outcomes. This helps establish personal accountability and provides metrics to self-evaluate progress.
- **Establishing an incentive and reward system:** This develops a stake among the employees in the organization's success and failure, closing the loop on accountability and organizational performance.

Principle 4. *Making strategy a continual process.* Strategy-focused organizations use a "double-loop" process that integrates the management of budgets and operations with the management of strategy. The balanced scorecard is used as a link between the two "loops." Three specific remedies are used to link the operations review cycle with the strategy review cycle.

- **Linking strategy and budgeting:** Stretch targets and strategic initiatives on the balanced scorecard link the conceptual part of strategy with the rigor and precision of budgets. Rolling forecasts are substituted for fixed budgets.
- **Closing the strategy loop:** Strategic feedback systems linked to the balanced scorecard provide a new framework for reporting and a new metric for monitoring strategy execution, one focused on strategy instead of operations.
- **Testing, learning, and adapting:** Using the balanced scorecard, managers can test the cause-and-effect relationships underlying an organization's strategy. These relationships can be modified to incorporate learning from experience and changed environmental conditions.

The emphasis on strategy as a continuous process, as opposed to a static and periodic statement of intent, keeps strategy current and relevant to an organization's environment. It also makes strategy easier to implement and change, when needed.

Principle 5. *Mobilizing change through executive leadership.* The buy-in of executive leadership is the underlying premise of a strategy-focused organization. Top management must understand that creating a strategy-focused organization is an organization change project. A successful change to a strategy-focused organization rests on performance of three critical activities by top management:

- **Mobilization:** An organization needs to understand why change is needed. In the mobilization phase, the organization is shaken up, or "unfrozen." A sense of urgency is established, a guiding coalition is formed, and a new vision and strategy is articulated for the entire organization to gather around.
- **Establishing a governance process:** The next phase defines, demonstrates, and reinforces the new cultural values in the organization. This is a democratic process, breaking existing silos and creating strategy teams, town hall meetings, and open communications.

- **Recognizing a new strategic management system:** This phase evolves as the organization begins to understand the process of being a strategy-focused organization. This phase essentially institutionalizes the new cultural values and new structures into a new system for managing. In other words, it "refreezes" the organization, albeit an organization that is more adaptable, flexible, and strategy focused.

COMMON PITFALLS

Pitfalls that impede the implementation of balanced scorecards to make firms strategy-focused usually fall in three categories:

1. *Transitional issues:* abandoning the project due to merger or acquisition, and/or change in leadership.
2. *Design flaws:* failing to integrate strategy into the scorecards, and not making scorecards detailed and multidimensional enough to be really balanced.
3. *Process failures:* these are exhibited in the following ways:
   - Lack of senior management commitment
   - Too few individuals involved
   - Keeping the scorecard at the top
   - A development process that is too lengthy
   - Treating the scorecard as a systems project
   - Hiring inexperienced consultants
   - Introducing the balanced scorecard only for compensation.

The message from the application of principles of the strategy-focused organization in several entities—across the public, private, and not-for-profit sectors—is that these principles work, and organizations achieve a tighter integration between their strategy and its implementation.

READING

2 | EXECUTION

LARRY BOSSIDY AND RAM CHARAN

SUMMARY PREPARED BY
CHRISTIAN F. EDWARDSON

Christian F. Edwardson is in the home remodeling business and a part-time consultant after spending more than 25 years in wood products research and development. His areas of research interest are related to the home building industry, especially green building technology. He is also interested in incorporating lean manufacturing principles in home remodeling and new construction. He received a B.S. and an M.S. in Wood Science and Technology from the University of Maine and an MBA from the University of Minnesota Duluth.

*T*he absence of execution is the biggest obstacle to business success today. Execution is a discipline that nobody has previously explained satisfactorily. Successful execution requires a specific set of behaviors and techniques that companies must master if they want a competitive advantage. Leading for execution is not difficult, but a leader has to be deeply and passionately engaged in the organization, and honest about its realities. Leaders at any company or level need to master the discipline of execution to establish credibility.

UNDERSTANDING EXECUTION

Three key points are useful to help understand what execution is:

1. *Execution is a discipline and integral to strategy:* It is a mistake to think of execution as the tactical side of the business. Execution is a systematic process of exposing reality and acting on it. Three core processes—the people process, the strategy

Larry Bossidy, and Ram Charan, with Charles Burck, *Execution: The Discipline of Getting Things Done.*
New York: Crown Business, 2002.

process, and the operations process—must be tightly linked for a company to execute effectively.

2. *Execution is the major job of the business leader:* The leader is in charge of getting things done by managing the three core processes with intensity and rigor. Picking other leaders, setting strategy, and running operations are the substance of execution that cannot be delegated. The leader sets the tone of the dialogue (the core of culture and the basic unit of work) in an organization.

3. *Execution has to be in the culture:* Execution is not a program; it is a discipline that must be understood by everyone in the organization. Execution requires education, practice, dedication, and reflection. Execution should drive the behavior of all leaders at all levels, beginning with senior leaders.

THE THREE BUILDING BLOCKS OF EXECUTION

The first building block of execution requires a leader to practice seven essential behaviors:

1. *Know your people and your business:* In companies that don't execute, leaders are usually out of touch with the day-to-day realities of the business. It's not that they lack information—they just aren't engaged with the business or where the action is. A leader (CEO) must go to operations and conduct business reviews. Managers may not like what you tell them, but they will respect that you care enough about the business to take time for the review. The review is useful for fostering honest dialogue and helping establish the personal connection critical to launching future initiatives.

2. *Insist on realism:* The heart of execution is realism. In order to execute, leaders must establish realistic, attainable goals with those who will carry them out. Avoiding realism because it is uncomfortable is a major mistake. By confronting reality, changes can be made so that execution is successful.

3. *Set clear goals and priorities:* Leaders who execute well focus on only a few priorities that everyone understands. The matrix organization requires a small number of carefully crafted, clear priorities to avoid conflicts over who gets what, and why. Along with clear goals, strive for simplicity in general; leaders who execute speak simply and directly.

4. *Follow through:* A major cause of poor execution is the failure of business leaders to follow through. If no one is held accountable for meeting goals, no one will take the goals seriously. A leader will set up a mechanism to monitor the progress of goal achievements assigned to others.

5. *Reward the doers:* People need to be rewarded if you want them to produce specific results. This seems obvious, but many companies do a poor job of linking rewards to performance. It is important to distinguish between those who achieve and those who don't, through base pay or in the administration of bonuses and stock options.

6. *Expand people's capabilities through coaching:* One of the most important jobs of leaders is to pass on their acquired knowledge and experience to the next generation of leaders. Coaching is a vital way of expanding the capabilities of everyone in

the organization. Coaching is teaching people how to get things done, and a good leader will regard every contact as a coaching opportunity.

7. *Know yourself:* Strength of character is critical to execution. *Emotional fortitude* is necessary to be honest with yourself, to deal honestly with business realities, and to assess people fairly. Emotional fortitude gives you the strength to hear the truth, to deliver the truth, and it enables you to deal with your own weaknesses. Emotional fortitude is the foundation of people skills and is made up of four core qualities: *authenticity* means who you are is what you do and say; *self-awareness* means you know your strengths and weaknesses; *self-mastery* allows you to keep your ego in check, take responsibility for your behavior, adapt to change, and be honest in all situations; and *humility* allows you to acknowledge your mistakes.

The second building block requires creating the framework for cultural change. It is important to recognize that people's beliefs and behaviors are equally or even more important than a company strategy or organizational structure. Changing culture is difficult and often fails because it is not linked to improving the business's outcomes. A set of processes (social operating mechanisms) is needed to change the beliefs and behaviors of people in ways that are linked directly to bottom-line results.

Operationalizing Culture

Clearly linking rewards to performance is the foundation of changing behavior. A company's culture will change if it rewards and promotes people for execution.

People should be rewarded both for strong achievements on numbers and adopting desirable behaviors. Linking rewards to performance is necessary to create an execution culture, but it must be implemented with the "social software of execution." The social software includes the values, beliefs, and norms of behavior (i.e., culture).

Social operating mechanisms are a key component of social software. *Social operating mechanisms are formal or informal interactions where dialogue occurs.* One difference between a meeting and an operating mechanism is that the latter are integrative. New information flows and working relationships are created because the interaction breaks down barriers among units, functions, disciplines, work processes, and hierarchies. A second difference is that social operating mechanisms are where beliefs and behaviors of the social software are practiced.

In the ever-changing business environment, the social operating mechanism is the constant, providing the consistent framework needed to create a common corporate culture. The social operating mechanism teaches people how to work together in constructive debate.

Robust dialogue is necessary in an execution culture. With robust dialogue, an organization will be effective in gathering and understanding information and using it to make decisions. For robust dialogue to occur, people must go in with an open mind and a desire to hear new information and choose the best alternatives. People should be encouraged to speak candidly. Informality encourages candor and invites questions and critical thinking. It gets the truth out. *Robust dialogue ends with closure,* that is, people agree about what each person has to do and when. Because robust dialogue has purpose and meaning, it brings out reality.

The culture of a company is defined by the behavior of its leaders. In the social operating mechanism, the leader has to be present to create and reinforce desired behaviors and robust dialogue. However, success in executing the desired cultural change depends on having the right people.

The third building block is having the right people in the right place. This is a job that should be handled by the leader and not delegated to someone else in the organization. If you claim that people are your most important asset, then it is critical that you understand what each job requires and what kind of people are needed to fill the job. The best competitive differentiator a company has is its people.

Many mismatches between people and their jobs result because the leaders do not know enough about the people they are appointing. A leader who is personally committed and deeply engaged in the people process will avoid this mistake.

It is the leader's responsibility to ask what specific qualities make a person right for the job. This means understanding the requirements of the job—the three or four non-negotiable criteria that a person must be able to do to be successful. A leader must have the emotional fortitude to confront a nonperformer and take decisive action. Finally, a leader must spend as much time and energy developing people as on budgeting, strategic planning, and other tasks. The payoff will be a sustainable competitive advantage.

Look for people who are good at getting things done. To build a company that has excellent discipline of execution, choose people who are *doers* (not just talkers). Search for leaders who have a drive for winning and who get satisfaction from getting things done. Good leaders will energize people, not through rhetoric, but by focusing on short-term accomplishments that lead to winning the game. Good leaders have the emotional fortitude to be decisive and are able to make difficult decisions on tough issues. The best leaders get things done through others. They do not micromanage the people they lead, nor do they abandon them. Finally, every leader who is good at executing will follow through. They ensure that people are doing the things they said they would, when they said they would.

It is not easy to get the right people in the right jobs. Traditional interviews don't work for finding the qualities of leaders who execute. It requires probing people to learn about how they think and what drives them. Developing leaders requires hands-on hiring. It is important to look for energy and enthusiasm for execution. Getting the right people in the right job is a matter of being systematic and consistent in interviewing and appraising people, and then developing them through candid appraisals and feedback to encourage improvement.

With the three building blocks in place, the foundation is established for operating and managing the core processes effectively.

THE PEOPLE PROCESS: MAKING THE LINK WITH STRATEGY AND OPERATIONS

Getting the people process right is necessary to fulfill the potential of the organization. This makes it more important than either the strategy or operations processes. A robust people process has three elements: It evaluates people accurately and in depth; it has a mechanism to identify and develop the leadership talent needed to execute its strategies; and it fills the leadership pipeline.

Evaluating people accurately and in depth will yield information about leadership qualities and business acumen. It may be necessary to replace an excellent performer with a person better equipped to take the business to the next level. It is important to have early feedback on behavior so that an unsuited person does not rise to a critical job in the future.

Four building blocks can be used to determine the organization's talent needs over time and for planning actions to meet the need:

1. *Linking people to strategy and operations:* The business leader must make sure that the right kinds and numbers of people are available to execute the near, medium, long-term, and operating strategy of the organization. A new strategy may require new people. A high performer in the current organization may not be able to handle the challenges of a new strategic future. It is tough, but necessary, to tell some people that they aren't capable of moving to the next level. The people process will force leaders to do what has to be done.

2. *Developing the leadership pipeline:* A leadership assessment summary tool is useful to develop a picture of the pipeline. The summary compares performance and behavior for a group of individuals and identifies those who have high potential and those who are promotable. A *continuous improvement summary* is similar to a traditional performance appraisal, but it captures information on development needs and helps the individual become a better performer. The essence of talent planning and developing a leadership pipeline requires analyzing succession depth and retention risk. *Succession depth analysis* shows if the company has enough high-potential people to fill key positions. *Retention risk analysis* may be used to learn if people are in the wrong job or at risk for leaving the company. Identifying the talent avoids the danger of organizational inertia; that is, keeping people in the same job too long and conversely, promoting people too quickly.

3. *Dealing with non-performers:* People who aren't meeting their established goals are *non-performers.* Failure to meet goals means they aren't performing at a level essential for the company's success and they need to be dealt with quickly and fairly. This may mean moving someone to a job the person is more suited for, but if you have to let someone go it should be done as constructively as possible. An important part of reinforcing the positive nature of the performance (execution) culture is preserving the dignity of people who leave jobs.

4. *Linking HR to business results:* The role of HR changes radically in an execution culture. HR is more important than ever in a recruitment-oriented mode and it can be a force for advancing the organization. The HR person must have the same characteristics as any effective manager; these include business acumen, understanding how a company makes money, critical thinking, a passion for getting things done, and the ability to link strategy and execution.

There is not one best system for having a robust people process, but certain rules are needed. The process must have integrity, honesty, a common approach and language, frequency, and candid dialogue. Candid dialogue is critical, as it is the social software of the people process.

THE STRATEGY PROCESS: LINKING PEOPLE AND OPERATIONS

The basic goal of any strategy is to be preferred by customers and achieve a sustainable competitive advantage, while making sufficient money to satisfy stockholders. The strategic plan must be an action plan used by business leaders to reach their business objectives. The strategy must be linked to the people process. If you don't have the right people in place to execute the strategy, you need a plan to get them.

The substance of any strategy can be summed up by a few key concepts and actions that define it. By pinpointing the key concepts or building blocks, leaders are forced to be clear as they discuss and debate the strategy.

A strategy will be effective only if it is constructed and owned by those who will execute it. Through the process of developing the plan using robust dialogue, the line people will learn execution. Discussing the business and environment creates excitement and alignment and in turn strengthens the process.

A strong strategic plan addresses nine key questions:

1. *What is the assessment of the external environment?* Businesses operate within a shifting political, social, and economic environment, and the strategic plan must define the external assumptions management has made.
2. *How well do you understand the existing customers and markets?* It is important to understand who makes the purchasing decision and their buying behavior. The sales approach used with an engineer, purchasing agent, or CEO (of a small company) will be significantly different.
3. *What is the best way to grow the business profitably, and what are the obstacles to growth?* Growth can be a result of new products, new channels, new customers, or acquisitions. Whatever direction your company takes requires understanding of the obstacles and taking action to overcome them.
4. *Who is the competition?* It is important to think critically about your competitors, neither underestimating nor overestimating them.
5. *Can the business execute the strategy?* The leader must make a realistic assessment of the ability of the organization to execute the plan. It is possible to increase your capability when you know the capabilities and understand what needs to be done.
6. *What are the important milestones in executing the plan?* Milestones help leaders decide if they have the right strategy. If the milestones are missed, the direction can be changed if the strategic plan is adaptable (as it should be).
7. *Are the short term and long term balanced?* Strategy planning needs to be done in the current environment. The plan must deal with what a company has to do between the present (short term) and the future time when the plan will give peak results.
8. *What are the critical issues facing the business?* It is important to identify the issues and impediments that can keep the company from reaching its objectives.
9. *How will the business make money on a sustainable basis?* An understanding of the drivers of cash, margin, velocity, revenue growth, market share, and competitive advantage is required.

The strategic plan developed according to these guidelines and questions will provide the basis for a robust dialogue linking the strategy to the people and operating processes. The plan is less about numbers and more about ideas that are specific and clear.

A critical part of developing and adopting the plan is the strategy review. The review is a good place for the leader to learn about the people involved and assess their potential for promotion. Five key questions should be critically addressed in the review:

1. Does each business unit team know the competition?
2. Does the organization have the capability to execute the strategy?
3. Is the plan scattered or focused?
4. Have the right ideas been selected?
5. Are the linkages with people and operations clear?

THE OPERATIONS PROCESS: MAKING THE LINK WITH STRATEGY AND PEOPLE

An operating plan provides the path for people to fulfill the strategy and achieve the end point where a business wants to go. The plan looks forward to how targets will be met. It addresses the critical issues in execution by building the budget on realities. The assumptions used in developing the plan are debated rigorously and trade-offs are made openly. Robust dialogue and debate are part of the social software that helps build the business leadership of the people involved.

The plan is built after the assumptions are agreed on. The process is done in three parts: setting targets, developing the action plan, and establishing follow-through measures after participants agree to the plan. The follow-through has three parts. The first is a memo (or other device) sent by the leader outlining what others agreed to accomplish. The second part of follow-through is a contingency plan. Companies that execute well have a contingency plan that deals with alternative scenarios, and this allows them to act quickly when faced with new situations. Finally, quarterly reviews help keep the plans up to date and synchronized and they show leaders who may need coaching to get things done.

If the operations process is run on the social software of execution, the people who must meet the targets have also set the targets. This avoids the traditional budget problem of disconnect from reality. Robust dialogue, debate, and review of the plan allow leaders to set meaningful stretch goals to maximize individual effort.

Conclusion

The discipline of execution is based on linking the core processes of people, strategy, and operations. It starts with the leader knowing what skills a job requires and having the right people in the job. Leaders need to be where the action is—learning the realities of the business from those in the trenches. Being honest both with yourself and others is critical to getting things done. Using robust dialogue to get at the heart of an issue brings reality to each of the core processes.

The people process has to be a top priority. Success in execution depends on having doers, and doers should be rewarded because the promise of meaningful compensation ultimately drives future performance. The long-term success of the business depends on having the right strategy process. The individuals who must execute the strategy should be driving the process. The critical issues facing the business need to be identified, debated, and resolved. The final strategic plan should be clear, concise, and understood by everyone involved. An operations plan for the year sets the stage for achievement.

In an execution culture, the leader must be personally involved in the three core processes. To run the business with reality knowledge requires the leader to be involved from the start through the follow-up. This involvement and follow-through allow leaders to know the capabilities of the people who work for them and the potential of the organization.

3

WHAT (REALLY) WORKS

WILLIAM JOYCE, NITIN NOHRIA,
AND BRUCE ROBERSON

SUMMARY PREPARED BY ALLEN HARMON

Allen Harmon is President and General Manager of WDSE-TV, the community-licensed PBS member station serving Northeastern Minnesota and Northwestern Wisconsin. He also currently serves as an adjunct instructor in the Labovitz School of Business and Economics at the University of Minnesota Duluth. Before joining WDSE, Mr. Harmon held a series of senior management positions in a regional investor-owned electric utility. He earned an MBA from Indiana University and has completed the University of Minnesota Carlson School of Management Executive Development Program.

INTRODUCTION

The list of companies currently at the top of their game churns constantly. Management thinkers offer a seemingly endless supply of silver-bullet cures that are half-heartedly adopted, quickly fail, and are soon abandoned. Managers await the latest autobiographies of business legends only to find that the experiences described and suggestions offered by these luminaries fail to translate easily into their own situations. By contrast, the Evergreen Project—a search for the "evergreen" source of business success—was conceived to replace blind faith, luck, and guessing with statistically rigorous analysis of the results of previously effective organizations. The results of that study produced the 4 + 2 formula for corporate success.

THE STUDY

An initial study of several hundred companies confirmed that, despite the caprices of the market, total return to shareholders (TRS) is useful as a primary metric of organizational performance. Successful companies, as measured by TRS, were found to be winners by almost every other measure.

From the initial group, 160 companies—four companies in each of 40 industry groups—were selected for extensive study. The companies in each group were, at the

William Joyce, Nitin Nohria, Bruce Roberson, *What (Really) Works: The 4 + 2 Formula for Sustained Business Success.* New York: Harper Collins, 2003.

start of the study in 1986, of comparable size, had achieved similar financial performance, and had similar prospects for the future. Failing companies and those conglomerates that defied classification were left out. Performance of the 160 companies was measured over two consecutive five-year periods, 1986–1990 and 1991–1995. Based on TRS performance, each company was labeled as a winner, climber, tumbler, or loser and assigned to one of four groups:

- **Winners:** Companies that outperformed their peers in both time periods
- **Climbers:** Companies that lagged their peers in the first period, but achieved performance better than their peers in the second
- **Tumblers:** Companies with better-than-peer performance in the first period, followed by under performance in the second
- **Losers:** Companies that lagged behind their peers in both time periods. This grouping of the companies would provide insight into cause-effect relationships. Accounting for the differences in performance was the next step.

Three distinct methodologies were used to unlock the answer to what really works from the 10-year performance of the companies studied. First, all publicly available information on the 160 companies was scanned for references to 200 established management practices, and the companies were scored on each practice using a scale from 1 (poor relative to peers) to 5 (excellent relative to peers). Scores were independently verified through alternate sources, such as former executives. A second set of studies by academic experts identified connections among management practices. Analysis of hundreds of documents concerning each of the companies—analysts' reports, newspaper and magazine articles, business school case studies—confirmed the results of the first two studies.

WHAT DOESN'T WORK

Of the 200 management practices surveyed, four popular approaches stand out for having *no* demonstrated cause-effect relationship to sustained superior performance. Over the period of the study, no correlation was found between total return to shareholders and a company's investment in technology. Despite their popularity, neither corporate change programs nor purchase and supply chain management practices contributed to superior TRS. There was no evidence that attracting better outside directors, an effort promoted as a means of improving corporate governance, improved TRS. If anything, it is better performance that attracts more astute outside directors!

WHAT DOES WORK—THE 4 + 2 FORMULA

In fact, most of the 200 practices studied turned out to be largely irrelevant to corporate performance. That is not to say that the vast majority of these practices are counterproductive, just that they are not essential to achieving superior performance. A compelling connection was found between sustainable high performance and just eight of the practices. *Four "primary" areas of management practice—designated in shorthand as strategy, execution, culture, and structure—proved essential to success.* Four "secondary" areas—talent, leadership, innovation, and mergers and partnerships—complete the set. Companies with high scores on each of the four primary areas and any two of the secondary areas had a better than 90 percent chance of being a Winner. This unique finding produced the *4 + 2 formula* in which four primary plus any two of the four secondary management practices are required for success.

THE FOUR PRIMARY MANAGEMENT PRACTICES

Strategy

Winning companies keep their attention and resources focused on growth of their core business through a *clear and focused strategy*. Positioning decisions, such as to be a product innovator, a quality leader, or a low-cost competitor, do not have a significant impact on whether the company will succeed or fail. Whether the planning process invited input from all levels of the organization or was the inspiration of the chief executive whether long-range budgeting and planning were a part of the process whether change was initiated in response to a takeover attempt or a change in management similarly had little effect.

What works well in the domain of strategy is:

1. Offering the customer a clear value proposition, rooted in an understanding of both the customer's needs and the company's capabilities.
2. Developing strategy from the outside in; what customers, partners, and investors say and do are more important considerations than relying on internal instincts.
3. Monitoring the marketplace and adapting the strategy to emerging trends; Winners have the ability to detect trends in their own and related businesses and to act on those that count.
4. Clearly communicating the strategy with both internal and external stakeholders, including customers; internal stakeholders give the strategy life, while communicating with customers encourages them to move from being "just" customers to true business partners.
5. Growing the core business; Winners achieve growth by focusing on their core business. When they do venture into other businesses, they do so before the growth potential of their core is exhausted.

Flawless Execution

Operational excellence—flawless execution in meeting the expectations of ever more demanding and sophisticated customers—can only be achieved through effort, study, and ingenuity. It will not, the Evergreen Project showed, be achieved through outsourcing operations; buying the latest enterprise resource planning (ERP), supply chain management, or customer relations management (CRM) software; or adopting a total quality management (TQM) program.

What *does* work in the pursuit of flawless execution?

1. Consistently meeting customer expectations. Winners need not deliver extraordinary products or services, but must *consistently meet their customers' expectations* in order to build trust.
2. Empowering employees on the front line of customer contact to respond to customer needs. This also requires keeping the organization's best employees in those front-line positions.
3. Eliminating waste and inefficiency, and then focusing the effort on the processes most important to meeting customer expectations.

Culture

Winning requires that virtually everyone in the organization perform to the maximum of their capabilities. Evergreen Project Winners created a culture dedicated to performance and then serving the customer by:

1. *Inspiring high performance by creating and supporting a culture that holds all employees, not just managers, responsible for corporate success:* The ideal culture empowers employees to make independent decisions to improve company operations, while building loyalty to the employee's team and the company.
2. *Rewarding achievement through praise and pay, while constantly raising expectations:* Once a winning organization achieves "best in class" performance, it ratchets the goal up to "best in show."
3. *Creating an environment that is challenging, satisfying, and fun:* Winners stay on the right side of the fine line between a high-performance environment and a high-anxiety environment.
4. *Establishing clear company values, presenting them to employees, living them, and making them a part of every communication with employees:* Good ethical behavior promotes good business.

Structure

Bureaucracy may have its place, but the Evergreen Project found that Winners focus full-time efforts on eliminating unnecessary bureaucracy. How the elements of the organization are arranged—functionally, geographically, or by product—matters not. Neither does the extent to which profit and loss responsibility is delegated to subordinate units, nor does the level of autonomy granted subordinate units to select their own unique structure. The structural attributes that *do* matter are:

1. *Simplicity:* Winners work to eliminate redundant layers, bureaucracy, and the behaviors that create and sustain them.
2. *Cooperation and information sharing across the entire organization:* Winners devote resources to break down walls between organizational fiefdoms.
3. *Putting the frontline first:* Winners place the best employees in positions where their decisions can make a difference, and keep them there.

THE FOUR SECONDARY MANAGEMENT PRACTICES

Talent

About half of the Winners in the Evergreen Project dedicated significant human and financial resources to building an effective workforce and management team. It was not the resources dedicated to building the highest quality human resources staff, maintaining a fast-track management development program, or implementing a 360-degree performance review system that made a difference. Instead, it was the effort devoted to the following that worked:

1. Promoting from within; filling mid- and upper-level positions with internal talent.
2. Offering top-quality training and education programs; committing resources to the programs that will develop candidates for internal promotion.

3. Designing jobs that challenge the best performers; decentralization and empowerment are tools for keeping people engaged.
4. Getting senior executives engaged in the competition for the best talent; recruiting isn't just for HR any more.

Leadership

The choice of a chief executive is crucial to the company's success. The Evergreen Project provides insight (contrary to many commonly held beliefs) into what leadership traits are consistent with becoming a Winner. The leader's decision-making style, be it independent or collaborative, is irrelevant. Personal characteristics—patient or impatient, visionary or detail oriented, secure or insecure—are irrelevant as well. Success is independent of whether senior managers make major decisions on the basis of qualitative or quantitative analysis. Instead, what does work in the domain of leadership is:

1. Strengthening management's relationships with people at all levels of the organization; Winners see these relationships as the foundation of positive attitudes toward the company and its goals.
2. Focusing management on spotting opportunities and problems early; encouraging managers to anticipate change rather than dealing only with immediate difficulties.
3. Motivating the board to take an active role in governing the company by requiring a significant financial stake; when board members have their own money at risk, they tend to seek and retain stronger chief executives.
4. Pay for performance; stock price need not be the only factor considered, but executive compensation should reflect performance against pre-established goals.

Innovation

The Evergreen Project provides the evidence. Barely half of the Winners were able to excel in this challenging area of management practice. Yet the potential payoffs for success—greater efficiency, new products, the opportunity to transform an industry—are difficult to ignore. Where new ideas come from makes no difference. For the companies that were successful, what worked was:

1. Introducing disruptive technologies and business models; success in innovation requires leading the industry and developing the innovative blockbusters that change the competitive landscape.
2. Using technological innovation both externally to produce new products and internally to improve efficiency.
3. Being willing to cannibalize existing products; Winners do eat their young in the battle to maintain their technological lead.

Mergers and Partnerships

In mergers and acquisitions analyzed by the Evergreen Project, 93 percent of the deals involving Winners created value, while only 9 percent of the Losers' deals did so. Why?

Losers sought mergers and acquisitions to achieve diversification, or to fix a weakness in their primary practices. What worked for the Winners was:

1. Acquisition of new businesses to take advantage of existing customer relationships; making the most of both their own relationships with customers and the relationships that came with the acquired company.
2. Entering businesses that are complementary to existing strengths; picking companies with compatible cultures and strengths that extend or complete the value they offer the marketplace.
3. In creating partnerships, entering businesses that draw on both partners' strengths; successful partnerships provide benefits neither partner could have achieved alone.
4. Developing the capacity to successfully identify, screen, and close deals; successful merger management is a significant business activity in itself.

KEEPING SIX BALLS IN THE AIR

The seemingly simple 4 + 2 model challenges managers to attend to no fewer than six key elements of their business at once. The task is certainly more daunting than simply applying the panacea of the day, but the results provide significant motivation to do so. Over the 10 years of the Evergreen Project study, investors in the average Winner saw their investment grow nearly tenfold; the average loser eked out only a 62 percent gain for the entire decade. Follow-up evaluation of over 40 of the original study companies for 1997–2002 affirmed the earlier study's conclusions.

PART

V ∥ FOCUSING ON THE HUMAN DIMENSION

Traditionally, many employees were promoted to supervisory and managerial positions based on their prior success in technical fields of expertise, such as engineering, accounting/finance, or sales. Often, they were ill prepared for the tremendous challenges of understanding the complexities of human behavior at work, and there was little information available to assist them. Approximately a half-century ago, the field of organizational behavior (OB) began to emerge, and its goal since then has been to establish an integrated field of knowledge based on a solid foundation of conceptual, theoretical, and research material. Borrowing initially from the fields of psychology, sociology, social psychology, and other domains, OB sought to identify the primary outcomes that organizations seek to obtain and the key causal factors that contribute to those outcomes. Although at one time focused on the academic preparation of future managers in college and university courses, several professors have become popular-press authors. Some of these have recently begun to share their insights and suggestions via practitioner-oriented "best-sellers."

Edward E. Lawler III is widely acknowledged as one of the country's premier experts on management. He is a distinguished professor of management and organization in the Marshall School of Business and director of the Center for Effective Organizations at the University of Southern California. Lawler received his Ph.D. from the University of California-Berkeley, was the recipient of a Lifetime Achievement Award from ASTD, and has been named a Fellow of the Academy of Management. He has prepared over 30 books, including *Pay and Organizational Performance, Managerial Attitudes and Performance, The Ultimate Advantage,* and *High-Involvement Management.*

Lawler, in his book *Treat People Right!,* suggests that treating people right is a challenging task, with payoffs for both organizations and their members. He portrays a "virtuous spiral of success" that moves beyond simply providing adequate working conditions and fair pay to induce new levels of sustained peak performance. Specific practices include "branding" the firm as a place for high achievers, recruiting and selecting high performers, and institutionalizing a leadership style that supports and rewards desired levels of individual and organizational performance. This is achieved through the integration of job design, reward systems, training programs, and a host of other recommendations.

Cindy Ventrice is the author of *Make Their Day!* Ventrice is a management consultant and workshop leader for Potential Unlimited in Santa Cruz, California, and a member of the National Speakers' Association of Northern California. As the basis for her book, she asked employees around the country to answer the question, "What kind of recognition makes your day?" She discovered that employees are often critical of existing programs and overblown special events. Ventrice suggests that there are four elements of effective recognition—praise, thanks, opportunity, and respect. These can be administered meaningfully, easily, and inexpensively to produce desired effects on morale, motivation, and profits.

Mihaly Csikszentmihalyi, the author of *Good Business,* is the C.S. and D.J. Davidson Professor of Psychology at the Peter F. Drucker School of Management at Claremont Graduate University and the director of The Quality of Life Research Center. His research interests include positive psychology, creativity, socialization, and the study of intrinsically rewarding behavior in work and play settings. Csikszentmihalyi is the author of *Flow: The Psychology of Optimal Experience, The Evolving Self: A Psychology for the Third Millennium,* and *Finding Flow: The Psychology of Engagement with Everyday Life.* He is a recipient of BrainChannels' "Thinker of the Year" award.

Csikszentmihalyi argues that workplaces can be dismal places when they have destroyed employee trust, given workers no clear goals, failed to provide adequate feedback, and taken away any sense of control. He suggests that CEOs need to recognize that the total fulfillment of a person's potential is what usually generates true happiness, and this begins with a philosophy and belief that the company will be operating successfully one hundred years from now. He articulates the eight central features underlying flow and suggests that managers can create the conditions for flow by making the workplace attractive, finding ways to imbue the job with meaning and value, and selecting and rewarding individuals who find satisfaction in their work.

Paul Lawrence and Nitin Nohria, in *Driven,* assert that employees act as they do because of a set of conscious choices made. These choices are affected by human nature and four innate drives: (1) to acquire objects of status; (2) to bond with others in long-term relationships; (3) to learn, grow, and make sense of the world; and (4) to defend themselves and others from harm. The key to attaining well-being is to balance the four drives, while never expecting that total balance and agreement are likely outcomes.

Paul Lawrence is the Wallace Brett Donham Professor of Organizational Behavior Emeritus at Harvard Business School. Many of his 24 books, including *Organization and Environment,* have focused on organizational design, organizational change, and the human aspects of management. Nitin Nohria is the Richard P. Chapman Professor of Business Administration and chairman of the Organizational Behavior Unit at Harvard Business School. He has co-authored or edited seven books, including *The Differentiated Network.*

1

TREAT PEOPLE RIGHT!

Edward E. Lawler III

Summary Prepared by Danielle DuBois Kerr

Danielle DuBois Kerr *is a compensation practitioner at Uponor, Inc. A majority of her career has been spent focusing on organizations' compensation and benefits needs. Her areas of expertise include market pricing, salary surveys, job analysis, salary structure design, benefits administration, and compliance. Danielle attained her Professional in Human Resources (PHR) certification from the Society of Human Resources Management and has completed course work toward her Certified Compensation Professional Designation through WorldatWork. She received a Bachelor of Business Administration degree from the University of Minnesota Duluth, with majors in both Human Resource and Organizational Management. She is a member of the Twin Cities Human Resource Association, WorldatWork, and the Twin Cities Compensation Network.*

In today's tough business environment, organizations and people can't succeed without the other. Organizations need to be successful so they can provide meaningful work and reward their people, but in order to be successful, organizations need high-performing people. Finding a mutually beneficial path that leads both parties to this joint definition of success seems difficult to find. However, there is a path that can lead both individuals and organizations to their goals. It is to "treat people right."

The challenge is to create organizational structures that provide employees with meaningful work and appropriate rewards, while motivating and satisfying them to behave in ways that help their organizations become effective and high performing. Both parties need to understand how the other operates in order to make informed decisions about the relationship. For example, an organization may treat its people right by investing in new training and development programs. However, for the training program to be successful, the individual must decide to take on additional responsibility for learning new skills and embrace the opportunity to manage his or her own career. Without a mutual commitment to the program, neither will succeed.

Edward E. Lawler III, *Treat People Right! How Organizations and Individuals Can Propel Each Other into a Virtuous Spiral of Success*. San Francisco: Jossey-Bass, 2003.

VIRTUOUS SPIRALS

Organizations that value and reward their people will motivate them to perform well, which in turn propels organizations to attain higher levels of accomplishment. When individuals and organizations achieve more and more of their goals, a virtuous spiral evolves. These spirals are the ultimate competitive advantage. They are win-win relationships that are hard-to-duplicate sources of positive momentum. The virtuous spiral begins with strategy, follows with organization design, and then proceeds through an iterative process of staffing–performance–rewards that continues onward.

Organizations that mishandle their human capital are susceptible to inverting this process, in turn creating a death spiral. During a death spiral, an organization will see both individual and organizational performance decline. These unwanted spirals can last for decades, or can be relatively fast and only last a few days.

How can a virtuous spiral be launched and a death spiral avoided? Simply being nice to people and treating them well are not enough. Organizations need to develop a wide array of human capital management practices that motivate people to excel and then follow through by rewarding them for high levels of performance. In turn, individuals need to make greater commitments to their own careers and organizations, at the same time becoming responsible for their own behaviors.

THE COMPONENTS OF AN EFFECTIVE ORGANIZATION

Before organizations can effectively establish human capital management practices, they need to lay the appropriate foundation for treating people right. The organization itself must be effective. This means that the organization must have alignment among four determinants of effectiveness:

1. Strategy: The master plan for the organization, which include its goals, purpose, products/services, etc.
2. Organizational capabilities: The factors that allow an organization to coordinate and focus its behavior to produce levels of performance required by its strategy. One example is the ability to manage and develop new knowledge.
3. Core competencies: A combination of technology and production skills that help define and create an organization's products/services, such as an organization's ability to miniaturize its products.
4. Environment: The context in which the organization operates. Examples include the business climate, the state of the economy, and the political and physical environments.

The organization must have a clear understanding of these factors before it can cultivate its human capital, organizational structure, reward systems, and processes. Once the organization lays its foundation for effectiveness, it can take steps to treat people right. Implementing the seven principles to treating people right will give the organization the capability of launching a virtuous spiral.

SEVEN KEY PRINCIPLES FOR TREATING PEOPLE RIGHT

1. Attraction and Retention

"Organizations must create a value proposition that defines the type of workplace they want to be so that they can attract and retain the right people." Creating a value proposition communicates who the organization is, what it wants, and what is has to offer. This allows an organization to attract and employ individuals who are aligned with its values and goals. Each organization should consider having multiple value propositions to attract and retain a diverse workforce. For example, rewards that are designed to retain core employees probably focus on encouraging individual commitment to the organization. Rewards for this group of employees usually include a stake in the organization through some type of stock ownership. On the other hand, some employees may not be interested in ownership, so it would be wise to develop a separate value proposition for this group. Overall, the propositions should be well thought out and focus on what the organization has to offer in order to attract and retain the right people needed to achieve a high-performing organization. In turn, a virtuous spiral could evolve.

2. Hiring Practices

"Organizations must hire people who fit with their values, core competencies, and strategic goals." This requires a clear and disciplined process that allows the organization to properly assess the competencies, skills, knowledge, personality, and needs of applicants. Objective data should be collected through assessment tools such as personality tests or knowledge exams. Another valuable tool for collecting data is background checks, as past behavior has been demonstrated to be the best predictor of future behavior. An organization that does not have effective hiring practices will have a very hard time reaching a virtuous spiral.

3. Training and Development

"Organizations must continuously train employees to do their jobs and offer them opportunities to grow and develop." Commitment to an organization's training and development program reinforces the value an organization places on creating a virtuous spiral. By doing so, employees' skills are essentially increased and a virtuous spiral is reinforced. Overall, supporting a training and development program is not only valuable to the organization, but also adds value to each employee as it helps ignite one's personal career spiral by providing the opportunity to learn, develop, and experience new things.

4. Work Design

"Organizations must design work so that it is meaningful for people and provides them with feedback, responsibility, and autonomy." Employee motivation, satisfaction, and performance are greatly influenced by this principle and can have a significant influence on the overall effectiveness of an organization. In order to influence these factors, organizations must make work involving, challenging, and rewarding for people. To do so organizations must:

- Avoid simplified jobs.
- Design enriched jobs that allow one to experience meaningfulness, have responsibility for outcomes of his or her behavior, and receive feedback about his or her results.

Not all work can be enriched to the fullest extent nor can all of the repetitive work in the world be eliminated. To combat this problem, an organization should consider making the work intrinsically satisfying, offer higher extrinsic rewards, or possibly outsource simplified, repetitive work to subcontractors. That said, paying attention to the way in which work is designed could have a significant impact on employees' motivation and satisfaction, which may in turn hinder or propel a virtuous spiral.

5. Mission, Strategies, and Goals

"Organizations must develop and adhere to a specific organizational mission, with strategies, goals, and values that employees can understand, support and believe in." Goals are a powerful motivator of behavior that can lead and direct an organization down a certain path. Accomplishment of goals gives people feelings of intrinsic satisfaction that cause them to reach for higher performance and to form a stronger commitment to the overall organizational mission and strategy. In turn, accomplishment sparks and carries the momentum of the virtuous spiral.

For the spiral to continue moving ahead, the established goals must be meaningful. Some may be noble and have a higher order mission, while others may be purely financial and performance driven. Both types have the ability to effectively influence individual and organizational results as long as there is a line of sight between the individual's behavior and the end result. For example, goals cannot be accomplished or even supported if they are hidden from the public eye. Employees must be committed to reaching goals and when they can see a direct connection between their behavior and the goal, attainment of the goal becomes more likely. In sum, when employees can understand, support, and believe in the developed mission and strategies, the potential for a virtuous spiral is greatly increased.

6. Reward Systems

"Organizations must devise and implement reward systems that reinforce their design, core values, and strategy." Reward systems are influential in obtaining a virtuous spiral. To be effective, the systems must reward performance; be properly aligned with the organization's design, core values, and strategy; and must motivate people to perform effectively. Several criteria should be considered when designing a reward system. First, the systems must have a clear line of sight between the desired outcomes and the individual behaviors needed to obtain those outcomes. Second, the size of the reward must be large enough to capture the attention of the employees and make a difference in their motivation. For example, average merit increases have been 3 to 4 percent over the past few years. If the reward were smaller than this, it might not capture their attention. However, a raise or a bonus of 10 percent is more likely to spark people's interest, in turn motivating certain behaviors. Third, if an organization has a pay-for-performance system in place, employees must possess the power, information, and knowledge they need to influence their performance. Finally, leadership must create credibility for their reward programs. This means being trustworthy and carrying out promises. If all criteria are designed properly, reward systems can be a powerful tool in becoming a high-performing organization.

7. Leadership

"Organizations must hire and develop leaders who can create commitment, trust, success, and a motivating work environment." Individual and organizational effectiveness can be greatly affected by leadership at all levels. So how can managers be most effective? The answer is simple: Set up win-win situations (in essence, virtuous spirals). Findings from The Ohio State University in the 1950s showed that the most effective managers focused on both organizational and individual results. Satisfying the wants and needs of both groups (managers and employees) can be a challenge; however, the responsibility should not reside on the shoulders of one person. The organization's leadership must be shared, including the responsibility for motivating employees and creating a vision.

CREATING A VIRTUOUS SPIRAL

Getting organizations to a point where they are ready to develop a virtuous spiral can be very challenging. It requires well-planned strategic actions to gain momentum. To start a virtuous spiral, a strategy must be developed by effective change leaders. Next, employees must be motivated to change and a vision should be created. Finally, all seven principles of treating people right need to be implemented. All steps must be set in place; one step simply cannot be omitted. Failure to do so leads to the risk of making all adopted principles dysfunctional. Once the spiral has begun, it needs regular checkups to make sure the organization is heading in the right direction. Depending upon changes within or outside the organization, changes may be needed to one or all of the steps used to initiate the spiral.

FALSE AND FRAUDULENT SPIRALS

As organizations develop their own spirals, false or fraudulent spirals can wreak havoc on the ability or potential to create a virtuous spiral of success. A false spiral occurs when an organization thinks a virtuous spiral has been initiated, when in fact the thought is simply an illusion. A good example of this was observed in the dot-com industry during the 1990s. In general, the market value of many dot-com organizations was greatly inflated. These companies believed they were in the midst of a virtuous spiral, when in fact their market values were too high. Eventually their stock prices collapsed and the majority of these dot-coms fell into a death spiral. Fraudulent spirals are another type of spiral that can cause destruction. These spirals can be easily mistaken as virtuous although they are created by deceitful activities. These practices were uncovered at several large corporations such as Enron, WorldCom, and Adelphia. Once fraudulent behavior surfaces, the organization almost always falls into a death spiral. Organizations must steer clear of these two types of spirals and focus their efforts on successfully implementing the seven principles mentioned earlier.

THREATS TO A VIRTUOUS SPIRAL

Once a virtuous spiral has been initiated, there is no guarantee that it will stay intact. Many internal and external threats can quickly turn the spiral in the wrong direction. One important and increasingly prevalent threat is environmental changes, including new competitors or industry regulations. Environmental changes are serious threats, which may call for new organizational strategies. This threat is so critical that the virtuous spiral model presented earlier was revised to take this threat into consideration. The new model again starts with an initial sequence of strategy–organizational design–staffing–performance–rewards, but then includes strategy change, organizational design change, and performance change, all of which are based on the fact that organizations need to pay attention to the environment and may need to react to changes by altering their initial foundation. The model then proceeds onward to iterative cycles of rewards–staffing–performance.

Environmental changes occur in many different forms and in many different frequencies. Depending upon these factors, each organization needs individually to assess when to react to the environment. When the timing is right, an organization will have the capability to change by tweaking the seven principles of "treating people right."

Environmental changes are just one type of threat to an organization's virtuous spiral. Others include:

- Economic downturn within a country
- Industry-specific economic downturn
- Mistakes or self-inflicted threats
- Fads or fashions

Any one of these threats can devastate an organization's financial performance. However, threats do not and cannot automatically cause a death spiral. A well-thought-out response to any threat can actually save an organization and launch it into a new virtuous spiral by causing it to rethink its strategy and re-lay its foundation.

Conclusion

Virtuous spirals can flourish in organizations that perform well and treat people right. Despite the numerous threats to an organization, virtuous spirals can be rekindled and launched into new directions. It is important to consider and recognize that organizations serve multiple stakeholders. Meeting financial performance goals is important, but so is satisfying customers, employees, stockholders, and community members. It must be remembered that organizations are made of people, they are created by people, and they exist to serve people. If organizations do not treat people right they should not (and often will not) exist.

2 | MAKE THEIR DAY!

CINDY VENTRICE

SUMMARY PREPARED BY JANNIFER DAVID

Jannifer David teaches Human Resource Management at the Labovitz School of Business and Economics at the University of Minnesota Duluth. Her courses include international human resource management, employee recruiting and selection, and introductory human resource management. Her research interests include international human resource management, the use of contingent workers and how they affect the work relationships of others within organizations, and the implications of workplace accommodations. She has published articles in Human Resource Planning, Journal of Leadership and Organizational Studies, Journal of Small Business Strategy, *and* Compensation & Benefits Review. *She received her Ph.D. in Labor and Industrial Relations from Michigan State University. Prior to her graduate studies she worked as a Human Resources Consultant for Mercer Human Resource Consulting.*

INTRODUCTION

Recognition is any form of personalized acknowledgment of an employee's accomplishments toward organizational goals. Well-designed employee recognition can lead to positive employee and organizational outcomes such as high employee morale, low turnover, and even higher productivity and profits. Employee recognition, however, involves more than the presentation of a plaque or certificate. *Effective recognition must meet the personal needs of each employee.* To ensure that employees receive this level of appreciation, managers should make an effort to create work environments that incorporate meaningful recognition as often as possible from a variety of sources.

Cindy Ventrice, *Make Their Day!: Employee Recognition That Works.* San Francisco: Berrett-Koehler, 2003.

WHAT IS EFFECTIVE RECOGNITION?

To deliver effective recognition, managers should consider its four key elements: praise, thanks, opportunity, and respect.

- *Praise* and compliments affirm that managers understand the accomplishments of their employees and how these accomplishments positively affect the organization's mission.
- Sincere *thanks* from managers make employees feel valued. Written thank you notes or other methods of showing appreciation and delivering thanks for employees that clearly state their accomplishments are excellent reminders of their manager's appreciation.
- Employees who have performed well should be provided *opportunities* to expand their knowledge and/or control over their work. These opportunities will make employees feel trusted by their managers and will likely lead to higher organizational loyalty, commitment, and increased efforts to perform well.
- *Respect* is critical to any integrated recognition effort. Managers should minimally strive for a work environment that is safe and pleasant. Beyond this they should make an effort to get to know each of their employees and show confidence in their capabilities to show that they respect them as people as well as workers.

Recognition can motivate people through either intrinsic or extrinsic sources. Both sources are valuable tools for managers to use. *Extrinsic recognition* encompasses any items that can be bestowed upon employees from others, such as bonuses, certificates, new offices, etc. Extrinsic rewards, if used properly, can work well but they are limited because they do not provide long-lasting effects. Intrinsic motivation, however, comes from within employees. Because employees are the source of this motivation and recognition, it is tailored to their needs and is therefore more powerful than extrinsic motivation. Sources of *intrinsic motivation* (feelings that come from within) include appropriate job design, valued purpose, and trust. Well-designed jobs provide opportunities for intrinsic motivation through the satisfaction that comes from performing the job tasks. Employees with a clear purpose for their jobs will have greater intrinsic motivation, as these employees will be able to see the value of their efforts. Trusting employees to do their work without micromanaging every detail imparts employees with respect as people worthy of trust and gives them an opportunity to decide for themselves how work should be done.

Managers must know who their employees are and what their individual needs are. Recognition must be tailored to individuals, and this can be facilitated by developing close relationships with each of them. For example, public recognition of achievement may work well for some employees, but may embarrass other employees who are extremely shy or introverted. Employees should be able to trust that managers are offering recognition because of sincere appreciation for their efforts and receive recognition that is personalized enough for them to see that management truly understands who they are as people. If this happens, then this recognition will retain its intended meaning and not become a negative interaction between employees and their managers.

WHO IS RESPONSIBLE FOR PROVIDING RECOGNITION?

Managers are the primary deliverers of extrinsic forms of recognition. Most employees see their managers as the main representatives of their organization. If their managers provide good recognition, then they are likely to think their organizations provide good recognition. Unfortunately, many managers are reluctant to give recognition because they feel that it is unnecessary, have had negative reactions to recognition provided in the past, are busy doing their daily work and don't feel they have time to give recognition, or fear backlashes for perceived favoritism in their recognition efforts. Employees, however, want recognition so as to obtain feedback on their efforts. Even negative feedback can be seen as recognition if it is offered as a developmental tool and imparts to employees a sense that management trusts they are capable of making the suggested improvements. To meet this employee need, managers ought to overcome their doubts about recognition.

Managers, however, are not the only important component of successful recognition programs. Organizations that are truly successful with recognition tend to have executive leadership that embraces and promotes recognition. Company executives should set examples of good recognition habits by getting to know their employees and regularly bestowing recognition on them. Recognition from top executives in organizations can be a particularly powerful motivator for rank-and-file employees, who may frequently feel they go unknown and unnoticed by high-level executives. When executives place high priority on recognition, they indicate to other managers and supervisors that recognition is an important part of the work environment. These managers and supervisors will strive to include recognition in their management styles and in the work environments of their employees. Finally, to solidify their public commitment to recognition, executives should recognize their mid-level managers' efforts to provide recognition for lower level employees, thus creating a waterfall effect. Through these efforts executives can ensure that their organizations have a culture of recognition that will improve employee loyalty and organizational performance.

Human Resource departments can contribute significantly to the success of recognition programs, but their roles are typically behind the scenes. HR departments have the professional knowledge to design high-quality recognition programs. They can also provide management with information regarding the success of recognition efforts through the design and administration of employee surveys. HR professionals, however, should not be the primary *deliverers* of recognition. HR professionals are not close enough to employees to provide the personalized recognition that is necessary for these interactions to be most effective. In addition to line managers and executives, co-workers and employees themselves are generally the organizational members closest to employees' efforts and they are best suited to provide this in-depth level of feedback.

Co-workers, while not a replacement for managerial recognition, are a powerful source. *Peer recognition*—formal or informal efforts by co-workers to praise employees for their positive contributions at work—can go a long way toward creating a pleasant work environment. Peer recognition efforts can be very informal, utilizing everyday items as signs of appreciation, such as giving tools as "fix it" awards to co-workers. Organizations can also implement formal peer recognition programs whereby co-workers can either directly reward employees with company-supplied awards or they can nominate their co-workers for company-wide awards. Either approach can help employees feel that they are appreciated and improve their everyday work environment.

Self-recognition provides another method of helping employees feel appreciated and rewarded. Organizations that promote self-recognition may develop programs for employees to highlight their accomplishments during the previous business cycle and share these accomplishments with other employees throughout the organization. Giving employees control over their own recognition ensures that employees will be recognized for those achievements that mean the most to them. This approach also helps management understand what aspects of work their employees value the most, which should assist management in developing other meaningful recognition opportunities for these employees.

HOW SHOULD MANAGERS DELIVER EFFECTIVE RECOGNITION?

Managers can develop, perhaps in conjunction with HR departments, recognition programs that consistently identify behaviors and performance worthy of recognition and reward employees accordingly. Delivering effective recognition requires managers to develop tools that address the need for recognition specific to each employee's contributions to the organization's mission, that give recognition consistently and fairly, and that make recognition an ongoing process. Recognition that specifically relates each employee's achievement(s) and/or behaviors to the organization's mission and values is most effective for improving employee morale. Therefore, organizations and managers should develop criteria for recognition that are directly related to the organization's mission and values. These criteria should be used consistently in determining who receives recognition as well as the magnitude of such recognition. Announcing these criteria will let employees know in advance what is going to be rewarded and help allay any fears of favoritism. Further, recognizing an employee for achievements and behaviors that foster the organization's mission and values helps impress upon the employee the importance of this mission.

To ensure consistency and accuracy of the recognition program, the criteria used in determining employee recognition should be based upon solid measurement techniques. Measuring organizational variables related to mission and values will help managers determine who should be recognized and reinforce within organizations that these goals are important. Measuring organizational outcomes will ensure that employees pay attention to these outcomes and strive to improve them. Measuring should be done carefully, however, as only measuring one dimension of an outcome may result in undesired employee behaviors. Measurements should be taken from multiple sources and using multiple methods to be certain that unintended and undesirable outcomes do not result from the measurement system. *Good measurements should be quantifiable, consistent over time, and provide an accurate picture of current conditions.* For more in-depth analyses qualitative data may be acquired through the use of interviews, focus groups, or observation, but these methods shouldn't be relied upon solely as a basis for a recognition program.

To set these ideas into action managers and supervisors should begin by trying to understand two aspects of their employees: (1) their unique contributions to the mission and values of the organization, and (2) how they prefer to be recognized. In addition to observing employees to learn how they are contributing, it is wise to sit down with them to discuss their contributions. During this conversation, managers should ask their employees how they think they are contributing to the organization's mission, what else they think they could be doing to foster the mission, and which of their tasks could be modified or eliminated because they do not currently contribute to the mission. Through this conversation, employees may come to learn more about how their jobs relate to the organization's mission and managers should learn which tasks their employees are most committed to, and therefore would be the best tasks for recognition.

To determine the best methods of recognizing each employee, managers should develop relationships with each of their employees to understand who they are. Learning what employees do in their nonwork time, identifying their career aspirations, and exploring other personal traits may provide valuable information about how they would prefer to be recognized. Beyond information gathered in this fashion, managers may be more straightforward and ask their employees through surveys about how they would prefer to receive recognition for various levels of exemplary performance.

Once managers have ascertained how their employees contribute and how they would prefer to be recognized, the final stage is the actual recognition. Managers need to take what they have learned and make a concerted effort to recognize their employees whenever these opportunities present themselves. When giving this recognition managers should follow some simple guidelines:

- **Recognition efforts should be commensurate with their employees' achievements.** Large achievements should be recognized with substantial rewards, while smaller achievements should also receive recognition, but on a lesser scale.
- **Past failures with recognition shouldn't be a reason to avoid giving recognition in the future.** Those employees who are not accustomed to receiving recognition may be wary at first, but continued efforts to provide them with personalized recognition will eventually lead to successful outcomes.
- **Recognition should be offered continually.** Grandiose recognition given at irregular intervals will not be as effective for employees as frequent, smaller recognition efforts.
- **Managers should constantly look for ways to allow recognition to come intrinsically from the job** and not make it always be dependent upon external sources.

To assist managers with these guidelines, it is often a good idea to develop a plan for offering recognition. Without such a plan, recognition may be sporadic and inconsistent with huge awards for relatively small deeds and fewer awards toward the end of the year because budgets have disappeared. If recognition is new to an organization or manager, then the best approach is to start small. A pilot program of recognition efforts can be a way to begin offering recognition before committing to a large program that could be unsuccessful. Pilot programs are typically offered in one area/unit of the company and studied to ensure that the results would be beneficial to the whole organization. First, managers should assess the levels of recognition and job satisfaction that currently exist. Employee surveys may be a useful tool for this. The results of these surveys will point out areas where successful efforts already exist and places where help is needed. Both of these pieces of information are worth noting, as successful efforts may be transplanted to areas of need.

The next steps in developing a plan are to determine the funding available and to set up a timeline for deployment of the plan. Funds may come from multiple sources such as bonus pools, training programs, employee events, and a manager's discretionary funds. Managers should make use of all possible resources. Realistic timelines for delivering recognition should be set that allocate recognition events throughout the budget year. By planning ahead, managers can ensure that recognition efforts don't begin with a bang and then dwindle out toward the end of the year, causing a demoralizing effect in employees. Finally, a good recognition program should have built-in opportunities to improve. Managers should observe how their recognition is received and modify it as needed.

Conclusion

A well-designed employee recognition program can help organizations improve many employee and organizational outcomes. Employees who receive quality recognition will be motivated to perform better and will, in the long run, have higher job satisfaction. Positive employee attitudes make their managers' jobs easier and make their organizations more successful. To achieve these outcomes managers should develop recognition programs that are personalized to the employee's unique needs and take into consideration his or her contributions to organizational goals. These employee recognitions will have the positive outcomes predicted for employees, managers, and their organizations.

3 GOOD BUSINESS

MIHALY CSIKSZENTMIHALYI

SUMMARY PREPARED BY KELLY NELSON

Kelly Nelson *is a General Manager, Human Resources with AK Steel Corporation, headquartered in Middletown, Ohio. She is responsible for the human resources programs of the organization's seven carbon, stainless, and specialty steel–producing facilities located in Pennsylvania, Kentucky, Ohio, and Indiana. In her position, she has daily opportunity to explore the "right" course of action and what framework provides the appropriate structure for the greater good not only of the organization, but for all stakeholders. A believer in enhancing human well-being, she receives the greatest intrinsic rewards as a parent to her son John, as a daughter, as a sister, as an auntie, as well as an enthusiastic student of human behavior.*

INTRODUCTION

Business leaders who manage their businesses to enhance the happiness of human beings provide an environment in which individual workers flourish and reasonable profits are made. Leaders who manage their organizations with a moral obligation toward the greater good share characteristics that, if more widely adopted, will lead to businesses truly making life happier for all.

Business leaders today have become the leaders of society—much like the nobility of the past. As leaders of society, it is incumbent upon business leaders to enrich the lives of individuals in society. This obligation goes beyond the focus of the quarterly financial review. It reaches all aspects of life because the careers that everyone follows, and how they feel about those careers, affect how they feel about themselves as individuals, family members, community participants, and contributors to society.

THE DUAL GOALS OF BUSINESS

As difficult as the balance is, today there are a number of CEOs who demonstrate that financially successful business enterprises can also contribute to human happiness. These individuals share common principles of good business and firmly believe that they have an obligation to society that is broader and has longer term significance than success

Mihaly Csikszentmihalyi, *Good Business: Leadership, Flow, and the Making of Meaning.* New York: Penguin Putnam, 2003.

based solely on financial strength. These CEOs embrace the *hundred-year manager philosophy,* which dictates leading the business enterprise and making decisions based upon the belief that the company will be operating successfully one hundred years from now.

The basis of human happiness is not universal, and this makes it more difficult to conduct a business in such a way that it ensures human happiness. It is generally agreed that happiness is, as Aristotle expressed it, the *summum bonum,* or the chief good. This philosophy holds that, while people desire other goods (such as money or power) because they believe those things will make them happy, they want happiness for its own sake. In fact, businesses are built on the premise that the goods and/or services produced will make people happy, so there will be a market for the products produced.

However, *the total fulfillment of a person's potential is what usually generates true happiness.* Total fulfillment depends upon the presence of two forces—differentiation and integration. The process of *differentiation* suggests that we are all unique individuals, responsible for ourselves, with the self-confidence to develop our uniqueness. *Integration* implies that, although we are unique individuals, we all are completely immersed in networks of relationships with other human beings, our environment, our culture, and our material possessions. A person who is fully differentiated and integrated becomes a *complex individual* and one most probable to develop true happiness.

The evolution of individual complexity changes throughout the stages of one's life. It culminates at the point where an individual has an appreciation for uniqueness and is in control of thoughts, actions, and feelings, while relishing dependence and interrelatedness to others, the environment, and the culture. Although the maturation of complexity is desired and is necessary for ultimate happiness, businesses who work to support complexity not only work for financial success, but the ideal that the business exists for a greater good.

THE BASES OF FLOW

Individuals who have developed complexity have the capacity truly to enjoy the work that they do. The total immersion one feels when completing tasks with no distinction between thought and action, or self and environment, is an element of flow, and *flow is an individual's full involvement with life.* Although individuals may feel flow from different life activities, eight conditions determine flow.

1. *Goals are clear.* The clarity of the goal allows individuals to focus their attention and to appreciate the completion of each step along the way to the goal.
2. *Feedback is immediate.* The individual knows internally whether each step is completed with the level of excellence acceptable to the individual. This can be provided by external sources; however, an individual who has achieved flow is able through knowledge and past experience to trust his or her internal standards.
3. *A balance between opportunity and capacity exists.* When the challenges faced by the individual are high and equal to the individual's skills, flow is possible.
4. *Concentration deepens.* As an individual focuses on the task at hand, his or her concentration deepens to the point that "thinking" is no longer necessary. Instead, the individual is focused and the process feels effortless.

5. *The present is what matters.* Concentration on the events at hand allows other worries and thoughts to be eliminated. The individual escapes in a positive manner by using his or her skill to accomplish the task.

6. *Control is no problem.* Because flow allows the individual to control his or her own performance and disregard environmental elements, the individual is in control and feels the power of his or her own control.

7. *The sense of time is altered.* The speed at which time passes depends upon two elements—how focused the mind is on the task and whether the individual's "clock" speeds up or slows down. Occasions of flow can either cause time to fly by or to appear to be passing in slow motion.

8. *The loss of ego prevails.* The final condition of flow is the individual's loss of ego. As workers completely focus on the task at hand and their skills and activities to complete their tasks, there is no concentration left over to focus on themselves. The consumption of oneself allows one to be self-less.

The ability to enter flow, of course, does not guarantee that the individual is happy or contented. However, it provides the opportunity to grow. Individual growth, in turn, adds more happiness and accomplishment to the individual's life.

The ability to enter flow fluctuates during the day. Each individual's internal clock provides opportunities at different times. The activities faced in the individual's day also determine the propensity to enter flow, as a function of challenges (high or low) and personal skill level (high or low). If a person's challenges are high and the person's skills are high, flow is possible. This is most often achieved when the individual is involved in favorite activities. On the other hand, when challenges and skills are both low, the individual is more apt to feel apathy, such as when one is lonely or passively watching television.

As the individual's challenge level increases, but his or her skills do not increase, the individual first feels worried and then reaches anxiety. If, when at a high challenge period, the individual's skill level increases, the individual moves from anxiety to arousal. In the state of arousal, such as when learning a new skill, the individual is alert and focused. As the individual's skill level increases, it is possible to move from arousal to the state of flow.

When employees' challenges and skills are low, they feel apathetic. If their challenges do not increase but their skill level does, it leads to boredom. As skills increase, boredom turns to relaxation, which leads to control as challenges increase to meet the skill level. From the point of control, it is possible to increase both the challenges and skill level to enter flow.

Prospective leaders challenge themselves and develop their skill levels to increase the times in which they experience relaxation, control, arousal, and flow. As the proportion of time spent in these areas increases, the individual experiences more opportunities to grow in his or her complexity, leading to still more happiness and contentment in life.

Although flow is important for personal development, flow may or may not be a part of an individual's workday. Most jobs were created to get the most productivity out of individuals, but not necessarily to bring out the best in them. Managers should seek to provide career opportunities and motivational conditions that bring out the best in people. Motivation toward work is determined by three conditions: (1) the type of job available, (2) the value the culture assigns to the job, and (3) the attitude the individual has toward his or her job.

Managers who build an organization that brings out the best in workers have three options:

1. Make the objective conditions of the workplace as attractive as possible;
2. Find ways to imbue the job with meaning and value; and
3. Select and reward individuals who find satisfaction in their work.

Although there have been general improvements in the workplace over the years, there are several reasons that workers still lack the opportunity for flow in their jobs. First, the goals of individual jobs have become more obscure. Many times the individual worker does not understand either the short- or long-term goals so although they may understand *what* they are doing, they do not understand *why*. It is difficult for workers to derive true satisfaction and accomplishment if they do not understand why they are doing what they are doing.

Second, *workers are rarely provided with clear, timely feedback*. The lack of feedback prevents employees from understanding that what they are doing is important and does matter to the organization. The skills of the worker are also not necessarily matched to the skills needed in the job, and this prevents the experience of flow. Also, workers feel a lack of control in setting not only the goals of the process, but also determining the rhythm of the process. Managers who want to allow workers to achieve their best must redesign the workplace to eliminate barriers to flow.

BUILDING FLOW INTO ORGANIZATIONS

It is possible for managers to redesign the workplace to encourage the growth of individuals to allow more flow. It takes a complete commitment from top management to create an environment that will foster flow. Because the profitability of flow does not appear neatly on a spreadsheet, it requires strong leaders who have achieved complexity and who understand business's duty to increase human well-being to redesign the workplace to achieve it.

It takes a leap of faith by top management to believe that redesigning the workplace will eventually result in improved financial results. It is especially important that top management commits to and believes in the fact that greater good results from improving the well-being of the individual.

To create an environment conducive to well-being, it is imperative that the organization's mission is understood by all participants and that individuals are provided the flexibility to adjust their individual goals to match the organization's goals. Managers must also allow individuals to fail without responding too harshly. Calculated risk-taking is important in challenging the individual and some risk-taking initiatives will result in either failure or lack of success. Individuals who are harshly criticized for risk-taking will learn to avoid risks (and the challenges they offer), and will fail to achieve flow.

Managers can best ensure that their workers understand the organization's true commitment to redesigning the workplace by communicating at every opportunity and by ensuring that feedback is provided. After managers ensure individuals are placed in appropriate jobs, given clearly understandable goals, and provided with appropriate feedback, the work conditions must also include the eight properties conducive to achieving flow. The details of each person's properties may be different, and so these should be handled in the work area of the individuals, with input and creation of the properties left to the individual and supported by the direct manager.

THE SOUL OF BUSINESS

Creating a nurturing environment in which individuals are encouraged to achieve flow lays the groundwork to be an organization that improves human well-being; however, it does not ensure it. It is imperative that the organization has soul. *Soul is demonstrated by the organization when it devotes energy to purposes beyond itself.* The goals adopted by the organization for the greater good or to benefit others (without financial reward to itself) show the organization's base values. Often the concept of soul of the organization is similar to beliefs supported by religions—giving donations, assisting the poor, supporting community events, supporting volunteerism, and fighting for what is right.

Managers who believe their obligation is to improve human well-being share five common traits:

1. They are *optimistic* in both their feelings about people as well as their thoughts about the future.
2. They have *integrity,* or an unwavering adherence to principles on which mutual trust can be based.
3. They have a high level of *ambition* coupled with the perseverance necessary to overcome obstacles.
4. They also have *curiosity and a desire to learn.*
5. They possess *empathy* and have a basic respect for others.

Managers who possess these traits also possess the *self-confidence* to pursue their dreams and to support the dreams of others. These are the managers who supply the soul of business.

CREATING FLOW IN LIFE

Business leaders can only provide the environment that is conducive to achieving flow. Everyone possesses the ability to achieve that state of challenge and accomplishment. It is important for people to build on their strengths by creating challenges to hone their own skills. It is also important to identify weaknesses and to strengthen them. In order to build on strengths and minimize weaknesses, it is important that employees pay attention. By paying attention, people will learn not only what their strengths and weaknesses are, but will see what is necessary to optimize them. Focusing attention to detail provides the greatest opportunity for learning and growth. Paying attention requires an investment of time. Individuals who lead others to greatness hone their use of time, develop healthy and challenging habits, and invest energy in their consciousness.

THE FUTURE OF BUSINESS

In order for an organization to contribute to human well-being while also achieving reasonable profitability, the leaders of the organization must have a vision beyond the organization itself. They must envision the organization within the framework of its environment and the human environment. The leaders must also have the intrinsic need to do what is right in relation to human well-being that is based on trust and respect for others. This will allow the leaders to encourage the personal growth of the workers and to provide opportunities for flow in the workplace. Finally, it is imperative that organizations provide goods or services that truly enhance the well-being of people, and that they operate in an ethical, responsible manner.

The principles of good business have historically been gleaned from our religious beliefs and from the principles of our parents. The leaders of today's business who manage their business for improved human well-being will provide examples to be followed by future generations of business leaders.

4 | DRIVEN

PAUL R. LAWRENCE AND NITIN NOHRIA

SUMMARY PREPARED BY GARY STARK

Gary Stark is a member of the faculty at Northern Michigan University, and previously taught at the University of Minnesota Duluth and Washburn University. He earned his Ph.D. in Management from the University of Nebraska. Gary's research interests include feedback-seeking behavior and self-evaluation. Prior to his academic life, Gary earned his B.S. and M.B.A. degrees at Kansas State University and worked in Chicago as a tax accountant.

THE CALL FOR A UNIFIED THEORY OF HUMAN BEHAVIOR

The nature of mankind has been debated since the time of the ancient philosophers. The work of Charles Darwin revolutionized the approach, but has been largely ignored by social scientists, who feared such an approach to social issues implied racism. The present state of the social sciences is too fragmented for any single discipline to address the challenge of a more complete understanding of human behavior. However, since Darwin's time there have been great advances in our knowledge of the social sciences and biology. It is time to synthesize this wealth of knowledge to create a unified theory of human behavior—one that must meet several very challenging criteria:

- It must work at several levels of analysis—individual to organizational to societal.
- It should not contradict the present knowledge of the social sciences and biology.
- It must be able to be tested empirically.
- It should be easy to teach, usable, and parsimonious.
- It should work in any cultural setting.

The present work is an attempt at developing this theory—one believed to meet these criteria. While the theory presented will require further testing, at the least it should stimulate new ways of thinking about human nature.

Paul R. Lawrence and Nitin Nohria, *Driven: How Human Nature Shapes Our Choices.* San Francisco: Jossey-Bass, 2002.

EVOLUTION OF THE BRAIN

Hominids split off from other primates around six million years ago, but there was very little development in human technology from that time until about 80,000 years ago. According to archaeological records there was, at that point, a very dramatic shift in human technology—from crude stone axes to needles, awls, scrapers, and the like. This revolutionary shift is known as the Great Leap. There is no consensus as to what caused the Great Leap, but contemporary understanding of innate skills, plus the limbic center and the frontal cortex of the brain, may shed light on the mystery.

Scientists now believe that evolution has selected several innate skills for humans, including habitat selection, food selection, danger awareness, intuitive psychology, orientation, justice, and an ability to remember important people. None of these skills alone would account for the Great Leap, but at that critical point in time these skills became connected in the human brain in such a way that humans could use all these skills simultaneously to deal with complex problems. Modern methods of electronically scanning the brain allow us to see that this work of sorting through complex concepts occurs in the frontal cortex.

To fully comprehend the role of the human brain in the Great Leap we must also understand the limbic center, which is the seat of emotions or the ability to experience feelings. The limbic center had previously been regarded as the most primitive area of the brain, but research by Antonio Damasio indicates that individuals who have all their rational faculties (most notably a fully functioning frontal cortex) but have sustained damaged to the limbic center experience a marked decrease in decision-making ability. They are able to solve complex problems and have fine memory and attention, but the inability to experience feelings renders them unable to make socially appropriate or personally beneficial decisions.

The limbic center plays a sophisticated role in "marking" incoming sensory messages for their relevance to human needs. Thus, when sensory information reaches the prefrontal cortex, where decisions are made, the limbic center has already done the job of eliminating several options from the decision.

Key in this "marking" theory is the idea that *the limbic center sorts sensory information based on human needs or drives.* The neuroscientists who have advocated this "marking theory" have not specified what those drives are, preferring to leave that work to social scientists.

Based on the accumulated work of biologists, anthropologists, psychologists, economists, and others, *the bases for many of the decisions in every fully functioning human are the needs to acquire, bond, learn, and defend.* These drives are the result of the natural selection process as they have allowed humanity to thrive and to propagate the species.

These drives were not fixed millions of years ago as many biologists believe, but instead were the product of Darwinian evolution. Indeed, this configuration of drives, specifically the emergence of the drive to learn and the drive to bond as primary rather than secondary drives, was the critical development responsible for the Great Leap. This configuration allowed humans to form complex social contracts that allowed humans as a collective to attain the adaptive ability that has made them the most dominant species on earth.

THE DRIVE TO ACQUIRE (D1)

One of the innate drives of all humans is the drive to acquire. Natural selection has favored those driven to acquire food, shelter, sexual consummation, and water. From an evolutionary standpoint, the drive to acquire seems the most obvious. This has led to the dominance of economic models of thought (and their corollary assumption that humans are driven only to acquire) in the social sciences. The economic model extends to say that human choice is based on the rational pursuit of self-interest.

There are instances where we can see some discord between the drive to acquire and rational self-interest and it is here we can see the role of emotion, or the limbic center. One example is food. Evolution has bestowed on humans a general attraction to foods with a high fat content. This is a derivative of our drive to acquire, as a diet high in fat helped our ancestors survive in times of food scarcity. Today, however, the unfettered drive to consume such food is at odds with rational self-interest—we know that such a diet increases our odds of a host of diseases, including heart disease and cancer. The eventual choice—to eat a certain food or not—reflects not only a rational choice, but a competition between emotions. The limbic center has been informed that eating has long-term negative consequences, but the limbic center also has been wired to drive us to eat.

The negative results of the drive to acquire (D1) are that one can never acquire enough, and that this drive may lead us to sacrifice absolute well-being for relative well-being. The constant drive to acquire ever more things leads us to increase our status to help ensure our ability to acquire. This drive is at the heart of conspicuous consumption. Evolutionarily, even in times of scarcity there was always some sustenance, but it went to those of highest status. While the futile battle to constantly increase status may lead to unhappiness, the job of our evolutionary needs is not to make us happy, but help us propagate. To propagate we must succeed against the competition.

On the positive side, the drive to acquire can also lead to cooperation. The drive to acquire can lead people to calculate comparative advantage and specialize labor in such a way as to increase the well-being of all parties.

It is tempting to explain all human behavior in terms of the drive to acquire. But we should note that even Adam Smith, the father of modern economics, did not believe this. He stated that moral sentiments are just as important to understanding human behavior as is the drive to acquire. This helps explain anonymous acts of charity, not cheating when cheating cannot be detected, and other behaviors at odds with rational self-interest.

THE DRIVE TO BOND (D2)

Human beings have an innate desire to bond with others. Early humans with this drive were more likely to pass these genes onto succeeding generations. Males were more likely to be selected as mates, females were more likely to nurture their children to adulthood, and children were more likely to avail themselves to such nurturing. Groups of individuals with this drive were more likely to form the cooperative bonds that helped the group face large challenges. The drive to bond accounts for the universal similarity of moral codes. Moral codes enhance adaptive cooperation.

The bonding drive is known by such terms as loyalty, friendship, love, fairness, empathy, and caring. There appears to be wide support suggesting that:

- People form social relationships very easily without evidence of material advantage.
- The breakup of social bonds is strongly resisted, even beyond any loss of material advantage.
- People spend a large amount of mental energy thinking about their social relationships.
- Many of the strongest human emotions, both positive and negative (such as elation, happiness, jealousy, and loneliness), are associated with bonding.
- People relatively deprived of social bonds are much more likely to suffer a wide variety of physical and mental pathologies.

The drive to bond can be shown to be separate from the drive to acquire. The strength of human bonds is determined *not* by the benefits *minus* costs of particular relationships, but by the benefits *plus* costs. That is, *sacrifices for the sake of a relationship seem to enhance that relationship.* Philosophically, we can all think of situations where the drive to acquire conflicted with the drive to bond. This universal conflict forms the appeal of art forms such as movies, literature, and plays that portray characters torn between such motives as love and money.

The drive to bond carries over to human interaction with social institutions. The growth of the human brain allowed humans the capacity to use symbols as abstractions of real events. When combined with the drive to bond, this allowed humanity to reinforce and extend social bonds with creeds, flags, songs, and ritual. Social institutions did not always exist. They were made possible by symbolization. These extended social bonds were key to developing the complex cultures and civilizations that allowed humanity to prosper.

With regard to work, Nobel laureate Herbert Simon points out that humans consistently exert more effort than is minimally required. Economists focus negatively on the shirking that occurs on jobs, but Simon points out that since shirking is the exception (and exceeding requirements is the norm), this demonstrates the human desire to see the success of the organization they are bonded to.

The dark side of the drive to bond is the common occurrence of a "we versus they" mindset in many groups. This may only result in friendly rivalry, but it can also take severe forms such as sabotage and even genocide.

THE DRIVE TO LEARN (D3)

Humans have an innate drive to learn about themselves and their surroundings. This drive is represented by such terms as wonder, curiosity, and inquisitiveness. The drive to learn is evidenced through the universality of religion as a means to explain gaps in such unobservable mysteries as the purpose of life and the nature of an afterlife. Further, humans have always been fascinated by games, puzzles, and humor even in the absence of material reward. Gaps between what humans think they know and what they observe cause a dissonance that they are driven to reduce.

The drive to learn forms the basis of such needs as mastery, achievement, efficacy, and growth. All of these topics relate to the importance of learning in job design. Jobs that are too simplified and specialized frustrate the drive to learn and may lead to unintended consequences as workers look to relieve boredom. On the other hand, since people are intelligent and have a drive to learn, if management simply empowers workers to make improvements, it is possible to harness these attributes to the organization's betterment.

Unfortunately the drive to learn can lead people to believe plausible, but inaccurate, stories and ideologies. This may be dangerous when it enables cult leaders to take advantage of followers. Once it is lodged in the human brain a belief is difficult to dislodge. Another downside to the drive to learn is that we sometimes pursue new knowledge so aggressively we ignore its destructive potential. The most dramatic example is the pursuit of nuclear technology.

THE DRIVE TO DEFEND (D4)

Humans have an innate drive to protect themselves, their knowledge, their accomplishments, and their valued possessions. This need manifests itself in the emotions of anger, fear, and alarm. This drive may have preceded the drive to acquire in evolution as evidenced by defense reactions in the simplest of creatures.

The drive to defend ties to other drives as we see evidence that humans defend the possessions they have acquired (D1), defend against threats to their loved ones or against threats to the relationships themselves (D2), and defend threats to their ideologies (D3). These threats and changes cause such reactions as resistance, caution, anxiety, denial, rationalization, and (if chronic) withdrawal, passivity, and helplessness.

More is known about the neurology of the defense drive than the other three drives. Evidence from other species and from electronic brain scanning of humans reveals that alarm-inducing messages can travel straight to the organs without passing through the cortex. Thus an individual can experience alarm without knowing why. This is why a defense reaction, such as fear or anger, can cause seemingly irrational behavior. In evolutionary terms this probably served as a valuable defense to physical dangers, but serves little purpose in today's world.

FREE WILL AND DIVERSITY

The independence of the four drives often forces them into conflict. When there is no conflict the body can go about much of its business with minimal consciousness. However, conflict forces these drives into the consciousness. These conscious decisions are what is known as free will. In this way human genes do not determine our behavior, but actually require the exercise of free will.

An important question becomes, *Why is there diversity among cultures?* The short answer is environmental contingencies. Recent research reveals that 99.9 percent of human genes are the same and there is little evidence that genetic differences account for differences in the way and rate at which civilizations emerged. Technological levels have differed based on differences in the resources on which civilizations depend— namely, easily domesticated plants and animals, but also mineral resources. The availability of resources eased the transition from hunter-gatherer societies to agrarian societies and set the trajectory for cultures to move on to more complex societies.

HUMAN NATURE IN ORGANIZATIONS

The four-drive model implies that an organization would do well to respect the needs to acquire, bond, learn, and defend in dealing with all organizational stakeholders. The beginning of the decline of GM and the rise of Japanese autos can be traced to management that paid factory workers well (met their acquisition needs), but generally ignored their learning needs by giving them mindless work. This thwarted any bonding with the organization through the stimulation of hostile or superior attitudes. Further, GM formed adversarial relationships (antithetical to the bonding drive) with suppliers—forcing short-term lowball bids (ignoring the security implicit in the drive to defend) without respecting supplier innovation (learning). The success of the Japanese auto industry in recent years can be attributed to those auto firms' respect for innate needs in their dealings with employees, suppliers, customers, and regulators.

An overemphasis on any of the four needs leads to a less successful organization, and an incomplete individual. *Respect for all four needs should lead to social contracts that leave all individuals and all parties fulfilled.*

PART
VI MOTIVATION

Anumber of readings contained in this edition of *The Manager's Bookshelf* attempt to focus the manager's attention on the social-psychological side of the organization. New concepts and suggestions for proactive management call our attention to the importance of recognizing that all organizations have a natural (human) resource that, when appropriately managed, can lead to dramatic performance effects.

Part VI has three readings. In *The Enthusiastic Employee*, authors Sirota, Mischkind, and Meltzer describe ideal employees. Their unbridled enthusiasm helps them outperform others, strive to achieve the impossible, and rally each other to work hard and make unusual contributions. Unfortunately, unenlightened *managers* often dampen the enthusiasm of these stellar performers and demotivate them. The answer lies in a three-pronged approach involving equitable treatment, opportunities for achievement, and the experience of camaraderie.

David Sirota holds a doctorate in social psychology from the University of Michigan; Louis Mischkind received his Ph.D. in organizational psychology from New York University. Michael Meltzer received his J.D. from Brooklyn Law School. All three are associated with Sirota Consulting, and they share background expertise in various aspects of opinion surveys, behavioral science research, and management assessments.

Most managers find themselves interested in the question "What motivates people to do their best?" In *Intrinsic Motivation at Work*, Kenneth W. Thomas addresses this question. Dr. Thomas highlights the fact that a large number of managers continue to rely upon extrinsic motivators—pay, benefits, status, bonuses, commissions, pension plans, and expense budgets—as a way to achieve high and sustained levels of employee motivation. The author suggests that a committed and self-managing workforce can be attained more easily and consistently through intrinsic motivation. Specifically, Thomas identifies the intrinsic rewards that are needed to energize a workforce, realize organizational commitment, and achieve self-management. The solution, he argues, lies in creating intrinsically motivating jobs.

Kenneth W. Thomas, Ph.D., is a professor of management at the Naval Postgraduate School in Monterey, California. He has been on the management faculty at UCLA, Temple University, and the University of Pittsburgh. He has done extensive work on conflict management and is the co-author of the Thomas-Kilmann Conflict Mode Instrument, which has sold over 3 million copies.

Based upon his observations of a large number of organizations (e.g., Southwest Airlines, the U.S. Marines, General Motors), Jon R. Katzenbach, in

Why Pride Matters More than Money, tackles the question "How do I motivate my employees?"—the question most frequently asked by supervisors, managers, and leaders. While conventional wisdom, as practiced in most organizations, suggests that money and intimidation are the keys to sustained performance, Katzenbach asserts that the real answer is to be found in the word *pride*. He asserts that neither money nor intimidation contribute to the long-term sustainability of an organization. With regard to money, Katzenbach states that it is not a motivator, and that pay-for-performance programs lead to self-serving behavior and ephemeral commitment to the organization. Instead, he notes that most employees are motivated by meaningful work, feelings of accomplishment, recognition/approval, and a sense of belonging and being a part of others in the work environment.

The author, Jon R. Katzenbach, was a senior partner and director of McKinsey and Company, a large U.S.-based consulting organization. He now directs his own firm, Katzenbach Partners, assisting organizations in such areas as workforce performance, team building, and leadership. Mr. Katzenbach is the author of several other books, including *Peak Performance, Teams at the Top, The Wisdom of Teams*, and *Real Change Leaders*.

1

THE ENTHUSIASTIC EMPLOYEE

DAVID SIROTA, LOUIS A. MISCHKIND, AND MICHAEL
IRWIN MELTZER

SUMMARY PREPARED BY SHELLEY OVROM

Shelley Ovrom is a human resources professional, having started her career in the private sector working as a recruiter for The Walt Disney Studios and Universal Studios. She recently made the transition to the public sector, currently working as a human resource analyst for the City of Azusa in California. In her current position, she is responsible for risk management, recruitment, and workers' compensation, as well as daily support for city employees, department heads, and the public. She is passionate about the importance of human resources in an organization and is thrilled to be working in a capacity that not only benefits an employee population, but an entire community.

Most people begin a new job with a sense of enthusiasm. They are typically excited about their work and their organization, eager to be part of a productive team, and reasonable in how they expect to be treated. This is the case for approximately 95 percent of any employee population. The other 5 percent should never have been hired, and managers spend an inordinate amount of time with these difficult employees. However, an even bigger problem lies in the vast number of workers who are not openly troublesome; they are individuals who have become indifferent to the organization and its purpose. They have learned not to expect too much and not to give too much. The most significant decline in employee morale typically begins about six months after being hired and occurs in approximately 9 out of 10 companies.

There are various approaches and theories of how to best tackle this problem. However, a strong argument can be made that the first step is to determine what workers really want. *The key question is not how to motivate employees, but how to sustain— and prevent management from destroying—the motivation and enthusiasm employees naturally bring to their jobs.* **Employee enthusiasm**, a state of high employee morale that derives from satisfying the three key needs of workers, results in significant competitive

David Sirota, Louis Mischkind, and Michael Irwin Meltzer, *The Enthusiastic Employee: How Companies Profit by Giving Workers What They Want,* Wharton School Publishing, 2005.

advantages for companies with the strength of leadership and commitment to manage for true long-term results. A highly effective method of creating and maintaining high levels of long-term organization performance is a **partnership relationship** in which employees work collaboratively, share common, long-term goals, and feel a genuine concern for other employees at work.

WORKER MOTIVATION, MORALE, AND PERFORMANCE

Many theories exist as to the differences in what employees want, explained by generational, racial, gender, or economic differences. Research indicates, however, that the percentage of people satisfied with their work is high for every group, with an average of 76 percent of all workers across all organizations generally enjoying the work they do.

Three-Factor Theory of Human Motivation in the Workplace

According to the three-factor theory of motivation, there are three primary sets of goals of people at work:

Equity

Employees want to be treated justly—in comparison to others—in relation to the three basic conditions of employment. These conditions are unrelated to a position in the company or to performance. The three basic conditions are:

- Physiological – decent working conditions and working environment
- Economic – satisfactory compensation and benefits
- Psychological – respectful and consistent treatment by management

Achievement

Employees want to take pride in their achievements; they want to do things that matter and do them well; they desire to receive recognition for their accomplishments; they want to take pride in the organization's accomplishments. Statistical analysis shows there are six primary sources that contribute to a sense of achievement:

- Challenge of the work itself
- Acquisition of new skills
- Ability to perform
- Perceived importance of the job
- Recognition received for performance
- Feeling proud of their employer

Camaraderie

Members of the workforce wish to experience **camaraderie**—the feeling that they have warm, interesting, and cooperative relations with others on the job. This includes the extent to which an organization functions not only as a business entity, but also as a community that satisfies the social and emotional needs of its employees. The impact that camaraderie can have on performance is often not recognized.

The overall relationship between morale and performance is reciprocal; each is both a cause and an effect of the other.

ENTHUSIASTIC WORKFORCES, MOTIVATED BY FAIR TREATMENT

Three important areas, as viewed by employees, define the issue of fair treatment:

- *Job Security* – In general, 60 percent of workers are confident in the security of their jobs, but this ranges widely across organizations, from a high of 90 percent to a low of 6 percent. Many workers have experienced layoffs and typically do not view them as a prudent business decision, but rather as simply inequitable treatment. Many U.S. companies now seem to use downsizing as a strategic maneuver rather than as a last resort compelled by economic necessity. This "strategy" violates a fundamental need of workers and, in doing so, severely damages the sense of equity that is necessary for effective organizations.
  Companies genuinely committed to their employees adhere to five basic principles in doing their best to provide employees with stable employment:

  1. They exhaust all possible alternatives before laying people off.
  2. When layoffs cannot be avoided, they first ask for volunteers.
  3. When layoffs cannot be avoided and there are no more volunteers, they act generously and decently. From an organizational standpoint, they're not doing it just for those who are let go, but for those who will stay.
  4. They communicate honestly, fully, and regularly throughout the entire process.
  5. They recognize the impact of downsizings on the survivors and take steps to minimize the negative impact.

- *Compensation* – This factor is extraordinarily important for worker morale and performance. Pay provides the material wherewithal for life and is also a measure of respect, achievement, and the equitable distribution of the financial returns of the company. It is a satisfier of both the equity and achievement needs.

- *Respect* – This is the nonfinancial component of equity, with *equality* being at the heart of respect—the treatment of each individual as important and unique without regard to any other characteristics, such as gender, race, income, or even perceived performance or contribution to the organization. This is a fundamental human need that has enormous consequences for human behavior and the effectiveness of organizations. Three broad levels of respectful treatment in organizations can be distinguished:

  1. Humiliating Treatment – This treatment is rare in most organizations at the present time. When it does occur, however, it can be devastating to people and their performance. This treatment comes in two forms: interpersonal, such as an employee's work being ridiculed by an immediate boss; and structural, such as formal organizational controls that allow workers absolutely no decision-making authority in the performance of their jobs. The consequences of this treatment show up most dramatically in labor conflict.
  2. Indifferent Treatment – This treatment is more common than blatant humiliation and is often better termed "benign neglect." It implies that

workers are not worthy of management's time and attention, thereby making workers feel insignificant. Indifferent managers are solely focused on the bottom line. The response of workers to indifference is less anger than it is disappointment and withdrawal.

3. Positive Treatment – There are many factors that contribute to the positive treatment of employees, including physical working conditions, job autonomy, and communication. Ultimately, employees need to feel that they are not just being tolerated, but are made to feel welcome and genuinely included.

ENTHUSIASTIC WORKFORCES, MOTIVATED BY ACHIEVEMENT

A critical condition for employee enthusiasm is a clear, credible, and inspiring organizational purpose. Research reveals a strong correlation between pride in the organization and the overall satisfaction of workers with that organization. The four main sources of pride, all of which reflect different facets of excellence, are:

- Excellence in the organization's financial performance,
- Excellence in the efficiency with which the work of the organization gets done,
- Excellence in the characteristics of the organization's products, and
- Excellence in the organization's moral character.

Success in this area consists of a combination of *purpose* (how an organization serves its customers) and *principles* (the moral character of the company). Any judgment about a company's principles must be based on its behavior in relation to *all* of its key constituencies.

One of the most important components of providing leadership is providing an organization with a purpose and principles of which employees can be proud, and to which they will willingly and enthusiastically devote their skills and energy. The basic points to keep in mind are:

- Purposes and principles must emanate from strongly held convictions of senior management.
- Statements of purposes and principles will be exercises in futility unless they are accompanied by a serious implementation plan.

In studies of group functioning, a useful distinction between three types of leadership exists: autocratic, laissez-faire, and participative. Of the three, research most strongly supports the participative method, which is an active style that stimulates employee involvement. A successful participative method is **self-managed teams (SMTs)**, which are teams of workers who, with their supervisors, are delegated various functions and the authority and resources needed to carry them out. The team operates like a small business whose members are highly involved in its management and in the sharing of its rewards. Effectiveness and job satisfaction are greatly enhanced by organizing teams, when possible, around identified customers and setting the primary goal of the teams to meet the needs of their customers.

External sources of satisfaction are feedback, recognition, and reward. Employees want to perform well, learn how to improve, and be recognized and rewarded for their achievements, which is among the most fundamental of human needs. There are four major means to recognize employees:

1. Compensation – differential compensation based on performance levels
2. Informal recognition – day-to-day recognition of performance
3. Honorifics – special awards for performance
4. Promotion – advancement to higher level positions for superior performance

To be most effective, organizations must think of recognition as a cluster of components that need to be used consistently with each other and with the organization's goals and values in mind.

ENTHUSIASTIC WORKFORCES, MOTIVATED BY CAMARADERIE

The quality of social relationships in the workplace—its social capital—is of enormous importance, not only because of the general need people have for camaraderie, but because cooperative relationships are critical for effective performance and, therefore, for a sense of achievement in one's work. An employee's greatest sense of satisfaction and accomplishment can come from interacting as a team toward common performance goals. Teamwork is needed for just about every job at every level. This cooperation is the glue that binds together the different parts of the organization. Groups, when structured and managed correctly, allow for the emergence and consideration of different perspectives, which is vital to solve problems and make good business decisions.

BRINGING IT ALL TOGETHER: THE TOTAL ORGANIZATION

To create and implement a truly significant and lasting organization change, the various components discussed cannot be thought of individually, but together as a system, one that is governed by an organization culture. The essence of the system and culture discussed is a partnership relationship. Partnership has both a vertical dimension, which consists of the relationships between workers and management, and a horizontal dimension, which are the relationships between individuals and between work units. Essentially, a partnership is people working together toward common goals. The partnership method is a high-involvement model, with the successful hallmarks including:

- Win-win – all parties recognize they have key business goals in common and that the success of one depends on the success of the other
- Basic trust – intentions of all parties are trusted
- Excellence – high performance standards are set for all parties
- Competence – the parties have confidence in each other
- Joint decision making – key decisions are made jointly
- Open communications – parties communicate fully with each other
- Mutual influence – parties listen to and are influenced by each other
- Mutual assistance – parties help each other perform
- Recognition – contributions by each party are recognized
- Day-to-day treatment – parties routinely treat each other with consideration and respect
- Financial sharing–parties share equitably in results

Partnership is highly effective because it harnesses the natural motivation and enthusiasm that are characteristic of the overwhelming majority of workers. Although some conditions may make partnership inappropriate, such as extremely contrasting individual differences, there is no evidence that the approach does not work when it is applied to certain types of work or in certain cultures. Certain adaptations may obviously need to be made, but the fundamental concepts are applicable everywhere as long as the actions for a partnership organization begin with, and are sustained by, senior management.

2

INTRINSIC MOTIVATION
AT WORK

KENNETH W. THOMAS

SUMMARY PREPARED BY SHANNON STUDDEN

Shannon Studden *is a native of Milwaukee, currently living in Duluth, Minnesota. She received her Master of Science degree in Industrial/Organizational Psychology from the University of Tennessee at Chattanooga in 1994. She has worked as an internal research consultant at Duracell, USA, in Cleveland, Tennessee, and has been a member of the faculty at Tennessee Wesleyan College and the University of Tennessee at Chattanooga. She has served as an adjunct instructor of Organizational Behavior at the University of Minnesota Duluth, and is currently Manager of Training at North Shore Mining Company.*

Traditionally, organizations have relied on extrinsic rewards such as salaries and bonuses to motivate employees. Rewards focused on employee behavior and depended on close supervision to determine who qualified for them and who did not. In a hierarchically structured organization, this was relatively easy to do, as multiple levels of managers with narrow spans of control were available to keep close watch over subordinates. Employees were fairly accepting of this watchdog approach because it meant they had a secure job with solid benefits.

The problem is that this type of reward system doesn't fit well with the changing face of organizations. The trend of eliminating layers of management has resulted not only in decreased employment security, but also in wider spans of control and less direct supervision of employees. This leaves supervisors with little time to micromanage employees' tasks.

The feeling of decreased employment security means that employees feel less loyal to their employers and are more likely than workers of previous generations to leave an unsatisfying job for a more attractive one, often several times in their lifetime. Therefore, to remain competitive, today's organizations need a better way to attract and retain the best employees.

Kenneth W. Thomas, *Intrinsic Motivation at Work: Building Energy & Commitment.* San Francisco: Berrett-Koehler Publishers, Inc., 2000.

The solution lies in creating *intrinsically motivating jobs*—jobs that generate positive emotions and are rewarding in and of themselves. This can only be accomplished by leading employees into the process of self-management.

THE PROCESS OF SELF-MANAGEMENT

Successful self-management is dependent upon four processes in progression: meaningfulness, choice, competence, and progress. First, employees commit to a *meaningful* purpose. Second, they are allowed to *choose* activities to accomplish the purpose. Third, after performing these activities, employees assess their own *competence*. Last, employees monitor their *progress* toward the purpose. These processes come together to create a continuous cycle. Ideally, an increased sense of progress leads back into an increased sense of meaningfulness and choice, and the process starts all over again.

BUILDING A SENSE OF MEANINGFULNESS

A meaningful job elicits a passion for its ultimate purpose. When we have a job that is meaningful, we spend more time thinking about it, feeling excited about it, and increasing our commitment to it. It means we try to get around obstacles in our way of reaching the purpose and keep focused on the outcome. Because what is meaningful to one person may not be meaningful to another, a leader's job is to match individuals with tasks that have meaning for them. To build meaningfulness, leaders should:

- **Provide a noncynical climate.** Cynicism punishes excitement and passion by trivializing positive emotions. If a cynical climate has existed in the organization in the past, leaders need to openly acknowledge past mistakes, admit to the reasons behind the cynicism, and emphasize that a new choice has been made to strive toward a more positive environment.
- **Clearly identify passions.** Employees need to identify what they care most about in their jobs. Leaders can talk with each employee individually about passions and dreams, then bring the group together to discuss the passions that they have in common. Identifying common passions leads to a shared vision and unifies the team through its values. Once these passions are openly expressed, the leader must allow the group to evolve in the direction of its passions, or cynicism will be even more firmly embedded in the climate than before.
- **Provide an exciting vision.** As the vision develops more fully, it should become more concrete to make it more real. A well-formed vision will also help later in assessing progress toward goals.
- **Ensure relevant task purposes.** All day-to-day tasks must contribute to the vision. Any tasks that do not contribute to the vision should be outsourced. This reinforces the fact that the organization is dedicated to the interests and passions of the group.
- **Provide whole tasks.** Whenever possible, employees should be able to see projects through from beginning to end. This allows for a greater source of pride in accomplishment and a better feeling for the team's overall purpose.

Special Advice for Leaders: Building Meaningfulness for Yourself

- **Create a noncynical climate for yourself.** Stop focusing on deficiencies.
- **Clarify your own passions.** Identify what really matters to you.
- **Craft your own vision.** This needs to be done before the team's vision is created, so that you can fit the vision not only to the passions of the team members, but also to your own.
- **Make your tasks more relevant.** Ask yourself what you could do at work that is meaningful to you.
- **Negotiate for whole tasks.** Make an attempt to take on the responsibility of an entire task when possible.

BUILDING A SENSE OF CHOICE

We experience a true sense of choice when our opinions matter, when we feel that we have flexibility in our behavior, and when we feel ownership of the outcome. When we are able to make choices, we accomplish the overall goal by deciding what works best for us. A sense of choice leads to initiative, creativity, and experimentation.

Leaders have more control over their employees' sense of choice than over the other three intrinsic rewards, because choice, and not meaningfulness, competence, or progress, is given to employees. To maximize a sense of choice, leaders need to provide them with basic guidelines and allow employees to make their own decisions within established limits. Additionally, leaders should:

- **Delegate authority.** Leaders must resist the trap of waiting to delegate until employees are more skilled. Waiting for ideal conditions only causes employees to become increasingly dependent, which makes them less capable of making decisions and creates a downward spiral of dependence. The only way for employees to become more competent decision makers is to have experience making decisions.
- **Demonstrate trust.** There are three keys to demonstrate trust. First, important decisions, rather than trivial ones, should be delegated. Second, employees must be left alone to carry out decisions. Monitoring the decision-making process diminishes the sense of choice. Third, trust can be demonstrated by encouraging employees to take on new responsibilities.
- **Provide security.** Employees need to feel that experimentation is acceptable, and that mistakes will be seen as learning opportunities rather than failures. The "zero-defects" mentality so prevalent in organizations today unfortunately leaves no opportunity for mistakes. As a result, employees keep mistakes to themselves, rather than presenting them to the team as opportunities for constructive learning. This secrecy increases the probability of falsifying records and blaming others, all of which act in direct opposition to the ultimate goal of intrinsic motivation. To minimize mistakes, leaders can try to match individuals to tasks within their abilities and provide help when asked. Once this is done, it is necessary to allow employees to make their own choices about the best way to reach their goals.

- **Provide a clear purpose.** To have meaningful work and make good decisions, workers need understanding of the bigger purpose, not just knowledge of tasks.
- **Provide information.** Leaders must provide employees with access to all relevant information so that they can make well-informed decisions.

Special Advice for Leaders: Building Choice for Yourself

- **Negotiate for the authority you need.** Tell your boss how giving you authority will help you or your team reach the purpose.
- **Earn trust.** Show that you are capable of self-management by your actions.
- **Don't yield to fear.** Unrealistic fears can keep you from thinking logically and intelligently.
- **Clarify your purpose.** Make sure that you understand why you are doing what you are doing.
- **Get the information you need.** Do you need more than you currently have? Personal contacts? A better information system? Access to information previously unavailable to you?

BUILDING A SENSE OF COMPETENCE

We feel a sense of competence when our performance meets or exceeds the standards we have set for ourselves. Performing well is, in itself, intrinsically rewarding. When creating a product, competence produces a sense of craftsmanship. When performing a service, competence produces a sense of responsiveness. Competence means that we are serving our purpose.

When people feel a sense of incompetence, it results in apathy, low effort, embarrassment, low job satisfaction, and anxiety. However, too much competence can also be a problem, as it results in a feeling of little challenge, boredom, and low job satisfaction. A leader's responsibility is to find the right balance for each employee's sense of competence. To achieve the balance, leaders can:

- **Provide knowledge.** Leaders need to provide specific job-related knowledge through discussions or training.
- **Provide positive feedback.** When a task is difficult, positive feedback allows employees to make necessary adjustments in their performance. Positive feedback increases the sense of competence, while negative feedback undermines it. Negative feedback is sometimes necessary; however, because people are more sensitive to negative feedback, leaders should concentrate on positives as much as possible.
- **Recognize skill.** Recognition increases a sense of competence.
- **Manage challenge.** Leaders need to find a fit between employee ability and task difficulty. The ideal task is one that the employee is capable of accomplishing with full concentration. High satisfaction results when this type of task is done well.
- **Foster high, noncomparative standards.** High standards build competence. Just as delegating trivial decisions diminishes a sense of choice, low standards diminish a sense of competence. A sense of competence comes after having achieved a sufficiently difficult goal.

Standards must be noncomparative. Comparing employees against each other sets average competence at "mediocre." Because the goal is for all employees to aim high, comparing them relative to each other is counterproductive.

Special Advice for Leaders: Building Competence for Yourself

- **Get the knowledge you need.** As a leader, it is your responsibility to engage in continuous learning.
- **Get the feedback you need.** Feedback lets you improve your own performance.
- **Recognize your own skill.** Acknowledge your own competence.
- **Manage challenge in your own work.** Say no when necessary. Take on more or increasingly complex responsibilities when things get too easy.
- **Set high standards for yourself.** A sense of competence comes when you feel that you have accomplished something worth accomplishing.

BUILDING A SENSE OF PROGRESS

When we feel a sense of progress, we feel that the task purpose is steadily being achieved, that things are on track. We feel part of something successful, resulting in excitement and enthusiasm for the task. When little progress is being made, however, a sense of frustration results. We feel a loss of control, resulting in a loss of commitment.

In some ways, progress is more important than the actual attainment of the goal. Reaching the goal is significant, but there must be progress along the way to serve as reinforcement. To help build a sense of progress, leaders must:

- **Build a collaborative climate.** Conflict can halt progress in its tracks. When conflict arises, collaboration allows all of the parties involved to get what they need. For collaboration to be successful, all parties must listen to each other, take each other's point of view seriously, and direct a great deal of energy into problem solving.
- **Track milestones.** Employees need reference points to measure progress. Breaking tasks into significant advances is especially important on long tasks, where progress is sometimes difficult to see.
- **Celebrate progress.** Employees need a special time to recognize that a milestone has been reached. Celebrations intensify the positive emotions that arise from a sense of progress. This can be as simple as pausing to acknowledge that a milestone has been reached, or as complex as an all-out party.
- **Provide access to customers.** One of the best ways to gauge progress toward a purpose or goal is to have contact with the people affected by it—the customers. Seeing customer satisfaction first-hand gives employees a sense of accomplishment. When customer contact is built into the job, it serves as an ongoing reinforcement of progress.
- **Measure improvements (and reduce cycle time).** Improvements are essential to a sense of progress. It is especially important that the right things are being measured—specifically, things that the leader and team care about. Measuring cycle time is particularly useful. Cycle time improvements result in teams having to cover fewer steps to reach their goals and encountering fewer obstacles along the way. These improvements create a sense of speed, which adds to the sense of progress.

Special Advice for Leaders: Building Progress for Yourself

- **Build collaborative relationships.** If you are experiencing noncollaborative relationships at work, share your desire to make the relationships more collaborative with the other persons, and ask them to join you.
- **Develop your own milestones** to increase your own sense of progress.
- **Take time to celebrate.** Think of celebrations as time for renewal. You need to pace yourself to avoid burnout and to keep your energy and passion.
- **Make contact with customers**—internal and external—as often as possible.
- **Measure improvements (and track intrinsic motivation).** Try to measure improvements in team progress, quality, and intrinsic motivation. Are employees still energized by their work tasks?

These four processes propel the change from an external, managerial-driven reward system to an internal, employee-driven reward system. The subsequent increase in intrinsic motivation is critical for organizations to succeed in the work environment of the twenty-first century.

3

WHY PRIDE MATTERS MORE THAN MONEY

JON R. KATZENBACH

SUMMARY PREPARED BY ANNEMARIE KAUL

AnneMarie Kaul is the Donor Recruitment Manager for the North Central Blood Region of the American Red Cross in St. Paul, Minnesota. She and her recruitment reps are responsible for recruiting sponsors and volunteers to ensure the acquisition of over 243,000 pints of blood each year. She also has several years of experience managing financial services operational departments. Her business expertise has been in the areas of leadership and customer service. She has a B.A. from the University of Minnesota Duluth and an M.B.A. from the University of St. Thomas in St. Paul, Minnesota.

Pride can be the key to unlocking the motivational spirit of any employee at any level and within virtually any enterprise. At the base of this building of pride is emotion. More specifically, it is critical to obtain the emotional commitment of associates, which in turn can lead to both positive and negative forms of motivation. The positive form of motivation is called institutional-building pride and the negative form is self-serving pride.

Companies that rely solely on monetary incentives to motivate employees will only realize short-term successes, because they are not taking advantage of the easily accessible building of pride that is a powerful motivating force. *Enterprises today must move beyond egos and monetary incentives to sustain not only employee satisfaction, but also economic performance and long-term growth.*

Jon R. Katzenbach, *Why Pride Matters More than Money: The Power of the World's Greatest Motivational Force.* New York: Crown Business, 2003.

WHY INSTITUTIONAL-BUILDING PRIDE WORKS

In the long run, a person who is allowed to pursue worthwhile goals and endeavors will be more motivated to work harder than a person only receiving monetary incentives. When associates take pride in their work, their job satisfaction increases, their productivity is higher, and the enterprise ultimately is more likely to succeed. One of the best reasons for using pride as a motivator is that it can be quickly learned and easily applied. Before leaders use pride to motivate, it is important that they understand the other reasons why instilling pride works so well to motivate others.

- The skills and knowledge for instilling pride are mostly teachable and can be readily learned.
- Pride begets pride; there is a closed loop of energy linking pride to work performance. The anticipation of higher performance feels good and generates the emotional commitment to obtain better results.
- The fundamental correlation between pride and performance can be found in any company that depends on humans.
- Leaders don't have to wait for real success before instilling pride in others. They can tap into past accomplishments as well as future expectations to trigger emotions.

DIFFERENCES BETWEEN SELF-SERVING PRIDE AND INSTITUTIONAL PRIDE

In companies that consistently perform better than their competition, pride is a primary driver of their higher performance. There is clear evidence indicating that in traditional larger companies, managers who instill pride also have better economic and market performance than their competitors.

Both categories of pride—self-serving and institutional-building—can be a factor in the production of good and bad results, but typically self-serving pride only produces short-term success.

Self-Serving Pride

Self-serving pride is all about power and money. The individual's thought process goes something like this: "The more you can earn, the more visible you are, the more powerful and well-off you become." Power and control are believed to be all-important, so typically a person who is motivated by this type of influence will switch allegiances such that there is no loyalty or commitment to the company. However, there *are* some advantages of self-serving pride, especially in situations such as in individual sports. Monetary awards not only serve as indicators of talent and achievement; they are a simple way to distinguish between performers and nonperformers.

Institutional-Building Pride

This type of pride is based on the character and emotional commitment of associates. With institutional-building pride, people are motivated to help others and work for the good of the enterprise. They place their efforts on more basic performance factors such as customer satisfaction, peer and mentor approval, developmental opportunities, and quality of work. These in turn build self-worth, group cohesion, and personal developmental happiness—factors that lead to success.

When further comparing the two types of pride, it is important to note that institutional pride has real strength because it can work across different types of organizations, even in companies where money is not a realistic source of motivation. For example, organizations such as the U.S. Marine Corps and Kentucky Fried Chicken (KFC) have been very successful, because they have integrated institutional-building pride into the workplace. It has been demonstrated over and over again that money may attract and keep people, but it does not continue to motivate them to excel. At the end of the day, it is the feeling of pride (self-serving or institutional-building) that prompts employees to do well.

SOURCES OF INSTITUTIONAL PRIDE

Institutional pride can come from many sources. The primary origins fall into three main categories—work results, work processes, and co-workers/supervisors.

- **Pride in the results of one's work.** This is often exhibited when employees feel good about what they have accomplished. This can arise from the product or service delivered or the kind of work done.
- **Pride in how work is done.** Employees can take pride in "doing something right." This refers to the set of values, standards, work ethic, and commitment that is applied to one's job.
- **Pride in co-workers and supervisors.** The people that an employee works with— supervisors, subordinates, or peers—can all provide job satisfaction.

Given the fact that these sources of "good" pride can be easily directed and controlled by leaders within corporations (as opposed to money), institutional-building pride should be the primary source of pride for the broader base of employees. *It is important to remember that what motivates upper level executives is very different from what motivates frontline employees, especially during difficult times.*

Why is this true? Top executives not only possess the business savvy in terms of schooling in business fundamentals, typically their individual goals are stated in terms of economic results and market share. As a result, their motivation is a function of performance logic and many rational factors. On the other hand, at lower levels, simple emotional factors from everyday occurrences are more important as a motivating source because on the front line, the performance statistics of the company are often less meaningful. The six most important nonfinancial elements of enterprise success that influence *all* associates are:

- Local company reputation
- Product/service attributes
- Customer satisfaction
- Work group composition
- Peer approval
- Competitive position

The good news is that these sources of pride result in the emotional commitment that motivates employees, leading to enterprise-wide success. Understanding the motivational differences between the top and the other levels of an organization is a critical challenge, but it can be learned. The enterprises that excel at engaging emotions employ leaders who are masters at cultivating institutional-building pride.

THE FIVE PATHS TO HIGHER PERFORMANCE

There are five distinct applications or paths that motivate higher performing groups in companies that have successfully developed emotional commitment.

- **Mission, Values, and Collective Pride (MVP)**—This is where companies use their rich histories of past accomplishments to instill pride.
- **Process and Metrics (P&M)**—Delivering value by measuring the right things and maintaining effective processes is a powerful source of pride.
- **Entrepreneurial Spirit (ES)**—High risk/high reward opportunities typically provide motivational direction on this path.
- **Individual Achievement (IA)**—Individual performance and personal advancement, rather than team performance, are the primary motivational sources.
- **Recognition and Celebration (R&C)**—Giving recognition and holding celebrations and special events are used to motivate others.

All of these paths lead to an emotionally committed workforce, which leads to a higher level of performance. Companies that desire to sustain an emotionally committed environment will be more successful if they integrate two of these paths, rather than concentrating on one. But what if you work for a company that does not appear to comprehend these concepts? What can a leader do as an individual to motivate the workforce?

IDEAS FOR INDIVIDUALS NOT IN AN INSTITUTIONAL-BUILDING COMPANY ENVIRONMENT

What if the company you work for is not a well-established enterprise—one whose size, market position, and growth prospects are not highly attractive? A manager in this situation can use the case study results of General Motors to identify successful key motivating features. The following three methods are not only useful, but also easy to apply.

1. *Keep it simple.* Use one or two concentrated themes and place great significance on local sources of pride that employees can easily understand.
2. *Develop one's own unique pride-building formula.* Strong pride-influenced managers should connect to their employees in any way they can (e.g., by tapping into their pride in the community, pride in their families, pride in a legacy).
3. *Make pride a priority.* Using pride on an everyday basis to motivate is the key to obtaining long-term results.

Pride-building people are aware that instilling pride along the way is the *only way* to gain long-term success from it. Therefore, it is more important for people to be proud of what they are doing every day than it is for them to be proud of accomplishing their goals and getting the wanted results. Good leaders appeal to emotions rather than rational compliance; that is why their internal compass is always pointing to pride.

Conclusion

The really good news is that a person does not have to work for a peak performance enterprise to experience pride and the motivation that comes with it. Institutional-building pride motivates people in almost any environment—from top-performing firms to traditional organizations to financially challenged companies.

The ability to instill pride can be learned and utilized, just like any basic performance management technique. What a manager must look out for, however, is trying to motivate employees solely by using sources that are more self-serving like monetary incentives and ego building. While money is economically necessary, it does not motivate one to excel in the long run. When a manager uses institutional-building pride sources, such as recognition, accomplishments, entrepreneurship, or team support, the general population of the workforce, especially people on the front line, is more likely to produce consistent and high-quality results.

At the base of pride-instilling motivation is emotional commitment. Employees want to feel connected to the cause, like providing the best customer service or not letting the team down. It is this connectedness to an overall objective that gives institutional-building pride its powerful force. *Managers must think beyond the compensation package.*

There are many peak-performing enterprises such as KFC, General Motors, and the Marine Corps that have clearly demonstrated that motivating by pride can lead to successful results. We should continue to look at these organizations for guidance. Pride is a powerful motivating force—one that has proven to result in improved success.

PART

VII

TEAMS AND TEAMWORK

As organizations attempt to find a distinctive "edge" and achieve their goals in a rapidly changing and highly competitive environment, more and more are experimenting with teamwork. In doing so, they are hoping to realize some of the synergies that flow from the creation of fully functioning teams. Many organizations, intrigued by the success of team-based structures in automotive assembly plants and elsewhere, have experimented with the use of employee involvement systems and problem-solving teams. Others have made radical changes in their technologies, and some have organized around work teams. Butler Manufacturing uses teams to assemble an entire grain dryer; Hallmark uses teams of artists, writers, accountants, marketers, and lithographic personnel to collaborate to produce Mother's Day cards, while another complete team works on cards for Father's Day.

All three readings in this section focus their attention on various facets of teams and teamwork. The first, co-authored by Frank LaFasto and Carl Larson, is titled *When Teams Work Best*. The second reading, by noted researcher/thinker J. Richard Hackman, explains the importance of managers *Leading Teams*. The third, *Beyond Teams*, was itself prepared by a team of authors—Beyerlein, Freedman, McGee, and Moran.

In *When Teams Work Best*, LaFasto and Larson draw upon a database of interviews with and observations by 6,000 team leaders/members. They identify the work knowledge (technical experience and problem-solving skills) and teamwork factors (openness, supportiveness, action orientation, and positive personal style) that comprise an effective team member. They also introduce suggestions for individuals to use to "connect" with other workmates, as well as discussing the five steps in problem solving and various roles for team leaders to play (focusing on the goal, ensuring a collaborative climate, building confidence, setting priorities, etc.). LaFasto and Larson previously published *Teamwork: What Must Go Right/What Can Go Wrong*.

In *Leading Teams*, author J. Richard Hackman contends that many organizations place too much emphasis on the leader as the primary cause of team behavior, as opposed to team self-management. His book identifies the five conditions necessary for team effectiveness (being a real team, having a compelling goal, having an enabling structure, feeling support, and receiving expert coaching). Hackman suggests that there are four levels of team self-management and urges organizations to evaluate team success on three measures: producing a client-desired product, growth in the team's own capabilities, and having a satisfying team experience.

J. Richard Hackman is the Cahners-Rabb professor of Social and Organizational Psychology at Harvard University, and he previously taught at Yale. He has been recognized with both the Distinguished Educator Award and the Distinguished Research Award from the Academy of Management. He has written several other books, including *Groups That Work (and Those That Don't)* and (with Greg Oldham) *Work Redesign*.

Beyond Teams lays out a simple premise based on research and case studies— that there can be a high organizational payoff from collaborative work systems. The authors identify 10 major principles that define collaborative organizations, including an emphasis on personal accountability, facilitation of dialogue, managing trade-offs, and "exploiting the rhythm of divergence and convergence." They also demonstrate the applicability of the 10 principles across manufacturing, product development, service, and virtual office settings.

Michael Beyerlein is the author or editor of 12 books on collaboration. He is the director of the Center for the Study of Work Teams at the University of North Texas. Craig McGee is a principal with Solutions; Linda Moran works for Achieve Global; and Sue Freedman is president of Knowledge Work Associates.

1

WHEN TEAMS WORK BEST

FRANK LaFASTO AND CARL LARSON

SUMMARY PREPARED BY SHANNON STUDDEN

Shannon Studden, a Milwaukee native, has an M.S. in Industrial/ Organizational Psychology from the University of Tennessee at Chattanooga. She is the Manager of Training for North Shore Mining Company, and was previously an instructor of Organizational Behavior at the University of Minnesota Duluth for several years. She also works as a Product Development Specialist with Emprove, a company that creates Web-based performance appraisal systems for the health care industry.

THE NATURE OF TEAMS

Teams differ from individual employees in that team members must not only work toward personal and team objectives, but must collaborate with other team members. The most effective teams are made up of people who have both technical skills and the ability to work with others to reach the team's goals.

A comprehensive study was conducted, and data were collected from over 6,000 individuals who work in teams. Each person assessed his or her team members, team leader, and organization. Five different functional levels emerged from the study: team members, team relationships, team problem solving, team leadership, and the organizational environment.

TEAM MEMBER CHARACTERISTICS

In order to achieve the team's goal, members need a combination of working knowledge and teamwork ability. In the area of working knowledge, members must have sufficient technical *experience* to provide practical knowledge related to the team's purpose. Members also need the ability to *problem solve;* this involves clarifying problems, helping

Frank LaFasto and Carl Larson, *When Teams Work Best: 6,000 Team Members and Leaders Tell What It Takes to Succeed.* Thousand Oaks, CA: Sage Publications, 2002.

others understand, developing ideas, providing suggestions, and making proactive decisions.

Key teamwork factors include openness, supportiveness, action orientation, and a positive personal style. *Openness* is the single most important factor in effective collaboration. It encompasses an individual's and the team's willingness to address issues and encourage exchange of ideas. Openness includes ensuring that team members have role clarity (specificity of individual roles as well as the role of the team as a whole), acknowledging and addressing performance issues (e.g., social loafing and a lack of accountability), communicating the quality of team results, and clearly identifying goals.

Supportiveness exists when team members have an interest in helping each other succeed. It includes behaviors such as encouraging, overlooking, helping, defending, being warm and caring, and giving team goals priority over individual goals. Defensiveness, the opposite of supportiveness, works against team effectiveness by taking energy away from the team goal. In the most effective environments, openness and supportiveness go together. In an open environment, it is possible to discuss controversial work issues. In a supportive environment, the *method* of discussion matters most.

Groups with a strong *action orientation* have a desire to do something (produce results). This requires encouraging others, suggesting strategies, and being willing to try. Action-oriented individuals and teams are more likely to emerge as leaders, perhaps proving the accuracy of the fundamental law of team success: *Action is more likely to succeed than inaction.*

A *positive personal style* reflects an underlying positive attitude. A team member with this type of attitude is typically energetic, optimistic, engaging, confident, and fun. A negative attitude, on the other hand, is exhibited by pessimism, defensiveness, and being difficult to work with. Just the presence of a few group members with negative attitudes can drain the energy from a team.

TEAM RELATIONSHIPS

Positive relationships help produce effective teams. These relationships develop when people come together, identify opportunities, share information, solve problems collectively, and develop inventive ways to collaborate. Key prerequisites for positive work relationships include:

- Being constructive.
- Acting respectful, trusting, nonthreatening, safe, and productive.
- Being focused on important issues, staying connected, and bringing out the best traits in others.
- Developing mutual understanding.
- Seeing another's point of view, feeling understood, and acting in a self-corrective manner.
- Being willing to make changes to improve the relationship; and trusting that each person is committed to the team.

Negative relationships, on the other hand, result in high costs to organizations by diverting progress away from goals and forcing managers to spend a great deal of time solving employee conflicts. Negative relationships often emerge when one or both parties are:

- Destructive.
- Disrespectful, cynical, suspicious, or threatening.
- Focused on superfluous issues.
- Engaging in power struggles.
- Uncertain about the other's points of view.
- Feeling as though their perspectives haven't been heard.
- Not making a committed effort toward concrete changes.
- Exhibiting only a limited commitment.

They are similarly negative when conditions around the parties are ambiguous or not self-correcting.

Team members can gauge these attributes in a relationship by answering these four questions:

1. Did we have a constructive conversation?
2. Was the conversation productive enough to make a difference?
3. Did we understand and appreciate each other's perspective?
4. Did we both commit to making improvements?

Handling conflict well is essential to positive relationships, but this skill is consistently identified as the greatest challenge in team interactions. Any conflict resolution between team members must include openness and supportiveness in order to be successful.

Feedback is frequently mishandled during the conflict resolution process. It requires caring and courage to deliver feedback; it requires courage and maturity to accept and appreciate it. Feedback rarely works because people tend to become defensive, which then eliminates the possibility of openness. When given and received well, feedback results in increased feelings of accountability, increased job satisfaction, and improved performance.

The Connect Model

Leaders and team members need to create and maintain positive interpersonal relationships. Both individuals in any relationship must participate actively in the process to ensure success. Participants are encouraged to:

- Make a strong commitment to the relationship.
- Tell why the relationship is important to you.
- Indicate to the other person that you're willing to work at the relationship.
- Optimize the other's safety (assert that you will not belittle the other person and will listen to him or her).
- Narrow the discussion to one issue and discuss it in a nonthreatening way.
- Neutralize defensiveness by asking the other person to tell you if he or she feels defensive.
- Explain and echo each perspective, by telling what you have experienced and how it makes you feel, and summarizing what the other person tells you.
- Change one behavior (what improvement each person could make).
- Track mutual results, picking a time to check in with each other at specified intervals.

TEAM PROBLEM SOLVING

Team members need to integrate different perspectives and funnel them into good decisions during the problem-solving process. There are three common denominators to effective problem-solving teams:

1. *Focus.* Members must have clarity of purpose and an understanding of the task at hand. It is important to have a concentrated joint effort to optimize energy. Ineffective teams have more scattered efforts and unclear objectives.
2. *Climate.* The best team climates are relaxed, informal, and fun. Members in these climates feel accepted, valued, and competent. Unhealthy climates, by contrast, are tense, critical, cynical, and formal. Bad climates develop because of personal agendas taking priority over group goals, political issues, dysfunctional behavior of group members, and inappropriate leadership styles.
3. *Communication.* Open and honest communication is essential for collaborative teamwork. Ineffective teams avoid problems and hope they go away. This can lead to bad decisions or the lack of a decision at all. None of these factors is related in any way to intelligence or rank in an organization. In fact, top management teams are consistently among the least collaborative problem solvers.

The Dynamics of Problem Solving

Problem solving involves the direction of expended energy. Mental, physical, and spiritual energy gets directed toward the goal, while drains take energy away from the goal. Successful teams are able to stay focused on the goal despite potential energy drains, while unsuccessful teams allow the drains to sap their energy. When drains take precedence, energies end up being expended on self-protection and counterproductive behaviors. Power struggles, political issues, and personality conflict diffuse group members' focus on their goals and tasks. In order to move energy toward the desired objective, the goal must be clear, elevating, compelling, and unifying. A common identity and values provide the team with immunity from energy drains.

Five Steps to Effective Problem Solving

Teams need to have a willingness to address problems systematically. The method of doing so is not as important as agreeing upon a method and sticking with it. In general, any successful problem-solving system should include first a thorough analysis of problems, then examination of issues, and finally a weighing of options.

The Single Question Format is one systematic method of solving problems. The main advantages of this format are (1) team members' attentions are concentrated on one problem, and (2) solutions are chosen only after thorough analysis. Five steps need to be addressed:

Step 1: *Identify the problem.* What one question do we need to answer?
Step 2: *Create a collaborative setting.* Determine the guiding principles for the problem-solving process, and identify the assumptions and biases possessed by group members.
Step 3: *Identify and analyze the issues and subquestions.* What must be determined before the process can be completed?
Step 4: *Identify possible solutions.* Come up with the two or three best options.
Step 5: *Resolve the single question.* Which is the best solution?

Cross-functional teams

Cross-functional teams combine members from different areas of an organization, or from different organizations altogether. The combination brings together many different backgrounds, areas of expertise, and perspectives. However, loyalties to different departments and organizations, as well as deeply divided time commitments and conflicting demands, can detract from progress on cross-functional teams. This increases the likelihood that energy will be directed away from the goal. Because of these factors, it is even more crucial to agree upon and commit to a common goal early in the team's formation.

THE TEAM LEADER

Leaders have a great deal of responsibility to ensure effective team functioning. There are six dimensions over which leaders have a great deal of control: focusing on the goal, ensuring a collaborative climate, building confidence, demonstrating sufficient technical know-how, setting priorities, and managing performance. Specific leader behaviors can ensure success on all six dimensions.

- When team leaders *focus on the goal,* they define goals in a clear and elevating way, set relatively difficult goals, help team members see their role in the goal achievement process, continually reinforce and renew the goal, and make adjustments to the goal only with clear justification.
- When leaders work to *ensure a collaborative climate,* they minimize barriers to open communication, bring up tough issues, show no tolerance for competitive or inappropriate behavior, reward collaborative behavior, publicly acknowledge the desired behaviors and outcomes, guide team problem-solving efforts, and manage their own ego and personal control needs.
- When leaders seek to *build confidence* in their team, they try to be fair and impartial, provide the team with positive experiences, keep team members informed about key issues and facts, demonstrate trust of team members, assign areas of responsibility based on members' skills and abilities, show a positive attitude, and acknowledge team members' efforts, contributions, and accomplishments.
- To *demonstrate sufficient technical know-how,* team leaders acquire and use the knowledge necessary for goal achievement, and recognize and acknowledge their own limitations.
- When it comes to *setting priorities,* team leaders stay focused on the question "What needs to happen for the team to move toward its goal?" They take on additional priorities only with careful consideration, reassess priorities when necessary, and thoroughly explain any reasons for changes in priorities to team members.

In the all-important domain of managing performance, team leaders discuss results in term of objectives, level of collaboration, management of people and resources, and personal development; give clear, constructive feedback on these four dimensions by addressing behavior, not people; and recognize superior performance.

IMPACT OF THE ORGANIZATIONAL ENVIRONMENT

The organizational environment encompasses the psychological atmosphere resulting from organizational processes. It affects how team members communicate and make decisions, whether they feel comfortable taking risks, how open they are, and whether they are ready to share and accept diverse ideas.

A good environment produces clarity, confidence, and commitment. Clarity drives confidence, and confidence drives commitment. Clarity of goals and priorities makes decisions easier, gives clearer understanding of roles, and produces clearer courses of action. Confidence helps team members commit to a decision, state their opinion, and take action. Commitment helps team members weather the difficult times that inevitably develop during any long-term process, and keep members' action orientation engaged in order to move toward the finish line.

There are three environmental dimensions that can support or hinder teamwork:

1. *Management practices.* Leadership is a primary factor in the shaping of the organizational environment. Managers must establish goals and priorities that are readily recognized at all levels of the organization. These priorities must be emphasized often and enthusiastically. It is also important to establish clear operating principles to guide team members' daily functioning. These principles should send clear messages to team members that leaders will avoid politics, and instead dedicate their energy toward the goal and being accountable for results.

2. *Structure and processes.* Changing objectives or methods of operation without creating structure and processes to support the change is a setup for failure. Structure affects decision making, information flow, intra- and interorganizational boundaries, and role clarity. Processes integrate skills, abilities, and information in order to produce an outcome. Effective structure and processes result in quality decisions, strong interpersonal connections, and the alignment of information, understanding, and effort. Repeating objectives and processes in a variety of ways fosters strong communication processes by reaching all employees. A good communication process assures team members that they will be kept informed.

3. *Systems.* Information systems and reward systems consistently present problems in the environment. Teams need reliable information to make effective decisions. Unreliable information systems lead to cynicism and caution in decision making. Reward systems are needed to encourage the team toward desired results. The traditional system of rewarding and recognizing individuals is incompatible with a team philosophy, as members attain results collectively. Just as they work as one body, teams must also be rewarded as one body.

2 | LEADING TEAMS

J. Richard Hackman

Summary Prepared by Katherine A. Karl

Katherine A. Karl is an Associate Professor in the Graduate School of Management at Marshall University in South Charleston, West Virginia. She received her M.B.A. and Ph.D. in Business Administration from Michigan State University with a major in Organizational Behavior and Human Resource Management. She has taught courses in human resource management, organizational behavior, labor relations, teams and teamwork, and leadership skills. Her research publications have focused on the topics of employment termination, job values, performance feedback, and the use of videotaped feedback in management education and development. Her consulting work has included teambuilding seminars, assessment centers, and employee satisfaction surveys.

INTRODUCTION

Common knowledge suggests that teams outperform individuals, and self-managing teams perform best of all. But, do they really? Not always, and not even usually. Work teams can outperform traditional work units, but they often perform much worse. Developing, supporting, and maintaining a highly successful team is a very beneficial but rare accomplishment. There is no magical recipe for team success. The best a leader can do is to help create conditions that increase the *probability* that a team will be effective.

WHAT CONDITIONS WILL FOSTER TEAM EFFECTIVENESS?

Teams have a greater chance of being successful when leaders (1) create a real team rather than a team in name only, (2) set a compelling direction for the team's work, (3) design an enabling team structure, (4) ensure the team operates within a supportive organizational context, and (5) provide expert coaching.

J. Richard Hackman, *Leading Teams: Setting the Stage for Great Performances.* Boston: Harvard Business School Press, 2002.

Creating a Real Team

First, leaders must make sure that the task is appropriate for a team. Some tasks are performed better when individuals work independently (e.g., creative writing). Second, the team should have clear boundaries. To work well together, team members need to have a clear and consistent sense of who they are. Third, it is important for leaders to clearly specify the team's level of authority. Here, there are four options: (1) teams who merely carry out the instructions of their manager (manager-led teams), (2) teams who perform the task as well as monitor and manage work process and progress (self-managing teams), (3) teams who perform, self-manage, and also design the team and its organizational context (self-designing teams), and (4) teams who do all the above as well as establish the overall direction of the team (self-governing teams). While it is possible for both self-managing and self-designing teams to make significant and valuable contributions to their organizations, the other two options are rarely successful. Manager-led teams, the first option, tend to be dysfunctional for both the people involved and the organization and invariably result in wasted human resources. The latter option, self-governing teams, are often bogged down in endless discussions about their values, purposes, and collective directions.

Finally, it is commonly held that teams should periodically introduce new members and remove existing members to prevent the team from becoming inattentive, careless, and too forgiving of one another's mistakes. In truth, teams with stable membership over a long period of time perform better than those that have constantly changing membership. Teams with stable membership are more familiar with one another, the team's work, the team's norms, team members' roles, and the work setting. As a result, team members are able to focus on getting work done rather than getting oriented.

Setting a Compelling Direction

Teams with no clear sense of where they are going have endless discussions and debates about the team's purpose. As a result they are unable to manage themselves efficiently or effectively. Teams are much more effective when someone in authority sets the direction for the team's work. A compelling direction—one that is challenging, clear, and consequential—energizes team members, orients their attention and action, and engages their talents.

In setting the team's direction, leaders have four choices. They can specify neither the ends nor the means, but that may result in disorder and undesirable behaviors and outcomes. They can specify both the ends and the means, but that is a waste of human resources. They can specify the means but not the ends, which is the worst case scenario. When this happens, the team's products or services rarely satisfy those who receive them, neither growth nor learning is experienced by team members, and the team's capabilities decline over time. However, *when leaders specify the ends but not the means, team members are able to take full advantage of the team's knowledge, skill, and experience to devise creative and effective ways of accomplishing the team's purposes.*

Enabling Team Structure

Three structural features are important for effective teamwork: task design, norms, and composition.

Team Task Design

When the team's work is designed to incorporate skill variety, task identity, task significance, autonomy, and feedback, the team is more likely to experience a state of collective internal motivation. Indeed, one of the benefits of creating teams to accomplish work is that the tasks assigned can be much larger and therefore more significant and meaningful. Autonomy can give teams the opportunity to excel by allowing team members to create new and improved work processes. However, there is always the risk that teams will use their autonomy in ways undesired by organizational leaders. Finally, feedback makes team learning and performance improvements possible.

Team Norms

Team norms are critical because they serve to coordinate and regulate member behavior. Two key norms that foster team effectiveness are (1) being active rather than reactive, and (2) clearly specifying a handful of critical things team members must do and things they must not do. Unfortunately, both of these require forethought, effort, and diligence because they contradict natural human tendencies. Groups and individuals tend to keep on mindlessly doing whatever they've done in the past and reacting to whatever demands their attention and response at the moment rather than actively scanning the environment for problems or opportunities. Groups and individuals also have a tendency to seek harmony and may do things that shouldn't be done in an effort to please others.

Team Composition

Leaders need to ensure each team member has strong task skills and at least adequate interpersonal skills. Additionally, the size of the group should be small (e.g., no more than six members). Finally, the composition of the team should strike a balance between homogeneity (for compatibility) and heterogeneity (for diversity of ideas).

A Supportive Organizational Context

A well-supported work team has (1) a reward system that provides positive consequences for good team performance (as opposed to individual performance), (2) an information system that provides accurate and reliable data and projections, (3) an educational system that provides critical training and technical assistance, and (4) the material resources necessary to carry out the team's work.

Unfortunately, providing these contextual supports is difficult, for it almost always involves changing the answers to the following questions: (1) Who decides? (2) Who is responsible? (3) Who gains? and (4) Who learns? In other words, providing teams with a supportive organization context often results in changes in the authority or privileges of currently advantaged organizational members.

One of the biggest challenges faced by those implementing teams involves changing reward systems so that recognition and reinforcement are contingent on excellent team performance. Team-based reward systems are critical in sustaining collective motivation and getting team members to think of "us" rather than "me." However, in most organizations performance appraisal and compensation systems are set up to measure and reward individual contributions, not team accomplishments.

Another critical challenge involves making changes in the accessibility of existing information and control systems. Providing teams with up-to-date and reliable information is not an easy feat for many reasons:

1. *The really good stuff is a secret.* To prevent key information from getting in the hands of competitors, some organizations keep information secret. Unfortunately, this "secret" information could often have been used by the team to improve its performance.
2. *Providers and users speak different languages.* The information is provided in a format that may make sense to the provider, but is either nonsensical or burdensome to the user.
3. *Information.* A flood is as bad as a drought. Due to improvements in information system technologies, teams may have more information available than they can adequately process. Too much information can be as much a handicap for a team as too little information.
4. *Information is power.* In many organizations, access to information is controlled by senior executives, and some of those executives are very reluctant to share information because doing so diminishes their sense of personal power.

Expert Coaching

The previously mentioned conditions—compelling direction, enabling team structure, and supportive organizational context—provide the foundation for exceptional team performance. No amount of coaching can make a team successful without a sound team foundation. However, when these conditions are favorable, coaching can be crucial to minimizing process losses and increasing process gains. *Process loss* occurs when a group accomplishes less than it theoretically should, given its resources and member talents. *Process gain* occurs when the collective efforts of the team exceed what the individual members could have achieved working independently.

What Should Be the *Content* of Team Coaching Interventions?

It is a common misconception that team coaching interventions should focus on improving interpersonal relationships. In truth, interpersonal conflicts are more often a consequence of, rather than a cause of, poor team performance. Thus, coaching interventions are more effective when the focus is on the team's task performance processes. More specifically, team coaching interventions should focus on (1) the amount of effort team members apply to their collective work, (2) the appropriateness of the performance strategies they utilize to accomplish their work, and (3) the level of knowledge and skill the team applies to its work.

Coaching that addresses effort is motivational in nature and seeks to build shared commitment to the team and its work and to minimize *social loafing,* or the tendency for team members to slack off. Strategy-focused coaching is consultative in nature and seeks to minimize thoughtless reliance on habitual routines and helps team members find or invent new performance strategies that are more appropriate to changing situational requirements and opportunities. Coaching that addresses knowledge and skill is educational in character and seeks not only to develop team members' knowledge and skills, but to prevent team members from failing to fully utilize the knowledge and skills of all its members.

When Should Coaching Be Provided?

The beginning of a team's life is a good time for motivational coaching. At this point the coach needs to get all team members to understand and accept that the team is collectively responsible for accomplishing the team's work. The beginning is the wrong time for strategy-focused coaching. A team needs to experience the task before it can benefit from strategy interventions. Thus, the midpoint of a team's work cycle is the best time for a strategy-focused coaching intervention. People don't learn well when they are in a hurry, preoccupied, or anxious. Thus, educational coaching is most effective at the end of work cycle when team members have some protected time.

Who Should Be the Coach?

It is not important that a team leader or advisor always serve as coach. Peer-to-peer coaching can also be effective. What is most important is that effective coaching be available to a team. Ideally coaching should be shared. It should be provided by a number of individuals at different times and for different purposes.

WHAT DO EFFECTIVE LEADERS DO?

Rather than focusing on traits (who the leader should be) or behavioral style (how the leader should behave), effective leaders know what to do. They make sure they have created a real work team with some stability over time. They know about providing a compelling direction, enabling team structure, supportive organizational context, and expert coaching.

Effective leaders also know when to do it. They pay close attention to timing. They move swiftly and assuredly when opportunities present themselves, but never try to force an intervention when the timing is not right. Astute leaders are aware that change initiatives are rarely successful during periods of equilibrium and that major interventions have a greater chance of success during turbulent times.

Effective leaders have both *emotional maturity and courage.* Leaders who are emotionally mature are more capable of dealing with their own anxieties and those of others. Courage is essential because creating the conditions necessary for successful team performance is usually a revolutionary endeavor and people, especially leaders, often get hurt in revolutions.

Finally, effective leaders neither micromanage nor totally abdicate their role as leader. To build teamwork, the leader needs to let the team work. Thus, the team's potential is rarely realized when leaders attempt to personally manage every aspect of the team's work. Equally wrong is the leader who merely stays out of the way, assuming that the magic of teamwork comes automatically. The bottom line is that a leader cannot *make* a team great. However, once the favorable conditions are in place—compelling direction, enabling team structure, supportive organizational context—a leader can help members take full advantage of those favorable conditions and thereby increase the chance that greatness will occur.

BEYOND TEAMS

MICHAEL M. BEYERLEIN, SUE FREEDMAN,
CRAIG MCGEE, AND LINDA MORAN

SUMMARY PREPARED BY DAVID L. BEAL

David L. Beal is a retired Operations Manager and Vice President of Manufacturing for Lake Superior Paper Industries and Consolidated Papers, Inc., in Duluth, Minnesota. Under his leadership, the all-salaried workforce was organized into a totally self-reliant team system using the principles of socio-technical design to create a high performance system. Dave teaches in the Labovitz School of Business and Economics at the University of Minnesota Duluth, where his areas of interest include designing and leading self-directed team-based organizations, teamwork, and production and operations management. He received his B.S. in Chemical Engineering from the University of Maine in Orono, Maine, with a fifth year in Pulp and Paper Sciences.

INTRODUCTION

The challenges organizations face today continue to grow as a result of a rapidly changing environment, not the least of which includes the proliferation of new technology, a dynamic global marketplace, and (more recently) the threat of terrorism. Contemporary organizations must be structurally flexible, capable of adapting to changing markets, and able to compete and win on a national and frequently international scale. *Collaborative Work Systems* (CWS) provide the fundamental principles and means to meet these challenges. Collaboration and CWS are not new; they are simply the principles and practices that make organizations and teamwork succeed. There are ten major principles for successful collaboration and a set of characteristics that collaborative organizations have that effectively apply these principles. Organizations that

Michael M. Beyerlein, Sue Freedman, Craig McGee, and Linda Moran, *Beyond Teams: Building the Collaborative Organization.* San Francisco: Jossey-Bass/Pfeiffer, 2003.

fail to embrace the collaborative work systems approach exhibit a contrasting set of defining characteristics.

Managers and employees at all levels working together can outperform individuals acting alone, especially when the outcome requires a variety of creative abilities, multiple skills, careful judgments, and the knowledge and experience that different employees possess in achieving organizational goals. CWS are the means to achieve these goals and not an end in and of themselves.

RATIONALE FOR COLLABORATIVE WORK SYSTEMS

Collaborative work systems put into practice a disciplined principle-based system of collaboration necessary to be successful in a rapidly changing environment. All organizations collaborate to some extent in order to achieve their goals, including how the organization serves its customers and meets its financial objectives. CWS carry collaboration to a much higher level and therefore outperform organizations that do not consistently apply the principles of collaboration as a disciplined practice, or do not make collaboration the means to achieve business objectives and the goals of the organization.

Organizations that not only value collaborative practices, but consciously apply and nurture these practices with passion and conviction at all levels create a definite competitive advantage over organizations that simply assume collaborative practices will occur. Strategic direction and leadership at the top of the organization are paramount to achieving CWS. While team-based organizations and self-directed work systems depend on collaborative practices, these organizations may not go far enough in the degree or variety of collaboration to reach the full potential that CWS have.

Collaborative work systems are a key strategy for achieving superior business results. While employees create value through collaborative practices, their ability to perform and to be highly productive are often limited by the barriers the organization creates. These barriers stifle the collaborative practices employees are expected to have. Key employees at all levels solve problems, make and act on important decisions, invent new practices and improved methods of doing business, build relationships, and strategically plan for the future. The effectiveness of their processes and practices and the work system the employees are in determines the degree to which they reach their full potential. A high level of collaborative capacity will stimulate both formal and informal learning and enhance the effectiveness of work done at all levels.

When collaboration becomes both a strategy and competency for achieving business goals and a major part of the organizational culture, then:

- Organizational barriers to a collaborative work system are broken down.
- Employees at all levels know when and how to collaborate to achieve business results without wasting valuable time and resources.
- Managers and leaders in the organization create systems that are highly flexible, functionally adaptable, and fast to react to a changing environment.
- The waste that occurs within a functional silo and between functional silos diminishes and is replaced with a high level of cross-functional cooperation.

- Teams become accountable for their results and hold themselves to a high standard.
- The organization becomes a highly interdependent, interacting, and interconnected system of processes and functions that continuously performs at a high level.

Collaborative work systems do not require formal teams or a team-based system (i.e., an organizational arrangement where teams are the basic unit of organizational structure), but their collaborative capacity and competency are enhanced by the use of these structures. Since teams are frequently the most common form of business collaboration, the design, management, and work processes that make collaboration within and between teams successful are important features to discuss.

THE PRINCIPLES OF COLLABORATIVE ORGANIZATIONS

The ten principles of collaborative work systems are:

1. *"Focus collaboration on achieving business results."* Collaboration is necessary to achieve the goals and strategies necessary for long-term success. It is not an end in itself, but a means to an end. This principle focuses the organization on a common goal where everyone understands their role in the broader context of achieving intermediate and overall corporate objectives. When collaboration is focused on achieving business results, everyone is focused on common goals and objectives and is in the business of getting results with very few self-serving obstacles. Employees know what needs to be done and can go about doing it in an efficient and effective manner. When collaborative efforts are not focused on business results, conflicts and disagreements will occur and employees may sub-optimize their own functional areas, sometimes at the expense of achieving overall organizational goals.

2. *"Align organizational support systems to promote ownership."* This principle stems from an understanding that all systems of support must be congruent with the goals and principles of the organization. If a collaborative work system is a defined strategy to achieve the goals of the organization, then all systems must support the who, when, where, and why of collaborative practices. These systems include management systems, organizational design, performance management systems, and information and communication systems. Support systems that create a sense of ownership have a much greater chance of success in creating a competitive advantage. When these systems are aligned, employees are rewarded for acting in a predictable and consistent manner toward achieving individual, intermediate, and overall corporate goals and objectives. When it is not working, employees are sent mixed messages that collectively produce organizational chaos and poor performance.

3. *"Articulate and enforce a few strict rules."* This principle applies to the policies, practices, and methods that drive decision-making within organizations. Everyone needs to understand what needs to be done within a framework of a few highly understood rules. These rules must be consistently applied and individuals held accountable for their application. The application of this principle gives individuals and teams of individuals a common understanding of what needs to be done without limiting their ability to accomplish it. It also allows them to break down barriers and make and act on important decisions toward the accomplishment of the goals and objectives.

Organizations with too many rules suffer from inaction and an unwillingness to take risks, while an organization with too few rules struggles from a lack of direction and consistency.

4. *"Exploit the rhythm of divergence and convergence."* This principle provides a balance between creating new and exciting ways of getting the job done, and the discipline necessary to get the job done. Both of these are processes by which participants are allowed to diverge with their ideas and generate different ways of getting the job done, and also converge to a level of agreement necessary to move forward to get the job done. Managing the process of divergence and convergence is important to goal accomplishment. The process also has a rhythm that is recognizable. As collaboration within and between teams and individuals at different levels and across functional boundaries occurs, complex activities take place toward the accomplishment of the stated goals and objectives. Each cycle accomplishes an intermediate objective that allows the next step or iterative cycle to occur. When the rhythm of divergence and convergence is effectively managed, new ideas and ways of getting the job done naturally occur, while the disciplined commitment to accomplish the objective in the expected time frame is achieved.

5. *"Manage complex tradeoffs on a timely basis."* Making timely and effective decisions requires the skills, knowledge, and a process for effective decision-making. When the collaborative unit is faced with complex, interrelated, or interdependent decisions, tradeoffs frequently have to be made between contradictory criteria or information. Managing these tradeoffs for effective decision-making sometimes requires specialized skills, knowledge, and information that the collaborative unit must recognize and acquire on a timely basis. When complex decisions are made on a timely basis, the collaborative unit can move forward with increased confidence.

6. *"Create higher standards for discussion, dialogue, and information sharing."* Collaborative processes can be very complex and highly important to goal attainment. These processes must be well managed by leaders that recognize the need for good organization, coaching, and facilitation skills. Higher standards mean that participants have direct access to relevant information, expert opinions, and advice, new and improved capabilities for effective decision-making, and a sense of excitement and commitment to be involved in a CWS. When the collaborative capacity of an organization is not increased through coaching or training of the participants, decision-making suffers, deadlines and expectations are more difficult to meet, and participants seek a safe haven by sticking to their own opinions and perspectives. Getting "out of the box" and taking a risk will become a rare event.

7. *"Foster personal accountability."* When organization members are personally accountable for their own role and responsibilities in the collaborative process, the capability of the collaborative unit will improve. Accountability means that participants will build capability to achieve goals by breaking down the barriers to goal attainment, putting the goal ahead of self-serving considerations, and tackling the tasks of getting the job done with confidence, risk taking, and timeliness. Participants simply do what needs to be done and act in support of the collaborative process. When there is a lack of accountability, participants fail to acknowledge their responsibility or mistakes, and they will usually act in support of their own self-serving interests.

8. *"Align authority, information, and decision-making."* This principle means that teams and participants have all the tools, including the authority to make important decisions, the skills, knowledge, and information for effective decision-making, and the resources and support to act and carry out the decisions they make for effective goal attainment. When these are present decisions are timely, well executed, and participants are committed with a high degree of responsibility for their participation on the collaborative unit. When authority, information, and decision-making are not aligned, participants experience a loss of both support and direction, a lack of ownership in the process, and chaos or confusion when decisions and plans have to be revisited.

9. *"Treat collaboration as a disciplined process."* This principle means that CWS organizations must recognize and support the principles as a strategy for goal accomplishment. Making collaboration a disciplined process requires the skills, knowledge, and training of a critical mass of participants that can pass on their expertise in successfully conducting collaborative processes. When organizations are competent at collaboration, they are able to manage multiple interdependent and interacting processes at the same time. These organizations will have good organization skills, the ability to quickly hurdle obstacles and break down barriers, easy access to relevant information, excellent communication skills, and the ability to make good decisions and act on those decisions in a timely manner. When collaboration is not treated as a disciplined process, meetings are not very productive or goal oriented, participants are frustrated by the lack of goal accomplishment, and managers with authority may try to micromanage the activities of the collaborative unit.

10. *"Design and promote flexible organizations."* The successful organization today must be quick to respond to all sorts of changing business conditions and structurally flexible in its ability to get the work done and compete in a dynamic business environment. Flexible organizations respond with different structures, both formal and informal to maximize the speed and effectiveness of what needs to be done to be successful. The increasing complexity and dynamic nature of competing in a global marketplace requires that organizations react with different structures based on the situation. These organizations break down the barriers that traditional organizations have in a way that improves their ability to compete and respond to changing business conditions. Information and decision-making are moved to those who have to take action, rather than those who control the action of others. Flexible organizations have leaders that decentralize decision-making for maximum effectiveness and manage the organization with a high level of cross-functional capability. When organizations are structurally inflexible, their collaborative activities are less effective, they waste valuable resources, and decisions take a lot longer to make and implement.

APPLICATIONS OF THE PRINCIPLES

Manufacturing facilities produce tangible products from physical materials with the support of functionally based staff organizations. They have become flatter in organizational structure, more flexible in their ability to get the work done in many different ways, and faster to react to the marketplace and remain competitive. As manufacturing organizations integrate vertically and horizontally to achieve a competitive advantage, they have also integrated new work systems such as "team based organizations," "high performance systems," "self-reliant teams," and "socio-technical systems." When properly applied, these principle-based systems can produce superior performance. All of these systems represent changes in how work is organized and how the empowerment of employees has moved leadership down to the productive process or shop floor. As organizations become flatter and more flexible, the opportunities to collaborate become more numerous. The leadership in organizations must make clear expectations of the "how" and "when" to formally and informally collaborate. The "when" occurs when more than one person is required to make a decision and when effective implementation requires the acceptance or the decision is executed by a group of employees.

Collaboration in service settings needs to occur when the skills, knowledge, and expertise needed resides in more than one employee, when the decisions or tasks are interdependent with other employees or parts of the organization, when decisions require the acceptance of a group of employees for effective implementation, and when multiple teams or areas need to share resources or have a common understanding for goal accomplishment. On the other hand, collaboration can be wasteful when there is not good direction or leadership for collaborative processes, when the practice of "command and control" of employees makes the empowerment of employees an abstract thought, and when management fails to share important information with employees or give employees direct access to information necessary to accomplish their tasks.

New product development creates unique and creative opportunities. Expertise in functional organizations is organized into silos as opposed to product or customer-based organizing structures. Another design is the team-based model, in which integration teams oversee the coordinated efforts and assignments of new product development teams. Global pressures, the threat of declining profit margins if new products are not developed, and the time to produce new products to pre-empt the competition are challenges these organizations face. The question is when, where, and who should collaborate to maximize the use of the valuable resources. It is also important to establish the training, expectations, and the time frame for effective collaboration.

The ten principles can also be applied in "virtual work settings." *Virtual organizations* are "groups of individuals working on shared tasks while distributed across space, time and/or organizational boundaries." They are unique in that they traverse organizational and functional boundaries that exist at multiple national and sometimes international locations. The participants in virtual settings are not located at the same site, but it is still possible to apply the principles of CWS to virtual work settings.

Conclusion

Collaborative Work Systems are principle-based systems that are consciously designed and nurtured for high performance. A CWS allows the creative capacities and talents of their employees to continuously increase through knowledge sharing and mutual support.

Individuals collaborating effectively in pursuit of common goals and objectives will consistently outperform individuals acting alone or in functional silos, especially when the task requires multiple skills, knowledge, different experiences, and creative abilities. As the work and the accomplishment of tasks become more complex, flexible organizational structures and collaborative practices must be carefully thought out and executed to meet the varied challenges the organization faces. When organizations apply the ten principles of collaboration, employee ownership and involvement increases, decision-making is more consistent and execution is more effective, positional power is replaced with knowledge and leadership, and employees learn and grow at a much faster rate. The organization is also quicker to respond to the business environment, more flexible in its ability to accomplish objectives in different ways, and flatter in an organizational structure that values cross-functional competencies.

PART

VIII LEADERSHIP

The 1990s was the "decade of the leader," a theme that continues today as the first decade of the twenty-first century nears an end. Nationally, we seem to be looking for the hero who can turn us around, establish a new direction, and pull us through tough times. Organizations are searching for visionary leaders—people who by the strength of their personalities can bring about a major organizational transformation. We hear calls for charismatic, transformational, and visionary leadership. Innumerable individuals charge that the problems with the U.S. economy, declining organizational productivity, and lost ground in worldwide competitive markets are largely a function of poor management and the lack of good organizational leadership.

Several years ago the concept of emotional intelligence (EI) emerged in the popular press. It was suggested that EI is an important leader characteristic, contributing to the leader's ability to manage more effectively not only his or her own behavior but also relationships with followers. In *Primal Leadership*, Daniel Goleman (author of *Emotional Intelligence* and *Working with Emotional Intelligence*), Richard Boyatzis, and Annie McKee draw upon their examination of EI and its role in the leadership process. A central question in their work asks how emotional intelligence drives organizational performance, that is, how does the EI of the leader spread through the organization such that it affects the bottom line? In answering this question, they highlight the contagiousness of emotions. Leaders whose personalities exude emotion—energy and enthusiasm—spread the same to their followers. Leaders whose personalities emit negativity transfer the same to their followers. Goleman and his colleagues argue that positive emotions are associated with organizational success, while negativity contributes to organizational hardships.

Daniel Goleman is the co-director of a consortium conducting research on emotional intelligence at Rutgers University; Richard Boyatzis is on the faculty at Case Western Reserve University; and Annie McKee serves on the faculty in the School of Education at the University of Pennsylvania. In recent years all three authors have conducted research on EI within the context of many organizations.

Jim Collins, in *Good to Great*, studied the 11 companies (out of 1,435) that had made a major transition from many years of mediocrity to many subsequent years of outstanding achievements. He discovered a series of contributors to success, including a culture of discipline, technology accelerators, a focus on doing things well, the importance of breakthrough momentum, the willingness to confront brutal reality while maintaining hope, and managing people well. In addition, he discovered that the great firms were typically led by "Level 5" executives—those who combined modesty/humility with a fearless will.

Jim Collins operates a management research laboratory in Boulder, Colorado. He previously held positions at McKinsey & Company and Hewlett-Packard, and was on the faculty at Stanford University's Graduate School of Business. He is the co-author of *Built to Last*, *Beyond Entrepreneurship*, and *Good to Great and the Social Sectors*.

Leadership for Everyone, by Peter J. Dean, introduces the L.E.A.D.E.R.S. Method. This acronym reminds managers to Listen to learn, Empathize with emotions, Attend to aspirations, Diagnose and detail, Engage for good ends, Respond with respectfulness, and Speak with specificity. Dean suggests that leadership self-development is possible if individuals use their everyday opportunities to practice these seven skills. However, it requires personal courage, honesty, humility, and persistent commitment to make it work. Peter Dean holds the O. Alfred Granum Chair in Management at The American College. He is the recipient of numerous awards for teaching excellence, the author of several papers, and a consultant to many Fortune 500 companies.

Barbara Kellerman received her Ph.D. from Yale University and subsequently held professorships at Fordham, Tufts, Fairleigh Dickinson, and George Washington Universities. She is currently the James MacGregor Burns Lecturer in Public Leadership at Harvard University's Kennedy School of Government. Before writing *Bad Leadership*, she published three previous books on leadership in the public sector. Her next two writing efforts will focus on followership and women leaders.

Bad Leadership dispels the simplistic notion that all leadership is positive. Bad leaders can be either ineffective (inappropriate means or ends) or unethical (failure to distinguish right and wrong). Kellerman identifies seven types of bad leadership: incompetent, rigid, intemperate, callous, corrupt, insular, and evil. She proceeds to identify a wide variety of ways in which leaders can improve their behavior, and tactics for followers to engage in self-help. In short, bad leaders can still become good leaders if they are willing to attempt making personal changes.

1

PRIMAL LEADERSHIP

DANIEL GOLEMAN, RICHARD E. BOYATZIS,
AND ANNIE MCKEE

SUMMARY PREPARED BY JOHN KRATZ

John Kratz is an instructor in the Labovitz School of Business and Economics at the University of Minnesota Duluth. He teaches business-to-business marketing, advertising and marketing communications, international marketing, and fundamentals of selling. He has over 20 years of experience working in consumer packaged goods sales and marketing, having served in a variety of business development and marketing management positions with Gage Marketing, MCI, Actmedia, The Pillsbury Company, and Land O'Lakes, Inc. His interest in emotional intelligence research lies in its potential application for improving sales force performance. He holds an M.B.A. from the University of Minnesota's Carlson School of Management.

INTRODUCTION

The ever-accelerating rate of change brought on by a globalizing world economy, a diversifying workforce, and technological innovation makes enormous demands on organizational leaders desiring to instill widespread change and encourage new organizational learning. Extensive field research indicates that most executive education and leadership development efforts fail to produce the anticipated results. The reason is not only because of *how* they are implemented, but also because of what they do *not* do. *For the most part, leadership-training processes do not take into account the power that emotion plays in influencing individual and organizational behavior.*

Leadership effectiveness is rooted in the ability to perceive, identify, and successfully manage the emotional states of ourselves as well as those of others. This is the essence of *primal leadership.*

Daniel Goleman, Richard Boyatzis, and Annie McKee, *Primal Leadership: Realizing the Power of Emotional Intelligence.* Boston: Harvard Business School Press, 2002.

WHAT IS EMOTIONAL INTELLIGENCE?

Emotional intelligence (EI) is a set of competencies that distinguish how people manage feelings and interactions with others. It is the ability to identify one's own emotions, as well as those of one's co-workers or employees. EI is separate from, but complementary to, academic intelligence (i.e., cognitive capacities measured by IQ). Emotional intelligence skills such as empathy and self-awareness are synergistic with such cognitive skills as analytical and technical proficiencies. Effective leaders have competency in both sets of skills. EI competencies are learned abilities rather than innate characteristics, with each one uniquely contributing to leader effectiveness.

EMOTIONAL INTELLIGENCE AND ASSOCIATED COMPETENCIES

EI consists of two sets of competencies, and four different domain areas. *Personal* competencies are those that determine how effectively people manage themselves, and *social* competencies are those that determine how effectively they manage their interpersonal relationships. The four domains of EI include self-awareness, self-management, social awareness, and relationship management. Each element influences individual, group, and organization performance. *Self-awareness and self-management are personal competence components, while social awareness and relationship management are social competence components.*

Self-Awareness
- **Emotional self-awareness:** Reading one's own emotions and recognizing their impact; using "gut senseé" to guide decisions.
- **Accurate self-assessment:** Knowing one's strengths and limits.
- **Self-confidence:** Having a sense of one's self-worth and capabilities.

Self-Management
- **Emotional self-control:** Keeping disruptive emotions and impulses under control.
- **Transparency:** Displaying honesty and integrity; trustworthiness.
- **Adaptability:** Showing flexibility in adapting to new situations or overcoming obstacles.
- **Achievement:** Demonstrating the drive to improve performance to meet inner standards of excellence.
- **Initiative:** Being ready and willing to act and seize opportunities.
- **Optimism:** Looking for, and seeing, the upside in events.

Social Awareness
- **Empathy:** Sensing others' emotions, understanding their perspective, and taking an active interest in their concerns.
- **Organizational awareness:** Reading the currents, decision networks, and politics at the organizational level.
- **Service:** Recognizing and meeting follower, client, or customer needs.

Relationship Management
- **Inspirational leadership:** Guiding and motivating with a compelling vision.
- **Influence:** Possessing a range of tactics for persuasion.

- **Developing others:** Bolstering others' abilities through feedback and guidance.
- **Change catalyst:** Initiating, managing, and leading in a new direction.
- **Conflict management:** Resolving disagreements.
- **Building bonds:** Cultivating and maintaining a web of relationships.
- **Teamwork and collaboration:** Cooperating with others and building effective teams.

EMOTIONS: THE PRIMAL DIMENSION OF LEADERSHIP

Some managers may view emotions and moods as trivial, but few would discount that they influence people's behaviors as they work with others. At its most basic level, the primal task of leadership is emotional—to generate good feelings in those they lead. Leaders who cannot distinguish and guide emotions in the right direction may fail in achieving intended outcomes when working with other people.

Resonant leaders are attuned to people's feelings and move them in a positive emotional direction. For example, a resonant leader may consciously choose to use self-deprecating humor to skillfully defuse tense situations or use warmth and empathy to communicate bad news. Resonance comes naturally to emotionally intelligent leaders. An EI leader makes work more meaningful for others by effectively connecting with others at an emotional level, thereby creating a more supportive and nurturing work environment.

The opposite of resonant leadership is *dissonant leadership:* being out of touch with people's feelings. Dissonant leaders alienate their colleagues because they lack well-developed personal and social competency skills.

THE NEUROANATOMY OF LEADERSHIP

Research reveals physical bases in the brain for people's interpersonal behaviors. The two types of intelligence, EI and IQ, are controlled in different parts of the brain. Cognitive and analytical intellect is controlled by the neocortex, the most recently evolved layers at the top of the brain, while the center of control for emotions is the limbic brain, the more primitive subcortex region of the brain. Although these neural regions managing rational thought and emotion are found in different areas of the brain, they have closely intertwined connections. *Understanding this interwoven relationship provides the foundation for understanding the concept of primal leadership.*

The limbic brain commandeers the rational region of the brain during emergencies to ensure safety or survival (i.e., alert drivers instantaneously brake sharply to avoid hitting a deer that jumps out in front of their car). The area of the brain responsible for this "fight or flight" response is the amygdala. The amygdala serves as an emotional radar, always on the alert for emotional emergencies. This subconscious survival mechanism, developed over 100 million years of human evolution, can be so overriding that it often "hijacks" our emotional response to present-day threats (i.e., when someone cuts us off while driving we tend to experience rage and may temporarily act out of character).

Extensive circuitry between the amygdala and the prefrontal area of the brain monitors emotional responses (feelings) to sensory perceptions, serving as a regulator that safeguards against potentially self-defeating behavior (i.e., recognizing that you need to take a couple of deep breaths before saying something you might regret).

Emotionally intelligent leaders monitor and regulate their feelings, and make effective decisions about how best to respond in any given social situation.

INADEQUECIES OF TRADITIONAL LEADERSHIP TRAINING

The problem with the content of most leadership training programs is that they are directed primarily at the rational-thinking part of the brain. That is, most leadership training, by its very design, limits potential learning because it ignores the emotional centers of the brain. Leadership training should address both the rational and emotional facets.

Some of the cited shortfalls of traditional leadership training include:

- Attempting to change only the person and ignoring the surrounding emotional culture.
- Driving the change process from the wrong organization level. Transformative leadership development must start at the top and must be viewed as a strategic priority.
- Ignoring many of the EI competencies.

The most successful leadership development initiatives are based on the idea that meaningful change occurs through a comprehensive process involving individuals in the organization, the teams in which they work, and the organization's culture.

Effective leadership development processes should be focused on intellectual and emotional learning. This can, in part, be achieved through the use of active participatory work, experiential learning and coaching, team-based simulations, and a mix of learning techniques.

SIX LEADERSHIP APPROACHES

Research drawn from EI assessments of nearly 4,000 executives identifies six distinct leadership styles requisite for creating resonance within organizations. The most effective leaders use one or more of these approaches, skillfully switching between the various styles depending on their analysis of the situation. The six distinct leadership styles, how they create resonance, and when they are best deployed are outlined below.

Visionary Leadership
- Builds resonance by moving people toward the firm's mission.
- Most effective when a firm needs a new vision or direction.

Coaching Leadership
- Connects what a person wants with the organization's goals.
- Best used to increase employee performance by building long-term capabilities.

Affiliative Leadership
- Creates harmony by connecting people to each other.
- Most appropriate for motivating employees during stressful times.

Democratic Leadership
- Gets commitment by valuing people's input and participation.
- Invaluable for building consensus and obtaining valuable input from employees.

Pacesetting Leadership
- Builds resonance by setting challenging goals.
- Most effective to achieve superior results from a motivated and competent team.

Commanding Leadership
- Reduces fears by providing clear direction during an emergency.
- Most appropriately used during a crisis or to jump-start a turnaround.

Conclusion

Primal leadership is a fundamental determinant of organizational effectiveness and superior business performance. Managers leading solely using their expertise and intellect miss a vital component of leadership. Neurological research indicates that the four core EI competencies are not innate talents; they are learned and teachable abilities, each of which can contribute to making leaders more effective. The most effective leaders skillfully switch between one or more of the six distinct approaches of EI leadership. Primal leadership operates best through leaders who create resonance by creating an emotional climate nurturing innovation, performance, and lasting customer relationships.

2

GOOD TO GREAT

JAMES C. COLLINS

W hat catapults a company from merely good to truly great? A five-year research project searched for the answer to that question, and its discoveries ought to change the way we think about leadership. The most powerfully transformative executives possess a paradoxical mixture of personal humility and professional will. They are timid and ferocious. Shy and fearless. They are rare—and unstoppable.

In 1971, a seemingly ordinary man names Darwin E. Smith was named chief executive of Kimberly-Clark, a stodgy old paper company whose stock had fallen 36 percent behind the general market during the previous 20 years. Smith, the company's mild-mannered in-house lawyer, wasn't so sure the board had made the right choice—a feeling that was reinforced when a Kimberly-Clark director pulled him aside and reminded him that he lacked some of the qualifications for the position. But CEO he was, and CEO he remained for 20 years.

What a 20 years it was. In that period, Smith created a stunning transformation at Kimberly-Clark, turning it into the leading consumer paper products company in the world. Under his stewardship, the company beat its rivals Scott Paper and Procter & Gamble. And in doing so, Kimberly-Clark generated cumulative stock returns that were 4.1 times greater than those of the general market, outperforming venerable companies such as Hewlett-Packard, 3M, Coca-Cola, and General Electric.

Smith's turnaround of Kimberly-Clark is one of the best examples in the twentieth century of a leader taking a company from merely good to truly great. And yet few people—even ardent students of business history—have heard of Darwin Smith. He probably would have liked it that way. Smith is a classic example of a *Level 5 leader*—an individual who blends extreme personal humility and intense professional will. According to our five-year research study, executives who possess this paradoxical combination of traits are catalysts for the statistically rare event of transforming a good company into a great one. (The research is described in Exhibit 1, "One Question, Five Years, Eleven Companies.")

"Level 5" refers to the highest level in a hierarchy of executive capabilities that we identified during our research. Leaders at the other four levels in the hierarchy can produce high degrees of success but not enough to elevate companies from mediocrity

◆ EXHIBIT 1 ◆

One Question, Five Years, Eleven Companies

The Level 5 discovery derives from a research project that began in 1996, when my research teams and I set out to answer one question: can a good company become a great company and, if so, how? Most great companies grew up with superb parents—people like George Merck, David Packard, and Walt Disney—who instilled greatness early on. But what about the vast majority of companies that wake up part-way through life and realize that they're good but not great?

To answer that question, we looked for companies that had shifted from good performance to great performance—and sustained it. We identified comparison companies that had failed to make that sustained shift. We then studied the contrast between the two groups to discover common variables that distinguish those who make and sustain a shift from those who could have but didn't.

More precisely, we searched for a specific pattern: cumulative stock returns at or below the general stock market for 15 years, punctuated by a transition point, then cumulative returns at least three times the market over the next 15 years. (See the graph.) We used data from the University of Chicago Center for Research in Security Prices, adjusted for stock splits, and all dividends re-invested. The shift had to be distinct from the industry; if the whole industry showed the same shift, we'd drop the company. We began with 1,435 companies that

(continued)

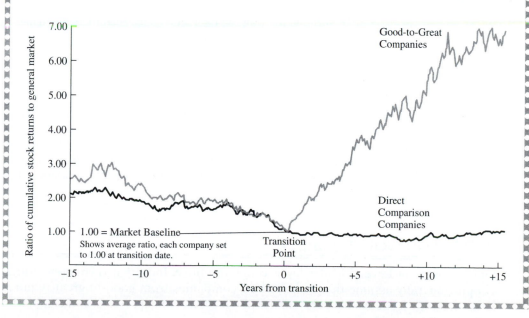

(continued)

appeared on the *Fortune* 500 from 1965 to 1995; we found 11 good-to-great examples. That's not a sample; that's the total number that jumped all our hurdles and passed into the study.

Those that made the cut averaged cumulative stock returns 6.9 times the general stock market for the 15 years after the point of transition. To put that in perspective, General Electric under Jack Welch outperformed the general stock market by 2.8:1 during his tenure from 1986 to 2000. A dollar invested in a mutual fund of the good-to-great companies in 1965 grew to $420 by 2000—compared to $56 in the general stock market. These are remarkable numbers, made all the more so by the fact that they came from previously unremarkable companies.

For each good-to-great example, we selected the best direct comparison, based on similarity of business, size, age, customers, and performance leading up to the transition. We also constructed a set of six "unsustained" comparisons (companies that showed a short-lived shift but then fell off) to address the question of sustainability. To be conservative, we consistently picked comparison companies that if anything, were in better shape than the good-to-great companies were in the years just before the transition.

With 22 research associates working in groups of four to six at a time from 1996 to 2000, our study involved a wide range of both qualitative and quantitative analyses. On the qualitative front, we collected nearly 6,000 articles, conducted 87 interviews with key executives, analyzed companies' internal strategy documents, and culled through analysts' reports. On the quantitative front, we ran financial metrics, examined executive compensation, compared patterns of management turnover, quantified company layoffs and restructurings, and calculated the effect of acquisitions and divestitures on companies' stocks. We then synthesized the results to identify the drivers of good-to-great transformations. One was Level 5 leadership.

Since only 11 companies qualified as good-to-great, a research finding had to meet a stiff standard before we would deem it significant. Every component in the final framework showed up in all 11 good-to-great companies during the transition era, regardless of industry (from steel to banking), transition decade (from the 1950s to the 1990s), circumstances (from plodding along to dire crisis), or size (from tens of millions to tens of billions). Additionally, every component had to show up in less than 30 percent of the comparison companies during the relevant years. Level 5 easily made it into the framework as one of the strongest, most consistent contrasts between the good-to-great and the comparison companies.

---

to sustained excellence. (For more details about this concept, see Exhibit 2.) And while Level 5 leadership is not the only requirement for transforming a good company into a great one—other factors include getting the right people on the bus (and the wrong people off the bus) and creating a culture of discipline—our research shows it to be essential. Good-to-great transformations don't happen without Level 5 leaders at the helm. They just don't.

NOT WHAT YOU WOULD EXPECT

Our discovery of Level 5 leadership is counterintuitive. Indeed, it is countercultural. People generally assume that transforming companies from good to great requires larger-than-life leaders—big personalities like Iacocca, Dunlap, Welch, and Gault, who make headlines and become celebrities.

◆ EXHIBIT 2 ◆

The Level 5 Hierarchy

The Level 5 leader sits on top of a hierarchy of capabilities and is, according to our research, a necessary requirement for transforming an organization from good to great. But what lies beneath? Four other layers, each one appropriate in its own right but none with the power of Level 5. Individuals do not need to proceed sequentially through each level of the hierarchy to reach the top, but to be a full-fledged Level 5 requires the capabilities of all the lower levels, plus the special characteristics of Level 5.

LEVEL 5 EXECUTIVE
Builds enduring greatness
through a paradoxical combination
of personal humility plus professional will.

LEVEL 4 EFFECTIVE LEADER
Catalyzes commitment to and vigorous pursuit
of a clear and compelling vision; stimulates
the group to high performance standards.

LEVEL 3 COMPETENT MANAGER
Organizes people and resources toward the effective
and efficient pursuit of predetermined objectives.

LEVEL 2 CONTRIBUTING TEAM MEMBER
Contributes to the achievement of group
objectives; works effectively with others in a group setting.

LEVEL 1 HIGHLY CAPABLE INDIVIDUAL
Makes productive contributions through talent, knowledge,
skills, and good work habits.

Compared with those CEOs, Darwin Smith seems to have come from Mars. Shy, unpretentious, even awkward, Smith shunned attention. When a journalist asked him to describe his management style, Smith just stared back at the scribe from the other side of his thick black-rimmed glasses. He was dressed unfashionably, like a farm boy wearing his first J. C. Penney suit. Finally, after a long and uncomfortable silence, he said, "Eccentric." Needless to say, the *Wall Street Journal* did not publish a splashy feature on Darwin Smith.

But if you were to consider Smith soft or meek, you would be terribly mistaken. His lack of pretense was coupled with a fierce, even stoic, resolve toward life. Smith grew up on an Indiana farm and put himself through night school at Indiana University by working the day shift at International Harvester. One day, he lost a finger on the job. The story goes that he went to class that evening and returned to work that very next day. Eventually, this poor but determined Indiana farm boy earned admission to Harvard Law School.

He showed the same iron will when he was at the helm of Kimberly-Clark. Indeed, two months after Smith became CEO, doctors diagnosed him with nose and throat cancer and told him he had less than a year to live. He duly informed the board of his illness but said he had no plans to die anytime soon. Smith held to his demanding work schedule while commuting weekly from Wisconsin to Houston for radiation therapy. He lived 25 more years, 20 of them as CEO.

Smith's ferocious resolve was crucial to the rebuilding of Kimberly-Clark, especially when he made the most dramatic decision in the company's history: sell the mills.

To explain: Shortly after he took over, Smith and his team had concluded that the company's traditional core business—coated paper—was doomed to mediocrity. Its economics were bad and the competition weak. But, they reasoned, if Kimberly-Clark was thrust into the fire of the *consumer* paper products business, better economics and world-class competition like Procter & Gamble would force it to achieve greatness or perish.

And so, like the general who burned the boats upon landing on enemy soil, leaving his troops to succeed or die, Smith announced that Kimberly-Clark would sell its mills—even the namesake mill in Kimberly, Wisconsin. All proceeds would be thrown into the consumer business, with investments in brands like Huggies diapers and Kleenex tissues. The business media called the move stupid, and Wall Street analysts downgraded the stock. But Smith never wavered. Twenty-five years later, Kimberly-Clark owned Scott Paper and beat Procter & Gamble in six of eight product categories. In retirement, Smith reflected on his exceptional performance, saying simply, "I never stopped trying to become qualified for the job."

NOT WHAT WE EXPECTED EITHER

We'll look in depth at Level 5 leadership, but first let's set an important context for our findings: we were not looking for Level 5 or anything like it. Our original question was can a good company become a great one, and, if so, how? In fact, I gave the research teams explicit instructions to downplay the role of top executives in their analyses of this question so we wouldn't slip into the simplistic "credit the leader" or "blame the leader" thinking that is so common today.

But Level 5 found us. Over the course of the study, research teams kept saying, "We can't ignore the top executives even if we want to. There is something consistently unusual about them." I would push back, arguing, "The comparison companies also had leaders. So what's different here?" Back and forth the debate raged. Finally, as should always be the case, the data won. The executives at companies that went from good to great and sustained that performance for 15 years or more were all cut from the same cloth—one remarkably different from that which produced executives at the comparison companies in our study. It didn't matter whether the company was in crisis or steady state, consumer or industrial, offering services or products. It didn't matter when the transition took place or how big the company. The successful organizations all had a Level 5 leader at the time of transition.

Furthermore, the absence of Level 5 leadership showed up consistently across the comparison companies. The point: Level 5 is an empirical finding, not an ideological one. And that's important to note, given how much the Level 5 finding contradicts not only conventional wisdom but much of management theory to date. (For more about our findings on good-to-great transformations, see Exhibit 3.)

Not by Level 5 Alone

Level 5 leadership is an essential factor for taking a company from good to great, but it's not the only one. Our research uncovered multiple factors that deliver companies to greatness. And it is the combined package—Level 5 plus these other drivers—that takes companies beyond unremarkable. There is a symbiotic relationship between Level 5 and the rest of our findings: Level 5 enables implementation of the other findings, and practicing the other findings may help you get to Level 5. We've already talked about who Level 5 leaders are; the rest of our findings describe what they do. Here is a brief look at some of the other key findings.

First Who: We expected that good-to-great leaders would start with the vision and strategy. Instead, they attended to people first, strategy second. They got the right people on the bus, moved the wrong people off, ushered the right people to the right seats—and then they figured out where to drive it.

Stockdale Paradox: This finding is named after Admiral James Stockdale, winner of the Medal of Honor, who survived seven years in a Vietcong POW camp by hanging on to two contradictory beliefs: his life couldn't be worse at the moment, and his life would someday be better than ever. Like Stockdale, people at the good-to-great companies in our research confronted the most brutal facts of their current reality—yet simultaneously maintained absolute faith that they would prevail in the end. And they held both disciplines—faith and facts—at the same time, all the time.

Buildup-Breakthrough Flywheel: good-to-great transformations do not happen overnight or in one big leap. Rather, the process resembles relentlessly pushing a giant, heavy flywheel in one direction. At first, pushing it gets the flywheel to turn once. With consistent effort, it goes two turns, then five, then ten, building increasing momentum until—bang!—the wheel hits the breakthrough point, and the momentum really kicks in. Our comparison companies never sustained the kind of breakthrough momentum that the good-to-great companies did; instead, they lurched back and forth with radical change programs, reactionary moves, and restructurings.

The Hedgehog Concept: In a famous essay, philosopher and scholar Isaiah Berlin described two approaches to thought and life using a simple parable: The fox knows a little about many things, but the hedgehog knows only one big thing very well. The fox is complex; the hedgehog simple. And the hedgehog wins. Our research shows that breakthroughs require a simple, hedgehog-like understanding of three intersecting circles: what a company can be the best in the world at, how its economics work best, and what best ignites the passions of its people. Breakthroughs happen when you get the hedgehog concept and become systematic and consistent with it, eliminating virtually anything that does not fit in the three circles.

Technology Accelerators: The good-to-great companies had a paradoxical relationship with technology. On the one hand, they assiduously avoided jumping on new technology bandwagons. On the other, they were pioneers

(continued)

(continued)

in the application of carefully selected technologies, making bold, far-sighted investments in those that directly linked to their hedgehog concept. Like turbo-charges, these technology accelerators create an explosion in flywheel momentum.

A Culture of Discipline: When you look across the good-to-great transformations, they consistently display three forms of discipline: disciplined people, disciplined thought, and disciplined action. When you have disciplined people, you don't need hierarchy. When you have disciplined thought, you don't need bureaucracy. When you have disciplined action, you don't need excessive controls. When you combine a culture of discipline with an ethic of entrepreneurship, you get the magical alchemy of great performance.

HUMILITY + WILL = LEVEL 5

Level 5 leaders are a study in a duality: modest and willful, shy and fearless. To grasp this concept, consider Abraham Lincoln, who never let his ego get in the way of his ambition to create an enduring great nation. Author Henry Adams called him "a quiet, peaceful, shy figure." But those who thought Lincoln's understated manner signaled weakness in the man found themselves terribly mistaken—to the scale of 250,000 Confederate and 360,000 Union lives, including Lincoln's own.

It might be a stretch to compare the 11 Level 5 CEOs in our research to Lincoln, but they did display the same kind of duality. Take Colman M. Mockler, CEO of Gillette from 1975 to 1991. Mockler, who faced down three takeover attempts, was a reserved, gracious man with a gentle, almost patrician manner. Despite epic battles with raiders—he took on Ronald Perelman twice and the former Coniston Partners once—he never lost his shy, courteous style. At the height of the crisis, he maintained a calm business-as-usual demeanor, dispensing first with ongoing business before turning to the takeover.

And yet, those who mistook Mockler's outward modesty as a sign of inner weakness were beaten in the end. In one proxy battle, Mockler and other senior executives called thousands of investors, one by one, to win their votes. Mockler simply would not give in. He chose to fight for the future greatness of Gillette even though he could have pocketed millions by flipping his stock.

Consider the consequences had Mockler capitulated. If a share-flipper had accepted the full 44 percent price premium offered by Perelman and then invested those shares in the general market for 10 years, he still would have come out 64 percent behind a shareholder who stayed with Mockler and Gillette. If Mockler had given up the fight, it's likely that none of us would be shaving with Sensor, Lady Sensor, or the Mach III—and hundreds of millions of people would have a more painful battle with daily stubble.

Sadly, Mockler never had the chance to enjoy the full fruits of his efforts. In January 1991, Gillette received an advance copy of *Forbes*. The cover featured an artist's rendition of the publicity-shy Mockler standing on a mountaintop, holding a giant razor above his head in a triumphant pose. Walking back to his office, just minutes after seeing his public acknowledgment of his 16 years of struggle, Mockler crumpled to the floor and died from a massive heart attack.

Even if Mockler had known he would die in office, he could not have changed his approach. His placid persona hid an inner intensity, a dedication to making anything he touched the best—not just because of what he would get but because he couldn't imagine doing it any other way. Mockler could not give up the company to those who would destroy it, any more than Lincoln would risk losing the chance to build an enduring great nation.

A COMPELLING MODESTY

The Mockler story illustrates the modesty typical of Level 5 leaders. (For a summary of Level 5 traits, see Exhibit 4.) Indeed, throughout our interviews with such executives, we were struck by the way they talked about themselves—or rather, didn't talk about themselves. They'd go on and on about the company and the contributions of other executives, but they would instinctively deflect discussion about their own role. When pressed to talk about themselves, they'd say things like, "I hope I'm not sounding like a big shot," or "I don't think I can take much credit for what happened. We were blessed with marvelous people." One Level 5 leader even asserted, "There are lot of people in this company who could do my job better than I do."

By contrast, consider the courtship of personal celebrity by the comparison CEOs. Scott Paper, the comparison company to Kimberly-Clark, hired Al Dunlap as CEO—a

---

◆ EXHIBIT 4 ◆

The Yin and Yang of Level 5

Personal Humility

Demonstrates a compelling modesty, shunning public adulation; never boastful.

Acts with quiet, calm determination; relies principally on inspired standards, not inspiring charisma, to motivate.

Channels ambition into the company, not the self; sets up successors for even more greatness in the next generation.

Looks in the mirror, not out the window, to apportion responsibility for poor results, never blaming other people, external factors, or bad luck.

Professional Will

Creates superb results, a clear catalyst in the transition from good to great.

Demonstrates an unwavering resolve to do whatever must be done to produce the best long-term results, no matter how difficult.

Sets the standard of building an enduring great company; will settle for nothing less.

Looks out the windows, not in the mirror, to apportion credit for the success of the company—to other people, external factors, and good luck.

man who would tell anyone who would listen (and many who would have preferred not to) about his accomplishments. After 19 months atop Scott Paper, Dunlap said in *Business Week:* "The Scott story will go down in the annals of American business history as one of the most successful, quickest turnarounds ever. It makes other turnarounds pale by comparison." He personally accrued $100 million for 603 days of work at Scott Paper—about $165,000 per day—largely by slashing the workforce, halving the R&D budget, and putting the company on growth steroids in preparation for sale. After selling off the company and pocketing his quick millions, Dunlap wrote an autobiography in which he boastfully dubbed himself "Rambo in pinstripes." It's hard to imagine Darwin Smith thinking, "Hey, that Rambo character reminds me of me," let alone stating it publicly.

Granted, the Scott Paper story is one of the more dramatic in our study, but it's not an isolated case. In more than two-thirds of the comparison companies, we noted the presence of a gargantuan ego that contributed to the demise or continued mediocrity of the company. We found this pattern particularly strong in the unsustained comparison companies—the companies that would show a shift in performance under a talented yet egocentric Level 4 leader, only to decline in later years.

Lee Iacocca, for example, saved Chrysler from the brink of catastrophe, performing one of the most celebrated (and deservedly so) turnarounds in U.S. business history. The automaker's stock rose 2.9 times higher than the general market about halfway through his tenure. But then Iacocca diverted his attention to transforming himself. He appeared regularly on talk shows like the *Today Show* and *Larry King Live,* starred in more than 80 commercials, entertained the idea of running for president of the United States, and promoted his autobiography, which sold 7 million copies worldwide. Iacocca's personal stock soared, but Chrysler's stock fell 31 percent below the market in the second half of his tenure.

And once Iacocca had accumulated all the fame and perks, he found it difficult to leave center stage. He postponed his retirement so many times that Chrysler's insiders began to joke that Iacocca stood for "I Am Chairman of Chrysler Corporation Always." When he finally retired, he demanded that the board continue to provide private jet and stock options. Later, he joined forces with noted takeover artist Kirk Kerkorian to launch a hostile bid for Chrysler. (It failed.) Iacocca did make one final brilliant decision: He picked a modest yet determined man—perhaps even a Level 5— as his successor. Bob Eaton rescued Chrysler from its second near-death crisis in a decade and set the foundation for a more enduring corporate transition.

AN UNWAVERING RESOLVE

Besides extreme humility, Level 5 leaders also display tremendous professional will. When George Cain became CEO of Abbott Laboratories, it was a drowsy family-controlled business, sitting at the bottom quartile of the pharmaceutical industry, living off its cash cow, erythromycin. Cain was a typical Level 5 leader in his lack of pretense; he didn't have the kind of inspiring personality that would galvanize the company. But he had something much more powerful: inspired standards. He could not stand mediocrity in any form and was utterly intolerant of anyone who would accept that idea that good is good enough. For the next 14 years, he relentlessly imposed his will for greatness on Abbott Labs.

Among Cain's first tasks was to destroy one of the root causes of Abbott's middling performance: nepotism. By systematically rebuilding both the board and the executive team with the best people he could find, Cain made his statement. Family ties no longer mattered. If you couldn't become the best executive in the industry, within your span of responsibility, you would lose your paycheck.

Such near-ruthless rebuilding might be expected from an outsider brought in to turn the company around, but Cain was an 18-year insider—and a part of the family, the son of a previous president. Holiday gatherings were probably tense for a few years in the Cain clan—"Sorry I had to fire you. Want another slice of turkey?"—but in the end, family members were pleased with the performance of their stock. Cain had set in motion a profitable growth machine. From its transition in 1974 to 2000, Abbott created shareholder returns that beat the market 4.5:1, outperforming industry superstars Merck and Pfizer by a factor of two.

Another good example of iron-willed Level 5 leadership comes from Charles R. "Cork" Walgreen III, who transformed dowdy Walgreens into a company that outperformed the stock market 16:1 from its transition in 1975 to 2000. After years of dialogue and debate within his executive team about what to do with Walgreens' food-service operations, this CEO sensed the team had finally reached a watershed: The company's brightest future lay in convenient drugstores, not in food service. Dan Jorndt, who succeeded Walgreen in 1988, describes what happened next:

> Cork said at one of our planning committee meetings, "Okay, now I am going to draw the line in the sand. We are going to be out of the restaurant business completely in five years." At the time we had more than 500 restaurants. You could have heard a pin drop. He said, "I want to let everybody know the clock is ticking." Six months later we were at our next planning committee meeting and someone mentioned just in passing that we had only five years to be out of the restaurant business. Cork was not a real vociferous fellow. He sort of tapped on the table and said, "Listen, you now have four and a half years. I said you had five years six months ago. Now you've got four and a half years." Well, that next day things really clicked into gear for winding down our restaurant business. Cork never wavered. He never doubted. He never second guessed.

Like Darwin Smith selling the mills at Kimberly-Clark, Cork Walgreen required stoic resolve to make his decisions. Food service was not the largest part of the business, although it did add substantial profits to the bottom line. The real problem was more emotional than financial. Walgreens had, after all, invented the malted milk shake, and food service had been a long-standing family tradition dating back to Cork's grandfather. Not only that, some food-service outlets were even named after the CEO—for example, a restaurant chain named Cork's. But no matter, if Walgreen had to fly in the face of family tradition in order to refocus on the one arena in which Walgreens could be the best in the world—convenient drugstores—and terminate everything else that would not produce great results, then Cork would do it. Quietly, doggedly, simply.

One final, yet compelling, note on our findings about Level 5: Because Level 5 leaders have ambition not for themselves but for their companies, they routinely select superb successors. Level 5 leaders want to see their companies become even more successful in the next generation, comfortable with the idea that most people won't even know that the roots of that success trace back to them. As one Level 5 CEO said, "I want to look from my porch, see the company as one of the great companies in the world someday, and be able to say, 'I used to work there.' " By contrast, Level 4 leaders often fail to set up the company for enduring success—after all, what better testament to your own personal greatness than that the place falls apart after you leave?

In more than three-quarters of the comparison companies, we found executives who set up their successors for failure, chose weak successors, or both. Consider the case of Rubbermaid, which grew from obscurity to become one of *Fortune*'s most admired companies—and then, just as quickly, disintegrated into such sorry shape that it had to be acquired by Newell.

The architect of this remarkable story was a charismatic and brilliant leader named Stanley C. Gault, whose name became synonymous in the late 1980s with the company's success. Across the 312 articles collected by our research team about Rubbermaid, Gault comes through as a hard-driving, egocentric executive. In one article, he responds to the accusation of being a tyrant with the statement, "Yes, but I'm a sincere tyrant." In another, drawn directly from his own comments on leading change, the word "I" appears 44 times, while the word "we" appears 16 times. Of course, Gault had every reason to be proud of his executive success: Rubbermaid generated 40 consecutive quarters of earnings growth under his leadership—an impressive performance, to be sure, and one that deserves respect.

But Gault did not leave behind a company that would be great without him. His chosen successor lasted a year on the job and the next in line faced a management team so shallow that he had to temporarily shoulder four jobs while scrambling to identify a new number-two executive. Gault's successors struggled not only with a management void but also with strategic voids that would eventually bring the company to its knees.

Of course, you might say—as one *Fortune* article did—that the fact that Rubbermaid fell apart after Gault left proves his greatness as a leader. Gault was a tremendous Level 4 leader, perhaps one of the best in the last 50 years. But he was not at Level 5, and that is one crucial reason why Rubbermaid went from good to great for a brief, shining moment and then just as quickly went from great to irrelevant.

THE WINDOW AND THE MIRROR

As part of our research, we interviewed Alan L. Wurtzel, the Level 5 leader responsible for turning Circuit City from a ramshackle company on the edge of bankruptcy into one of America's most successful electronics retailers. In the 15 years after its transition date in 1982, Circuit City outperformed the market 18.5:1.

We asked Wurtzel to list the top five factors in his company's transformation, ranked by importance. His number one factor? Luck. "We were in a great industry, with the wind at our backs." But wait a minute, we retorted, Silo—your comparison company—was in the same industry, with the same wind, and bigger sails. The conversation went back and forth, with Wurtzel refusing to take much credit for the transition, preferring to attribute it largely to just being in the right place at the right time. Later, when we asked him to discuss the factors that would sustain a good-to-great transformation, he said, "The first thing that comes to mind is luck. I was lucky to find the right successor."

Luck. What an odd factor to talk about. Yet the Level 5 leaders we identified invoked it frequently. We asked an executive at steel company Nucor why it had such a remarkable track record of making good decisions. His response? "I guess we were just lucky." Joseph F. Cullman III, the Level 5 CEO of Philip Morris, flat out refused to take credit for his company's success, citing his good fortune to have great colleagues, successors, and predecessors. Even the book he wrote about his career—which he penned at the urging of his colleagues and which he never intended to distribute widely outside the company—had the unusual title *I'm a Lucky Guy.*

At first, we were puzzled by the Level 5 leaders' emphasis on good luck. After all, there is no evidence that the companies that had progressed from good to great were blessed with more good luck (or more bad luck, for that matter) than the comparison companies. But then we began to notice an interesting pattern in the executives at the comparison companies: They often blamed their situations on bad luck, bemoaning the difficulties of the environment they faced.

Compare Bethlehem Steel and Nucor, for example. Both steel companies operated with products that are hard to differentiate, and both faced a competitive challenge from cheap imported steel. Both companies paid significantly higher wages than most of their foreign competitors. And yet executives at the two companies held completely different views of the same environment.

Bethlehem Steel's CEO summed up the company's problems in 1983 by blaming the imports: "Our first, second, and third problems are imports." Meanwhile, Ken Iverson and his crew at Nucor saw the imports as a blessing: "Aren't we lucky; steel is heavy, and they have to ship it all the way across the ocean, giving us a huge advantage." Indeed, Iverson saw the first, second, and third problems facing the U.S. steel industry not in imports but in management. He even went so far as to speak out publicly against government protection against imports, telling a gathering of stunned steel executives in 1977 that the real problems facing the steel industry lay in the fact that management had failed to keep pace with technology.

The emphasis on luck turns out to be part of a broader pattern that we came to call *the window and the mirror.* Level 5 leaders, inherently humble, look out the window to apportion credit—even undue credit—to factors outside themselves. If they can't find a specific person or event to give credit to, they credit good luck. At the same time, they look in the mirror to assign responsibility, never citing bad luck or external factors when things go poorly. Conversely, the comparison executives frequently looked out the window for factors to blame but preened in the mirror to credit themselves when things went well.

The funny thing about the window-and-mirror concept is that it does not reflect reality. According to our research, the Level 5 leaders *were* responsible for their companies' transformations. But they would never admit that. We can't climb inside their heads and assess whether they deeply believed what they saw in the window and the mirror. But it doesn't really matter, because they acted as if they believe it, and they acted with such consistency that it produced exceptional results.

BORN OR BRED?

Not long ago, I shared the Level 5 finding with a gathering of senior executives. A woman who had recently become chief executive of her company raised her hand. "I believe what you've told us about Level 5 leadership," she said, "but I'm disturbed because I know I'm not there yet, and maybe I never will be. Part of the reason I got this job is because of my strong ego. Are you telling me that I can't make my company great if I'm not Level 5?"

"Let me return to the data," I responded. "Of 1,435 companies that appeared on the *Fortune* 500 since 1965, only 11 made it into our study. In those 11, all of them had

Level 5 leaders in key positions, including the CEO role, at the pivotal time of transition. Now, to reiterate, we're not saying that Level 5 is the only element required for the move from good to great, but it appears to be essential."

She sat there, quiet for a moment, and you could guess many people in the room were thinking. Finally, she raised her hand again. "Can you learn to become Level 5?" I still do not know the answer to that question. Our research, frankly, did not delve into how Level 5 leaders come to be, nor did we attempt to explain or codify the nature of their emotional lives. We speculated on the unique psychology of Level 5 leaders. Were they "guilty" of displacement—shifting their own raw ambition onto something other than themselves? Were they sublimating their egos for dark and complex reasons rooted in childhood trauma? Who knows? And perhaps more important, do the psychological roots of Level 5 leadership matter any more than do the roots of charisma or intelligence? The question remains: can Level 5 be developed?

My preliminary hypothesis is that there are two categories of people: those who don't have the Level 5 seed within them and those who do. The first category consists of people who could never in a million years bring themselves to subjugate their own needs to the greater ambition of something larger and more lasting than themselves. For those people, work will always be first and foremost about what they get—the fame, fortune, power, adulation, and so on. Work will never be about what they build, create, and contribute. The great irony is that the animus and personal ambition that often drives people to become a Level 4 leader stands at odds with the humility required to rise to Level 5.

When you combine that irony with the fact that boards of directors frequently operate under the false belief that a larger-than-life, egocentric leader is required to make a company great, you can quickly see why Level 5 leaders rarely appear at the top of our institutions. We keep putting people in positions of power who lack the seed to become a Level 5 leader, and that is one major reason why there are so few companies that make a sustained and verifiable shift from good to great.

The second category consists of people who could evolve to Level 5; the capability resides within them, perhaps buried or ignored or simply nascent. Under the right circumstances—with self-reflection, a mentor, loving parents, a significant life experience, or other factors—the seed can begin to develop. Some of the Level 5 leaders in our study had significant life experiences that might have sparked development of the seed. Darwin Smith fully blossomed as a Level 5 after his near-death experience with cancer. Joe Cullman was profoundly affected by his World War II experiences, particularly the last-minute change of orders that took him off a doomed ship on which he surely would have died; he considered the next 60-odd years a great gift. A strong religious belief or conversion might also nurture the seed. Colman Mockler, for example, converted to evangelical Christianity while getting his M.B.A. at Harvard, and later, according to the book *Cutting Edge,* he became a prime mover in a group of Boston business executives that met frequently over breakfast to discuss the carryover of religious values to corporate life.

We would love to be able to give you a list of steps for getting to Level 5—other than contracting cancer, going through a religious conversion, or getting different parents—but we have no solid research data that would support a credible list. Our research exposed Level 5 as a key component inside the black box of what it takes to shift a company from good to great. Yet inside that black box is another—the inner development of a person to Level 5 leadership. We could speculate on what that inner box might hold, but it would mostly be just that, speculation.

In short, Level 5 is a very satisfying idea, a truthful idea, a powerful idea, and, to make the move from good to great, very likely an essential idea. But to provide "10 steps to Level 5 leadership" would trivialize the concept.

My best advice, based on the research, is to practice the other good-to-great disciplines that we discovered. Since we found a tight symbiotic relationship between each of the other findings and Level 5, we suspect that conscientiously trying to lead using the other disciplines can help you move in the right direction. There is no guarantee that doing so will turn executives into full-fledged Level 5 leaders, but it gives them a tangible place to begin, especially if they have the seed within.

We cannot say for sure what percentage of people have the seed within, nor how many of those can nurture it enough to become Level 5. Even those of us on the research team who identified Level 5 do not know whether we will succeed in evolving to its heights. And yet all of us who worked on the finding have been inspired by the idea of trying to move toward Level 5. Darwin Smith, Colman Mockler, Alan Wurtzel, and all the other Level 5 leaders we learned about have become role models for us. Whether or not we make it to Level 5, it is worth trying. For like all basic truths about what is best in human beings, when we catch a glimpse of that truth, we know that our own lives and all that we touch will be the better for making the effort to get there.

LEADERSHIP FOR EVERYONE

PETER J. DEAN

SUMMARY PREPARED BY REBECCA M. CARLSON

Rebecca M. Carlson received her BBA in Organizational Management and Finance from the Labovitz School of Business and Economics (LSBE) at the University of Minnesota Duluth. During her undergraduate career, she participated in the LSBE Financial Markets Program and participated in the University's Undergraduate Research Opportunities program, resulting in a paper entitled "Interorganizational Trust: Trust, Routines, & Institutionalization." She is now employed by Piper Jaffray in Minneapolis, Minnesota, as an equity research analyst covering medical device and diagnostic companies in the health care sector. For recreation, she enjoys spending time with friends and family, traveling, and participating in outdoor activities.

HOW TO LEAD

Everyday interactions are opportunities to lead, and all members of an organization may establish themselves as leaders, teachers, and/or mentors. These leaders will then be viewed as proactive and effective contributors to any effort/team in which they participate. There are increased numbers of opportunities for individuals to practice leadership because organizations are changing from formal to cross-functional, there are fewer managerial ranks, and the percentage of knowledge workers has increased. Managers, or "everyday leaders," have the adaptability and flexibility to become forward-looking in order to put today's actions in a strategic context. By embracing self-development and responsiveness, everyday leaders put aside their personal and internal distractions in order to be receptive to others. Further, when they effectively manage their emotions and put their self-concept aside in order to respond objectively, quiet leaders will emerge on an organization-wide basis. In order to become an everyday leader, managers should practice seven essential skills.

Peter J. Dean, *Leadership for Everyone: How to Apply the Seven Essential Skills to Become a Great Motivator, Influencer, and Leader.* New York: McGraw-Hill, 2006.

L.E.A.D.E.R.S. METHOD

*Everyday leaders should practice the L.E.A.D.E.R.S. Method because it contains the skills necessary for them to become effective in today's organizational setting. It is an acronym for the seven critical leadership skills, including **L**isten to learn, **E**mpathize with emotions, **A**ttend to aspirations, **D**iagnose and detail, **E**ngage for good ends, **R**espond with respectfulness, and **S**peak with specificity.* On a daily basis and during typical interactions with others, everyday leaders should receive feedback, assess and analyze it, and then give feedback. Receiving feedback includes listening, empathizing, and attending to the aspirations of others. Assessing and analyzing the situation includes diagnosing and detailing, while giving feedback is comprised of engaging for good ends, responding with respectfulness, and speaking with specificity.

Receiving Feedback

To receive feedback efficiently and effectively, everyday leaders should listen to learn, empathize with emotions, and attend to aspirations. When these elements of feedback are practiced together, everyday leaders will interpret a situation realistically and strive for complete understanding. Receiving feedback using these three critical leadership skills sets the stage for the assessment and analysis process, which includes diagnosing the situation and detailing it prior to giving constructive feedback.

Listen to Learn

Everyday leaders should first listen to learn in everyday interactions in order to capitalize on their opportunity to lead. By using active listening, managers will be leading in a collaborative and comprehensive style, increasing their own and their group's ability to engage in two-way learning. Active listening includes not only hearing what is said, but also includes recognizing the other's tone, having an open mind, and avoiding distractions. In order to listen to learn, everyday leaders must acknowledge the following prerequisites:

- monitor self-awareness and practice self-regulation,
- become aware of their own and others' intellectual and emotional capacity,
- have the courage to hear conflict as creative energy,
- demonstrate a willingness to deal with problems, and
- indicate one has the ability to work toward a joint understanding.

Active listeners must learn the barriers to active listening so they do not jump to conclusions. This also allows them time to check for understanding. Barriers to active listening include lacking self-discipline or objectivity, becoming overemotional, missing tone, faking attention, and listening only for the next time one may speak. When putting these listening principles into action, everyday leaders will be demonstrating respect verbally, vocally, and visually, for they will be using eye contact, facing the speaker, assessing the whole message, minimizing interruptions, reducing filters, and using pauses effectively. Other actions everyday leaders may take in order to listen to learn include clarifying, restating, encouraging, justifying, and summarizing others' messages. Everyday leaders will be able to critically diagnose the situation and make an appropriate decision. Rewards for active listening include:

- learning extensively about the current situation,
- codifying thoughts,

- problem solving,
- making productive decisions, and
- gaining confidence in everyday leadership.

Once an everyday leader genuinely listens, he or she is one step closer to showing empathy, the next step in the L.E.A.D.E.R.S. Method.

Empathize with Emotions

During their everyday interactions, everyday leaders should also empathize with others' emotions. Having listened to learn, everyday leaders will have gained an understanding that will allow them to empathize with the emotions of others and not judge them. Empathy includes considering others' needs, feelings, and emotions by aligning one's own feelings with the other person's, creating openness and acceptance. Everyday leaders also know that by offering empathy they are not showing sympathy, which implies a perception of helplessness. Everyday leaders, well versed in the four areas of emotional intelligence (self-awareness, self-management, empathy, and social/relationship management) and on the eight categories of emotions (anger, sadness, fear, enjoyment, love, surprise, disgust, and shame), are well-equipped to use this skill. To empathize with emotions, everyday leaders should:

- recognize emotions by assessing verbal and nonverbal cues,
- reflect on the emotion in a nonthreatening way,
- show the other person that he or she is understood,
- move the conversation to address and resolve the emotion,
- tune out distractions,
- identify feelings you think the person is experiencing,
- probe the other person to reveal the cause of his or her feelings,
- respond with empathetic comments, and
- ask the other person to clarify if needed.

Once the everyday leader has empathized with the other's emotions by seeking to know the area of emotional distress, learning the emotion itself, reflecting the emotion, and paraphrasing it, he or she will be able to discuss the content that has become overshadowed by the emotion. This content will provide an opportunity for everyday leaders to attend to the person's aspirations.

Attend to Aspirations

The final component of receiving feedback is attending to aspirations. Everyday leaders should cultivate a productive work environment by fostering people's natural tendency to grow. Limitations decrease productivity and creativity, leading people to leave the company if they feel their professional and personal growth is being hindered. People will feel secure and, therefore, more likely to increase their productivity if they are allowed to aspire within a conducive environment. In order to attend to aspirations, roadblocks that need to be overcome include:

- lack of clear vision, mission, or values in an organization,
- misalignment of employees' values with the organization's, and
- misunderstanding others' levels of need.

Once these roadblocks have been overcome through listening to learn, empathizing with emotions, and attending to aspirations, everyday leaders attend to others as individuals because they understand that each person's needs and motivations may differ. Recalling Maslow's hierarchy of needs, we realize that many never reach self-actualization because they are too busy tending to their other needs such as food, drink, sex, safety, love, and esteem. Highly self-actualized people assimilate work into their self-identity, and everyday leaders can facilitate this process by aspiring toward goals of growth and development, increasing responsibility, and providing a conducive work environment for others to do the same. How exactly does an everyday leader attend to aspirations, so work is integrated into one's self-identity?

- Be conscious of individual people's ability, education, background, motivations, and goals.
- Allow members to participate in decision making and make suggestions through constructive feedback in order to set challenging work goals.
- Facilitate trust formation among organizational members.

A key part of attending to aspirations is giving and receiving feedback in order to engage in participative decision making and goal setting. When giving feedback, everyday leaders avoid excess and blindness, which is presuming we know what's best for the other person. Guidelines everyday leaders live by when giving and receiving feedback include:

1. Giving feedback

   - accept self and others,
   - gauge the receiver's readiness and create immediacy,
   - be descriptive,
   - don't state the obvious,
   - give feedback on what can be changed and don't overload the receiver, and
   - share experiences with the receiver.

2. Receiving feedback

   - state what you want feedback on,
   - check what you heard,
   - share your reactions to what you heard,
   - utilize it to improve, and
   - discount destructive feedback.

Moreover, success is based on the commitment of everyday leaders who focus on the person and intrinsic rewards even if the organization structure focuses on extrinsic rewards. Their focus is on goal setting and constructive feedback in order to push forward.

Assessing and Analyzing

Now that an everyday leader has received a clear picture of the situation, he or she is ready to assess and analyze the feedback through diagnosing and detailing by shifting to a cognitive mode within the L.E.A.D.E.R.S. Method. Everyday leaders need to sort through the information they gathered during listening to learn, empathizing with emotions, and attending to aspirations in order to give constructive feedback.

Diagnose and Detail

Within the workplace, one key way everyday leaders apply the process of diagnosing and detailing is during performance improvement. They seek out knowledge to narrow the gap between existing and ideal performance by using diagnostic questions to uncover areas that need more detail. First, they will identify the accomplishment by determining if it is caused by a specific behavior and then by comparing it to the end purpose of the job. Once this has been completed, everyday leaders will apply the three criteria of an accomplishment. Questions they may ask during diagnosis include:

- Is the accomplishment a measurable quality, quantity, or cost?
- Is the accomplishment observable?
- Is the accomplishment reliable, whereby two or more observers come to the same conclusion?

Everyday leaders should also practice the following ten sub-skills associated with detailing when sorting through the feedback they received:

- discern what is expected and what is observed;
- question without being threatening;
- reinforce what you want to have happen again;
- make sure you and the other person are ready, willing, and able to have the conversation;
- ensure the consequences are clearly understood;
- align yourself verbally, vocally, and visually to the message;
- make sure the person understands what needs to be done;
- probe for chronic problems;
- deflect sudden changes in emotion; and
- paraphrase complexity by addressing the emotion first and the complexity second.

By implementing these ten detailing skills and applying the three criteria of an accomplishment during diagnosis, everyday leaders will determine the root causes of a situation, leading to joint understanding, participative decision making, and cooperative goal setting. Everyday leaders are now prepared to give feedback by engaging for good ends, responding with respectfulness, and speaking with specificity.

Giving Feedback

Giving constructive feedback begins with engaging for good ends, which includes ethical decision making. When everyday leaders respond with respectfulness, they create openness while maintaining consideration for the other person's rights. Finally, when responding with respectfulness, everyday leaders align their remarks verbally, vocally, and visually in order to speak with specificity.

Engage for Good Ends

Three enemies in the workplace include egoism, relativism, and lack of freedom of speech. Rejection of ethical egoism implies there is a non-egoistic foundation for judging right from wrong. Regarding relativism, certain universal principles transcend local customs. Everyday leaders challenge others by practicing freedom of speech, as well as by implementing ethics and professional integrity. They will also maintain motivation by applying policy consistently and practicing concern for others. Engaging for good ends includes everyday leaders maintaining and creating balance between standards of virtue such as integrity, productivity, and responsibility.

- Integrity involves fair play with a sense of justice and actions to establish long-term relationships.
- Productivity is prudent competence at work to achieve goals.
- Responsibility is characterized by the fortitude to practice courage and overcome fear in order to keep promises.

Everyday leaders must also internalize the universal rules and utilitarianism. Universal rules include the principle of universality (your action becomes universal law), principle of reversibility (treat others as you wish to be treated), and principle of respect for persons. Everyday leaders should also practice utilitarianism by considering which action produces the greatest good for whom. By examining consequences, resolving conflicts of interest, and recognizing primary stakeholders, everyday leaders maintain confidentiality, provide truth, use power correctly, and deny inappropriate requests. Further, everyday opportunities to apply this skill include cases involving employee rights, sexual harassment, whistle blowing, selection, termination, evaluations, safety, quality control, and environmental protection. Overall, engaging for good ends includes everyday leaders practicing ethical decision making by:

- listing the facts and defining the issues on all organizational levels,
- identifying all relevant stakeholders,
- determining possible alternatives,
- acknowledging implications for each alternative,
- considering practical constraints, and
- deciding which action should be taken.

Respond with Respectfulness

Once everyday leaders have engaged for good ends through ethical decision making, they will respond with respectfulness. When everyday leaders respond respectfully to others, they behave in ways that honor the other's intrinsic worth, are sensitive to power differences, resolve all conflicts honestly, create a good reputation for dependability, and practice courage in upholding these standards. Everyday leaders also minimize prejudice by speaking to increase the ethical and social contact among alien groups, by responding with a climate of equality, by vigilantly communicating to increase a positive attitude, and by practicing consciousness-raising techniques in all conversations. Individuals' behavioral responses can be categorized as people-focused, task-focused, control-focused, or image-focused. Everyday leaders strive to do the following at appropriate times:

- meet the human and social needs while providing an opportunity for personal growth (people-focused),
- focus on continuous improvement and teamwork while thinking strategically (task-focused),

- get results by taking control and being urgent while charging into action (control-focused), and
- provide worth and seek acceptance while driving to please others (image-focused).

Everyday leaders' self-concepts increase when they become aware of how to shift among the four major behavioral responses, maximizing respectfulness in their responses. Further details of each type of everyday leaders are as follows.

People-focused everyday leaders are socially skillful and demonstrate patience; however, they may not use time well and may even lose sight of their own course. They need preservation of the status quo, and their key tools include preparing before change, taking shortcuts, and receiving reassurance. Task-focused everyday leaders thoroughly examine the situation and follow methods; however, they may feel the effects of paralysis by analysis and may get stuck in their old ways. They need precision and ready access to facts, and their key tools include opportunities created by others and a standard methodology.

Control-focused everyday leaders are impatient and desire change; however, they move too fast and may take control where they shouldn't. They need difficult assignments and the opportunity to explain why they do what they do, and their key tools include opportunity for advancement and freedom from supervision. Image-focused everyday leaders guide in their sphere of influence through statements of principle and fairness and are willing to hear other people's positions; however, they may accept unreasonable demands and may not act in fear of losing approval. They need objectivity and democracy, and their key tools include popularity and public recognition of their ability.

Each type of everyday leader solves problems in a different way, and if one can learn to identify which situations warrant which type of problem solving, their leadership will be far-reaching. While people-focused leaders solve problems by observing, implementing, researching, and applying, task-focused leaders analyze, investigate, evaluate, plan, and critique. Control-focused leaders problem solve by being pragmatic, exercising efficiency, and by reacting competitively and in a domineering manner. Last, image-focused leaders' problem solving can be characterized by supportiveness, experimentation, trust, and instinct. Moreover, by honing the ability to identify when each type of leadership is most applicable to the problem at hand, managers will be able to respond with respectfulness.

Speak with Specificity

While responding with respectfulness, everyday leaders should align their remarks verbally, vocally, and visually in order to speak with specificity. All three should be considered because the spoken word reveals leadership by indicating what we know and don't know. When the verbal, vocal, and visual aspects of speaking are aligned, understanding is enhanced and confidence and credibility are projected. Everyday leaders know that while the verbal element (words) leads, the vocal and visual elements trail behind. Considerations for the verbal element include word choice, meaning, pronunciation, sentence arrangement, vivid language, structured repetition of the residual message, and avoiding the use of jargon.

The vocal element is "how" one says words and everyday leaders should use proper breath support to vary their tone, volume, pace, and pitch. Alignment of this element with the other two improves believability and articulation while eliminating a monotone sound and non-words. Everyday leaders know they are the visual aid. The visual element includes utilizing facial expressions and eye contact, which enhances everyday leaders' credibility and shows sincerity. Gestures, when used properly, also amplify words while a non-slouching posture shows dignity. Physical movement, dress, and humor also establish a good first impression and help build rapport. These are some behaviors that everyday leaders use to hold a listener's attention:

- Begin with the conclusions, so the listener knows where you are coming from.
- Translate the benefits as soon as possible.
- Use examples to repeat your point, using specific conversations.
- Avoid too many details.
- Don't overestimate the other person's knowledge.
- Consider the many meanings a word can have.
- Don't forget to listen, because communication is a cooperative effort.

Conclusion

Everyday leadership is about individuals finding ways to become influencers, mentors, and teachers. Managers are encouraged to become everyday leaders by following the L.E.A.D.E.R.S. Method, which is a map for everyone to practice leadership everyday. Applying these seven leadership skills in order to receive feedback accurately, diagnose and detail the information, and give constructive feedback, managers have the building blocks for being an everyday leader. *Through self-development, individuals can seize the potential in everyday interactions to apply these seven leadership skills in order to put their actions into a strategic context, aligning themselves with their group and their organization as a whole.*

4 BAD LEADERSHIP

BARBARA KELLERMAN

SUMMARY PREPARED BY WARREN CANDY

Warren Candy is Senior Vice President for Allete/Minnesota Power, a diversified electric services company headquartered in Duluth, Minnesota, where he is responsible for the electric, water, gas, and coal business units in Minnesota, Wisconsin, and North Dakota. His interests include high-performance organizational systems, sustainable organizational design, leadership development, and sociotechnical systems implementation. He received his diploma in Production Engineering from Swinburne Institute of Technology in Melbourne, Australia.

INTRODUCTION TO "BAD" LEADERSHIP

What does "bad leadership" mean? Is bad leadership automatically immoral or unethical? Or does it mean leadership that is incompetent or ineffective? What is to be done to maximize good leadership and minimize bad leadership? Can we fully understand the impact and role of leadership within our organizations without acknowledging its dark side? What role do followers play in supporting and enabling bad leadership? Why do people hold idealized visions of their leaders and defer power and control to them? Why do competent people sometimes behave badly when leading? Finally, can there ever be any form of "leadership" without "followership"?

Over the past several decades a "leadership industry" has developed within the United States that is based on the proposition that leadership, as a body of knowledge, is a subject that can be studied and a skill that can be learned by any and all people. To support this industry, definitions of leadership have evolved to the point where they are always undeniably positive and always have leaders as people of competence and character.

For example, in 1978, James MacGregor Burns stated that leadership occurs when people use resources to attain goals by engaging their followers and satisfying their needs. Warren Bennis, in 1989, suggested that a leader creates shared meaning through integrative goals, speaks in a distinctive voice so as to differentiate him- or herself,

Barbara Kellerman, *Bad Leadership: What It Is, How It Happens, Why It Matters.* Boston: Harvard Business School Press, 2004.

exhibits the capacity to adapt, and demonstrates his or her integrity. John Gardner noted that leadership is different from coercion. People who use coercion are judged as bad.

Therefore, all "leadership" has become synonymous with "good" leadership. This should not be surprising since there is a natural preference to want to go through life accentuating the positive and eliminating the negative in order to be as healthy and happy as possible. Recognizing and accepting the negatives of human nature goes against this tendency and is not something we naturally or easily acknowledge.

However, we need to think more broadly about the concept of leadership, not so much as a "thing" to be learned, but as an integral part of the human condition. It has not only a positive side, but also a "dark side," or in the context used here, a "bad side"!

Leadership is a complex interaction that needs to be thought of in shades of gray, black, and in terms of how people actually go about exercising power, authority, and influence.

Additionally, we need to understand that *leadership does not exist in isolation* or in the abstract. Without followers there is no leadership; leaders and followers are interdependent. There cannot be "good" leadership without "good" followers or, conversely, "bad" leadership without "bad" followers.

WHAT IS "BAD" LEADERSHIP?

Often leaders are assumed to be all powerful and independent. However, we must remember that leaders do not act alone. A leader chooses a particular course of action and then in some way gets others to go along, or, more subtly, encourages the led to "choose" the course that the group will follow. That followers matter is a presumption that is now widely shared.

There's something odd about the idea that somehow leadership can be distinguished from coercion, as if leadership and power were unrelated. There is no leadership without followership. Leaders cannot lead unless followers follow, either passively or actively.

Two fundamental categories of bad leadership exist—ineffective and unethical. *Ineffective leaders* are generally judged ineffective because of the inappropriate means they employ (or the appropriate means that they fail to employ) rather than the ends they pursue. *Unethical leadership* occurs when people fail to distinguish between right and wrong. Ethical leaders put their followers' needs before their own; unethical leaders do not. Ethical leaders exemplify private virtues such as courage and temperance; unethical leaders do not. Ethical leaders exercise leadership in the interest of the common good; unethical leaders do not. Most people are familiar with ineffective and unethical leaders. These leaders tend to disappoint us because they are inept or corrupt, and not because they are inherently evil.

Bad Leadership

Bad leadership is mainly a result of leaders behaving poorly because of who they are and what they want, and then acting in ways that do harm. This harm can be intentional or can occur as a result of carelessness or neglect. Seven types of bad leadership have become prevalent in today's organizations: incompetent, rigid, intemperate, callous, corrupt, insular, and evil.

- Incompetent Leadership – the leader and at least some followers lack the will or skill (or both) to sustain effective action or to create positive change.
- Rigid Leadership – the leader and at least some followers are inflexible and unyielding. Although they may be competent, they are unable or unwilling to adapt to new ideas, new information, or changing times.
- Intemperate Leadership – the leader lacks self-control and is aided and abetted by followers who are unwilling or unable effectively to intervene.
- Callous Leadership – the leader and at least some followers are uncaring or unkind. Ignored or discounted are the needs, wants, and wishes of most members of the group or organization, especially subordinates.
- Corrupt Leadership – the leader and at least some followers lie, cheat, or steal. To a degree that exceeds the norm, they put self-interest ahead of the public interest.
- Insular Leadership – the leader and at least some followers minimize or disregard the health and welfare of "the other"—that is, those outside the group or organization for which they are directly responsible.
- Evil Leadership – the leader and at least some followers commit atrocities. They use pain as an instrument of power. The harm done to men, women, and children is severe rather than slight. The harm can be physical, psychological, or both.

WHAT IS "BAD" FOLLOWERSHIP?

To fully understand the role of leadership in organizations of today we must understand leadership as two contradictory things: good and bad. Just as we have bad leaders, we also have bad followers; just as we have good leaders, we have good followers.

Bad followers commit themselves to bad leaders. They do so knowingly and deliberately, and generally mirror bad leaders for a variety of complex reasons.

Good followers are true partners with leaders. They think independently, engage in self-direction and self-control, follow through on their own, and fulfill their responsibilities willingly.

Individual Versus Group Needs

People do not exist in organizations in isolation, so they are driven to satisfy a wide variety of both individual and group needs and expectations. Among the most compelling explanations for the willingness of followers to obey authority is the need that people have to *keep things simple*. Even bad leaders often satisfy the most basic human needs, in particular safety, simplicity, and certainty. Leaders, even bad ones, can provide a sense of order and certainty in a disordered and uncertain world. The construct of the leader itself is a manifestation of our preference for simple as opposed to complex explanations.

Groups also go along with bad leaders to gain important benefits for themselves collectively. Leaders maintain order, provide cohesion and identity, and do the collective work. Hierarchy, it turns out, is the natural order of things since as societies increase in size, they become even more dependent on leaders to order, organize, and carry out their collective activities. There will always be leaders, and there will always be those tasked with getting the group's work done.

For reasons that are now quite clear, followers have good and sound reasons for following, even when their leaders are bad. To meet their needs as individuals and a member of groups, followers usually conclude that it's in their interests to go with the flow.

FROM BAD TO BETTER, HOW LEADERS AND FOLLOWERS CAN IMPROVE

We cannot stop, slow, or change bad leadership by attempting to change human nature. Exhortations to do good works are often ineffective. And we cannot expect to reduce the number of bad leaders until we reduce the number of bad followers.

Leaders and followers will change only when they decide that it is in their best interest to do so. When the cost/benefit ratio of bad leadership tips in favor of good leadership then change will occur!

From the research and analysis of many real-life examples of "bad" leadership specific actions have been identified that can be used by leaders and followers alike to limit, correct for, and prevent bad leadership and followership.

Ideas for Leadership Self-Help

- Share power and work with others collaboratively in meaningful ways.
- Don't believe your own hype: "For leaders, to buy their own publicity is the kiss of death."
- Get real, stay real, and stay in touch with reality.
- Compensate for your blind spots by acquiring in-depth knowledge, or support, in areas of weakness.
- Stay balanced, because balanced leaders develop healthier organizations, and make more thoughtful and effective decisions.
- Remember the mission, your reason for existence, and use it as your compass during difficult times.
- Stay healthy; physical and mental health are critical.
- Be reflective and develop self-knowledge, self-control, and good habits through quiet contemplation.
- Establish a culture of openness in which diversity and dissent are encouraged.
- Bring in advisers who are both strong and independent.
- Avoid groupthink, encourage healthy dissent, minimize excessive cohesiveness, and strive for frank and open discussions to realistically appraise alternative courses of action.
- Get reliable and complete information, and then disseminate it.
- Establish a system of checks and balances. For example, limit the tenure of leaders, rotate responsibilities, hold regular performance reviews, and use multiple metrics.
- Strive for stakeholder balance by connecting with all constituencies and not just a chosen few.

Ideas for Follower Self-Help

- Empower yourself to take action and don't merely "go along."
- Be loyal to the whole, and not to any single individual.
- Be skeptical, realizing that leaders are not gods and are subject to errors and omissions that need to be highlighted and discussed.
- Take a stand.
- Pay attention; do not contribute to bad leadership through deliberate or inadvertent inattention.

- Find allies, since there is always strength in numbers when working with other like-minded individuals.
- Develop your own sources of information to verify correct and complete information, remembering always that the interests of leaders and followers do not always coincide.
- Take collective action.
- Be a watchdog; do not abdicate responsibility for oversight and for minding the store.
- Hold leaders accountable to all stakeholders through transparency, open discussions, and meaningful participation.

PART

IX

THINKING
INCLUSIVELY
AND ACTING CIVILLY

A wide range of biases (such as racism, ageism, and sexism) are unfortunately still entrenched in pockets in some segments of society and—sadly—exhibited in its organizations. Despite powerful federal and state laws, potent corporate policy statements, widespread efforts at enlightenment, and extensive training programs, many public and private organizations still have, for example, a limited number of female upper-level managers. A number of different groups within society find themselves singled out and subjected to discriminatory treatment. (See, for example, the class-action allegations of lower pay and limited promotional opportunities for women at Wal-Mart as discussed in "People problems on every aisle," *Workforce Management,* February 2004, pp. 26–34.) Professors R. W. Griffin and A. M. O'Leary-Kelly recently edited a book entitled *The Dark Side of Organizational Behavior* (Jossey-Bass, 2004). Part Two of this book ("Discrimination and the Dark Side") contains three excellent essays reflecting current thinking and research focused on discrimination, sexual harassment, and sexual orientation discrimination in the workplace.

Many interesting books and articles have been written on the rapidly changing demographics in the United States, and the implications that those trends have for businesses and organizations. The popular press reminds us almost daily that diversity in the workplace is not only increasingly common, but also a critical factor for success in the twenty-first century marketplace. A consequence of these dramatic demographic trends is the need for constructive response.

The three readings included in this part highlight the importance of building an organizational environment that values *all* of its members as a way of achieving organizational enhancement. In essence, these three readings encourage all of us to think in new ways about organizations and the people who are its members.

The Inclusion Breakthrough argues that every employee should be valued as a vital component of the organization's success. Authors Miller and Katz suggest a unique view of diversity, one in which fair treatment gets redefined to mean that every employee gets treated according to their needs so that they can do their best work. Diversity exists within every individual, and should therefore be leveraged through a culture of inclusion so as to best create a competitive advantage. This can be achieved, the authors contend, through a four-stage process of laying a foundation for change, mobilizing the effort, institutionalizing it, and sustaining the change.

The authors are top executives of the Kaleel Jamison Consulting Group. Frederick Miller (President and CEO) served on the Board of Directors for the American Society for Training and Development, and was the editor of *The Promise of Diversity*. Judith Katz (Executive Vice President) has written extensively on change management, oppression and diversity, and inclusive organizations. Her previous book was *White Awareness: Handbook for Anti-Racism Training*.

In the second reading, *Straight Talk About Gays in the Workplace*, author Liz Winfeld discusses issues such as the costs associated with an inequitable workplace, best practices in advertising, and domestic partner benefits pertaining to the growing visibility of gays and lesbians in the workplace. The author highlights some of the progressive practices engaged in by many of today's organizations as they deal with gay, lesbian, bisexual, and transgender issues in their work environments.

Liz Winfeld is an expert and consultant who focuses on domestic partner benefits, sexual orientation, and gender identity. She is frequently a keynote speaker on these topics at special events and conferences for many large U.S. organizations such as Ford, Kaiser Permanente, Shell Oil, and Prudential.

Choosing Civility is a handbook that identifies and expounds on 25 rules that the author, P. M. Forni, believes essential to allow us to live well among others. The author contends that civility has increasingly been pushed aside as people live their hurried lives, lives that seem propelled by e-mails, cell phones, and multitasking. Through examples, Dr. Forni advises managers and leaders to think twice before asking for favors, give constructive criticism, respect the opinions of others, care for their employees, and accept and give praise graciously. The 25 rules are equally relevant to both work organizations and social relationships.

P. M. Forni is on the faculty at Johns Hopkins University where he teaches a course on civility. He is the cofounder of the Johns Hopkins Civility Project. Dr. Forni's work has been aired on the Baltimore affiliate of National Public Radio, and in the *New York Times*, *Washington Post*, and the *Times of London*.

1

THE INCLUSION
BREAKTHROUGH

FREDERICK A. MILLER AND JUDITH H. KATZ

SUMMARY PREPARED BY KRISTINA A. BOURNE

Kristina A. Bourne *holds a Ph.D. in organization studies from the University of Massachusetts in Amherst, where she also obtained an M.B.A. and a Women's Studies Graduate Certificate. She received a Bachelor of Business Administration with a concentration in marketing and a Bachelor of Arts with a concentration in French and economics from the University of Minnesota Duluth. Dr. Bourne is currently an Assistant Professor of Organizational Behavior at the University of Wisconsin-Eau Claire. She has published articles in* Organizational Dynamics *and* Research in Multi-Level Issues. *Her academic interests include gender and organization. She is currently working on research in the area of women business owners and on several collaborative research projects focusing on work–family and alternative work arrangements.*

An *inclusion breakthrough* is a powerful transformation of an organization's culture to one in which *every* individual is valued as a vital component of the organization's success and competitive advantage. In the past, diversity has been seen as something that must be managed, tolerated, or molded to fit the dominant culture. Even those organizations that embrace diversity usually see it as an end in itself, rather than connected to the main mission of the organization. Such views create a *diversity in a box* strategy for most organizations, limiting the potential and power of diversity. With an inclusion breakthrough, differences are understood as mission-critical, not something extra linked only to human resource policies and practices.

Underpinning an inclusion breakthrough is the assumption that *diversity can be found in all individuals.* Everyone has his or her own unique backgrounds, experiences, and perspectives. Hiring people from different backgrounds, however, is not enough if the organization values sameness in ways of thinking, style, and behavior. Organizations

Frederick A. Miller and Judith H. Katz, *The Inclusion Breakthrough: Unleashing the Real Power of Diversity.* San Francisco: Berrett-Koehler, 2002.

can break out of the diversity in a box model by transforming their culture to one that values and supports the various dimensions of diversity, and unleashing its power.

Barriers to inclusion, ranging from blatant disregard for differences (such as the lack of accommodations for people with disabilities) to more subtle forms (such as exclusion from the afternoon golf game) are still widespread. Change efforts, however, should not stop at leveling the playing field by breaking down these barriers. Creating an environment where all people can be more productive means raising the playing field by continually examining processes to ensure that everyone feels valued for their contribution to the organization's success. *Leveraging diversity requires a culture of inclusion to support it.*

THE FUNDAMENTALS OF AN INCLUSION BREAKTHROUGH

An inclusion breakthrough is a cycle—each element builds on the previous to raise the entire bar of expectations for organizations. This cycle positively impacts organizations by continuously increasing job satisfaction, attracting and retaining talented individuals, developing thriving communities, and tapping into market potential. Creating a culture of inclusion requires organizations to examine the following five key processes:

- Defining a new set of competencies
- Aligning policies and practices
- Leveraging a diverse labor force
- Connecting with the local community
- Increasing value to the marketplace

Defining a New Set of Competencies

Organizations today are plagued with incompetence such as inadequate communication skills, underutilized assets, internal rivalry, turnover of talented workers, and lack of cooperation across units. To unleash creativity and enable people to perform at their highest level, organizations must require new competencies and develop infrastructures that support them.

Working collaboratively and partnering across a diverse pool of people requires an environment in which individuals feel their unique perspective contributes to the overall success of the organization. People's experience of an organization is often based on the behavior of their immediate supervisor and members of their work group. A culture of inclusion, therefore, requires *all* people, no matter what position or level in the organization, to demonstrate the following new *inclusive competencies:*

- Greet others genuinely
- Understand difference as a force for new ideas and resolve disagreements
- Listen to each team member's ideas and perspectives
- Share information clearly and honestly
- Ensure that everyone understands the overall vision and how each task relates to it
- Realize that every member has a contribution to make

- Understand that others' experiences and perspectives can add innovative ideas
- Encourage quiet members to share their thoughts
- Respect other team members' time and personal/family responsibilities
- See mistakes as learning opportunities for improvement

These key competencies create a workplace that encourages communicating across differences, resolving conflict, and valuing every individual as a contributor to the overall mission. These new competencies, however, are not static and must be continuously re-evaluated in light of changes in the external and internal environment.

Aligning Policies and Practices

Developing a new set of inclusive competencies will only be effective if they are integrated into the formal rules and policies of the organization, requiring both the written and unwritten practices to change. Even the so-called soft policies, those that help people feel connected to and supported by the organization, must be re-evaluated to enable individuals to feel respected for their unique contribution while working in diverse situations. Old assumptions must be abandoned. For example, no longer is the office Christmas party "everyone's holiday."

In order to achieve an inclusion breakthrough, organizations must go beyond what they are already doing, raising the bar of the old baseline of actions to new levels. Table 1 lists current and updated policies and practices that allow people from a variety of social identity groups to perform at their highest level. The goal is not to treat everyone the same. *Fairness gets redefined as treating everyone according to their needs so that they can do their best work.*

Leveraging a Diverse Labor Force

Just having people who represent diverse social identity groups in the organization is not enough; an environment must be created that unleashes that diversity. Diversity in a box creates a situation where everyone is expected to fit within its walls. Dismantling these limits creates an environment where people feel safe to bring forward new ideas and perspectives when their difference is valued and respected as integral to the organization's strategic mission.

The Biases Among Us

Unleashing the potential of a diverse workforce requires organizations to address the barriers preventing everyone from succeeding. Organizational practices reflect societal and individual belief systems. Racism, sexism, heterosexism, ageism, and other prevalent "isms" are like a boulder of oppression that builds momentum as it rolls down the hill. Condescending and patronizing comments maintain the dominance of the one-up group. Sexism is prevalent when men are admired for leaving early to go to their child's school activity, while women are judged negatively for leaving early to pick their child up from daycare. Systematic racism exists when white women express concern about their organization's glass ceiling, while ignoring the fact that more women of color are concentrated at the lower levels. Doing nothing allows the boulder of bias to roll on. The only way to have a true inclusion breakthrough is to stop this boulder of oppressive beliefs with sustained, positive action.

TABLE 1   The Old and the New Baselines for Inclusive Policies and Practices

Addressing Issues Relating to . . .	*The Old Baseline*	*The New Baseline*
Age	• Recruits young people • Values the experience of people who are 50 and older	• Recognizes that young people are investments in the future • Develops young people quickly • Extends the retirement age • Includes 50+ people in high-potential groups
Lesbians, Gays, and Bisexuals	• Creates an environment that is safe for people to come out • Offers domestic partner benefits	• Invites people's partners to company events • Encourages people to talk about their personal lives • Offers benefits that take into account the unique needs of lesbians and gays • Recognizes that not all customers are heterosexual
Nationality	• Offers additional pay for language skills • Recruits people from different countries	• Recognizes a variety of holidays and customs • Includes representatives from all the organization's geographic locations on board of directors and senior management team • Develops local talent
Organizational Hierarchy	• Values and respects people at the lower levels • Provides career development opportunities for all people	• Recognizes that all people contribute to the organization • Listens to all voices at all levels • Creates participatory decision-making processes
People of Color	• Actively recruits and retains people of color • Has minimal representation at all levels • Acknowledges differentiation between groups (e.g., African American, Latinos)	• Demonstrates a critical mass throughout organization • Acknowledges multiracial identity • Develops two-way mentoring across racial lines (versus one-way mentoring to fit into old culture)
People with Disabilities	• Complies with the Americans with Disabilities Act • Provides medical benefits that address disabled people's particular needs • Recognizes the contributions of people with disabilities	• Creates an environment where people feel safe to express their unique needs • Proactively recruits and retains people with disabilities • Represents people with disabilities in marketing campaigns • Provides more funding for accommodations
White Men	• Ensures that white men are included in inclusion efforts • Recognizes that there is more than one type of white man	• Develops two-way mentoring so white men can learn about their own diversity and expand their perspective • Acknowledges work/family issues

(*continued*)

Women	• Shows representation at all levels • Addresses sexual harassment • Acknowledges the structural barriers to women's advancement • Values the work women do at all levels	• Eliminates subtle forms of harassment • Addresses the sticky floor (i.e., barriers that keep women of color at the bottom) • Develops two-way mentoring across women and men • Applies flexible scheduling to all levels of the organization • Includes men in parental polices

Attracting and Retaining a Talented Workforce

Hanging on to new talent is difficult in today's high-turnover environment. Most people change jobs and/or organizations every few years, making recruitment and retention of talented individuals a strategic priority. When people walk out the door in a year or two, they take with them their talent and training, often heading to the competitor's door. The traditional strategy of "bringing them along slowly" doesn't work when employee turnover is high. Further, "outsider status" must be eliminated. People of color, people with an accent, and people from other social identity groups must not be ignored or made to prove that they can fit in. All members must be nurtured and developed, because all members create value for the organization.

An Employer of Choice

Becoming an employer of choice means asking why, given complete freedom, people would work for your organization. The following are key characteristics that talented individuals from diverse backgrounds report as significant in selecting an employer.

- The leaders are highly knowledgeable and inspirational.
- The organization is positioned for growth.
- Policies support work, life, and family integration.
- Ample growth and development opportunities exist (e.g., educational support).
- People feel respected by their colleagues.
- The environment is physically and emotionally safe.
- People are recognized as business partners (e.g., profit-sharing programs).
- People have access to all job-relevant information.
- Roles, responsibilities, performance expectations, and reward systems are openly stated.

If organizations want their employees to invest their time and energy into the organization, then organizations need to invest their time and energy into those people; this is the new two-way employment agreement.

Connecting with the Local Community

To be competitive, an inclusion strategy should not only focus on the inside of the organization, but the outside. Attracting talented people requires attractive communities in which they will live. The quality of the water supply, school systems, transportation, and other community resources must be high. Organizations should go beyond a one-way relationship with local communities based on tax breaks and other incentives to investing in educational, recreational, and health facilities. Organizations are, after all, dependent on local communities for people, suppliers, distributors, customers, and investors.

Increasing Value to the Marketplace

Diversity in a box places customers outside of its walls. An inclusion breakthrough sees customers as central players in the organization's success. Traditionally, diverse customers are segmented into niches, which treats social identity groups as monolithic categories. Leveraging diversity in the marketplace requires organizations to expand their view of customers and link them to their core business strategy. The range of tastes and preferences within each social identity category must be recognized. Tapping into this market potential requires more than the token representative of each social group. *All* people in the organization must have the competencies to understand the unique features of each social group.

BUILDING AN INCLUSION BREAKTHOUGH

Creating an environment in which all members of the organization feel supported to perform at their highest level requires a methodology for an inclusion breakthrough. Most organizations will go through four phases: laying the foundation for change, mobilizing change efforts, making change an everyday activity, and sustaining and challenging the new change.

Phase I: Laying the Foundation for Change

The most important piece of the foundation is the support from the top. Senior executives must lead and model the new competencies and provide resources to help people change to new, and initially uncomfortable, ways of behaving and interacting. Senior leaders need to link the change to the core business mission by creating an organizational imperative that clearly describes how a culture change will positively impact the organization as a whole, thereby creating value for each individual.

Laying the platform for change also requires a comprehensive organizational assessment that examines and documents a baseline of the current culture, resources, practices, and opportunities. Assessment is itself a tool for change; asking people about their experiences and concerns opens a space for change to occur. Data can be collected from surveys or by focus groups that assemble people by different social identities—part-time workers, individuals over 55, Asian-American managers—providing a forum for a diversity of views. Senior leaders must be receptive to honest and frank feedback about the organization's culture.

Senior leaders cannot create the change alone; learning partners should be selected to share their experiences and perspectives with senior leaders on a continuous basis. These individuals should not be seen as token representatives for differences, but as vital partners in the change effort, who offer insights to voices in the organization that otherwise go unheard. Further, a change leadership team, including individuals from various social identity groups and the dominant group, should be created to broaden the scope of the efforts.

Phase II: Mobilizing Change Efforts

This phase begins with developing an initial 12- to 18-month plan to implement the widespread culture change. At this stage, senior leaders should provide frequent and clear communication so that everyone in the organization is aware of the forthcoming changes. For example, the CEO can send a personal letter to each employee that describes the inclusion breakthrough as mission-critical. A core group should be selected to model the changes by integrating the new competencies into their everyday work lives. Intense education sessions will also allow groups of people in the organization to learn the new competencies. For example, human resource staff will need to learn how to integrate the new inclusive policies. Further, managers at all levels will need to integrate the new skills for leveraging diversity into their behaviors. Managers can often resist the culture change because in order for them to have climbed to their current position, they had to follow the rules of the old culture, with which they became comfortable.

Breaking down both overt and subtle forms of discrimination is also an integral component of this phase. For example, organizations need to take a close look at the gender wage gap, lagging advancement opportunities for people of color, and disregard for the family needs of lesbian and gay members. Processes must be created to address these forms of discrimination.

Finally, networking groups and buddy systems should be formalized. In one organization, a networking system was established in which each group linked its existence with the overall mission, was supported by a senior executive (usually not from the group's primary identity group), and belonged to an overall group of networks, which regularly meet to align each group's activities with business objectives. After two years, the benefits of such a networking system included new talented recruits, new relationships with business partners from various social identity groups, and new products that met the needs of different customers. In buddy systems, the success of new hires is both the responsibility of the new employee and the established team member, who are matched in the recruiting process.

Phase III: Making Change an Everyday Activity

For the culture change to become a core part of the organizational mission, a longer term strategic plan must be developed to integrate the new diversity concepts into every aspect of the organization, especially training and education. Managers, with their vital role in training and mentoring, must practice the new behaviors and hold their direct reports accountable for them. As new competencies get cultivated, effective performance-measuring systems must be established and formalized in order to verify that people's, including managers', behaviors align with the new inclusion policies and practices.

In one organization, a comprehensive plan to make the inclusion breakthrough an everyday reality included mandatory education sessions on the organizational imperative for every employee, a multi-day training on leveraging diversity for managers, a reorganization of managers according to the new competencies, and the identification of change agents to model the new skills in their teams. Just two years after the changes were made, people felt more than twice as favorable toward their managers and were more committed to the organization.

Phase IV: Sustaining and Challenging the New Change

An inclusion breakthrough is not static; rather, it is a dynamic process that must be continually re-created. Periodic reviews allow organizations to assess the change progress. Revisiting the organizational imperative will show where advancements have been made and where gaps are still present.

Leadership groups will evolve, bringing in new ideas and perspectives. Communication of the new culture should remain open both internally and externally. *To be successful, an inclusion breakthrough must be ever changing and continuously improving as people, strategies, customers, and environments change.*

BREAKING DIVERSITY OUT OF THE BOX

Diversity in a box may feel more comfortable in the short run, but breaking out of the box will set free the organization's underutilized human potential. Stepping out of the box opens a space for individuals to feel respected, valued, and supported so they can perform to their highest level. Changing one organization at a time just might change the world by unleashing the real power of diversity.

2

STRAIGHT TALK ABOUT GAYS IN THE WORKPLACE

LIZ WINFELD

SUMMARY PREPARED BY LINDA HEFFERIN

Linda Hefferin is a business management professor at Elgin Community College. She obtained her Ed.D. in Business Education from Northern Illinois University in DeKalb, Illinois. Dr. Hefferin is a strong advocate of diversity on her campus and is a founding member of MAGIC, the Multi-cultural and Global Initiatives Committee, whose mission is to "prepare individuals to succeed in a diverse society by providing and supporting multicultural learning experiences in an inclusive environment."

SEXUAL ORIENTATION AND GENDER IDENTITY CHANGES IN THE WORKPLACE

The changing landscape of the workplace now includes the issues of sexual orientation and gender identity. The presence of gays and lesbians is much more visible than at any time in the past. In 1990, only about 25 percent of Americans reported having a gay acquaintance. By 2000, the percentage had increased to over 50 percent.[1] According to the Gill Foundation in 2003, the percentage of straight people who say they know at least one gay is 90 percent; these data indicate that there is an increased awareness of sexual orientation in the workplace.[2]

The issue of gays and lesbians in the workplace gained attention in 1992 when Lotus became the first publicly traded company to offer same-sex domestic partner benefits. While this event was seen as a win for sexual orientation rights, gender identity issues have more recently come to the forefront. As of 2004, several states had passed laws inclusive of sexual orientation and/or gender identity for the purposes of employment, housing, public accommodations, and credit.

Liz Winfeld, *Straight Talk About Gays In the Workplace: Creating an Inclusive, Productive Environment for Everyone in Your Organization* (3rd ed.). Binghamton, NY: Harrington Park Press, 2005.

[1] Harris Interactive/Witeck-Combs, "New Harris Interactive/Witeck-Combs Internet survey confirms gays and lesbians are among heaviest Internet users," April 2000. Available online at www.witeckcombs.com.

[2] Statistics available online from the Gill Foundation at www.gillfoundation.com.

A basic understanding of terminology is important in order to be able to discuss any topic intelligently. Here are some important definitions to know regarding gender identity.

Transgender is the degree of gender disagreement between a person's biological sex and his or her gender identity; included are transsexuals, intersexuals, cross-dressers, transgenderists, and androgynes. **Transsexuals** are people whose gender identity does not match their biological sex. They are motivated to change their sex so that it matches their gender identity. **Intersexuals** are people whose biological sex attributes may be male or female or a mixture of both, but whose gender identity is flexible and they are comfortable with that flexibility. **Cross-dressers** are people whose gender expression is at odds with their biological sex. While most cross-dressers are males who dress as women, there are also female cross-dressers. **Transgenderists** are transsexuals who choose not to have sex-reassignment surgery but often take part in hormone therapy that causes certain sex-characteristic changes. **Androgynes** (from androgynous) refers to people having both male and female sexual characteristics.

WHAT ELSE IS CHANGING IN THE WORKPLACE?

- The 2000 U.S. Census reported 15 million persons self-identified as gay/lesbian, even though this is thought to be an undercount since there was no box to check to indicate sexual orientation.
- Gallup reported in December 2003 that 79 percent of Americans believe that gays should be allowed to openly serve in the military.[3]
- Sixty percent of heterosexual adults report believing that employees with same-sex partners should be eligible for workplace benefits available to spouses.
- More than 7,000 organizations offer domestic partner benefits (DPB) to same-sex or same- and opposite-sex couples and their families. Only 100 such organizations were reported on January 1, 1992.
- The percentage of organizations including the words "sexual orientation" in their nondiscrimination policies has increased 7 to 10 percent every year for the past 10 years. Currently, 157 organizations also include "gender identity" or "gender identity/expression" in their nondiscrimination policies. This number was less than 20 three years ago.

WHAT'S AT STAKE IN DOLLARS AND CENTS?

The gay market segment is one of the fastest growing demographics for products and services in the United States.[4] Buying power for the lesbian, gay, bisexual, and transgender (LBGT) community was $451 *billion* in 2002, and is projected to reach $608 billion by 2007; this is a cumulative increase of more than 34 percent.

---

[3]Frank Newport, "Iraq, economy remain most important problems," Gallup News Service, Gallup Polls, December 13, 2005. Available online at www.gallup.com/polls.

[4]Witeck-Combs/Harris Interactive, "HRC public report," February 2004. Available online at www.witeck-combs.com.

WHAT IS THE COST OF AN INEQUITABLE WORKPLACE?

A simple formula can be used to estimate the cost of an inequitable workplace. Assuming a 10 percent non-heterosexual population, a company employing 5,000 people has 500 people who are not heterosexual. Also assume a cost of 10 percent to estimate the amount of productivity decline associated with the absence of a safe and equitable workplace. If the average salary is $40,000 and the average loss of productivity per non-heterosexual worker is $4,000 ($40,000 $\times$ 10 percent), then the annual loss to the company is estimated to be $2 million ($4,000 $\times$ 500).

Individuals do not work at their best when they work in fear, yet data show that discrimination is still prevalent in the workplace. Witeck-Combs reports that for the second year in a row, while there is more openness of lesbian, gay, bisexual, and transgender (LGBT) issues at work, LGBTs reported little change in the amount of discrimination they witnessed or personally experienced. Forty percent of LGBTs reported facing some form of discrimination on the job; this included being fired, harassed, pressured to quit, or denied a promotion because of their sexual orientation or gender identity. Further, a greater percentage (52 percent) of heterosexuals reported hearing jokes about LGBTs than they did in 2002 (45 percent).

WHAT DOES SAME-SEX MARRIAGE MEAN IN BUSINESS?

Regardless of an individual's personal opinion regarding same-sex marriage or civil unions, the status of same-sex relationships affects every professional charged with ensuring that the organization's policies and actions fall within the realm of the law, and it is important to understand the legal issues of same-sex relationships in order to make informed decisions.

For example, assume an employee brings in a marriage license for a same-sex marriage and the organization currently does not offer domestic partner benefits. Does this matter concern management? Yes, it most certainly should, because more than organization-offered benefits are involved. Many other issues that fall under state and federal marriage status are affected; such as Family and Medical Leave Act (FMLA) and pension plans. Gays who marry will expect to be treated as heterosexual married employees and will expect benefits ranging from tuition reimbursement assistance to pretax flexible spending accounts.

SUPPLIER DIVERSITY

Supplier diversity programs that actively support sexual orientation and gender identity are relatively new. IBM recently unveiled the first procurement and diversity program directed at LGBT-owned companies. Long known for its inclusiveness, IBM added the words *sexual orientation* in its nondiscrimination policy in 1976. As a result of this supplier diversity program, IBM is demonstrating cutting-edge inclusion, enhancing its profitability by building presence in the LGBT community, improving its competitive advantage for labor and patronage, and taking full advantage of its greatest resource: all its people, gay and straight, who work for it.

On the other hand, companies like Cracker Barrel learned the hard way that they needed to change their approach regarding their sexual orientation policy. In the 1990s it was common practice for employees to be fired, and the reason given was the "employee is gay." The company once circulated a memo stating that all Cracker Barrel employees must exhibit "normal" heterosexual values.[5] Cracker Barrel changed its nondiscrimination policy to include sexual orientation in 2003 in response to boycotts, protests, and a campaign by shareholders.

BEST PRACTICES IN LGBT ADVERTISING

The first companies to respond with gay advertisements were in the liquor and cigarette industries. The list is much longer today and includes companies such as Apple, AT&T, American Airlines, Disney Corporation, Calvin Klein, Levi's, Crate & Barrel, Barnes & Noble, America Online, American Express, Visa, Wells Fargo, Wachovia, John Hancock, E*Trade Financial, United Airlines, Avis, Verizon, SBC Communications, Subaru, Volvo, Jaguar, Mercedes-Benz, Land Rover, Saturn, Ford, Absolut, Glaxo-SmithKline, and Merck.

In May 2003, one ad by Volvo featured two men and a baby; another ad showed a pregnant woman embracing her pregnant partner—each with the headline, "Whether you're starting a family or creating one as you go." The text of each ad reads, "Some families are carefully planned. Others, you just meet along the way. Whoever makes up your family, think about making Volvo a part of it."

According to Thomas Andersson, Executive Vice President at Volvo, "We're targeting people with modern family values. It's a value set, and the Volvo-minded consumer is very diverse. 'Family' is much more than the traditional family."[6]

WHAT ELSE CAN BE DONE?

Several strategies are available to effectively deal with sexual orientation and gender identity in the workplace. Here are a few ideas to consider:

- Incorporate nondiscrimination policies
- Offer education
- Provide domestic partner benefits
- Make employee networks/alliances available
- Market to the LGBT community
- Start internal and external outreach programs
- Supply knowledgeable internal resources and reference libraries

Some companies resist adding the words *sexual orientation* or *gender identity* to their policies because they fear that they will lose customers. They think that customers might view their inclusive policy as tacit approval and withdraw their business.

For many years women and racial minorities were excluded from many businesses because of fear that clients would prefer not to be served by them. But firms did start

---

[5]Michael Markowitz, "Shareholders' power is the new weapon in fight for equality," *Newsday,* January 4, 2004.

[6]Michael Wile, "Volvo bids for gay families," *The Commercial Closet.* Available online at www.planetout.com.

to diversify and clients did accept it. In fact, in the long run, the moral choice is the lucrative one as well. As major cultural changes take place, it pays to be the leader rather than attempting to catch up and in the process make excuses as to why you are behind.

Walt Disney Corporation was the target of a large boycott by a religious organization when they first implemented domestic partner benefits. However, the boycott failed, and the company posted better-than-expected profits and revenues compared to the previous year's fiscal period. Americans have shown time and time again that they do not believe in discrimination; in fact, they boycott to stop it.

While numbers continue to change, as of March 2004, 75 percent of the Fortune 500 organizations included sexual-orientation language in their nondiscrimination language. More companies are reporting that they are adding gender identity or gender identity/expression to their policies.

Management support of all sexual orientation and gender identity strategies is essential. The support needs to be verbal, written, and in the form of management's actual physical presence whenever possible. This presence sends the message that a solid connection exists between the organization's values and diversity support.

WHERE DO WE GO FROM HERE?

Some people are straight, some are gay, some are bisexual, some are asexual, and some are transgender. None are superior to anyone else based on their sexual orientation or gender identity. Modern workplaces continue to recognize the human aspects of diversity, yet more progress is necessary before we all respect and appreciate each other for these differences.

3 | CHOOSING CIVILITY

P. M. FORNI

SUMMARY PREPARED BY KELLY NELSON

Kelly Nelson is a General Manager of Human Resources, at AK Steel in Ohio. In order to maintain her goal of civility, she keeps a set of the rules in her planner, next to her son John's picture. That provides focus for the most important reason for civility—achieving and maintaining meaningful, respectful relationships.

The **coarsening of America**, or the decline in the quality of social interaction, is an age-old concern, exacerbated by the information overload provided in today's world. Lives are made more complex and more remote by our busyness and lack of meaningful interaction with others. This can be cured by adhering to one guiding principle:

"A crucial measure of success in life is the way we treat one another every day in our lives."

INTRODUCING CIVILITY

As a society, we need to base our behavior on respect, restraint, and responsibility. The result of those behaviors is **civility**. Life can be difficult, but it is not unbearable and it is made infinitely better by meaningful, respectful communication with others. Civility helps us learn to be happy and to live well with others.

To be fully human, we must be able to imagine others' hurt and to relate it to the hurt we would feel in their position. That process of **consideration** is the result of imagination on a moral track—a function of empathy and moral values in action. **Empathy** is our ability to feel, to a certain extent, what others feel and to identify with them. Empathy is housed within civility, but it does not go far enough. Civility involves actively improving the lives of others through fostering harmonious and caring relationships. Civility requires us to use our intellect and our social skills to better ourselves, our communities, and our societies.

P. M. Forni, *Choosing Civility: The Twenty-Five Rules of Considerate Conduct.* New York: St. Martin's Press, 2003.

What is civility? Among other things, it is:

- Respect for others
- Politeness
- Fairness
- Etiquette
- Morality
- Compassion
- Courtesy
- Kindness
- Tolerance
- Sincerity
- Trustworthiness
- Going out of one's way

It is complex and it belongs within the realm of ethics. Civility is a form of goodness. Courtesy, politeness, manners, and civility are all forms of awareness. Civility takes all of the forms of awareness and molds them into active interest and action in the well-being of others.

Civility, courtesy, politeness, and manners are not synonyms. Courtesy suggests excellence and elegance in bestowing respect and attention. It also suggests deference and some degree of formality.

Politeness may sometimes be questioned with suspicion, particularly if a person's behavior is so polished that it indicates a façade. However, true politeness is a positive attribute and is a part of civility.

Manners refer to behavior in social interaction, when we handle others with care. Manners, too, are an important part of civility, but do not encompass all of what civility is.

Our lives are composed of events over which we have little or no control. We do, however, have complete control over how we *react* to life's events. We are makers of our own happiness. In order to choose civility, each of us must choose to make and keep our own happiness. Creating personal happiness provides a basis for us to make positive, caring relationships.

ACHIEVING CIVILITY

Other persons can be a source of happiness when we have positive relationships. We can all learn to be decent and caring for others. How do we learn to do this?

Step 1: Discipline our ego to look beyond the narrow confines of its immediate needs;

Step 2: Practice respect, restraint, concern, and benevolence;

Step 3: Learn to love and accept love from others.

Civility also involves self-control in both emotions and actions. It is not self-denial; it is self-expression, which is much different than that. **Self-expression** is a balance between self-effacement and self-indulgence. The balance allows us to be free from impulsive selfish reactions.

The restraint that comes as a result of the balance allows us to forgo actions whose effect is short-lived and choose, instead, the actions that will have a positive effect into the future. **Restraint** is the art of feeling good later. Civility may limit our immediate gratification, but it provides a satisfying sense of contentment from knowing we are making good, positive choices in our interaction with others.

The self-restraint within civility is not weakness when being faced with an adversarial circumstance. Instead, it encourages us to be sensitive and assertive at the same time—to practice respect for others while dealing with the situation at hand.

RULES OF CIVILITY

The rules of civility are profound in their simplicity. The challenge of achieving civility is to abide truly by the rules. This must come from the core of one's being.

1. Pay Attention
2. Acknowledge Others
3. Think the Best
4. Listen . . . Really Listen
5. Be Inclusive
6. Speak Kindly
7. Don't Speak Ill
8. Accept and Give Praise
9. Respect Even a Subtle "No"
10. Respect Others' Opinions
11. Mind Your Body
12. Be Agreeable
13. Keep It Down (and Rediscover Silence)
14. Respect Other People's Time
15. Respect Other People's Space
16. Apologize Earnestly and Thoughtfully
17. Assert Yourself
18. Avoid Personal Questions
19. Care for Your Guests
20. Be a Considerate Guest
21. Think Twice Before Asking for Favors
22. Refrain from Idle Complaints
23. Give Constructive Criticism
24. Respect the Environment and Be Gentle to Animals
25. Don't Shift Responsibility and Blame

Upon reading these rules, some people may be inclined to think they already follow them. However, true civility is deeper than that. To pay attention, one must constantly be aware of others around them. For example, is someone coming to a door that can be opened for them? Is someone looking very forlorn, but people continue to go on about their business without a sincere inquiry into their well-being?

When we listen, we must not listen just to have our turn to speak. Instead, we need to plan our listening, give the other person's words our complete attention, show the person we are listening, and be a cooperative listener. To be a cooperative listener, we must decide what is important in the material being communicated, and what is not.

By acknowledging others and by listening, we are including them. Every person desires to be included by others—family, friends, and co-workers. Even though this is an innate desire, some people have difficulty becoming included. Seek them out. Include them in your interactions.

Speaking kindly is the heart of civil behavior and involves both the spoken words as well as body language. First, you must decide if you need to speak at all. If so, an unhurried pace at a moderated volume that remains on point is necessary. If there is a conflict, be fair, and stick to the topic. Don't attack the other person. Never use profanity or seek to embarrass others. Perhaps most importantly, *think before speaking*.

Although compliments are fairly common, it is difficult for many to accept praise graciously or give praise meaningfully. Don't pay a compliment unless it is sincere; when you do give one, start with thoughts of the person in mind. Word the compliment carefully and specifically, but don't be patronizing. It's important to give compliments even if you feel the other person already knows your thoughts, so look for small reasons to compliment others. Remember to give compliments to your family, your co-workers, your acquaintances, and friends. When complimented, accept it graciously with a sincere "Thank you."

A rule of civility that many may find difficult is respecting—*truly* respecting—others' opinions. When other people disagree with us, it is easy to dismiss their thoughts as wrong. It is also easy to assume that others share our opinion, so we don't ask them what theirs is. Remember that opinions are not facts. It is important not to treat your own opinion as if it is fact.

Our time and everyone else's is in high demand. That is why it's important to respect other people's time. This involves being punctual and giving people reasonable amounts of time to discuss the issue at hand. It's also important when communicating with others to ask if it is a convenient time for them. If so, it is still important to only take the amount of time that is necessary.

Ones who live in civility do not forgo their right or obligation to assert themselves. This often involves learning to say "no" in a civil way, thereby respecting the person with whom you are communicating. It is important to be able to disagree without being disagreeable.

Treating our guests courteously and being a courteous guest is a balance between showing delight in the occasion and respecting privacy. Provide your guests some space, allow them to help in small chores if they wish, and allow them to feel in charge of their own time. When you are a guest, never assume that additional guests or pets are welcome and always ensure you leave their space as undisturbed as possible.

Delivering constructive criticism is a mainstay to improvement and must be handled with care. When providing constructive criticism, identify the issue rather than attacking the person. Describe what you have observed, and show that you understand how the person may feel. Suggest a solution or volunteer to assist in the process of finding one. Finally, treat the exchange kindly, remaining calm and empathetic throughout.

It is possible to be civil and remain true to one's beliefs. We must not lose sight of our own standards of behavior and accept responsibility and blame they are is ours to accept.

ACHIEVING A CIVIL SOCIETY

Past generations have moved from all working toward the survival of the community to being "self" centered. Civility moves us away from "self" and toward the improvement of others. As each person embraces and practices the rules of civility, society is improved. The guiding principle to this achievement is to *treat one another in a civil way every day of your life.*

PART
X | ORGANIZATIONAL CHANGE

A philosopher once noted that a person never steps into the same river twice, for the flowing current is always changing. Contemporary organizations have their own "river"—a turbulent environment around them. Consequently, managers of today's organizations are being called on to integrate their operations with a rapidly changing external environment. To bring about this integration, they must often adapt their organization's internal structure, processes, and strategies to meet these environmental challenges. The ability to manage change is far different from the ability to manage and cope with the ongoing and routine side of the organization.

Experts frequently advise American managers to invest in research and development (R&D) to keep their product mix current. Some companies (e.g., 3M) derive as much as 25 percent of their revenues from products introduced in the past five years. Nevertheless, many critics charge that one of the reasons for the decline in the competitiveness of U.S. industry revolves around its failure to innovate at sufficiently high levels. Clearly, organizations need to manage change, stimulate renewal, and develop organizational cultures in which change can thrive.

Robert E. Quinn is the M. E. Tracy Collegiate Professor of Organization Behavior and Human Resource Management at the University of Michigan, and also the co-founder of the Center for Positive Organizational Scholarship. He has written a trilogy of books that focus on the positive tensions associated with excellent performance—*Deep Change, Change the World*, and *Building the Bridge as You Walk on It.*

Dr. Quinn believes that understanding change is the foundation for building a better world. He suggests that each of us faces a core dilemma: Make deep and significant changes within ourselves, or face a slow but certain death. The solution to this dilemma lies in practicing the "fundamental state of leadership," which involves eight practices of increasing integrity—reflective action, authentic engagement, appreciative inquiry, grounded vision, adaptive confidence, detached interdependence, responsible freedom, and tough love. To effect change, Quinn says, requires that leaders become results-centered, internally driven, other-focused, and externally open.

Clayton M. Christensen, professor of business administration at the Harvard Business School, and Michael E. Raynor, a director at Deloitte Research (the research arm of Deloitte Consulting) teamed up to write *The Innovator's Solution*. *The Innovator's Solution* is a sequel to *The Innovator's Dilemma*, authored by Dr. Christensen. In this later book, Christensen and Raynor explore how managers become blinded by "disruptive innovations" because of their preoccupation with their existing businesses and most profitable customers. In *The Innovator's Solution*, the authors reveal how organizations that are capable of sustaining growth get beyond this crippling dilemma. These organizations have managed to create a "disruptive growth engine." By drawing upon organizational examples, Christensen and Raynor identify and discuss the forces that cause managers to make bad decisions and they suggest how to make disruptions succeed.

The third reading in this part focuses on the work of Edward E. Lawler III and Christopher Worley. Dr. Lawler is on the faculty at the University of Southern California and director of the Center for Effective Organizations. He has a Ph.D. from the University of California, Berkeley, and has held faculty appointments at Yale and the University of Michigan. Dr. Lawler has a long and distinguished scholarly career contributing extensively to the organizational sciences. He is the author or co-author of several other popular management books, including *Rewarding Excellence, The Ultimate Advantage,* and *The New American Workplace*. Chris Worley holds a Ph.D. from the University of Southern California and is a research scientist for the Center for Effective Organizations.

The authors of *Built to Change* argue that contemporary (B2Change) organizations need to be designed and structured so as to stimulate change in the context of today's global economy. Specifically, B2Change firms should maintain a close connection to their environments, reward employee experimentation with new ideas, search out and learn about new practices and technologies, make a strong and vocal commitment to the improvement of performance, and do "whatever it takes" (ethically) to gain competitive advantages. Two major strategies for accomplishing continual change are the Commitment to Development and the Travel Light approaches.

1

BUILDING THE BRIDGE
AS YOU WALK ON IT

ROBERT E. QUINN

SUMMARY PREPARED BY PETER STARK

Peter Stark teaches Strategy, Managing Change, Entrepreneurship, and International Marketing courses in the Labovitz School of Business and Economics at the University of Minnesota Duluth. Peter is an ABD doctoral student in organizational change at Pepperdine University. He has previously taught at several institutions in the United States, Mexico, and China, and is a frequent visiting instructor with the Helsinki School of Economics in Finland. He is an international consultant working with many global companies. His research interests include the application of systems theory and chaos theory to the process of understanding and dealing with the embedded ontological arche-types that inhibit culture change in organizations.

THE BASIC IDEA AND CONCEPT PATH

Leadership, rather than being a set of tool-like behavioral patterns to be enacted through emulation, is best portrayed as a state of *being* ("who we are") rather than a means of *doing* ("what we do"). Many people spend most of their time in the "normal life state." They tend to be comfort-centered, externally driven, self-focused, and internally closed. As a consequence, many organizations reflect the embedded selfishness, insecurity, and lack of courage inherent in this state of being. Fortunately, anyone can transform their state of being and enter the extraordinary **fundamental state of leadership** in which they become results-centered, internally directed, other-focused, and externally open. These individuals become role models for others to emulate, and hence they stimulate positive organizing approaches and more productive social systems.

Robert E. Quinn, *Building the Bridge as You Walk on It: A Guide for Leading Change.* San Francisco: Jossey-Bass, 2004.

There is a strong link between an individual's personal transformation to the fundamental state of leadership and subsequent organizational transformation. *Anyone who aspires to leadership must engage in a continuous and, perhaps most importantly, courageously and consciously intended learning journey*. This requires that they wed their individual ability to let go of ego needs-based control and venture into uncharted territory with their capacity for inspired, authentic leadership. Leaders who undertake this journey of self-transformation enable the positive creation of a more productive community capable of creating, leveraging, and enduring change.

Five major conclusions about leadership can be offered:

1. Extraordinarily positive organizations (productive, flourishing communities) are reflections of (and are brought about by) extraordinary states of being among their members; they are consequently capable of creating, leveraging, and enduring great change. Without such states of being present among an organization's leaders, organizations will entropy (decline).
2. Leadership has nothing to do with position and power. It is about your fundamental "state of being" (who you are), not what you do or what you have. Leadership is realized not in what the leader does but in what others do as a consequence of the leader's state of being.
3. The normal state of being for most individuals is comfort-centered, externally driven, self-focused, and internally closed. Leadership in the "normal state" isn't really leadership at all—it is a self-interested rationalization in support of socially normed organizational coping strategies. The fundamental state of leadership is results-centered, internally directed, other-focused, and externally open.
4. Entering the "fundamental state of leadership" requires those who aspire to leadership to experience deep, revitalizing personal change in which they challenge and change many, if not all, of their basic beliefs and assumptions in pursuit of greater awareness and authenticity.
5. Organizations change only when the leaders among its members change. The creation of extraordinarily positive organizations/productive communities is contingent upon a leader's acceptance of and engagement in a process of deep personal change.

How, then, should one fundamentally "be" in the context of a catalytic and systemic organizational process? It must be noted that human beings are complex paradoxes of qualities, attributes, and behaviors. Leadership, then, is the effect on others that emerges from the confluence of these creatively tense paradoxes. Positive traits and tensions tend to exist and operate as part of a larger, more complex, reciprocal system. Integrating the oppositions of eight polarities of being (spontaneous/self-disciplined, compassionate/assertive, mindful/energetic, principled/engaged, realistic/optimistic, grounded/visionary, confident/flexible, and independent/open) suggests eight creatively tense states from which a more dynamic and more accurately representative view of the state of leadership emerges. These practices serve as "guard rails" on the path and are both realistic and idealistic in conception and application. In *striving* for the integrated path, one is in the fundamental state of leadership.

PRACTICES FOR ENTERING THE FUNDAMENTAL STATE OF LEADERSHIP

The eight integrated but creatively tense and seemingly paradoxical practices individuals can engage in for entering the fundamental state of leadership are:

- *Reflective action* – the practice of integrating the realm of personal identity (who we are) with the realm of action (what we are doing). This person acts and learns simultaneously.
- *Authentic engagement* – the practice of increasing our integrity by engaging the world of action with genuine love for what we are doing. This person is authentically engaged (ethical, while also highly involved).
- *Appreciative inquiry* – the practice of gaining the capacity to see the best in the world and what is possible. These persons are optimistic, constructive, realistic, and questioning, which allows them to help others surface possibilities that previously have been less recognized.
- *Grounded vision* – the practice of integrating the present with an image of a positive future. Such leaders are grounded, factual, hopeful, and visionary.
- *Adaptive confidence* – the practice of letting go of control and moving into a state of action learning. The adaptively confident person is concurrently flexible, confident, secure, experimental, and open to feedback.
- *Detached interdependence* – the practice of considering one's relationships from a very high level of maturity. This leader combines independence, a strong sense of purpose, and strength with humility and openness.
- *Responsible freedom* – the practice of being aware of and acting in regard to the intimate connections between freedom and responsibility. The practitioner of responsible freedom is spontaneous, expressive, self-structuring, self-disciplined, empowering to others, and responsible.
- *Tough love* – the practice of living in the balance of being both simultaneously compassionate/concerned and assertive/bold. The tough love practitioner is assertive, challenging, bold, compassionate, and concerned.

DEVELOPING LEADERS

Leaders are developed through a two-step process: changing ourselves, and choosing to enter the fundamental state of leadership. In the first step, all change requires and begins with self-change and requires making a personal choice to change. The second step is helping others to do the same. Leadership development similarly involves these interdependent, mutually reinforcing phenomena. Developing leaders is not just imparting a set of concepts or teaching a toolkit of strategies and behaviors; *it is encouraging people to engage in the process of deep change in themselves and then inviting others to do the same.*

Self-change can be viewed as a nine-stage path or spiral:

- Precontemplation: increasing information about one's self—one's own problems (self-deceptions), negative routines, and self-defeating behaviors. This involves consciousness raising (becoming aware that we don't know what we don't know).
- Social liberation: increasing social alternatives for behaviors that are not problematic.

- Emotional arousal: experiencing and expressing feelings about one's problems and solutions.
- Self-reevaluation: assessing feelings and thoughts about one's self with respect to a problem.
- Commitment: choosing and committing to act; belief in one's own ability to change.
- Countering: substituting new and positive alternatives for problem behaviors.
- Environment control: avoiding stimuli that elicit problem behaviors.
- Reward: rewarding one's self, or being rewarded by others, for making appropriate and positive changes.
- Helping relationships: Enlisting the help and support of someone who cares to aid in preventing you from relapsing.

The fundamental state of leadership has significant implications. First, it redefines what leadership means. It is not authority and not a set of easily imitated attributes or skill sets. It is, instead, a state—a way of being that has the ability to profoundly change the systems that it is a part of. Second, it redefines what it means to develop leaders. Leadership development is first and foremost self-change, which requires an understanding of the stages and strategies inherent in this process as well as the ability to support others as they go through them.

There really is no way to teach what it means to be in a fundamental state of leadership. The best way is simply to be what you wish to evoke from others. However, the fundamental state of leadership is an inherently fragile and episodic phenomenon; it is difficult to get into and difficult to stay in.

We attract others into the fundamental state of leadership, then, by our own change process in pursuit of our own uniqueness and ever-increasing integrity. *It is one's courage to engage in the process and not one's success in mastering it that attracts others.*

THE INNOVATOR'S SOLUTION

CLAYTON M. CHRISTENSEN, MICHAEL E. RAYNOR,
AND SCOTT D. ANTHONY

SUMMARY PREPARED BY WARREN L. CANDY

Warren L. Candy *is a Senior Vice President at Allete Minnesota Power, a diversified electric utility located in Duluth, Minnesota, where he is responsible for generation, transmission, distribution, mining, and customer operations in Minnesota, Wisconsin, and North Dakota. His interests include sustainable organizational design, leadership excellence, and socio-technical systems. He received his Bachelor of Science degree in Production Engineering from Swinburne Institute of Technology in Melbourne, Australia.*

SUSTAINING CORPORATE GROWTH

Research and observation of hundreds of both successful and unsuccessful growth-oriented businesses have resulted in the identification of a number of key theories and practical responses for creating and sustaining new growth in business. Growth is important to all management teams because companies create shareholder value through profitable growth. However, approximately 1 company in 10 is able to sustain the kind of growth that translates into above average increases in shareholder returns for more than a few years at a time. It's hard to know how to grow, but pursuing growth the wrong way can be worse than no growth at all.

As the core business approaches maturity, investors demand new growth, and executives develop seemingly sensible strategies to generate it. Although they often invest aggressively, many times their plans still fail to create the needed growth fast enough. Probably the most daunting challenge in delivering growth is that once you fail to deliver it, the odds of ever regaining past levels of success are very low. It has been shown that of all the companies whose growth has stalled, only 4 percent are able to successfully reignite their growth, even to a rate of 1 percent above GNP!

Clayton M. Christensen, Michael E. Raynor, and Scott D. Anthony, *The Innovator's Solution: Creating and Sustaining Successful Growth.* Boston: Harvard Business School Press, 2003.

What *can* make the process of innovation more predictable comes from an understanding of the forces that act upon those individuals and the management teams building the business. When comprehended and properly applied, these forces can powerfully influence what managers can choose to do, and what they cannot choose to do.

A dearth of good ideas is rarely the core problem in a company that struggles to launch exciting new-growth businesses. The problem is in the shaping process itself. The major obstacle for growth-seeking managers is that the exciting growth markets of tomorrow are most likely small and off the radar screen today. Managers who understand these forces, and learn to harness them in making key decisions, will develop successful new-growth businesses much more consistently than historically seemed possible.

FUNDAMENTAL ISSUES AND PRINCIPLES

The following set of issues highlights some of the most important decisions that need to be addressed by managers. The answers to the underlying questions, and the essential principles supporting them, can guide managers as they successfully grow new and profitable businesses.

Outperforming your Competition

A key management question is always "What could our competition do to outperform us?" A natural follow-up question becomes "What courses of action could actually give *us* the upper hand?" A new market entrant is more likely to beat the incumbent with disruptive innovations, rather than with sustaining innovations. *Disruptive innovations* occur where the challenge is to commercialize a simpler, more convenient product that sells for less money, a product that appeals to a new or unattractive customer set. This compares to *sustaining innovations,* where the goal is to deliver a better product that is sold for more money to an already attractive set of customers.

Disruptive innovations don't attempt to bring better products to established customers in established markets. Rather, they disruptively redefine the market by introducing products and services that are not as good as the currently available products, but instead offer other benefits such as being simpler, more convenient, less expensive, and more appealing to a new, or less demanding, customer group.

This distinction is important for innovators seeking to create new-growth businesses. Whereas the current leaders of the industry will almost always triumph in battles of sustaining innovation, successful disruptions are most likely to be launched by the new entrant companies.

Identifying Desired Products

Managers appropriately ask the questions, "What products should we be developing?" "Which improvements will our customers want?" and "Which new products will be rejected out of hand?" Managers need to rethink their perceptions and opinions of why customers actually use or don't use their products and services. In reality, customers "hire" products to do specific jobs that regularly arise in their lives and that need to get done under specific circumstances. Companies that target their products at the circumstances in which customers find themselves, rather than the customers themselves, can launch predictably successful products.

Identifying Best Customers

As managers create new business ventures, they must ask themselves "Which initial customers will constitute the most viable foundation upon which to build a successful business?" The first step is to find the ideal customers for low-end disruptions. They are the current users of the mainstream products who seem disinterested in offers to sell them improved performance products. They may be willing to accept improved products, but they are often unwilling to pay for them.

A *new-market disruption* is an innovation that enables a large population of people who previously lacked the money or skill to now begin buying and using a product, and doing the job for themselves. However, a product that purports to help non-consumers do something that they weren't already prioritizing in their lives is unlikely to succeed.

Internal vs. External Activity

A key decision for the long-term sustainability of any organization revolves around the activities required to design, produce, sell, and distribute products and services—Which ones should be done internally? Which ones should be done externally by partners and suppliers?

Traditionally this decision has been made around the organization's core competency model, which suggests that if something fits your core competency, then you should do it inside the organization. If it is not a core competency and another firm can do it better, then you should rely on them to do it. The problem with this approach is that what might seem to be a non-core activity today might become an absolutely critical competence to have mastered in a proprietary way in the future, and vice versa. The real question to be asked, and the decision to be made, is "What do we need to master today, and what will we need to master in the future, in order to excel on the path of improvement that customers will define as important to them?"

Core competence is a dangerously inwardly looking notion. Competitiveness is far more about doing what *customers* value than it is about doing what you think you are good at. Staying competitive as the competition shifts requires a willingness and an ability to learn new things rather than to hold onto what has been successful in the past.

Avoiding the Commoditization of Products

As organizations grow, they need to maintain strong competitive advantage and attractive profits within a marketplace that, over time, is trending toward commoditization. *Commoditization* is a natural and inescapable process that occurs as new markets coalesce around proprietary products that become increasingly difficult to differentiate from the competition. Attractive future profits can often be found elsewhere in the value chain, in different stages or layers of value added, usually in the places where previously profit was hard to attain.

Considering Disruptive Growth

One ongoing responsibility for all management teams is to ensure that the optimal organizational design and structure is in place to facilitate ongoing business growth. Many potentially successful innovations fail not because of market forces, but because the management of the organization is not up to the task. Those capabilities that were assets in sustaining circumstances become liabilities when disruption is needed. To be confident that managers can handle the new challenges placed before them, executives need to examine in detail the types of actual problems that they have had to deal with in the past, and diminish their emphasis on broad leadership attributes that are believed to be inherently important (e.g., good communicator; results oriented). By focusing on a person's ability to learn and adapt, managers can avoid the trap of assuming that those skills that are important today are those that will still be required in the future. In many ways this results in a paradox: *The managers that corporate executives have come to trust most today because they have consistently delivered the needed results in the core business cannot be trusted to shepherd the creation of new business ventures tomorrow.*

Establishing a Strategy that Works

Most questions that are raised about strategy focus on its substance. However, the crucial question really relates to the *process* of strategy formulation, that is, using the right process in the right circumstances. Although senior management can become obsessed with finding the right strategy, they can actually wield greater leverage by managing the processes used to develop the strategy, and by making sure that the right process is used under the right circumstances.

Within organizations there are essentially two types of strategies—deliberate and emergent. *Deliberate strategies* are the product of a conscious and analytical plan based on rigorous analysis of data. *Emergent strategies* are responses to unanticipated opportunities, problems, and successes that were unforeseen in the deliberate strategy-making process. The emergent process should dominate in circumstances where the future is hard to read and in which it is not clear what the right strategy should be. Alternatively, the deliberate process should dominate once a winning strategy has become clear and effective implementation is crucial.

PREFERRED SOURCES OF CAPITAL

As companies seek to grow and expand, three key issues emerge for senior management to consider. These focus on (1) identifying whose investment capital will help the firm succeed, (2) determining whose capital might be the "kiss of death," and (3) exploring what sources of money will help the firm most at different stages of its development. The best resource for facilitating success in a growth-oriented business is money that is "patient for growth but impatient for profit." By contrast, money should be impatient for growth in later stage, deliberate-strategy circumstances after a winning strategy has emerged.

THE ROLE OF SENIOR EXECUTIVES

One reason that many soaring hot-product companies flame out is that the key initial resource, the founding team, fails to institute the processes or the values that will help the company continue to develop and initiate disruptive products and services. The CEOs of all companies play a critical role in sustaining the growth of the business.

Senior executives have three roles to play in ensuring repeated disruptive growth in their organizations. First, they must stand astride and manage the interface between the disruptive growth businesses and the mainstream businesses. Second, these executives must shepherd the internal processes that repeatedly create new organizational growth. Third, they must sense when circumstances are changing and respond appropriately.

The larger and more complex a company becomes, the more important it is for senior managers to train employees at every level to act autonomously. Doing so will help them make prioritized decisions that are consistent with the strategic direction and business model of the organization. Senior management's role is to decide when to keep their hands off the new business, and when to get involved.

Conclusion

Managers need to know how to use a key number of theories and principles to create and sustain continuous organizational growth. An integrated body of theory derived from the successes and failures of hundreds of different companies has been developed, and each of these address a different aspect of the "innovator's dilemma."

3

BUILT TO CHANGE

EDWARD E. LAWLER III AND CHRISTOPHER G. WORLEY

SUMMARY PREPARED BY MARTHA GOLDEN

Martha Golden *is a graduate of the Labovitz School of Business and Economics at the University of Minnesota Duluth, where she double majored in Organizational Management and Human Resource Management. Martha is currently a manager at Wintergreen Northern Wear, a handmade clothing manufacturer in Minnesota. She looks forward to starting her professional career with a progressive change-oriented organization. Martha currently lives in Duluth and enjoys proximity to the North Shore of Lake Superior.*

INTRODUCTION

Change is everywhere and occurs more rapidly every day. Every organization needs to pay attention to change in order to survive. Organizations continue to struggle with change because they traditionally have been encouraged to be stable, constant, and methodical. Most organizations view change as a necessary, or in some cases unnecessary, evil. Change is seen as difficult, disruptive, and too often ineffective. Today's organizations need to adopt a group of short-term competitive advantages in their organizational design that assumes change is a normal activity and become *B2change* (built to change) *organizations*.

LEADERSHIP

Effective leadership is critical when organizations experience change. The larger and more significant the change the greater need there is for a leader who can guide the organization through the change. B2change organizations employ *shared leadership* for three reasons. It can replace rigid hierarchies and spread decision making across many people; it can help an organization build a large pool of leaders at all levels to draw from; and it supports more effective change management. Being an effective manager and an effective leader is attractive to B2change organizations because managers with shared leadership skills can switch between roles as needed as they react to the organization's changing environment.

Edward E. Lawler III and Christopher Worley, *Built to Change: How to Achieve Sustained Organizational Effectivencws.* San Francisco: Jossey-Bass, 2006.

HUMAN CAPITAL MANAGEMENT

Globalization has raised the level of competition and opened new markets, which challenges organizations to deal with a global consumer base. Being able to change rapidly and react to their environments means that firms need to invest a significant amount in their human capital. The way a firm is organized, and the quality of its management, staff, and employees, can prove to be a significant competitive advantage. B2change organizations begin to compete, in part, on the basis of intangible assets and their staff, instead of tangible goods.

How individuals react to change is a major barrier that organizations encounter when considering change initiatives. People need a reason to change and most organizational structures have been designed around stability, which is a natural resister to change. Past efforts have shown that large-scale change operations are usually unsuccessful and ultimately have little effect. However, competitive pressures dictate that an organization must change. If it does not, it will likely become extinct. *The best competitive advantage an organization can have is the ability and willingness to change.* Every part of an organization's design, every department, every policy, and every employee needs to be committed to change and the implementation of the change strategy. B2change organizations are so reliant on their human capital that it should command as much as or more attention than the organization's financial or other physical assets. Recruiting individuals who already possess the ability and willingness to change is critical.

Two key human resource strategies are employed by B2change organizations. The *Commitment to Development* strategy involves hiring individuals who are skilled, but who are willing and able to change and develop regardless of where the organization goes. This strategy avoids the high cost of turnover, yet it is expensive to maintain and may even slow down change while people learn new skills. The other option is the *Travel Light* strategy, which allows companies to obtain new talent when needed and discard it when the need ends. This allows for a flexible workforce that can shift core competencies quickly. Unfortunately the organization may not be able to find the exact talent it needs or find it when it needs it, and this tends to lead to a disloyal workforce short in leadership and management. The approach that works best depends on the rate of change in the organization's environment.

Effective decision making is a challenging process to manage for many organizations, and even more so for B2change organizations. It is most effective to allow decisions involving operations and existing processes to be made at the level the processes are centered on, and managed with input from employees. By contrast, strategic decisions that concern the entire organization ultimately need to be made at the top, but B2change organizations seek input from all levels. All decisions need to be communicated to everyone they will affect as soon as possible to reduce confusion and create accountability.

REWARD SYSTEMS

Once an organization has decided whether it is a Travel Light or Commitment to Develop organization and has identified its core employees, it needs to define the reward system. Quantity and mix are the key factors in a successful reward system.

For B2change organizations, designing a reward system that will attract and retain the type of individuals they need is an important part of human capital management. Along with an appropriate reward system, B2change organizations need to have a complex performance management system in place so that they can quickly determine if they have the correct mix of employee skills to match their current and near-future environment. An organizational reward system should motivate its employees to perform in ways that support the strategic intent and requirements. B2change organizations need to offer the rewards that employees value highly, so that they will be willing to do what is asked of them. A clear connection has to be established between the reward and the behavior required to obtain it; this is called a line-of-sight approach, or *organizational transparency*. As B2change organizations change, their reward systems will change and employees need to be able to see that what they are told about the changes will actually appear. It also creates a level of accountability. B2change reward systems need to be tied to individual, team, business unit, or organizational performance in order to motivate performance so that they maintain the core competencies and capabilities.

B2change organizations stay away from seniority-based reward systems and base their reward structure on bonuses. Giving bonuses enables them to reward individual or team performance and can result in the retention of highly effective people. Bonus systems can even be tied into change goals that the organization sets for itself and its employees. They also provide the clearest line of sight between what the employees are doing and what they are being rewarded for. Profit sharing and stock ownership are two bonus reward programs that companies can use. B2change organizations can also implement a person-based pay reward system. People are rewarded for their skills and knowledge, not just their job. This leads to the further development of the labor force as employees work to improve their capabilities. This can lead to high levels of motivation and the ability of the organization to develop and improve employee competencies and capabilities quickly and efficiently.

THE BUILT-TO-CHANGE MODEL

The Built-to-Change Model consists of three primary organizational processes that revolve around an organization's *identity*, which is the core values, beliefs, and behaviors that an organization will try to keep constant. It originates in the company's culture and describes the way a company does business. An organization's identity reacts to *environmental scenarios* that represent a variety of possible future business conditions. The processes of *strategizing, creating value*, and *designing* are the main contributors to an organization's effectiveness. These processes help an organization to decide how to react to the changing environment.

Strategizing, in the B2change Model, describes the way an organization decides where to focus in respect to product, service, and market. The organization's *strategic intent* is its guide to creating value and overall design. Ironically, a B2change organization needs to have a stable identity—but one that is committed to change. Five elements of strategic intent help to identify what an organization needs to do to accomplish its objectives.

1. The breadth of an organization's activities
2. The aggressiveness of its operations

3. The way it orchestrates change
4. The differentiated features of its products and services
5. The logic for making profits

Orchestration is the most important of these five, as it describes how all the rest fit together. It is the most challenging for organizations to implement, but the most critical investment if a company wants to become a B2change organization. Only through tremendous orchestration will a company be able to embrace a strategic change. When an organization's strategic intent describes a path that is proximate to both its environment and its identity, the organization achieves *critical configuration*. Critical configuration refers to the importance of specifying the relationships between an organization's environment, identity, and strategic intent, all of which determine performance.

The strategizing process a B2change organization should follow has three phases. Phase 1 is the strategic review, consisting of an identification of the causes of an organization's current performance and an analysis of the current strategy's appropriateness for the future. Phase 2 is the strategic choice. This phase works with the information developed in the strategic review and decides whether a change is necessary. Phase 3 is the strategic change. If the organization decides that its strategy does need to change, then this phase is the reconfiguration point. If a strategic change is necessary, it is essential to inform all members of the organization so that they are as involved as possible, so that they, too, are committed to the change. Again, the orchestration step emerges as a critical capability for a B2change organization.

Finding the best approach to creating value is the major consideration when designing and structuring an organization. The top designs put as many employees as possible in contact with the external environment to ensure the powerful feedback from customers that can be a source of motivation for change. This approach to organizational design leaves no room for rigid, fixed job descriptions. B2change organizations are in an environment of continuous change, and having their employees unable to change with them because of their confining job descriptions is costly and inefficient. Individuals and teams who are known by what they *can* do instead of being known for their *job* encourages employees to be flexible and more adaptable to change initiatives. B2change organizations utilize temporary teams to build relationships and to help employees develop skills they may not already have. Virtual teams, business units, matrices, and front-back structures are some types of team-based relationships that B2change organizations can use. All have their advantages and disadvantages and can be utilized effectively for B2change companies.

Creating value is a critical part of the B2change Model because it details how an organization creates competencies and capabilities. Core competencies are defined as the combination of technology and production skills that underlie the product lines and services of an organization. They are based in science, technology, and engineering and can be found in an organization's staff. Capabilities are the clearly identifiable and measurable value-adding activities that describe what the organization can do. Processes, routines, behaviors, and systems constitute the major part of capabilities and can be found anywhere in the organization. By constantly improving competencies and capabilities, they can be leveraged to result in a competitive advantage for the B2change organization.

The last process of the B2change Model is designing. To perform effectively, an organization designs processes and structures that allow it to create the appropriate competencies and capabilities it needs. It is a constant process that modifies and adjusts all parts of an organization. *Dynamic alignment* exists when all of the pieces in the designing and creating value process are evolving in the same direction and in support of the strategic intent. There are three questions at the foundation of an effective dynamic alignment that must be considered at the beginning of the design process. They are:

1. What kind of information do you collect and how do you communicate it?
2. How do you measure individuals, units, and the organization as a whole?
3. Who should be involved in making decisions?

Information on how the business operates, the organization's environment, and how it is currently performing are the three most important kinds of information that an organization needs to collect. Communicating the information to everyone in the organization will connect the employees to their environment, which will help bring about the changes needed. B2change organizations concentrate on measuring predictors of performance. Measuring individuals, teams, business units, the total organization, and key processes is a difficult task. B2change organizations look at all of these parts and determine if what they are doing presently will continue to allow them to perform effectively in the future. There are many different options that the B2change organization can employ to measure these organizational parts and they are detailed extensively in the book.

CREATING A VIRTUOUS SPIRAL

Creating a *virtuous spiral* is the goal of B2change organizations. This state exists when everything comes together in such a way that critical configuration and dynamic alignment equally coexist for extended periods of time. They are very unusual and almost impossible to duplicate. IBM, Nike, Microsoft, Procter & Gamble, and GE are organizations that have found the virtuous spiral path and have continued on it for many years. Unfortunately, a rapidly changing environment is the biggest hazard for virtuous spirals and sustained effectiveness. It is for this reason that successful B2change organizations are difficult to maintain. Creating a B2change organization is a daunting prospect, but it is becoming more and more important in today's increasingly competitive business environment. Using a Built-to-Change Model can help organizations adapt to their surroundings and give them the competitive edge they need to gain or sustain organizational effectiveness.

PART
XI | INTRA-ORGANIZATIONAL DYNAMICS

In part, organizational culture is all about the relationships that exist among organizational members, and how people connect and interact with one another as they carry out their organizational roles. In this section, two book summaries (*Who Really Matters* and *It's All Politics*) are presented with each one providing insight into the internal and interpersonal workings of organizations.

According to Art Kleiner in *Who Really Matters*, it is common to see in corporate mission statements and in various other organizational communications the claim that "we make our decisions on behalf of our shareholders." All too often, Kleiner notes, these words are taken at face value and assumed to be spoken with sincerity. Yet the author argues that all organizations have one motive in common, and that motive is to promote the wants and needs of a "core group of people"—those "who really matter." In many instances (but not always) this group of people is those who are positioned atop the corporate hierarchy. In *Who Really Matters*, Kleiner gives his readers clues on how to identify the core group and the nature of its mission. Edgar H. Schein, professor emeritus of management at MIT, observes that this book "Provides a much-needed new perspective on leadership, power, and authority in showing clearly how core groups unconsciously guide and control organizations."

Art Kleiner is the Director of Research and Reflection at Dialogos, a Cambridge, Massachusetts, consulting firm. He also teaches in the interactive telecommunications program at New York University. His consulting and writing work is primarily centered on the human impact of management and technology.

In *It's All Politics*, Kathleen Kelley Reardon notes that hard work and potential are not the only keys for an individual's movement upward and ultimately to the top of the organizational hierarchy. Those who make it—the winners—and those who don't—the losers—differ from one another in terms of their political skills and the use of those skills. Those who make it upward successfully manage their relationships with those who are capable of rewarding them with key organizational moves.

Kathleen Kelley Reardon is a professor of management in the Marshall School of Business at the University of Southern California. She is an expert in the areas of persuasion, negotiations, and politics. Dr. Reardon is also the author of *The Secret Handshake*.

1

WHO REALLY MATTERS

ART KLEINER

SUMMARY PREPARED BY CATHY A. HANSON

Cathy A. Hanson is the Director of Human Resources for the City of Azusa, California. She is responsible for labor relations, compensation, recruitment and selection, training and development, as well as safety and risk management. Prior to moving to the public sector, she worked for Fortune 500 companies in human resources for both corporate and manufacturing sites. Her assignments included a new team-based manufacturing plant start-up, a plant closure, and a merger and acquisition. She has a Bachelor of Business Administration from the University of Minnesota Duluth and a Master of Business Administration from the University of Southern California.

INTRODUCTION

Every organization has a **core group**. This consists of people who influence the direction of the organization, determine how decisions are made, and affect who will be the most influential in making those decisions. This group may be different from the group of people the organization publicly states it is designed to serve, such as the customers, the public, or the shareholders. The organization will do whatever it takes to meet the needs and wants of this group.

WHAT IS A CORE GROUP?

Normally, the core group will be made up of the organization's top executives, along with others in the organization. Some of the members are in the core group by the organization's choice, while others attain their status because of their role in the organization. In some organizations, membership can frequently change. Size of the core group can vary from very small to relatively large. No matter who these key people are, they set the organization's direction and influence the decisions made on behalf of the organization. The power of the core group comes from the authority bestowed to it from the other employees within the organization. The direction in which the organization moves will

Art Kleiner, *Who Really Matters: The Core Group Theory of Power, Privilege, and Success.* New South Wales, Australia: Currency, 2003.

depend on where the employees of the organization perceive the core group wants it to go. When faced with a decision, the employees will consider how core group members would make the decision by asking themselves, "What would X think? What would Y do?" Then, they act accordingly.

COMMON CORE GROUP

Core groups can be identified by who belongs to them or how they behave. For example:

- Noncooperation within the organization. Parts of the organization either ignore each other or compete with each other. Employees of these areas end up modeling this behavior in similar but smaller ways, such as on project teams, thereby perpetuating the behavior throughout the organization. Energy and time spent on resolving these conflicts or trying to get the other's attention take away from the ultimate purpose and goals of the organization.
- Protection of the organization's bureaucracy. For example, a newly appointed vice president of finance might want to streamline the accounts payable process, but is continually thwarted by long-term employees who continue to "do things they way we've always done them," despite the direction from the VP.

Core groups that demonstrate behavior such as this reduce the organization's effectiveness and distract the employees.

BEING PART OF THE CORE GROUP

Various positions have power solely based on the hierarchy of the organization. The core group, however, gets its power from the authority bestowed on it by the employees of the organization. As part of the core group, an employee will enjoy several things others in the organization only dream about. Some of these "perks" include:

- Being viewed as critical to the organization's fate
- Being taken seriously on matters beyond their expertise
- Feeling commitment from the organization that their wants and needs will be met

By contrast, if employees are *not* one of the core group members, they will have a different relationship with the organization. Sometimes referred to as employees of "mutual consent," the organization will not meet their every want and need, but it will provide them with some level of satisfaction. In return, they will provide their talents and knowledge to help the organization reach its goals and objectives as determined by the core group.

CORE GROUPS AND LEADERSHIP OF ORGANIZATIONS

Effective core groups possess a unique type of knowledge specific to organizations of their type—the knowledge of the types of problems to be solved and the knowledge of the unique way their organization solves these problems. When these two parts are accepted, internalized, and demonstrated by the core group, the organization as a whole accepts and internalizes them. Employees below the core group can then use this knowledge to make decisions that reflect the organization's goals and objectives. This type of knowledge is sometimes referred to as "core competencies" or an "integrated learning base." When employees within the organization develop core competencies, the organization as a whole runs more smoothly and reaches the goals set by the core group.

However, core group members can also distract the organization from its goals and objectives. This happens when something that the core group members say is "amplified" throughout the organization. In addition, subordinates will take what is said and make assumptions about what to do with it. For example, a passing comment about a new product may lead to financial and human resources being spent on the project because people think that's what the core group wants. In order to minimize wasted time, effort, and financial resources, the core group must minimize the distortion in the messages it sends.

MEASUREMENTS AND INCENTIVES

Organizations often utilize performance measures and compensation incentives to motivate their employees. These organizations will state that these measurements and incentives are intended to focus employees on the ultimate goals and objectives of the organization and to motivate performance. In reality, however, only what is *perceived* to matter to the core group will be measured. As these measurements flow down from the core group to the employees, they flow down through layers of supervision, with each layer putting its spin on what the measurements mean and how the core group is interpreting them. Conversely, the results of these measures will flow up through the layers, with each putting its spin on them, and ultimately this will reach the core group. Examples of these measurements include financial targets and production goals, and the numbers will often take on a life of their own. When that happens, the masses will forget about the intent of the measurement and focus on the measurement itself, thus reducing the effectiveness of the measurement. In order to prevent this from happening and for the measurements and incentives to accomplish what they were intended to do, employees must feel free to question them and receive feedback from the core group. When this happens, the organization learns as a whole and the measures can be adjusted to reflect the true goals and objectives of the organization.

THE CEO AND CORE GROUP

The CEO of an organization is also constrained by the wants and needs of the core group. Members within the core group may have conflicting goals that the CEO is forced to deal with. However, the CEO can help the core group become more effective by the processes he or she is able to influence. These include:

- Information and communication channels within the organization
- Tolerance or lack thereof for creativity and the failures that accompany them
- The process by which employees are hired, fired, promoted, demoted, etc.
- The quality of the leadership provided by the CEO

By actively influencing these processes, the CEO can enable the organization to become efficient and effective while working with the core group.

CAN ALL EMPLOYEES OF AN ORGANIZATION BE IN THE CORE GROUP?

The simple answer is "yes." However, this is no small undertaking. First and foremost, the organization must instill a culture that places the employee's well-being and success equal to that of the financial well-being of the organization. Organizations who are successful at this have a structure that not only emphasizes both the human and financial systems, but also continually works to improve these systems. When these systems are successful employees feel involved, committed, and an integral part of the organization.

CORE GROUPS AND CAREERS

Like our parents in our early lives, core groups influence us early in our careers. After continually being told to "look both ways before you cross the street" we no longer need our parents to tell us to do so; we begin to tell ourselves. It's the same with core groups. *The core groups we're exposed to early on continue to influence us throughout our careers.* They influence how we perceive organizations should work, how things get done, and who should do what. We internalize our early experiences with core groups and take them with us as we progress throughout our careers. These experiences can either help or hinder us.

UNHEALTHY CORE GROUPS

Just like an unhealthy personal relationship, we can have unhealthy relationships with core groups. This happens when we know what the core group believes or does is wrong, but continue to encourage and empower them. By doing this, employees sacrifice themselves in the process. The only way to break out of an unhealthy core group relationship is for the employee to remove him- or herself. This can only effectively happen when the employee has "equity" with the organization. Equity is built over time by individuals and comes in different forms. Types of equity include, but are not limited to:

- Financial – having enough money and/or resources to be able to walk away from the organization and the unhealthy core group.
- Reputation – being able to easily develop and nurture relationships throughout the organization.
- Capability – being able to enhance an employee's skill base.

By developing and nurturing the various types of equity, an employee can influence the direction of the core group. The more varied the types of equity possessed by an individual the greater the possibility to influence the organization through the core group.

In the end, all forms of equity have two things in common.

1. Equity gives an employee influence within the organization.
2. Equity grows exponentially.

Initially, employees who are developing equity will find that they will develop confidence in a particular area of equity. This happens as they begin to realize they are able to influence the organization by utilizing this skill. As time goes on, employees will begin to realize their equity is sustainable. For example, early in a career they may work hard to develop relationships and eventually realize they're good at it. Later in their career they may continually develop new relationships through the old relationships they have built without much effort on their part. When organizations assist employees to develop various types of equity, the organization as a whole becomes stronger.

WHEN CORE GROUPS GO BAD

There have been numerous stories over the years of various core group members taking over an organization and running it into the ground, while the top executive (and other core group members) leave with huge severance packages and move on to the next unsuspecting organization. This can only happen when the core group continually sends a message to the organization that the organization *only* exists to make and withdraw money from the organization. The employees of the organization must also buy into the message even if individually they would have some reservations. There are signs that an organization may be in trouble. These include:

- Secrecy at the top levels of the organization
- Unhealthy levels of debt
- Conflicts of interest
- Lack of governance

In order to keep an organization on track, the core group must realize and emphasize the long-term health of the organization and what affects it. Additionally, core group members can encourage the organization to be open and transparent, whereby corruption would be easily spotted if not altogether deterred.

Not many organizations reach this level of dysfunction. Some organizations demonstrate this on a much smaller scale. For example, organizations may exhibit questionable accounting practices, inappropriate attention to "perks," or an unhealthy emphasis on hierarchy (implying that some employees are more worthy than others).

WHEN CORE GROUPS FIGHT

One of the most destructive things that can happen to an organization is when the core group splits over an issue and takes opposing sides. Instead of focusing on the ultimate goals and objectives of the organization, employees begin to focus on the argument and who is on what side. During this time, employees are left to try to figure out who really is running the organization, who they should be loyal to, etc.

In order to put an end to the fight, members of the core group have to remember they are there for a greater purpose. They also must remember that they have to work together in order to reach the organization's goals and that no one can do it alone. The employees, on the other hand, must begin to see that there is one leadership team and that they no longer need to worry about who will win.

INFLUENCING THE ORGANIZATION AND THE CORE GROUP

Influencing the organization and the core group can be done only if you understand how the core group's priorities are perceived and how they differ from its intentions. To do that, the organization and the core group must be evaluated objectively while not triggering any fear or mistrust in the organization. This takes relationship and reputation equity in addition to guts and a keen awareness of the organization's environment. This is no easy task. There are several things that are **NOT** effective when trying to influence the core group. These include:

- Trying to force the core group into submission
- Rebelling
- Becoming passive-aggressive and gossiping about the core group to others throughout the organization in order to get a point of view across
- Putting yourself down
- Participating in an innovative operation that is concealed from the core group

Before you begin trying to influence the core group, you should ask yourself several questions. These include Why do you want to do this? Who will do this with you? What support do you have? What is the outcome you're hoping for? How will you know you're successful? The most effective way to begin is to gather a group of co-workers who feel the way you do and create a **shadow core group**. The purpose of the shadow core group is to begin to develop awareness within the organization and the core group. In order to begin influencing the core group, the shadow core group should:

- Begin to widen the shadow core group to include core group members.
- Determine how the core group defines success and show the core group how this project will help them obtain their success.
- Pick the right time to ask for formal permission for the project.
- Be cognizant of how you interact with the core group.
- Determine who influences the core group and ensure they are included.
- Identify core group members who deviate from the norm and are moving in the desired direction.
- Demystify what the core group wants and needs and what people perceive it wants and needs.
- Try out these things in safe environments first until you feel comfortable.

CORPORATE GOVERNANCE

There are two types of corporate governance:

1. The fiduciary model – the shareholders come first.

2. The stakeholder model – money just comes when you take the constituents seriously.

Both have weaknesses when used exclusively. The stakeholder model's weakness comes from trying to please all the stakeholders at once, since no organization can do this effectively. The fiduciary model's weaknesses come when certain creditors or shareholders have leverage over the corporation. Their interests can overtake the organization's priorities. Additionally, the fiduciary model claims to be the map for the future by encouraging executives to make better decisions. This is not always the case and can lead the core group to focus on increasing the share price at all costs. Therefore, *a third model of governance is needed—one that aligns the purpose of the core group with the long-term needs of the organization.* This would begin with selecting the right Board of Directors. The Board members would focus not only on share price, but on the other goals and objectives of the organization. Once the Board is in place, a core group can emerge that can focus on things other than the share price that will make the organization successful.

NOBLE PURPOSE

An organization with **noble purpose** *is one that has an awareness of its destiny and understands the role it needs to fulfill.* It understands its greater purpose in life. This type of organization will dedicate its resources to an end goal that transcends its current purpose. The core group must embrace the organization's noble purpose or it won't have a chance of success.

Summary

Core groups are an inevitable part of organizational life as well as life in general. We need to discover what they are, how they work, what motivates them, and what sustains them in order to work effectively within an organization. Understanding the challenges faced by core groups and particularly how they influence the decisions we make help us influence the core groups we deal with on a daily basis. Ultimately, these core groups converge with the core groups in society and influence the world in which we live. By understanding them, we can then hope to influence the world in which we live and work.

2 | IT'S ALL POLITICS

KATHLEEN KELLEY REARDON

SUMMARY PREPARED BY ANNEMARIE KAUL

AnneMarie Kaul is the Donor Resources Manager for the St. Paul Blood Center of the American Red Cross. She and her recruitment representatives are responsible for recruiting sponsors and volunteers to ensure the acquisition of over 235,000 pints of blood each year. She also has several years of experience managing financial services departments at Securian Financial, Inc. Her business expertise has been in the areas of leadership and customer service. She has a BBA degree from the University of Minnesota Duluth and an MBA from the University of St. Thomas in St. Paul, Minnesota.

POLITICS: IS IT REALLY A BAD THING?

Most people consider workplace politics as a necessary evil. The words themselves are usually associated with negative feelings, such as anger, anxiety, and fear. Moreover, people usually attribute politics to a whole host of problems including missed promotional opportunities, terminations, and even smaller decisions such as who gets the best office. In fact, many people sling around the word *politics* as if it was mud. But truth be told, it is a well-known fact that politics, in general, is a part of life and those who can overcome their fear and learn how to be more politically astute have a higher rate of success and satisfaction. The downside is that, even though politics plays an important role in one's life, rarely do we see a college class focused on learning how to become politically skilled. However, the good news is that we can learn how to enhance our political competencies on our own. Politics can be a positive influence in our lives; we just need to observe and practice it.

THE DEFINITION OF POLITICS

Quite simply, politics is the positioning of ideas in a favorable light by knowing what to say, and how, when, and to whom to say it. There are five key areas of political development: intuition, insight, persuasion, power, and courage. To increase one's political acumen, developing and strengthening skills in these five areas is essential.

Kathleen Kelley Reardon, *It's All Politics: Winning in a World Where Hard Work and Talent Aren't Enough.* Currency Books, 2005.

Letting Intuition Be the Guide

People who are born with natural intuition are a very rare breed. The good news, however, is that anyone without natural instincts can develop them just by observing those who are intuitive and then replicating certain behaviors. Therefore, it is important to be able to identify these general characteristics of an intuitive person.

A person using intuition is constantly *unpredictable* and does not work on the premise of going with the status quo. For example, instead of the typical greeting, "Hi, how are you?" an intuitive person would more likely quickly assess the social level of the passing individual and customize a more appropriate response. If the other person is more reserved, a simple head nod would suffice. An intuitive person will make others feel comfortable, yet keep them guessing by varying his or her behavior.

Another trait of an intuitive person is the ability to use **gut feelings** to make quick decisions. This person acts on a hunch or a feeling versus analyzing the facts. The trouble with pure intellect is that it allows us to take in only a small portion of the relevant information. On the other hand, intuitive people tend to multi-track, which means taking in information from gestures, tone of voice, and other nonverbal cues in addition to the words. They process the message at a deeper level, resulting in more effective communication.

In addition to unpredictability and the use of feelings, being empathetic is another key ingredient to enhance political intuition. **Empathy** is being sensitive to the changing feelings of another person. Getting connected to people and how they think will place a person in a better position to guide future outcomes of almost any interaction.

Here are some common, straightforward guidelines to improve your intuition skills:

- Ask a lot of questions.
- Don't make assumptions.
- Learn how things are normally done.
- Read between the lines.
- Look for differences between verbal and nonverbal communication.

Political Insight: It's About Thinking

Another component of politics is knowing what to do after you predict what is about to happen. This is called **political insight**. Political insight is typically 99 percent perspiration and 1 percent inspiration. Essentially, it is using creativity to respond to typical situations. Insightful people demonstrate the following behaviors:

- Being patient
- Looking at problems from all angles (using the mind-mapping technique)
- Choosing the best option after considering the positives and negatives
- Considering possible choice points or reactions of others
- Using the concept of framing to position ideas in an appealing manner to others
- Not making assumptions

More specifically, it is important to develop political insight *before* and *during* interactions with others. Advance work primarily involves managing the perception of others and being prepared for different reactions. Some tactics to include in this prep work are:

- Getting to know people and forming alliances
- Testing an idea or concept on a select audience

- Preparing a response prior to negative reactions
- Possessing a solid track record in your field of work

During an interaction, thinking on your feet helps to glean political insight. Responding in the moment is critical, but many people feel inadequate in this area of political interaction. In the context of political strategies, responding properly to problems, personal attacks, and hidden agendas holds the key to creating a favorable outcome. The following guiding principles can be used to defuse negative conversations:

- Know when to confront, when to back off, and when to ask for support.
- Recognize when to apologize.
- Give credit to others.
- Divert attention away from sensitive or unresolvable issues.
- Paraphrase what was said in a favorable context.

Understanding how to proceed in a politically charged environment by doing up-front homework can virtually save a person's job, and at a minimum save a person's credibility and reputation.

Understanding Persuasion

Political influence can be more important to bring about change in the workplace than the standard methods of authority, culture, or expertise. **Persuasion**, one of the most important components of influence, is the ability to position ideas in an appealing manner so others will accept them. Interestingly, whether specifically at work or generally in life, many people consider persuasion as the "high road" of manipulation, which is actually a form of deception. To be an astute student of politics, both persuasion and manipulation techniques should be well understood.

Listening to really understand the actual meaning of a message and taking time to formulate thoughts *before* responding wields great power and influence. Knowing when the content of a message is relevant, called **conversational coherence**, and how to introduce a new topic, called **topicality shift**, are also necessary skills to enhance persuasive ability.

These preparation steps are critical to enhance political persuasion:

- Understanding what motivates the other person so as to connect the message to those interests
- Determining how much should be said and the way it should be said
- Ensuring that the information is reliable and relevant

Common Persuasion Strategies

There are many methods and approaches to persuade others. The approach that is most effective will depend on each person and situation. Typically, however, the three more commonly used strategies are reciprocity, scarcity, and authority.

Reciprocity is doing a favor for someone *now* in order to have it returned *later*. Skilled politicians are very good at giving help up front to get things accomplished in the future. **Scarcity** is the ability to create a high demand by providing scarce resources. People want what they can't have. An example of this strategy was the Tyco Beanie

Baby craze of the late 1990s. **Authority** is becoming an expert in a certain field, preferably in a field that is inadequately filled. Thus, a person becomes a "niche" player.

Whether a person's strategy encompasses any of the three just described or a combination of others, it is helpful to keep the following suggestions in mind:

- Keep your work visible to the right people.
- Be in a position to be noticed.
- Make sure the project goals are in line with the company's goals.

How Does Political Power Work?

In order to get ahead in the workplace it is paramount to understand how political power works and to learn how to gain this power. Accomplishments alone are not enough; selling yourself is the key.

Power can easily be gained and lost, so cultivating and maintaining it should be a continual process. During this process, it is important to keep in mind that it is the *perceptions* of others that essentially create and sustain the somewhat nebulous power. In other words, if a person feels powerless, it is because that person has allowed someone else's perception to influence how he or she thinks, feels, and behaves. Fortunately, by following the power strategies listed below, people can improve and maintain their power base.

- Maintain appearances, including attire, office décor, handshaking, gestures, etc.
- Maintain relationships by getting to know the people who can help you (be charming and humorous).
- Enhance communication by listening and then adapting one's style to fit another's style.
- Assess the power of your position within the hierarchy of the organization.
- Seek out advisors.
- Be sure to thank people who help you and remember to help them, too.
- Increase knowledge by learning about the company's culture and real goals.
- Manage your reputation by acquiring the skills to do the job well, and ensuring that others know about it.

Political Power: Courage versus Suicide

Most people would agree that in order to increase power, a person must take risks and not be afraid to make misjudgments or mistakes. *But the question is: When does political courage become political suicide?* The answer lies in one's intentions. If a person is taking a stand based on true beliefs and feelings, then showing courage by speaking out is the smart and necessary option. On the other hand, if the intent is artificial or self-centered, eventually these actions will lead to career suicide. Of course there are varying degrees between doing what is best for the company and what is best for the person. Political courage should not lead to self-destruction or the destruction of others. *One must assess the real risks and rewards before moving too quickly, keeping in mind that achieving the goal is not always as important as the way it is reached.*

Before jumping into a politically charged situation, the following questions should be evaluated and answered honestly.

- Do I have the needed support?
- Is my track record sufficiently developed?

- Am I up for the challenge right now?
- What are the win-win and no-win options?

Ultimately, having the strength and stamina to proceed with caution is the key. It is up to each individual to personally reconcile his or her motives with the risks and rewards to make this type of decision.

POLITICAL BOUNDARIES

To some extent, all organizations mold and shape their political direction by the nature of their culture. A company's political environment should be carefully analyzed prior to employment whenever possible. By doing this up-front work, a person will be in a better position to react when faced with political choice points. It is good practice to establish a personal "comfort zone" when dealing with politics, since many individuals who do not do so end up confused and misunderstood.

From a corporate culture perspective, smart organizations will intentionally influence their political direction. Good organizations encourage positive politics. They develop and communicate a set of values that can be adopted at every level—from the mailroom clerk to the CEO. Two examples of politically smart companies are Mars and Nokia. Both of these firms put a high priority on rewarding associates who demonstrate a strong work ethic. They also support workplace principles such as responsibility, mutuality, and freedom of expression.

THE POLITICAL GAME

Staying on top of the political game can make all the difference between hiding out on the bench (frightened to take risks) and getting out on the field to score the necessary points to stay ahead. The good news is that anyone can nurture and strengthen their political savvy to actually win the game. The process to improve political know-how requires only two simple actions: observing and practicing. Equipped with enhanced intuition and persuasion skills, a not-so-politically adept person can take more control over his or her life and make some highly astute political decisions and useful connections. Moreover, having the knowledge of the political culture in the workplace and the courage to abide by personal political boundaries will provide the necessary strength to face and overcome political adversity. The opponent is no longer a threat but an adversary.

PART
XII | MANAGERIAL DECISION MAKING

Managers at all levels of organizations make decisions. Some of these are relatively trivial and some are powerfully significant. Some managers make decisions frequently and others engage in the process more infrequently. Some managers make decisions intuitively and others follow a more systematic process. Nevertheless, in a systems framework, all decisions eventually affect the success of the enterprise. It is critical to discover useful frameworks for how managers should approach the decision process so as to avoid common errors and increase the probability of success. This becomes increasingly true for "high-stakes" decisions with large potential payoffs, or when managers are faced with crisis situations.

Paul C. Nutt, in *Why Decisions Fail*, asserts that up to two-thirds of all decisions are either failure-prone or based on questionable tactics. He examined 400 top-level strategic decisions and 15 monumental fiascoes to identify the three most common blunders that managers make—rushing to judgment, misusing resources, and failure-prone tactics. Under these conditions, managers often make the bad decision undiscussable such that no one can learn from it. He concludes by suggesting alternative tactics that decision makers can use to avoid these traps, including owning up to past mistakes.

Nutt is a professor of management sciences and public policy and management at The Ohio State University's Fisher College of Business. He received his Ph.D. from the University of Wisconsin–Madison, and was named a Fellow in the Decision Sciences Institute. Nutt serves on the editorial board for several publications, including the *Strategic Management Journal*. He is the author of six other books, including *Managing Planned Change* and *Making Tough Decisions*.

Authors Murnighan and Mowen, in *The Art of High-Stakes Decision-Making*, point out that managers often need to make key decisions under tight time pressures and incomplete information, but still must use a systematic process for doing so. They start by asking managers to analyze their situation based on (1) whether or not a problem really exists, and (2) whether or not action needs to be taken. Next, they describe a variety of classic traps that decision makers fall into, including time snares, decision myopia, illusions of causality, and hindsight bias. Finally, they prescribe a seven-step (SCRIPTS) process for approaching and analyzing complex, high-risk decisions that focuses on Search, Causes, Risks, Intuition, Perspectives, Time Frame, and Solving the Problem.

J. Keith Murnighan is the Harold H. Hines Jr. Distinguished Professor of Risk Management in the Kellogg School of Management at Northwestern University, and a specialist in negotiations and decision making. He has a Ph.D. in Social Psychology from Purdue University, and is a Fellow in the Academy of Management. His co-author, John C. Mowen, is Regents Professor and Noble Chair of Marketing Strategy at Oklahoma State University. His Ph.D. is from Arizona State University, and he is a past president of the Society for Consumer Psychology. Professor Mowen specializes in managerial and consumer decision making.

Malcolm Gladwell, a staff writer for *The New Yorker*, has a remarkable record in his book publishing career. He has written two popular books that have each sold over a million copies. The first, *The Tipping Point*, explained how simple ideas and trends can snowball into veritable social epidemics that have tremendous positive inertia to them. The second book, *Blink!*, suggests that on-the-spot decision makers can be extremely successful at identifying familiar patterns based on very limited information (in the blink of an eye). They do this by using their "adaptive unconscious" to zero in on a few highly salient details, and by using the process of "thin-slicing" to find patterns in situations based on narrow samplings of information. As a result, Gladwell suggests that managers should learn to trust their intuitive decisions, while also controlling their snap judgments.

1

WHY DECISIONS FAIL

Paul C. Nutt

Summary Prepared by Paul C. Nutt

Paul C. Nutt is a professor of management sciences in the Fisher College of Business at The Ohio State University. He received his Ph.D. from the University of Wisconsin–Madison and a B.S.E and M.S.E from the University of Michigan. His research interests include organizational decision making, leadership, and radical change. He has written over 100 articles and 7 books on these topics that have received numerous awards from the Decision Sciences Institute, The Academy of Management, INFORMS, The Center for Creative Leadership, AAMC, FACHE, and others. He is a Fellow in the Decision Sciences Institute. Trade discussions of his work have appeared in the Wall Street Journal, Fast Company, *and PRI's* Marketplace. *He serves on several editorial review boards and regularly consults for public, private, and not-for-profit organizations on strategic management, decision making, and international business.*

INTRODUCTION

With the rash of recent corporate scandals, the public rightfully wonders if corporate managers are able to make sound decisions. The answer is unnerving. Based on a multi-decade study of real-life organizational decisions, about *half of all business decisions end in failure.* Vast sums of money are spent to make decisions that result in no ultimate value for the organization. Worse yet, some managers make the same mistakes over and over again. Research shows that failed decisions share three common blunders: managers rush to judgment, misuse their resources, and repeatedly use failure-prone tactics to make their decisions.

A STUDY OF DECISION MAKING

A 25-year research effort developed a unique database of more than 400 decisions made by top managers in private, public, and not-for-profit organizations across the United States. A wide variety of decisions has been studied, from purchasing equipment to

Paul C. Nutt, *Why Decisions Fail: Avoiding the Blunders and Traps That Lead to Debacles.* San Francisco: Berrett-Koehler, 2002.

renovating space to deciding which products or services to sell. About half of the decisions were not fully used after just two years—one of the key indicators of failure. One-third of the decisions were *never* used. These failure figures would be even higher if it were possible to study a random selection of decisions. The "story behind the story" of EuroDisney, the Firestone tire recall, the Denver International Airport (DIA), Quaker's acquisition of Snapple, Shell's disposal of the Brent Spar oil platform, and other equally devastating decision debacles were studied and documented, providing insights into why decisions fail. Lesser known failures were found to have the same features as the debacles, except they didn't attain the notoriety. Failure could not be blamed on events that can't be controlled, such as fickle customers and down markets. Instead, *failure typically stems from blunders that point unsuspecting decision makers toward traps that ensnare them.* In this sense, most of these decision-making failures are actually preventable.

THE BLUNDERS

Three deadly blunders led to failed decisions and debacles. The *rush to judgment* blunder crops up when managers identify a concern and latch onto the first remedy that they come across. Managers seem to believe that concerns and solutions come in pairs. They fear the threat of an unresolved concern—and they do so with good reason, as higher executives are quick to question them and pressure them for an answer. As the pressure mounts, managers find it nearly impossible not to grab the first solution that they find. However, *failure is four times more likely when decision makers embrace the first idea they come across without taking the time to investigate what is motivating their action and then seeking out possible remedies.*

The second blunder—*misuse of resources*—occurs when managers spend their time and money during decision making on the wrong things. For example, decision makers collectively spend millions of dollars to defend hastily selected ideas with a defensive evaluation and devote little or nothing to other aspects of decision making, such as gathering intelligence about the concerns prompting action, finding who may block action, setting expectations, and uncovering actions that can meet expectations.

The third blunder is *failure-prone tactics*. Two-thirds of the decisions studied applied failure-prone tactics. Success can increase by as much as 50 percent when better tactics are used. Following good decision-making practices costs very little, especially when compared to the costs of a debacle.

One blunder often leads to another. A rush to judgment skips important decision-making steps so no time or money is spent on them. Failure-prone practices often seem to be quick, so using them appears to be a pragmatic way to save money.

FAILURE TRAPS AND WAYS TO AVOID THEM

Managers that blunder find themselves caught in one or more traps. When trapped, managers are apt to make a bad call that makes failure likely. The blunders create traps and these traps bring about failure that crops up in all failed decisions. Seven common traps were uncovered:

- Not taking charge by reconciling claims
- Failing to deal with the barriers to taking action

- Providing or receiving ambiguous directions
- Engaging in a limited search and no innovation
- Misusing evaluation
- Overlooking ethical questions
- Failing to learn

Not Taking Charge by Reconciling Claims

To start a decision-making effort, powerful and influential stakeholders make a claim and attempt to get it endorsed. Other claims are overlooked. If decision makers buy into a claim without looking further, they are apt to get trapped. The initial claim often omits what aroused the claimant, it may be disconnected from the concerns of people, it may fail to identify their perceived needs or their considerations, and it may neglect to suggest perceived opportunities. The relationship of a concern or a consideration with a claim's arena of action may be suspect, as in Smithburg's beliefs about the connection of an acquisition with the need for defensive restructuring for Quaker. Adopting the implied arena of action (e.g., an acquisition) is ill-advised when such a motivating concern or consideration is used to defend it. The concerns and considerations motivating a claim are seldom spelled out, leading people to speculate about what they may be. In the debacles studied there were no attempts to analyze the claim or to uncover competing claims, although gathering this kind of intelligence is highly and widely recommended.

Instead, decision makers select among the claims being offered by a select group of powerful insiders and forge ahead with the selected claim, and its implied arena of action. When decision makers are silent about their concerns and considerations, people make their own judgments about what a decision is really about and its importance. These judgments often elude the decision maker. Skeptics and people who have something to lose each are handed a platform to raise objections. To discredit the decision and the decision maker, opponents call attention to what seems to be an error, faulty logic, or a misrepresentation to question the legitimacy of a claim, and its arena of action. The decision-making effort must then scale this slippery slope to be successful. Many of the debacles studied had hidden concerns, suggesting very different claims than the ones pushed by decision makers. At Ford, officials expressed surprise when told that many insiders were troubled by the company's failure to recall the Explorer and fix its tendency to roll over. Ford's leaders also say they were unaware of the public's very negative reaction to the company's tactic of stonewalling recalls.

Decision makers can avoid this trap by finding a claim that stakeholders can support. Insight into people's concerns and considerations broadens one's views of what needs fixing and suggests an arena of action that stakeholders can support. Demonstrating awareness of people's views gives any decision-making effort legitimacy. Stakeholders who understand the arguments presented and see how they point to an arena of action that accounts for important things are more apt to support the proposal. When people see a claim as valid, momentum is created as word spreads to others.

Failing to Manage Forces Stirred up by a Decision

Decision makers in the debacles studied implemented a preferred course of action with either an edict or with persuasion. When using an edict, the best one can hope for is indifference—that people either do not care enough to resist or will believe that resistance is futile. If the edict fails, decision makers may resort to persuasion, now trying to explain why the decision has value. This is fouled by the previous power play, even if power is applied incrementally. Using persuasion from the outset is somewhat more effective. Selling an idea with persuasion can work if stakeholders are indifferent to what decision makers want to do. Persuasion has little effect, however, on people who believe they have something to lose. There are better ways to get a decision adopted.

Edicts and persuasion fail because neither manages the social and political forces stirred up by a decision. The decision makers in the debacles had no idea what enflamed their opponents and assumed it stemmed from self-serving interests. People's worries fester and grow when their interests and commitments are ignored. Being more forthcoming about reasons and motives can neutralize opposition. Involving potential critics in the decision-making process at least clarifies their views for you. And involvement may shift the critic from a position of opposition to one of support.

Successful decision makers push implementation to the front of their decision-making efforts to uncover and manage people's interests and commitments. If power must be shared, teams can be created and involved in making the decision. People are more apt to disclose their interests when they are in such an arrangement. Even when disclosure is limited, the act of negotiating a solution promotes ownership in the agreed-upon plan that increases its prospect of success. Even when not forced to do so, savvy decision makers use participation because it improves the chance of a successful implementation. Another effective approach, called networking, helps demonstrate the necessity of acting. Current performance is documented, and credible performance norms are identified. Using this information, key stakeholders are shown the importance of a decision by decision makers, collecting and managing interests with each encounter. People are more likely to be supportive when networking makes them aware of performance shortfalls and the level of performance that is possible. *Networking makes the need to act credible.*

Ambiguous Directions

Direction identifies the expected results of a decision. In failed decisions, directions are either misleading, assumed but never agreed to, or unknown. Using economic benefits to justify the arena is both misleading and dangerous. Critics were given a platform to question the arena. Opponents of the Denver International Airport (DIA) asked if there was a better way to spend $500 million to produce economic gains for the greater Denver area. Misrepresenting the expected benefits provides an opportunity to attack the decision. Being clear about what is to be gained by having an arena puts a "best face" on such projects. Many major infrastructure projects, such as mass transit systems, are put in jeopardy when champions trumpet "economic benefits" as the expected outcome. Debacles often had bloated or unrealistic expectations that made them failure-prone.

Directions that were not understood by key players pose difficulties. Thwarting a takeover seemed to be Smithburg's aim in masterminding Quaker's acquisition of Snapple. It became the implicit direction behind the key decision, but this was never codified or explained. Smithburg's failure to be clear about his aims prompted insiders to make their own assumptions. It is easy to see how people could assume a different direction. What about profit? Insiders who assumed that a profit direction guided the

Snapple purchase would find the decision wrong-headed. Thwarting a takeover would make the rationale behind Smithburg's decision clearer and would prompt other questions, but at least would steer people away from looking for profit-enhancing ideas.

Being clear about expected results was often set aside in the debacles by a rush to find a remedy. Fearing criticism, decision makers act as if they must have a way to deal with a claim as soon as one is acknowledged. The need to disarm the real or the potential critic makes it hard to admit doubt. Doubt can be a powerful positive force pushing one to think deeply about what is needed. The leaders substitute an answer (the acquisition of Snapple) for thinking about the aim of profit possibilities. The idea (the Snapple acquisition) eliminated discussion about what might create profits at Quaker and what would be the best way to realize this aim. The idea and its assumed benefits displaced the need to think about the results the company hoped to produce. People will see these benefits differently and form different impressions about what is wanted. Without clarity about the reasons for taking action, disputes arise as people push courses of action that deal with their idiosyncratic notions of expected results. Such disputes are a prime cause of conflict in decision making. The recommended action is discussed but not the hoped-for results that prompted it. People pushing a preferred course of action often fail to tell others what results they are trying to realize. Setting an objective clears away this ambiguity and conflict. Being clear about what is wanted also mobilizes support and guides the search for answers.

Limited Search and No Innovation

Decision makers often embrace a quick fix. Having an "answer" eliminates ambiguity about what to do, but keeps the decision maker from looking for other ideas that could be better. Smithburg was wedded to buying and turning around companies. Shell was drawn to deep-sea disposal of waste materials because it was legal.

Decision makers that avoid a quick fix are confronted with a new challenge: the allure of current business practices. It is difficult to move away from the tangible to the unknown. In the debacles, many of the proposed actions copied the business practices of others to reduce time and cost. These costs are almost always underestimated, as is the time to do the required tailoring.

Decision makers drawn to a quick fix or to "how others do it" are also pulled away from innovation and search. The search for ideas, and for an innovative one that provides "first mover" advantage, is often waylaid by the desire for a quick fix and the lure of current business practices. When a clear direction is set, however, conducting a search and seeking an innovative response reduces the risk of failure.

Misusing Evaluations

Once a quick fix is uncovered, many decision makers strike a defensive posture and collect information to argue for its adoption. More time and money were spent doing this type of evaluation than all the other decision-making activities combined. Smithburg knew Snapple's price, but little else. Shell officials spent huge sums on "evaluations." It was hardly a surprise that each commissioned evaluation spoke glowingly of the idea. The money spent on defensive evaluations that justify such actions would be better spent to find a more beneficial action.

Evaluation is valuable when used to compare the benefits of a preferred course of action to performance norms and to determine the risk in realizing the benefits. Expected results must be clear before such an evaluation can provide pertinent information. If one adopts a profit direction for the Snapple decision, best and worst case assumptions about sales and product synergies can be analyzed to determine risk. This would have exposed the Quaker board to factors that limit synergies (the incompatibility of distribution and manufacturing for Snapple and Gatorade) and sales (public dislike of Snapple Products) lowering revenue projections and the likelihood of turning a profit. Such an evaluation can be used to uncover the level of risk in the purchase decision and strip away ambiguity and conflict. Factors that drive revenues and profits upward and downward were ignored in the debacles, so risk was hidden. Substituting benefit and risk assessments for defensive evaluations improves the prospect of success.

Ignoring Ethical Questions

Tough decisions pose ethical dilemmas. The DIA supporters ignored questions about who pays, who benefits, and who decides. Many large-scale infrastructure projects such as sports arenas, rapid transit systems, and arts centers share this failing.

Values that lurk behind an ethical position were never understood in the debacles. Shell executives saw their disposal plan as pragmatic. Others saw it as unethical. When the actions of decision makers appear unethical it can prompt whistle-blowing by insiders or boycotts by outsiders, as in the Shell case. Even when these extreme reactions are avoided, decision makers plant the seeds of distrust when their behavior appears to be unethical to insiders or to outsiders.

To avoid distrust, whistle-blowing, and boycotts, these ethical issues must be confronted. To do this, people should be encouraged to speak out and pose ethical questions during decision-making deliberations. Create forums for ethical concerns to be voiced, explore options uncovered in the decision-making effort, and offer mediation to those who disagree. The forum allows a decision maker to look for values behind the positions of people who oppose them. The decision maker can often affirm these values and make a minor modification in a claim or a preferred course of action to carry on much as before. Had Shell officials affirmed the values of the groups that opposed them by addressing disposal questions they would have cut the ground from under the arguments of Greenpeace and blunted any attempted boycott. If this fails, offer mediation. Shell officials could have held hearings and conferences to find out what their critics were saying, looking for unwarranted criticisms and misunderstandings to be diffused. At best, new insights can develop. If not, the leaders can take steps that show they considered the views of their critics—a position that boosts the legitimacy of a proposed action. Companies using mediation win lawsuits involving whistle-blowing. Companies without it usually lose them.

Failing to Learn

Guiding decision makers away from failure-prone tactics requires learning. But learning is thwarted when managers have no tolerance for mistakes and errors, or a failed decision. In such an environment, people conceal bad outcomes. To make things worse, chance events make outcomes muddy. Good decision-making practices cannot guarantee good outcomes, because of chance events. Bad luck, such as when product demand falls below expectations because of unexpectedly bad weather, can be mistaken for bad decision-making practices. Good luck, such as windfall profits due to favorable increases in interest rates or consumer interest in a product, can cover up failure-prone decision-making practices.

A failed decision puts people in a no-win situation when there is no tolerance for failure. Individuals in such a bind have but two options: own up or cover up. An own up approach makes the day of atonement today; a cover-up makes it tomorrow or perhaps never. Put in this bind, people will seldom own up to a failure and likely will delay the day of atonement as long as they can. Several acts of deception are necessary to pull this off. Offsetting bad news with good news sidetracks potentially threatening questions. The cover-up is two tiered: the distorted good news and the blatant act of creating misleading information. These games of deception become undiscussable in the minds of the presenters because to reveal them would also reveal the "lose-lose" position created for the organization. There must be a cover-up of the cover-up to cover one's tracks. Put in this situation, people engage in a paradoxical behavior; *they make undiscussable the key aspects of a decision from which others need to learn.*

The real culprit in this process is the perverse incentive that keeps decision makers from owning up. A perverse incentive always has this effect, making it difficult for people to come forward with their insights about what happened and why. Subordinates are often aware when things are going badly, but they are not inclined to share what they know in a punishment-driven environment. Many higher-ups make it clear they tolerate no opposition to their pet projects. In each case, perverse incentives create barriers to learn why a decision went wrong and how to avoid a similar failure in the future. It is essential to create an environment in which decisions can be openly discussed so as to avoid this blame-finding mentality.

IMPLICATIONS FOR MANAGERS

The prospect of decision-making success dramatically improves when managers avoid the traps discussed above. To do so, managers should probe to uncover hidden concerns, take steps to manage the social and political forces that can block an idea, identify the results wanted, search widely and encourage innovation, and estimate benefits linked to expected results along with the risk in realizing them. Ethical dilemmas often go undetected as decisions are made and crop up later, causing responsible people considerable embarrassment. This can be avoided if decision makers encourage ethical questions to be voiced as the decision-making effort unfolds. Perverse incentives get people to adopt a defensive posture that blocks learning how to improve decision making. Perverse incentives must be rooted out and a win-win environment created before learning can occur.

2 | THE ART OF HIGH-STAKES DECISION MAKING

J. Keith Murnighan and John C. Mowen

Summary Prepared by Linda Rochford

Linda Rochford is Associate Professor of Marketing at the University of Minnesota Duluth. Her interests include formulating and implementing marketing strategy and the development and marketing of new products. Her work has been published in such outlets as the Journal of Product Innovation Management *and the* Journal of the Academy of Marketing Science. *She has held various technical, marketing, and management positions for 3M and Cargill. She earned her Ph.D. in Marketing, M.B.A. and B.S. in Chemistry from the University of Minnesota.*

INTRODUCTION

Managers can benefit from a systematic method for making *high-stakes decisions—those nonroutine, high-risk decisions, often made under time pressure with ambiguous or incomplete information, that have serious consequences.* Equally important, managers need to recognize barriers to effective decision making. Awareness of these barriers is the first step in making sound decisions.

SCRIPTS is an acronym for a seven-step process for making sound, high-stakes decisions. It includes these phases:

1. *Search* for signals of threats and opportunities.
2. Find the *causes*.
3. Evaluate the *risks*.
4. Apply *intuition* and emotion.
5. Take different *perspectives*.

J. Keith Murnighan and John C. Mowen, *The Art of High-Stakes Decision Making: Tough Calls in a Speed-Driven World.* New York: John Wiley & Sons, 2002.

6. Consider the *time* frame.
7. *Solve* the problem.

To truly appreciate this structured method, it's important to understand the conditions that impede good decision making and how the seven-step process is designed to minimize or eliminate these impediments.

EXAMINING THE STEPS

Is There a Problem?

The first step is searching for signals of threats and opportunities. The process of accurately identifying the problem is critical for good decision making. The most basic issue here is whether there in fact even *is* a problem. Is the decision maker actually facing a threat or opportunity? Decision makers face four possible scenarios. They may:

- Correctly diagnose that a problem exists and take action to solve the problem.
- Correctly determine that no problem exists and take no action.
- Mistakenly decide a problem exists and take action when there really is no problem, resulting in a "needless blunder."
- Mistakenly ignore a problem that exists and fail to take action, producing a "missed opportunity."

The challenge is to avoid "needless blunders" and "missed opportunities." Even if a decision maker is fortunate enough to avoid these pitfalls, there is still the danger of getting behind the *power curve*. The power curve refers to the compounding effects of delaying action. A familiar example is the huge long-term difference between investing a fixed amount for retirement at age 25 versus 45. The total amount of interest earned favors early investors and penalizes those that wait until later. Because reaching a decision, acting on that decision, and seeing results from the action all take time, there is a time lag before the intended effect is realized. The size of the lag increases to a point beyond which it is simply not possible to catch up. This produces a *zone of false hope,* the point at which action has been taken too late to have an impact on the problem. For example, failing to respond in a timely fashion to a new product introduction from a competitor can put a company in the zone of false hope where there is no chance of recapturing the ground lost in the market, and the odds of success for the firm have dropped significantly.

Threshold for Action

The power curve and the need for timely problem identification and action raise the issue of how to set the threshold for action, or "set the trigger" for decision making. The trigger metaphor illustrates how decision makers have to weigh the amount of evidence or information necessary before taking action. A "sticky trigger" requires a preponderance of evidence before acting—for example, the decision to go to war should require a sticky trigger because of the tremendous political, economic, and human risks and consequences from taking such action. A "hair trigger" might be set for a decision where the failure to act has great consequences. A "hair trigger" might be set for product recall where the public's safety is at risk. Johnson & Johnson's handling of the Tylenol product tampering is a situation where it was better for them to overreact to protect the public (and they did just that). Johnson & Johnson's handling of the Tylenol situation—a combination of rapid product recall and production of a tamper-resistant package—may have seemed costly and extreme at the time, but because of the rapid and extensive action taken on the problem, public trust in the Tylenol brand was quickly re-established and even strengthened. Finally, a "neutral trigger" is set for problems where it is not necessary to be neither particularly conservative, nor particularly aggressive in response.

Barriers to Sound Decision Making

One of the biggest challenges faced by decision makers is the tendency to overestimate the probability of success. The *overconfidence bias* blinds managers to signals of threats, increasing the risk of making an error in one of two ways: (1) failing to collect necessary information, and (2) influencing how the trigger is set. In other words, since overconfident people assume that things will turn out well, they are lax in their search for opportunities and threats in the situation analysis. They tend to underestimate the risk of the threats and overestimate the odds of success in exploiting opportunities or overcoming threats.

Decision makers fall into this trap when they base decisions on incomplete information—the *illusion of correlation* (e.g., focusing on the number of correct forecasts by Wall Street pundits rather than asking how many of the forecasts were incorrect). A dramatic example of failing to look at all of the information is demonstrated by the *Challenger* spacecraft disaster. NASA decision makers looked at O-ring failure caused by burn-through from the rocket fuel at different launch temperatures. However, they didn't consider the other half of the picture—how often was there no burn-through at different launch temperatures. When the complete picture is examined, what looked like almost equal odds of having failure above and below 65 degrees launch temperature produced a radically different outcome—100 percent failures at lower temperatures and about a 20 percent chance of failure above the temperature threshold.

Once threats and opportunities have been identified, the SCRIPTS model calls for determining the underlying cause. Treating a symptom of a problem rather than taking action on the underlying cause will only delay solution and risk getting behind the power curve. A single cause can generate many symptoms, may share symptoms with other causes, and there may be more than one root cause, particularly for high-stakes decisions. In other words, determining causality can be very difficult. Most high-stakes problems are caused by a number of complex factors. What otherwise might be a fairly benign event can act as a tripwire on this set of complex factors to create a serious and dramatic event. The *tipping point* is the threshold event—often a seemingly trivial or minor factor—that pushes the system into failure.

Decision makers must guard against *illusions of causality,* inaccurately attributing causes to problems. An example of the illusion of causality is the *illusion of performance*— giving oneself credit for good outcomes and attributing poor outcomes to anyone else in greater proportion than is merited by the facts. Another example is *hindsight bias* that leads decision makers to retrospectively overestimate how well a problem or outcomes from a problem could have been anticipated.

One technique for identifying problem causes is *root-cause analysis.* A fundamental part of root-cause analysis is dissecting the sequence of events leading up to the problem, including both human decision making and physical systems and processes.

After identifying the problem and its cause, the consequences of taking action—risk assessment—should be considered. Risks can include social or monetary risk for the decision maker, risk to life and health, information risk, as well as catastrophic "sink the boat" risk. Risk analysis helps to determine where the threshold for action—the decision trigger—is set.

Risk assessment can be plagued by distortions of probability estimates and outcome evaluations. Distortions can occur for a number of reasons. More recent, more familiar, or more vivid information is more easily accessible and remembered—the *availability bias*—making this the information that is inappropriately used in determining potential outcomes. The law of decreasing margin effect suggests that the first loss or gain has more impact than subsequent losses or gains. Consequently, decision makers are apt to take more risks to try to break a losing streak—often taking reckless chances—and are very conservative about making decisions that could risk interrupting a winning streak. Decision makers can also be blinded to very real risks by "summit fever"—the temptation to achieve their goals so tantalizingly close that very unreasonable risks are undertaken.

Using Intuition and Multiple Perspectives

Relying on intuition for high-stakes decisions seems risky. However, intuition can be valuable if used carefully. Intuition can be used to validate decisions made using rational decision making or when the rational decision-making process does not lead to a clear decision. Intuition may be the only option in crisis situations where there is no time for a more time-consuming, rational process. The systematic decision model calls for the use of guided intuition to make fast, experienced based decisions under very short time deadlines.

It makes sense to look at problems and potential decisions through various frames of reference to counteract the normal tendency to confirm one's own frame or perspective. Multiple professional perspectives should be used to help place the decision maker in the role of other organizational stakeholders—such as engineering, production, legal, accounting, marketing, and even competitors—and to ensure that the ethical dimensions of the decision are fully explored.

It's About Time

One of the most interesting challenges in decision making is how managers use and view time. High-stakes decisions are often characterized by time pressure. Different cultures may view time as a linear concept—one event following the next in a sequential fashion. Most western cultures consider time linear. Other organizational cultures—agricultural societies, academic institutions—view time as circular because the same sequence of events takes place year after year. Procedural time is perhaps the most unpredictable because the ending point is dependent on completing a particular process where unforeseen circumstances can compress or extend the time needed to finish a process. An example of procedural time is a surgery. Even if the average length of time for a procedure is two hours, the surgery isn't finished until all of the necessary procedures have been completed, which could vary considerably around the average. Consider the frustration of a linear time–oriented individual working in a circular time–oriented organization. The linear-oriented individual may be frustrated that more speed and effort are not put into solving problems that the organization may consider as temporary and cyclical.

Even without different perspectives on time, decision makers face time traps. Time traps are the present versus future time trade-offs made in confronting problems. Decision myopia, time snares, and time fences are all examples of time traps.

Decision myopia is associated with overvaluing present outcomes over future outcomes. These managers want immediate gratification. This can lead to short-term thinking at the expense of the long-term health of the individual or organization. *Time snares* are related to decision myopia. Time-snared decision makers let short-term positive outcomes cause an action that leads to long-term negative outcomes. For example, General Mills was criticized for boosting quarterly sales by shipping much larger orders to customers than the customer had asked for. At some point, customers will rebel against carrying extra inventory, and this can affect the buyer–seller relationship. Sales may drop significantly as customers simply don't need to or want to buy any more goods.

Time fences, on the other hand, occur when an action that would lead to long-term gains is stopped because it also causes short-term negative outcomes. For example, the political will to balance the federal budget almost always runs up against a time fence. Most politicians do not want to face the short-term sacrifices needed in order to achieve the longer range benefit.

High-stakes decisions often must be made under time pressure. Time pressure creates a number of effects on decision makers that can make for poorer decisions. For example, decision makers under time pressure will increase the speed with which they process information for a decision, but they will compensate by reducing the amount of information considered. Decision makers under fire will also tend to let emotions carry them away, which interferes with more rational analysis or guided intuition. To minimize the negative effects of time pressure on crisis decision making, organizations should preplan responses to potential problems and utilize dress rehearsals of crisis situations to practice responses.

Solving the Problem

The entire SCRIPTS process culminates with solving the problem. The first step in solving the problem is setting the threshold for action. The *risk ratio* is used to quantitatively set the trigger and is defined as follows:

$$\text{Risk ratio} = \frac{\text{the value of a needless blunder}}{\text{the value of a needless blunder} + \text{the value of a missed opportunity}}$$

The risk ratio is then adjusted qualitatively based on each of the risk factors identified previously. This is an important step, as not all risks can be assigned financial values.

The second step in solving the problem is to determine the probability of successfully responding to the problem. This is accomplished by identifying the specific actions and milestones that need to take place, as well as the probability of achieving each of these. The conditional probability is calculated to compute the overall probability of achieving the expected outcome across multiple milestones. The results of such an estimate are often sobering due to the tendency to overlook the conditional nature of the outcome.

The last step in solving the problem is to compare the likelihood of success to the risk ratio. This is called the *confidence margin*. The decision maker should not proceed if the likelihood of success is less than the risk ratio (i.e., if the confidence margin is negative). If multiple alternatives have positive confidence margins, the alternative with the greatest confidence margin should be the best choice.

Conclusion

Novice and veteran decision makers can learn and gain from examining their past decision-making experiences as a vehicle for developing new ways of thinking. Master decision makers practice their decision making on lower-stakes decisions in order to learn from the process. Then, when a real crisis arises, they can have a higher expectation of responding coolly and creatively. This is perhaps one of the most valuable lessons and benefits of practicing a systematic problem-solving and decision-making process.

READING 3 | BLINK!

MALCOLM GLADWELL

SUMMARY PREPARED BY CHERI STINE

Cheri Stine holds a bachelor's degree in Human Resource Management from the University of Minnesota Duluth. First and foremost, Cheri is a wife to her husband Dan and a mother to her two young children Kayla and Carter. She has owned and operated her own distributorship for an internationally known paper-crafting products company called Stampin' Up!® for over five years. She provides training for new distributors, markets her business locally, and teaches her customers to use the products that she offers to tap into their creativity and to touch people's lives in a meaningful way.

INTRODUCTION

In today's society, we are instinctively skeptical of quickly made decisions. We consider them to be reckless and not well thought out. The quality of a decision is believed to have a direct relationship with the amount of time and effort we spent making the decision. In fact, for this reason, decision makers in all walks of life spend countless hours, days, weeks, and even years trying to reach decisions that they could have reached in two or three seconds if they had trusted their instincts. *Despite common belief, decisions made very quickly can be every bit as good as decisions made cautiously and deliberately.* In fact, in many situations they can be better.

HOW WE PROCESS INFORMATION

In life and in business, we are constantly faced with situations in which we have to make sense of a large amount of new and confusing information in a short amount of time. *Therefore, our brains have developed two separate and very different ways to process information and render decisions, each of which is valuable under different circumstances.* These two forms of decision making are conscious and unconscious.

Malcolm Gladwell, *Blink!: The Power of Thinking Without Thinking.* New York: Little, Brown, 2005.

Conscious Decision Making

Processing information and rendering decisions on a conscious level is intentional. It is typically a slow process and entails gathering information, employing logic, and coming up with a definitive answer to a problem, with the action following the decision. It is used in situations where a person knows that a problem exists or an answer is needed. Examples of processing information in this conscious way include when businesses gather market information and analyze it to make strategic decisions, or when people explore their choices among health care providers. In each of these situations, some quantity of information is gathered and analyzed, and a decision is made based on the result of that analysis. This way of making decisions requires substantial time. However, in situations where more time is available and when good information is available, we can reach well thought out and appropriate decisions if we don't fall prey to the following problem areas:

- Inundation with irrelevant information
- Overanalysis of pertinent information
- Overlooking a critical piece of information

Conscious research and analysis is a commonly used and useful tool to decision makers everywhere. However, it is not appropriate for every situation nor should it be used in every situation. Our brains make unconscious decisions all the time that change our lives and businesses without doing formal research, and those decisions are just as good if used appropriately.

Unconscious Decision Making

In situations where conscious decisions are being made, some degree of unconscious decision making is also taking place. *However, making unconscious decisions, also known as rapid cognition, is very different from conscious decision making.* The biggest difference is that the thought process is not intentional. The individuals making decisions on this level, more often than not, don't even know that they are doing it. Decision makers may feel their heart race, or their palms begin to sweat . . . but may not know why it is happening or what it means. Nevertheless, even before the first piece of relevant information is gathered or analyzed, decision makers may have a "gut feeling" about what they should do. This gut feeling is the result of their unconscious analysis of the situation, which is made by tapping into their experiences, skills, knowledge, and other such factors that are readily accessible but not easily communicated.

This gut instinct can be a highly useful tool in making decisions, especially in situations where decisions need to be made quickly and no time is available to conduct research. However, many are skeptical of this quick decision-making process and don't trust decisions reached through snap judgments or gut feelings because they are deemed hasty. In the world of business, this could be a serious handicap. By not being able to respond quickly, many strategic business opportunities could be missed due to a company being bogged down in extensive research and analysis rather than taking advantage of a timely opportunity based on "a gut instinct." Often decision makers will have a "feeling about a decision" and will still spend days, weeks, months, or even years researching the situation, only to come up with what their initial instincts had already told them so long ago.

However, a word of caution should be heeded in trusting your instincts. Although often accurate, there are some inherent problems associated with decisions of this type:

- Relevant information may be difficult to decipher quickly.
- Individuals may be slow to react due to interpretation problems.
- Snap judgments can overlook important information.

Despite these problems, our brains are capable of rapidly gathering information deemed valuable in assessing a situation and then quickly sending the analysis of that information to the rest of the body so that it can react appropriately. In addition, processing information in this way typically allows the brain to reach conclusions and begin to react to a situation before we are even aware that a problem exists. Our brain's ability to unconsciously process information allows us to react far sooner than we would be able to if we relied solely on our conscious ability to make assessments and reach conclusions. Other examples of situations in which our brains engage in rapid cognition include carrying on a conversation with another person, reacting in an emergency situation, and breathing.

ADAPTIVE UNCONSCIOUS

The part of our brain that reaches these conclusions very quickly is called the *adaptive unconscious*. This portion of our brain operates like a supercomputer that efficiently processes lots of data that is needed to keep us functioning on a daily basis. It allows us to make judgments quickly without requiring a lot of additional information and allows us to respond quickly to varying situations. Some functions of the adaptive unconscious are:

- Warning us of danger
- Setting goals
- Initiating action in a sophisticated and efficient manner

During our daily life it is common for us to switch back and forth between conscious and unconscious decision making depending on the situation. An example of conscious decision making is when you decide to invite a co-worker for dinner. You think about it, you decide that it would be fun, and then you invite the individual to join you. There is a deliberate thought process involved in making the decision to extend the invitation to the co-worker. This process may take a few moments or many weeks, but the invitation does not occur until after the decision is reached. The very next moment, however, you could get into an argument with that same co-worker, which would be an example of unconscious decision making. Most likely you did not walk into the co-worker's workspace with the intention of arguing. Nevertheless, through the process of communicating with that person, your unconscious mind perceives a "problem" and causes you to react to something that was said or done, and an argument ensues. You reach the decision to argue unconsciously; therefore you often are not aware that you are arguing, or why, until after the situation is over. The decision to argue is made by the adaptive unconscious portion of your brain and happens very quickly, even before you are aware that something has happened to cause you to respond.

Thin-Slicing

In order to have a better understanding of how rapid cognition works, we need to recognize that a little information goes a long way and our brains are extremely adept at picking up on the minute details in any situation. This concept is called *thin-slicing*. Thin-slicing refers to the ability of our unconscious mind to find patterns in situations and behavior based on very narrow slices of experience. The color of a label on a product, the slight raising of a person's eyebrow, and many other thin slices of information all play a part in our decision-making process. The way in which we make decisions to buy a certain product or talk to a person is determined by information that is both gathered by and stored in our brains. Body language, stereotypes, skills, and experiences are just a few of the things that the brain uses to analyze a situation and make snap decisions. The ability that our brain has to thin-slice situations is amazing. During this process, our brain will observe and dissect a concept, idea, interaction, or experience into its smallest parts in as little as a matter of seconds. In doing so, it has the ability to recognize patterns or overriding themes that are then used to make a prediction or decision based on minimal information. Thin-slicing is a necessary component to rapid cognition because it is essential for the brain to be able to process information quickly. That can happen only when it takes that information in small ("bite-sized") pieces.

Problems with Rapid Cognition

Rapid cognition is often an accurate and useful tool for decision makers. *However, errors in snap judgments do occur for three common reasons:*

1. Ideas, experiences, and attitudes cause altered perceptions.
2. Too much information clouds the ability to thin-slice.
3. Too little information can make it difficult to see the big picture.

By having an awareness of these common errors, decision makers will be better equipped to avoid them and improve the quality and speed of their decisions.

Conclusion

By taking steps to understand and educate the unconscious mind, we can and will improve our ability to make faster and more useful judgments. Although snap judgments take place in a matter of seconds, they can be just as useful if not more so than those we reach through lengthy analysis and research if we allow them to do their job. However, the key to successful decision making lies in knowing when to rely on rapid cognition—and when additional information or research is needed. Decision makers, businesses, and individuals can become more responsive and adaptable by becoming more comfortable with trusting their gut instincts rather than relying on extensive analysis every time a decision-making opportunity presents itself. The quicker response time will allow them to be more able to take advantage of time-sensitive situations by being responsive and flexible in situations that would have ordinarily led them to conduct time-consuming research and analysis and miss out on opportunities that require quick responses.

PART

XIII ETHICS AND VALUES

Almost daily, newspaper and television reports appear that document unethical activities engaged in by organizations, their executives, and their employees. The corporate world has been rocked by reports of scandal and corruption. Simultaneously, the past several years have seen an increase in the number of schools of business that have introduced ethics courses into their curricula. A large number of organizations are actively discussing ethical behavior, developing codes of conduct or codes of ethics, and making statements about the core values of their organizations.

A number of books have explored the ethical dilemmas that managers face, the core principles that guide ethical decision making, and the need for linking corporate strategy and ethical reasoning. However, questions still surround which values ethical leaders should hold, and how those values could be conveyed to their employees. The four books in this part address the need for managers to be ethical and credible.

In *Moral Intelligence*, Doug Lennick and Fred Kiel, two leadership experts with an international audience, introduce and define the essence of moral intelligence. The authors illustrate how the best-performing organizations have leaders with a strong moral compass. Through their book they illuminate ways that managers can build moral skills such as integrity, responsibility, compassion, and forgiveness. Included in their book is an inventory that can be used to assess where you and your organization currently stand with regard to its own level of moral intelligence.

Moral Intelligence is a co-authored book. Doug Lennick worked for and still serves as an advisor to American Express Financial Advisors' CEO, focusing on workforce culture. Today he is a managing partner of the Lennick Aberman Group. Fred Kiel (Ph.D.) is a co-founder of KRW International. He consults with senior executives of several Fortune 500 firms, focusing on leadership excellence.

Greed and corporate corruption are the backdrop for the second reading in this section on ethics and values. *Saving the Corporate Soul & (Who Knows?) Maybe Your Own* was written by David Batstone, who was a founding editor of the magazine *Business 2.0* and a contributor to several newspapers (*New York Times, Chicago Tribune, San Francisco Chronicle*). His writings have focused on ethics, business, spirituality, and culture. In this book, Batstone discusses eight principles for the creation and preservation of integrity and profitability. The central theme of the book suggests that corporate and personal success can be achieved without the sacrifice of one's soul. Confronting the current furor over corporate irresponsibility, Batstone discusses what is necessary for the revitalization of today's corporations and their managers.

Warren G. Bennis joins Robert J. Thomas in the authorship of *Geeks & Geezers*. Warren Bennis is professor and founding chairman of The Leadership Institute at the University of Southern California. He has made the study of leadership a major vocation, having authored 27 books on leadership and change. His co-author, Robert J. Thomas, is an associate partner and senior fellow with the Accenture Institute for Strategic Change. He is also the author of *What Machines Can't Do*. Bennis and Thomas have also collaborated on the book *Crucibles for Leadership*.

Geeks & Geezers presents a detailed description and differentiation between the leadership philosophy and style of our youngest and oldest leaders. The Geeks (the youngest leaders) are under the age of 35; they matured in front of the computer screen during the dot-com era. The Geezers (our oldest leaders) are over the age of 70 and matured during the Great Depression and World War II. The authors discuss the processes through which each of these leader groups emerged, and the role which that era played in shaping their values and leadership styles. It appears as though regardless of one's generation, virtually every leader has experienced at least one transformational experience—what is called a "crucible"—a make-or-break experience and a significant leadership-defining event.

Authentic Leadership is the last reading in this section on ethics and values. Drawing upon his 20-year leadership position at Medtronics, a world-leading medical technology company, Bill George offers lessons on leading with heart and compassion—a guide for character-based leadership. He identifies what he believes to be five essential dimensions of authentic leadership—purpose, values, heart, relationships, and self-discipline—and discusses how they can be developed.

Bill George is the former chairman and CEO of Medtronics. The Academy of Management recognized Mr. George as Executive of the Year, and the National Association of Corporate Directors and *Business Week* recognized him as Director of the Year. Currently, he serves as executive-in-residence at Yale University and sits on the boards of Goldman Sachs, Novartis, and Target.

1 MORAL INTELLIGENCE

DOUG LENNICK AND FRED KIEL

SUMMARY PREPARED BY ADAM SURMA

Adam Surma is a store manager with Target Corporation. Adam has held several positions with Target overseeing guest service and logistics operations in three Minneapolis Target stores. Primary management responsibilities include team development, corrective action, and store process execution. Adam received a Bachelor of Business Administration degree from the University of Minnesota Duluth with a major in Organizational Management. He belongs to the honorary business fraternity of Beta Gamma Sigma and spends much of his free time volunteering with the Southwest Metro Animal Rescue Adoption Society.

INTRODUCTION

Today's high-profile accounting scandals, corporate misconduct, and well-publicized accounts of abuses of executive power have left organizations as a whole facing a serious crisis of employee and stakeholder lack of confidence. In addition to a solid business model, efficient production, and world-class marketing, organizations in today's market need a strong grasp of the concept of moral intelligence to attract and maintain high-performing employees and build stakeholder confidence. Though organizations have known for years the importance of vision statements, corporate value credos, and emotional intelligence, morality as such has only recently been added to the mix of essential management paradigms and practices that define a successful and high-performing organization.

Moral intelligence is the mental capacity to determine how universal human principles should be applied to our values, goals, and actions. This capacity is similar to a person's cognitive, creative, or emotional capacity in that it is a sliding scale, as everyone sits somewhere along the continuum exhibiting different degrees of moral intelligence. Though many cultures and religions stress different behavioral and mental characteristics as being important or virtuous, all cultures share a simple set of universal human principles on which moral intelligence is based. The knowledge that killing another human is wrong, treating others as one would like to be treated,

Doug Lennick and Fred Kiel, *Moral Intelligence: Enhancing Business Performance and Leadership Success.* Pennsylvania: Wharton School Publishing, 2005.

and commitment to something greater than one's own self are all principles that numerous studies have confirmed to be common among humanity at large. *Aligning the values, goals, and actions of one's self and organization to consistently deliver morally "right" decisions strengthens worker loyalty, increases job satisfaction, and ultimately leads to increased long-term performance.*

THE COMPONENTS OF MORAL INTELLIGENCE

Moral intelligence as a mental capacity develops in every person from their earliest days as an infant. Although each person's individual life experience growing up plays a factor in their moral development, the overwhelming source of information for their internal moral compass is hardwired from birth. Nature, not nurture, is our primary guide; studies have shown that as a species, humanity has used social groups as a survival mechanism, relying on our "moral nature" to help each other find food, shelter, and comfort. This is the basis for a set of universal human principles that we all share.

In studying the many skill sets and other factors that go into moral intelligence, four principles were found to relate most strongly to high performance both personally and organizationally when examined under the lens of morality: integrity, responsibility, compassion, and forgiveness. Each of these principles is made up of **moral competencies** that are the actionable components of each skill set, which, if followed, lead to a more morally intelligent person or organization. These skill sets of competencies, more than any other, were found to build trust, respect, and a highly effective group of individuals. They include:

- Integrity. This principle is the cornerstone of any moral character. It involves doing what you said you would do, and following through on promises even when they are difficult. In business, integrity is what builds strong partnerships and convinces subordinates to entrust their confidences within a leader. The behavioral competencies involved in this skill set that can be practiced and honed to increase proficiency are keeping promises, standing up for what is right, telling the truth, and acting consistently within your own principles.
- Responsibility. This skill set also plays a large role in being morally intelligent. Taking on power as a leader necessarily means taking on responsibility. Accepting responsibility for personal choices, embracing those choices as you serve others, and admitting mistakes and failures are part of this principle.
- Compassion. Actively caring about others as a leader and organization may be the trendy thing to promote in modern organizations, but there are also real results to be reaped from doing this in a morally intelligent manner. Showing employees that you care builds fierce loyalty, even when the organization as a whole may be going through hard times. It is one of the few intangible assets of an organization that will keep workers feeling good about their jobs, even when losing them may be an option.
- Forgiveness. Forgiving may be the hardest thing for many to do in the demanding world of perfect results. It encompasses not only forgiving others for their mistakes, but focusing on the morality of letting one's own mistakes go. Mastering this skill will help develop an organizational culture that encourages risk and new ideas as people know that possible failures will be forgiven.

LIVING IN ALIGNMENT

Although everyone has a hardwired sense of universal human principles, this does not mean everyone always acts on them in a positive and morally correct manner. Having a foundation of the four principles of moral intelligence is just the first step; it is our moral compass pointing us in the direction that we know deep down is correct and true. To complete our sense of well-being and moral consistency we have to align our moral compass with both our goals and behavior. When our actions and behavior lead to obtaining our goals in a morally constant manner we have stayed true to the principle of moral intelligence and consequently increased our own sense of worth while by building trust and respect among the people around us.

Developing and maintaining a large group of moral competencies in the four principles allows for more control of your alignment between what you believe (moral compass), what you would like to accomplish (goals), and what you actually do (behavior). The Alignment Model shows how moral intelligence moderates the relationship between how we set our goals (based on what we know is right) and how we behave (based on our goals).

MISALIGNMENT

Sometimes knowing what is right and what needs to be done to accomplish this is not enough. Emotions play a role in determining if the person or group of people is strong enough to make the moral decision. Two types of variables must be guarded against if moral intelligence is to be observed.

- Moral Viruses. Moral viruses are negative beliefs that develop that conflict with the universal human principles that make up the foundation of our moral compass. These viruses infect the moral compass such that goals form that are not normally allowed under moral intelligence. Common viruses include beliefs such as "I'm not worth much," "Might makes right," and "Most people can't be trusted."
- Destructive Emotions. A more common yet still dangerous variable that prevents us from acting in a manner consistent with our goals is *destructive emotions*. This

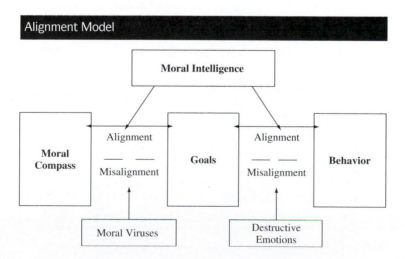

phrase is a catchall for negative emotions that cloud our judgment and mask our sense of morality; greed, racism, jealousy, and fear can turn even the most morally intelligent person from alignment.

With such dire consequences for both leaders and organizations who fall prey to these two negative factors, we must constantly monitor and realign our moral compass with the goals and behaviors we wish to adopt. Actively inquiring and physically creating lists and documents stating and comparing beliefs, goals, and actions both help to keep us honest to our universal human principles. The alternative is a dissatisfied, confused, and ultimately underperforming workforce.

Conclusion

Moral intelligence is based on universal human principles of right and wrong, and these are largely hardwired into each of us at birth. It is the guidance for our moral compass, which in turn helps us set our goals and guide our behavior to be consistent with our goals. Though the alignment model shows us how to form and act upon a fundamental moral foundation, atrocities and misdeeds occur on a daily basis. This straying from the moral path is found in varying degrees of alignment decay brought about through moral viruses and destructive emotions. These negative factors can be long term and severe enough to take years to correct.

A structured approach to identifying goals and determining behavior is the best way to develop and maintain a moral culture. Frequent review and challenging of actions, goals, and beliefs leads to open dialogue and quicker identification of possible moral viruses that may have crept into the concept of living in alignment unnoticed.

Moral intelligence is a concept that leaders and organizations alike can no longer ignore. It is a vital part of an organization's culture, and when paired with a solid business model it can produce real long-term results in terms of increased job satisfaction, higher worker productivity, and stronger stakeholder confidence in knowing what the organization is doing is "right."

2

SAVING THE CORPORATE SOUL & (WHO KNOWS?) MAYBE YOUR OWN

DAVID BATSTONE

SUMMARY PREPARED BY GARY P. OLSON

Gary P. Olson is Executive Director of the Center for Alcohol and Drug Treatment, Duluth, Minnesota. He is responsible for the overall direction of this regional not-for-profit corporation. His areas of interest include corporate strategy, employee participation, and effectiveness. He received his M.B.A. from the University of Minnesota Duluth.

INTRODUCTION

Public concern over corporate irresponsibility is deep and widespread. Corporate scandals have filled the headlines, ruined careers, and bankrupted retirement accounts. Yet millions of workers, from clerks to executives, rely on corporations for their livelihood and investors count on them to grow and prosper. At the same time, public markets have had unrealistic expectations for growth, leading to a short-term vision by executives and compromising long-term sustainability.

Ultimately, the confidence and trust of employees and the public are as important to the success of the corporation as quarterly performance. This can only be achieved and maintained when the corporation acts in a principled way. Substantial evidence supports the notion that principled corporations outperform the market over the long term. A principled company will strengthen its reputation, avoid costly legal battles, and more effectively manage its business network. In a principled corporation, profits do not overshadow its other priorities, particularly its reputation. A corporation that embraces the following principles will be a better place to work, to do business with, and to invest in:

David Batstone, *Saving the Corporate Soul & (Who Knows?) Maybe Your Own.* San Francisco: Jossey-Bass, 2003.

- The interests of corporate leaders are closely aligned with those of their customers, employees, shareholders, and communities.
- The company's operations are open and visible to all stakeholders.
- The corporation is a positive force in the communities in which it operates.
- Products are accurately represented, and there is a commitment to customers before and after a sale.
- Workers are treated as valued team members.
- The corporation fully accepts responsibility for its environmental impact.
- The corporation is committed to diversity in its workforce and markets.
- The transnational corporation will apply the same principles overseas that inform its activities at home.

PRINCIPLED LEADERSHIP

Corporate workers make decisions every day that affect employees, customers, and the community at large. Without leadership and support from the executive and board level to act in a principled way, their decisions may undermine the integrity of the corporation and lead to unexpected or even disastrous consequences. In other words, *principled leadership starts at the top.*

The personal interests of corporate leaders should be aligned with those of employees, customers, shareholders, and the communities in which they do business. Their actions should support the viability of the corporation in a responsible way. If trust and confidence among employees are lacking, investor confidence can also suffer. When corporate leaders display integrity, don't cut corners, and act responsibly, that trust can be earned.

One indication of principled leadership is whether or not the business model is built for both present and future earnings. Is it sustainable? An example of an unsustainable business plan is when growth targets are based on shareholder expectations rather than actual consumer demand. Unrealistic growth targets can lead to ill-advised marketing, capital investments, and other expenditures. Customer surveys and actual orders can be used to develop sales projections, giving a more realistic estimate.

In many corporations, executives reap the rewards while employees bear most of the risk. Both shareholder value and jobs have suffered while executives cashed in their stock options and companies went bankrupt. Bonuses have been paid to executives following wage concessions from workers. A principled corporation links executive compensation with company performance. The way directors and executives report their compensation is also important, particularly in the areas of share ownership and stock options. Holding periods for stock options, for example, can ensure that executives place the interests of the corporation above personal gain. Finally, excessive wage gaps between executive and nonexecutive employees can indicate something other than a long-term strategy on the part of leadership.

Since the ultimate control over the character of a corporation takes place at the board level, the integrity and independence of the board is crucial. It is the board's responsibility to protect the interests of all the stakeholders: employees, customers, shareholders, and the public. Although management representation is important, the CEO alone should not recruit board members, and board members should be expected to disclose any conflicts of interest and business relationships with the corporation on whose board they might serve. Employees can and should have a representative on the board, since they have the most to lose. Finally, shareholders should have a democratic process to influence company policy when corporate boards get off track.

TRANSPARENCY

The most important relationships a corporation can have are based on trust. Shareholders must have confidence that the results reported by the company are genuine. Employees who are expected to stake their careers and personal security on a company need to trust its commitment to value. Customers expect to get what they pay for and trust the company to stand behind their products.

One of the biggest problems corporate integrity has faced has been in the area of financial reporting. Clear, accurate, verifiable company reports, access to information by employees and shareholders, and rational accounting practices are critically important. A transparent corporate culture is enhanced when reports to employees and investors disclose details on operations, finances, and other important affairs. Shareholders count on independent auditors to report accurately a company's performance and avoid conflicts of interest. A company committed to transparency will ensure that accounting assumptions are clear, real earnings are reported, cash flows are detailed clearly, and write-offs are fairly stated. Transparency means operating with honesty, integrity, and openness so that a company's operations can be judged realistically by anyone who cares to look.

Participation by employees in key decisions is another aspect of transparency. Not all decisions are open for debate, but the rationale behind those decisions can be shared. When ideas are in the earliest stages of consideration, wide input is encouraged as part of the decision-making process.

Finally, when a company makes promises, it needs to stand behind them. Trust is built when the promises made by an individual employed by the company are honored even if it hurts the company in the short term.

COMMUNITY

Corporations rely on the resources, labor, and infrastructure of the communities in which they operate. A single-minded focus on profitability can lead to a disregard of the source of their success. Insensitivity to the interests of community can lead to a backlash by employees and customers that can damage the company's reputation and limit its opportunities.

The ways in which a corporation builds a relationship with the community are wide-ranging. Structured programs that encourage employees to become involved in community projects have been very successful. These programs can improve employee satisfaction as well as improve the company's image. Direct investment in community development is another way corporations can build support. The goal is to build social capital: community support that can come to the aid of the corporation at critical moments.

It is as important to assess the return on investment for community engagement, as is any other enterprise activity. Sometimes the development of its own workforce is a primary consideration. In other situations, it is the correlation between the resources invested and the goals of the program.

CUSTOMER SERVICE

A company that presents its products honestly and serves its customers beyond the initial transaction builds loyalty and support. Marketing campaigns that focus on obfuscation more than clarification are a sign of corporate dishonesty.

There are a few simple questions that can determine the level of customer care.

- Can the promises a company makes about a product be delivered?
- When a company fails to deliver on its promises, can it make it right?
- Does a company respond in a meaningful way to customer feedback?

Customer loyalty and retention are at the top of the list of management challenges, but customers need a good reason to believe in a company. Trust and fairness at each point of contact with a company will determine whether that loyalty is earned. Each component of customer service should be broken down and evaluated and all employees of the company should interact with customers periodically. Decision making should be pushed to those employees closest to the customer and employees should be rewarded for acquiring new customers and retaining them.

THE VALUE OF WORKERS

The extent to which workers are treated as partners in the business enterprise can be critical to long-term success. Historically, workers have been viewed as a capital expense, but when employees align their personal interests with those of the company this relationship can result in a significant competitive advantage. This is particularly true when superior quality is important in a product or service.

There are many ways to achieve this objective: profit-sharing, participation in governance, involvement in decision making, creation of career advancement opportunities, employee stock ownership programs (ESOPs), and others. Perhaps the ultimate form of employee participation is worker ownership of the company. Since the U.S. government declared employer contributions to ESOPs tax deductible, the trend toward employee ownership has accelerated. Although most employee-owned companies are small, some large corporations like United Airlines are majority-owned by workers.

Although no company can guarantee job security or compensation, employee involvement can minimize the human cost of the business cycle. When workers become true partners and that partnership is fully supported by the company's structure, then everyone is more likely to pull in the same direction. Enhancing the role of employees as stakeholders in the company can alter the labor-management paradigm, build trust and confidence, and improve company performance in important ways.

RESPECT FOR THE ENVIRONMENT

Ignoring the impact of the corporation's activities on the environment can lead not only to unplanned expense, but can also undermine the company's reputation and the public trust. There have been a number of high-profile cases of environmental damage caused by corporations that led to serious consequences, both financially and to the company's reputation.

Until recently it was seen as government's role to protect the environment through regulation, and the firm's job to operate within those guidelines. The consumer-led environmental movement has given the environment a new and important position as a virtual corporate stakeholder. Important public interest groups now work together with government, but often go considerably further in their concern for the environment. Consumers are also making decisions about products and companies based on their environmental record. *These changing social values present the corporation with a powerful challenge.*

Though it can be difficult to meet both consumers' expectations and the demands of militant environmentalists, a number of large corporations have begun to look beyond the regulations to address these social concerns. These companies have moved beyond a compliance mentality toward an outcome-informed process of environmental management.

One of the terms used to describe a merger between business and environmental concern is *sustainable development*. Corporate goals and strategies for achieving sustainability start with pollution control and compliance with existing regulations. The participation of external stakeholders and the creation of environmental management systems within the firm are important additional steps. In order to be effective, sustainability needs to be a key factor in planning and integrating management systems that consider the environmental impact of product development and production each step of the way.

DIVERSITY

Diversity is not just about skin color, gender, sexual orientation, or religion. Diversity is not a euphemism for affirmative action. *Diversity is about reflecting the values and cultures of the customer and the community in which you operate.* Sometimes companies must make a special effort to avoid a narrow-minded view of who is a desirable employee or customer. This is simply a sound business practice.

To achieve a balanced workforce, managers should be evaluated on their track record for hiring, retaining, and promoting minorities and women. Any process that excludes individuals, customers, or employees in an arbitrary way needs to be examined and corrected. This is certainly true when trying to diversify the customer base. Some of the essential steps in a diversity effort are to:

- Establish a physical presence in an underrepresented community
- Build strong connections with local interest groups
- Work to strengthen the neighborhood
- Recruit and employ representatives from the community
- Design products and services that meet local needs

THE GLOBAL PERSPECTIVE

A principled corporation that operates globally should apply the same principles overseas that inform its activities at home. The rights of workers, respect for the community, protection of the environment, and fair trading practices are equally important for the transnational corporation. Developing nations can provide valuable assets to the corporation, yet they should not have to sacrifice genuine economic development in the process. There is no question that transnational corporations can contribute to the improvement of standards of living in impoverished economies. If those corporations operate transparently and engage the population of the country in which they operate, they may be able to avoid some of the pitfalls that await the insensitive or unaware.

3

GEEKS & GEEZERS

WARREN G. BENNIS AND ROBERT J. THOMAS

SUMMARY PREPARED BY STEPHEN B. CASTLEBERRY

Stephen B. Castleberry (Ph.D.) is a professor of marketing at the University of Minnesota Duluth where he teaches courses in research, selling, and ethics. He was the previous holder of the UARCO Professor of Sales and Marketing Chair at Northern Illinois University and has served as department chairperson at two universities. He has published over 30 refereed journal articles in national publications on topics such as sales teams, sales training, listening, and ethics, and is co-author of the text Selling: Building Partnerships. *He serves on the editorial boards of several journals, has done consulting work for international as well as regional businesses, and owns a publishing company. He also appeared in eight segments of a PBS special on personal selling called* The Sales Connection.

Individual factors such as class, intelligence, wealth, beauty, and genetics have long been studied for their influence upon leadership traits. What has not been studied as much is the influence of another demographic factor, the era in which the leader matured as an adult. An interesting distinction, for example, can be seen when one compares environmental influences from the era of the early 1950s with that of the 1990s.

GEEZERS AND THE ERA OF LIMITS

Geezers, highly successful leaders who are now over 70 years old, were in their maturing years (mid to late twenties) during 1945–1954. Interviews with 25 geezers revealed the following environmental influences and characteristics:

- Although there was great hope and promise after World War II, this was tempered by fears of nuclear war and a stock market crash.
- To be successful in business it was important to be a team player and follow the company's rules and norms. Firms were highly respected by employees.
- Level of experience was highly correlated with respect. Those who worked hard, were patient, and learned the ropes were rewarded. Advancement took time.

Warren G. Bennis and Robert J. Thomas, *Geeks & Geezers: How Era, Values, and Defining Moments Shape Leaders.* Boston: Harvard Business School Press, 2002.

- Americans trusted institutions. For example, organized religions had substantial influence in communities.
- It was assumed that most men would choose one career and have a traditional family. Work–life balance was missing, with families being treated as secondary in importance when compared to the firm's wishes.
- Raised during the Depression, geezers sought financial security in order to offer their families a better life than they had growing up.
- Many were war veterans who exhibited service-based maturity and had practical, goal-oriented attitudes and philosophies.
- Heroes were numerous and widely available (e.g., FDR, Ghandi, Winston Churchill) and their presence had profound impacts on the ideas and behaviors of citizens.
- Leaders were more comfortable leading alone and stressing a "command and control" mentality.

GEEKS AND THE ERA OF OPTIONS

Contrast that portrait of geezers with what life was like for *geeks,* those successful leaders under 35 years old, who experienced their maturing years (mid to late twenties) during 1991–2000, and you'll find a world of difference. Based on interviews with 18 geeks, the following highlights the types of environmental influences and characteristics of leaders that matured during that era:

- An expectation of lifetime employment for the "loyal company man" of the 1950s was replaced with contract workers, part-timers, and a lack of corporate loyalty toward workers, as companies downsized and outsourced in a never-ending cycle of cost reductions.
- Opportunities seemed endless, and included ones like becoming an entrepreneur and getting rich overnight in the dot-com craze. Newly emerging leaders were impatient to realize their ambitions.
- Women flocked into the workforce.
- It was a period of great economic prosperity.
- Institutions went through drastic changes. Organized religion lost much of its importance, the definition of what constituted a "family" changed, and public education was in crisis as evidenced by falling test scores.
- They feel a responsibility to the communities that surround them and fully expect to change the world into a better place.
- They don't expect to stay with one company all their lives. They saw what happened to their parents, who were jettisoned out of companies to which they had been very loyal.
- They don't expect to remain in one career all their lives. In fact, they expect to have something closer to nine different careers.
- Success is defined as being challenged, having power, and charting history.
- Lessons are learned primarily from life, not from formal instruction or from reading "the classics."
- Balance between work and personal life is of paramount importance.
- Heroes, of which there are very few contemporary ones, tend to be people with whom they have had personal contact (a coach or parent). It's just too easy for

"traditional" heroes (e.g., politicians) to be discredited in the ever-present world dominated by the media and Internet.

CRUCIBLES OF LEADERSHIP

Emerging leaders enter life's trials and opportunities with leadership skills based upon individual factors and the influences of the era in which they lived while maturing as a young adult. But how do these people become truly gifted leaders? By a crucible. The *crucible* is a metaphor that calls to mind the melting pots and caldrons that alchemists employed in their attempts to change worthless metals into gold. In leadership terms, *crucibles are those transforming events or situations that radically change a person's leadership abilities and skills.* Crucibles are where leaders start asking themselves elemental questions, like "Who do I want to be? Why I am here on earth?" "How should I relate to people?" Every one of the 43 leaders studied had experienced at least one such crucible.

Crucibles are not necessarily painful, and therefore emerging leaders may even seek them out. For example, working with a chosen mentor can be a crucible. Arthur Levitt, Jr. created crucibles for himself by constantly seeking out new challenges in the form of new careers that would stretch and grow his leadership skills. For Geoff Keighley, his unpainful crucible was discovering his own power and uniqueness, while pretending to be a magician at a birthday party in the second grade. For Liz Altman, it was spending a year in Japan, whose culture shocked and challenged her.

In other situations, crucibles represent difficult circumstances that test and mold. For example, Sidney Rittenberg was put in a Chinese prison on charges of spying. For Mike Wallace it was the sudden death of his oldest son. Vernon Jordan credits the many racial slurs he encountered from a Georgia governor as his crucible. Not surprisingly, World War II was a crucible for many of the geezers in the study.

THE OUTCOMES OF CRUCIBLES: LEADERSHIP COMPETENCIES

1. Adaptive Capacity

Truly successful leaders come through their crucibles, not with a sense of bitterness or frustration, but with a vision about who they are or who they might become. It is this *adaptive capacity* that sets them apart from non-leaders who experience the same types of crucibles. Even when failure occurred during a crucible, it was seen as a friend, not a foe. Why? Because the leader finds new abilities, new appreciation, and new resolve for future encounters. The leader often creates a story around the experience that instills resolve and reminds the leader of the lessons learned. This story is almost always shared with others and can become a legend.

2. Engaging Others by Creating Shared Meaning

What good is it to have a vision unless others know about it and agree with it? That's why one of the very first jobs of successful leaders is to communicate their vision to followers and have them buy into it, even to the point of accepting the vision as their own. Leaders convert an inspiring personal vision into a shared meaning for their followers.

3. A Distinctive Voice Loud Enough to Provide Leadership

Leaders have self-confidence and are aware of their abilities. They know who they are and have the emotional intelligence to know how to relate to their followers effectively. Their "voice" stands out in a distinctive way for others to hear.

4. Integrity and a Strong Sense of Values

All leaders studied had a strong set of values, which includes components such as a desire for justice, an appreciation for the value and rights of all people, a compelling desire to do the right things, and integrity. Their integrity—a critical component of success—is composed of three components:

- **Ambition.** The drive for gain and growth. The focus can be on rewards for the individual, the good of the community, or both.
- **Competence.** The skills component of integrity, it includes expertise in critical leadership skills.
- **Moral compass.** The ability to differentiate good and evil and the recognition that we do not live our lives alone.

All three components must be present and in balance for true integrity to be present. *While it is easy to understand the dangers of unbridled ambition and lack of competence, less recognized is the danger of having a moral compass, but having no ambition or competence.* An example would be Huey Long or Father Charles Coughlin, who had a great moral compass, but lacked competence or ambition to achieve goals, leading people into false dreams and follies.

ANOTHER TRAIT OF SUCCESSFUL LEADERS: BEING PUPPIES

When examining the geezers in this study, an additional trait was identified: neoteny. *Neoteny* is the youthful, almost puppy-like quality that attracts others to oneself. It is to have energy, to stimulate and enjoy being stimulated, to be curious, to have a contagious laugh, and to feel alive. Charisma may in fact be an outcome of neoteny. It is probably the neoteny of successful older leaders that attracts younger people to seek mentoring relationships with them. It can also be a reason that many older leaders actually enjoy mentoring younger people, because many young people exhibit neoteny, too.

THE LEADERSHIP MODEL—A SUMMARY

Based on results of interviews with the 43 geeks and geezers, a model of leadership emerged. Leaders are the product of individual factors in the context of the era during which they reached maturity. They go through a life-transforming event or experience called a crucible, which gives meaning and direction to life and leadership. This results in improved competencies in adaptability, engaging others in shared visions, finding their own distinctive powerful and effective voice, and integrity.

One can find many examples, beyond the 43 persons interviewed for the study, who display the leadership model in action. For example, September 11, 2001, provided a crucible by evoking life-changing leadership skills for leaders like New York Mayor Rudolph Giuliani and President George W. Bush.

HOW CAN WE INCREASE THE POOL OF LEADERS?

There are many people who have the capacity to be great leaders, but they have never had the opportunity to test their skills or utilize them. Here are some suggested ways to increase our pool of available leaders:

- **National level**—Increase the opportunities for service (Peace Corps, Teach for America, AmeriCorps, City Year programs).
- **Firm level**—Invest in leadership training, encourage employees to spend time reflecting on lessons learned in day-to-day activities, systematically rotate employees through various departments, provide life-work balance for geeks who seek it, and offer sabbaticals.
- **Individual level**—Learn how to learn, build networks across generations and cultures, stay active through exercise, be optimistic, spend time thinking and reflecting, find ways to practice leadership, and strive to develop one's own level of neoteny.

4

AUTHENTIC LEADERSHIP

BILL GEORGE

SUMMARY PREPARED BY RANDY SKALBERG

Randy Skalberg is an assistant professor of taxation and business law at the University of Minnesota Duluth where he has taught courses in Corporate and Individual Tax, Business Law, and Corporate Ethics. He holds a B.S.B. in Accounting from the Carlson School of Management at the University of Minnesota, a J.D. from the University of Minnesota Law School, and an L.L.M. in Taxation from Case Western Reserve University in Cleveland, Ohio. He has served as an in-house Tax Counsel to Fortune 500 corporations including Metris Companies and The Sherwin-Williams Company, and also served in the tax department at Ernst & Young's Minneapolis office. He is admitted to practice law in Minnesota, as well as before the U.S. Tax Court.

AUTHENTIC LEADERSHIP

Authentic leadership involves those actions taken by people of high integrity who are committed to building enduring organizations relying on morality and character. It means being your own person as a leader. A leader's authenticity is based not only on differentiating right and wrong (the classic "moral compass") but also on a leadership style that follows qualities of your heart and mind (passion and compassion) as well as by your intellectual capacity. All too often, society has glorified leaders based on high-style and high-ego personalities instead of personal qualities that provide for true quality leadership.

DIMENSIONS OF A LEADER

An authentic leader practices the five dimensions of leadership: Purpose, Values, Heart, Relationships, and Self-Discipline. *Purpose* focuses on the real reasons people choose to become leaders—not the trappings of power, the glamour, or the financial rewards that go with leadership. *Values* provide the "true north" of a leader's moral compass. Failure of leadership values lies behind the failure of Enron, but more importantly, leadership

Bill George, *Authentic Leadership: Rediscovering the Secrets to Creating Lasting Value.* San Francisco: Jossey-Bass, 2003.

values have been critical in the growth of virtually all of America's long-term corporate success stories. An example of *Heart* in leadership is provided by Marilyn Nelson, CEO of Carlson Companies. She took over an organization bordering on crisis from previous years of "hard-nosed" management and created a program called "Carlson Cares," which has resulted in both corporate growth and an improved bottom line. The *Relationship* dimension debunks the myth that a great leader needs to be distant and aloof to prevent the relationship from interfering with "hard" decisions. An authentic leader creates close relationships as part of leadership. The existence and fostering of such relationships is actually a sign of strength in leadership, not an indicator of weakness. Consistency is the hallmark of *Self-Discipline* in a leader. Consistency enables employees who work with the leader to know where he or she stands on important issues and to rely on even the most difficult decisions the leader has made.

LEADING A BALANCED LIFE

One of the key characteristics of authentic leadership is the focus on the journey rather than the destination. The leader must recognize that a career is rarely a straight-line path to success (and most likely should not be), but rather it is a journey wherein all of the leader's experiences contribute to overall success.

This concept of success implies not merely financial or professional success, but the overall success that comes from leading a *balanced life*—one that recognizes the importance of work, family, friends, faith, and community service, with none of them excluding any of the others. Leaders who subordinate everything else in life to their work do not develop organizations as well as those who live a more balanced life. Living such a life and allowing their employees to do so as well creates higher levels of commitment to the organization and, in turn, improves the organization's bottom line. *Balancing work, family, social, and spiritual aspects of your life and providing a meaningful amount of time to each provides the leader with richness in life* that is unavailable to someone who chooses an 80-hour week and is simply a "company person." The balance between work and family life is a substantial challenge, especially in today's two-career families. One of the challenges every leader will face is the impact of increased time demands from the organization on his or her family. The "delicate balance" between work and family life continues to be very difficult to achieve.

In addition to work/family balance, friendships are important. True friendships offer a place to share your emotions outside your family and without workplace involvement. This sharing process is an important part of the process of personal development. Equally important is the mentoring process. Contrary to the traditional view of mentoring, where an older person provides one-way advice to a younger person, true mentoring is a two-way process where both parties learn from each other. This two-way process acknowledges that mentoring is not merely the older generation telling "war stories," but a process where younger employees and students can provide insight into the questions that young leaders have about the business world. Finally, community service is an essential part of authentic leadership. Through community service, leaders have an opportunity to work with people of lesser economic means. *Getting in touch with people helps develop both the heart of a leader and sensitivity for the difficulties of the lives of others.*

ORGANIZATIONAL MISSION AS MOTIVATION

A common phrase in today's business world (some would say almost a mantra) is "maximizing shareholder value." While that might be an appropriate goal for a company seeking a white knight in a takeover battle, it is fundamentally flawed as a long-term business model. The best way to create real long-term value for a company's shareholders is to be a *mission-driven organization*—one that utilizes its mission statement as an integral part of managing the organization, not merely a plaque that hangs on the CEO's wall. The best organizations have a corporate mission that inspires creative employees to develop innovative products and provide superior service to the customer. This strategy creates a self-sustaining business cycle. In Medtronic's case, this mission is to "alleviate pain, restore health, and extend life" of the patient consumer, which creates demand from physicians who are the immediate customers.

CUSTOMER FOCUS

Every company's purpose boils down to serving its customers well. If it does this better than any of its competitors, and does it over the long term, it will ultimately create more shareholder value than its competitors. *Customer-focused quality* relies for its success on measurements that focus externally on customers, and uses customer feedback as the ultimate measurement of quality. The role model for customer focus must be senior management. If senior management is focused on internal operations instead of on customer service, the company will eventually fail to an environment that empowers and rewards employees who provide high-quality sales and service to the customer.

TEAM-FOCUSED MANAGEMENT

CEOs are given credit when companies succeed, but it is largely a myth that the CEO is primarily responsible for the success of a company. Many of the great corporate success stories of the past 25 years—Intel, Nokia, Hewlett-Packard, Microsoft, Coca-Cola, and Pepsi—have all been managed by a team at the top, not merely by a single high-powered CEO. Upon being named CEO of Medtronic, Bill George immediately proposed a partnership (as opposed to a traditional boss–subordinate relationship) with Vice Chair Glen Nelson. This was critical to Medtronic's success. Nelson, an M.D., brought a critical perspective on the relationship of the practice of medicine and technology to the management team, while George brought experience in high technology management from his previous employer, Honeywell.

PITFALLS TO GROWTH

There are seven key pitfalls to sustainable corporate growth: lack of mission, underestimation of core business, single-product dependence, failure to spot change, changing strategy with changing culture, ignoring core competencies, and over-reliance on growth through acquisition. Avoiding each of these pitfalls requires disciplined leadership to recognize the problem and aggressively solve it without immediately retreating into a dangerous cost-cutting mode. This type of leadership in the face of inevitable criticism from securities analysts and the media will provide inspiration to the organization and rejuvenate its growth.

OVERCOMING OBSTACLES

A key obstacle for Medtronic involved litigation in the implantable defibrillator market. A former Medtronic employee held patent rights to the first implantable defibrillator and went to work for Eli Lilly, a Medtronic competitor. Lilly used the patents to prevent Medtronic from developing its own defibrillator, a product that was critical to its core pacemaker business. Medtronic and Lilly litigated this patent claim to the U.S. Supreme Court, where Medtronic won the right to develop its implantable defibrillator. Even after this victory though, Medtronic still had to negotiate a cross-licensing agreement with Lilly, clear FDA approval, and face the challenge of another competitor (Guidant) that reached the market with a dual chamber defibrillator prior to Medtronic. This 15-year struggle proved worthwhile, however, since Medtronic now enjoys greater than 50 percent market share in the implantable defibrillator market.

ETHICAL DILEMMAS

Socially responsible organizations need to confront directly the issue of ethical standards in international business. Medtronic discovered shortly after acquiring the Italian distributor of Medtronic's Dutch pacemakers that the distributor was depositing large sums in a Swiss bank account, presumably to pay off Italian physicians who were Medtronic customers. George confronted the recently hired president of Medtronic Europe about the account and terminated him for violating Medtronic's corporate values. The termination caused uproar within Medtronic Europe, but in the 12 years since this incident, the Dutch pacemaker subsidiary has responded with outstanding performance.

A second crisis arose in Japan, where two Medtronic-Japan managers were arrested and put in jail for giving airline tickets to a physician so that he could give speeches at two international transplant conferences. The arrests were part of a series of arrests of executives of foreign pacemaker manufacturers apparently based on the Ministry of Health's frustration at its inability to force the manufacturers to reduce prices in the Japanese market. The two managers were eventually released from jail following a guilty plea and returned to work. But George took the critical step in visiting Japan to reestablish confidence in Medtronic-Japan's employees and meet with officials from the Ministry of Health. This visit led to the creation of an industry-wide code of conduct approved by the Ministry of Health. Medtronic continues to be a leader in the medical device industry in Japan and has not agreed to mandated price concessions.

GROWTH BY ACQUISITION

In the fall of 1998 Medtronic engaged in a series of acquisitions costing a total of $9 billion. Medtronic's growth had been in sharp decline, so George decided to make a series of bold moves. These included the acquisition of Physio-Control, a manufacturer of manual defibrillators used in hospitals. George had to overcome internal resistance to the Physio-Control deal, as well as others, based on a poor history of acquisition integration at Medtronic. After overcoming that resistance in the Physio-Control deal, the groundwork was set for two more acquisitions in 1998 and 1999—Sofamor Danek, the world's leading spinal surgery company, and AVE, the leader in the U.S. stent business.

By late January 1999 Medtronic had completed five acquisitions at a total cost of $9 billion. Next Medtronic faced the more difficult task of integration. Most acquisitions that fail do so not from financial issues or lack of strategic vision, but rather from cultural clashes within the newly merged entities. Medtronic took a proactive approach to integration focusing on four key issues: leadership of the business, financial leadership, business integration, and cultural integration. George formed integration teams for each company led by a Medtronic executive and including Medtronic employees and employees from the acquired company.

SHAREHOLDERS COME THIRD

George's executive philosophy was described in an article in *Worth Magazine*, quoting him as saying, "Shareholders come third." George expected some backlash from the article, but surprisingly received none. The theory is simple. Customers are first, employees are second, and shareholders come third. Only by truly meeting the needs of the first two stakeholder groups does the successful company have any chance of satisfying the shareholders. *The key to meeting shareholder expectations is transparency.* Medtronic is completely transparent about every corporate event inside the company with respect to shareholders, a policy that can be contrasted with the Kozlowski-led Tyco, which hid major corporate expenditures from its own board of directors, much less the shareholders.

CORPORATE GOVERNANCE

The key to improved corporate governance is to restore power to boards of directors to govern corporations. The board should play an important role as a check on the company's executives and a means of ensuring long-term as opposed to short-term focus. One key to creating this type of board is to have a majority (perhaps two-thirds) of truly independent board members that have no business relationship to either the corporation or the executives. This will ensure that the directors can truly act independently of the CEO, not merely as "inside" directors who serve at the pleasure of the CEO.

PUBLIC POLICY AND RISK TAKING

Medtronic found itself cast in a leadership role in reform of the U.S. Food and Drug Administration. The key issue in the reform movement was the steadily increasing approval time for new drugs. Drugs that were already in use in foreign countries were taking months, and in many cases years, to be approved in the United States. and American patients were dying without access to life-saving medications. George presented his ideas about the need for reform at the Food & Drug Law Institute in Washington, D.C., and went on to work with the late Senator Paul Wellstone to generate bipartisan support for the Food and Drug Modernization Act of 1996. Today, new drugs are approved in less than 6 months, as opposed to 29 months at the height of the FDA's delay problems.

SUCCESSION PLANNING FOR THE CEO

One of the most critical and often overlooked steps in a CEO's career is succession. Almost as many CEO succession processes fail as succeed. If the board working with the incumbent CEO fails to identify a qualified and appropriate internal candidate, they are often forced to look outside the organization for a "star" CEO, a process that more often than not fails, as happened at Xerox and Maytag. One of the key factors is a lack of clarity on the CEO's part about how and when he or she will step aside. The CEO should identify a retirement date well in advance (Bill George announced his retirement date one year in advance), develop a succession plan, and make the transition as seamless as possible. This transition method is critical not only to employees and shareholders who desire consistent leadership, but also to the new CEO who knows when he or she will take over. This prevents the new CEO from being forced to choose between waiting around and moving on to other opportunities.

SUCCESSION PLANNING FOR THE CEO

PART

XIV

EMOTIONS AT WORK

Topics of interest to managers encompass a wide array of themes, and these are constantly changing and evolving. This section includes a sampling of topics that have received substantial attention in recent years, all focusing on employee emotions, feelings, and attitudes. The topics in this section include employee mindfulness, compassion, toxic experiences at work, the positive psychology underlying authentic happiness, and the need for employees to find meaning in their (work) lives. These readings are designed to raise issues, provide an opportunity for reflection on oneself, and stimulate conversations regarding the balance between emphasis on corporate profits and employee (and personal) needs.

Resonant leaders recognize the importance of the "soft" side of management. Their stresses and sacrifices place them at risk of a downward spiral into dissonance. Resonant leaders, however, rely on three major ingredients—mindfulness, hope, and compassion—to overcome the negative effects of stress in their own work lives while also stimulating continuous renewal throughout their organizations. In effect, they recognize that their leadership role includes an astute management of both their own emotions and the emotions of others.

Resonant Leadership was written by Boyatzis and McKee. Richard Boyatzis is a professor with joint appointments in the Departments of Organizational Behavior and Psychology at Case Western Reserve. Annie McKee is the co-chair of the Teleos Leadership Institute, and also teaches at the University of Pittsburgh's Graduate School of Education. They, along with Daniel Goleman, are the authors of the best-seller *Primal Leadership*.

Toxic bosses and organizational cultures exist in many workplaces even in this enlightened era, and their impact is often compounded by the presence of combative customers, impossible deadlines, and unexpected tragedies. The results of this insidious organizational toxicity include lower productivity, job stress, workplace sabotage, and labor–management disputes. *Toxic Emotions at Work* by Peter J. Frost provides a description of the positive roles that toxin handlers can engage in to reduce and even minimize the adverse impacts of toxic pain. They can listen with compassion, facilitate the discussion of emotions, intercede on behalf of colleagues, and reframe painful situations. Frost concludes his book with a three-stage model for managing toxicity that identifies strategies for prevention, intervention, and restoration.

Peter J. Frost received his Ph.D. from the University of Minnesota, and served as the Edgar F. Kaiser Professor of Organizational Behaviour on the Faculty of Commerce of the University of British Columbia. In addition to *Toxic Emotions at Work*, he is the co-author of many other books, such as *HRM Reality, Doing Exemplary Research, Organizational Reality*, and *Reframing Organizational Culture*. In 2003, Peter Frost received the George R. Terry Book Award from the Academy of Management for *Toxic Emotions at Work*.

The third book included in this section is *Authentic Happiness*, by Martin Seligman. The book draws upon psychological research on "positive psychology" to suggest that happiness can be cultivated by individuals if they choose to identify and draw upon their existing "signature strengths," such as humor, optimism, kindness, creativity, and generosity. The resulting positivism can serve as a buffer against negative life events and misfortunes, help individuals attain their personal growth goals while improving the world around them, and move them toward achieving authentic contentment. Putting it more simply, Seligman argues that good character coupled with optimism leads to lasting happiness.

Martin Seligman is the Fox Leadership Professor of Psychology at the University of Pennsylvania, where he has initiated work on learned helplessness, depression, optimism and pessimism, motivation, personality, and positive psychology. He is the former president of the American Psychological Association. Included in his bibliography of 20 books and 170 articles are *Helplessness, What You Can Change and What You Can't, Abnormal Psychology*, and *Learned Optimism*.

Viktor Frankl is one of the world's best-known survivors of the Holocaust's Nazi concentration camps in World War II. He attributed his survival under horrifying conditions to a driving search for meaning in a seemingly hopeless situation, and reported his lessons learned in his book, *Man's Search for Meaning* (named by the Library of Congress as one of the 10 most influential books of the twentieth century). Alex Pattakos, in *Prisoners of Our Thoughts*, has distilled Frankl's 30 books down into seven core principles: choose your attitude, commit to meaningful goals, find meaning wherever you are, recognize how you work to defeat yourself, search for insight and perspective while laughing at yourself, learn to shift your focus of attention, and make a difference in the world. Pattakos shows us how to connect with others so as to create and experience meaning in our lives.

Alex Pattakos is the founder of the Center for Personal Meaning in Santa Fe, and also a principal of The Innovation Group. He is a speaker, writer, facilitator, and consultant to corporate clients on the Fortune 500. He is a strong advocate of "community building" in a wide range of settings, an adjunct professor at Penn State University, and author of the books *Intuition at Work* and *Rediscovering the Soul of Business*.

1 | RESONANT LEADERSHIP

RICHARD BOYATZIS AND ANNIE MCKEE

SUMMARY PREPARED BY BEVERLY FRAHM

Beverly Frahm is founder and principal of Frahm Consulting located in Danville, California. She specializes in human resource management and organization and leadership development. Her previous internal management positions and her work with consulting and coaching clients have given her the opportunity to work with and learn from leaders at all levels. She has done research on leadership, executive coaching, and emotional intelligence, exploring the unique experiences of individual research participants as leaders and coaches. Her life is enriched by her relationships with family, friends, nature, and the great outdoors.

INTRODUCTION

Leadership is often an emotional roller coaster ride. It can be exciting, stressful, powerful, consuming, energizing, lonely, frustrating, rewarding, influential, overwhelming, and exhausting. The personal sacrifice that comes with the leadership role can be overwhelming and destructive.

While leadership has never been easy, the ride is intensified by our ever-changing and uncertain world of challenges and dangers and by organizations that are becoming more global, complex, and confusing yet leaner. Leaders today face new and greater challenges and higher levels of stress and pressure.

Organizations are realizing that greater results are achieved through **resonant leaders**, those who create and sustain resonance and effectiveness. Dissonant leaders who are emotionally unaware, volatile, and reactive do not fit into those organizations.

Now, a new kind of leadership is required—resonant leadership.

GREAT LEADERS ARE RESONANT LEADERS

Resonant leaders are great to work with and get the desired results. They give of themselves *and* care for themselves. They have a personal vision for their lives, work, future, and who they want to be. They have an agenda for learning and a process for

Richard E. Boyatzis, *Resonant Leadership: Renewing Yourself and Connecting with Others Through Mindfulness, Hope, and Compassion.* Boston: Harvard Business School Press, 2005.

continuous renewal. They focus on the future, lead with mental clarity, and inspire others with a clear and meaningful vision.

They are awake and aware of themselves, others, and their surroundings. They are compassionate, empathetic, mindful, hopeful, and optimistic. They manage their own attitudes, behaviors, and impulses and recognize, understand, and manage their own emotions and the emotions of others. They establish positive relationships, bring out the best in others, and encourage fun, reflection, and self care. They build trust, create excitement about the present, and stimulate hope for the future. In essence, they have developed emotional intelligence.

THE SACRIFICE SYNDROME—A SLIPPERY SLOPE

Over time, the burdens of leadership and its associated exhaustion take their toll. *Those who give too much of themselves and receive too little for too long become victims of the **Sacrifice Syndrome***. They fall into *dissonance* and lose their effectiveness.

Some of the same factors that contribute to their effectiveness can lead them down the slippery slope of the Sacrifice Syndrome. It starts as leaders are striving to achieve, putting their work and organization ahead of their own best interests. They have little or no time for friends or family.

Once in the Syndrome, leaders become its victim and go into a downward spiral. Their judgment is impaired and they lose emotional intelligence. They numb out. They close off from others, shut down, and become difficult to deal with. They misuse power, inflict stress on others, and create dissonance and suffering. They become ineffective—mindless and clueless about what is going on around them and with them. They miss real goals. Life may lose its meaning. Their high state of constant alert and stress weakens the nervous and immune systems. Eventually their career, relationships, and physical and mental health are negatively impacted.

Leaders set themselves up to fall into the spiral trap when they do not take care of themselves. They have a personal and professional responsibility to manage the pressures of their role so they can prevent the Sacrifice Syndrome. They must learn and develop skills and practices so they can counter the effects of stress and personal sacrifice and build and sustain resonance and effectiveness.

There are organizations that encourage individual self-sacrifice, and train and reward people to achieve results at any cost. They overvalue achievement, undervalue interpersonal skills, and tolerate dissonance and bad behavior. Their environments are full of tension. Their leaders create dissonance and the spiral continues. Especially then, individual leaders must be able to maintain themselves and make choices that are in their own best interests.

DISSONANCE

When leaders do not create and sustain resonance, they fall into dissonance. It happens as a result of power stress, a type of stress that is sometimes blinding and often chronic, that goes along with being a leader. This stress is exacerbated by loneliness at the top, continuous self-sacrifice, and failure to allow time for recovery. Even though they may sense something is going wrong, they ignore it and keep going.

Even the most effective leaders can become dissonant, especially during difficult and trying times. They lose their patience, become nervous and driven, often over-working and undervaluing themselves and others. Their behavior causes others to feel threatened and frustrated. Dissonant leaders behave in ways that may threaten and frustrate others. They create a dissonant climate in which people become less effective and helpless; complaints and infighting increase.

When in dissonance, it takes more energy to focus; decision making is more difficult, confidence levels decrease, relationships become less fulfilling and ignored, values fall by the wayside, and spiritual and emotional lives diminish. The dissonant leader disconnects from self and others.

People sink into dissonance and remain there because of

- The Sacrifice Syndrome – unchecked power stress and personal sacrifice
- Defensive Routines – bad habits that keep them in denial
- Organizations – tense environments that encourage dissonant behaviors

THE CYCLE OF SACRIFICE AND RENEWAL

Leaders must be able to recognize their destructive patterns and take steps to renew themselves holistically so they do not go into the spiral of the Sacrifice Syndrome. They must regulate their own cycle of sacrifice and renewal, countering the effects of power stress and personal sacrifice.

Those who have fallen into the Sacrifice Syndrome can break out of it. For some, however, it may take one or more wake-up calls, such as a medical illness, loss of a significant relationship, being passed over for a promotion, or loss of their job, in order for them to do so. They must then begin a process of renewal and intentional change.

KEYS TO RENEWAL

Renewal is an ongoing process, a way of life that requires conscious daily efforts and practices. Three key elements of renewal are mindfulness, hope, and compassion. Renewal begins with mindfulness.

Mindfulness is a conscious awareness of self, others, and the way in which we work and live. Mindful people are awake and tending to themselves, their lives, and their environment. They are aware of their thoughts, emotions, and bodily sensations. They listen to their inner voice as it tells them when something is right or wrong. They are able to recognize and respond to power stress early on.

Mindfulness must be learned and practiced. Without practice it can decline slowly without our noticing it, leaving us unaware, clueless, and shut off from others. We become mindless leaders, left out of meetings or excluded from membership on the management team because of it. Mindlessness can derail careers and destroy marriages, families, and other important relationships, leaving the individual more alone and empty.

The capacity for mindfulness can be developed through reflection, practice, and supportive relationships.

Reflection involves taking time to stop, quiet the mind, and pay attention to what is going on inside our mind, body, heart, and spirit. It may include practices such as meditation, mental imagery, nature walks, and journaling.

Supportive relations and connections with others provide another source of reflection that helps leaders learn and counter the stress and loneliness of leadership. The leader must, however, make the effort and take time to develop and nourish the relationships and maintain the practices.

Slipping into Mindlessness

Even successful leaders at the peak of their careers can lose touch. Over the years, their drive and ambitions overpower them; they develop irritating patterns and behaviors that alienate others. They become more self-protective and self-centered, losing sight of organizational goals. Getting caught in the Sacrifice Syndrome, they shut themselves off from others. They slip into *mindlessness*. Some reasons for this are tunnel vision and multi-tasking, shoulds, fragile self-esteem, and the imposter syndrome.

Tunnel Vision and Multi-tasking

Although the ability to focus and multi-task are considered strengths, when carried to the extreme they lead to exhaustion, unpredictable emotional responses, and mindlessness. Subtle patterns, early warning signs, and new opportunities are missed. Eventually, the ability to focus and to multi-task declines.

Shoulds Lead to Compromises and Mindlessness

When people get on a track of doing what they think they should do to become what they want to be, they can get stuck there; *they become the role and lose touch with themselves and what really matters to them.* They get lost and lose their sense of fulfillment about their work and home life. They deny that they are having problems; they become defensive, angry, and go into fight or freeze mode. Their emotions paralyze them and mindlessness sets in.

Fragile Self-Esteem and the Imposter Syndrome

When leaders possess fragile levels of self-esteem, they feel insecure and afraid. They fall into the *imposter syndrome* and become defensive and disconnected; they focus on overachieving, proving their worth, shutting down, and hiding so they are not found out as being less than what they want to project. Their battle results in bad behavior.

Hope is an emotional state that enables us to believe in ourselves and our visions. It is cultivated by developing an attainable vision and a dream one believes is feasible. Hope inspires leaders to move toward goals and dreams and inspires others to go with them. It also inspires leaders to face their situation, to correct their mistakes, and to make a fresh start. Hope arouses compassion.

While hope inspires, it also hurts when used by leaders to create an illusion of hope and to manipulate others.

Compassion implies understanding other people and their wants, and feeling motivated to act on our feelings about them. Listening leads to understanding, which in turn sparks compassion. Compassionate leaders create a positive work environment wherein the leader and his or her people are able to sustain effectiveness longer. Compassion is contagious, and as it spreads it positively impacts the organization.

Leaders who have slid into dissonance must reignite their own compassion. However, they also need to draw on the compassion of others in order for renewal to occur. During their decline into dissonance, others may have given up on them and walked away. They need to reach out and reconnect with those who are still willing and able to support them.

INTENTIONAL CHANGE

In order to create and sustain effectiveness, leaders must engage in intentional change and continuous self renewal. *Intentional and sustainable change involves a process of deep personal discovery and the creation of a learning and development plan.* The process requires mindfulness, compassion, and hope.

Coaching and Intentional Change

Personal transformation is essential. In order for transformation to occur, leaders have to recognize the need for change and have the inspiration and courage necessary to do the work. They must be honest with themselves, and admit to and face their shortcomings. They must recognize and be accountable for their contributions to the situation, develop a plan for change, and focus on making the necessary changes. They need to develop more constructive habits, attitudes, and behaviors.

While transformation is a personal process, it needs the connection and support of others. Relationships are essential, and friends, bosses, peers, spouses, and coaches can be helpful. Many leaders appreciate and benefit by the safe and confidential environment, guidance, honest feedback, and confrontation that a coach can provide. In turn, the leader learns to coach.

Coaching others and being coached helps leaders stay connected with others instead of being lonely and isolated. Being a compassionate coach helps leaders on the path of renewal.

LEADERSHIP CHOICES

Leadership is more than planning, organizing, and controlling. It is also about the body, mind, spirit, and heart. Along with the new kind of leadership necessary for today's world, there is a new language along with concepts and skills that must be learned, integrated, and managed. They are mindfulness, hope, compassion, resonance and renewal, intentional change, and emotional intelligence. The impacts of power stress and the Sacrifice Syndrome must be acknowledged and managed.

Leaders can *choose* to be great leaders. They can become great by learning from others, engaging in a personal transformation process, renewing themselves, and sustaining resonance.

2

TOXIC EMOTIONS
AT WORK

PETER J. FROST

SUMMARY PREPARED BY GARY J. COLPAERT

Gary J. Colpaert received a B.A. in Business Administration from the University of Minnesota Duluth and a Master's degree in Health Care Administration from the University of Wisconsin in Madison. He worked for the U.S.S. Great Lakes Fleet, with his responsibilities there including marketing, sales, and running the day-to-day operations of the commercial fleet. After leaving Duluth, Gary held the position of Vice President–Clinical and Support Systems at Children's Hospital of Wisconsin and then became the Executive Vice President of the Blood Center of Southeast Wisconsin. Gary is currently the Administrative Director of the Eye Institute in Milwaukee. He has developed and implemented internal coaching programs, a Winning at Work program, and a Leadership Intensive Program. He leads a men's group whose members are interested in leading an authentic life of leadership and service, and he also has a meditation practice that includes a yearly 10-day period of silence.

OVERVIEW

Work organizations and their leaders sometimes take actions—intentional and unintentional—that produce emotional pain in their employees. That pain can become toxic and thus have a negative effect on the organization. Alternatively, there is a meaningful role for compassion in an organization, and managers face the task of handling toxic emotions and their consequences for those people who experience pain in the workplace. In short, *compassionate companies can improve their toxin-handling practices.*

Organizations by their very nature create a regular supply of emotional pain. New bosses, mergers, layoffs, stifling or confusing policies, salary decisions, and even the way

Peter J. Frost, *Toxic Emotions at Work: How Compassionate Managers Handle Pain and Conflict.* Boston: Harvard Business School Press, 2003.

that changes are communicated can all be sources of emotional pain felt by all organizational members. If the pain cannot be dissipated it will, at a minimum, become a source of decreased productivity and a toxic condition that renders significant negative consequences for the organization and its staff.

Most organizational leaders lack the awareness to encounter and neutralize toxins and therefore an informal structure of toxin handlers emerges that takes on the difficult (often unsupported) work of maintaining emotional homeostasis. The large amount of emotional pain caused by organizations, the unrecognized value of engaging this pain, and the already heavy workload of toxin handlers puts the organization at risk for not having the capacity to deal with the emotional pain it creates.

SPECIFIC SKILLS NEEDED BY AN EFFICIENT TOXIN HANDLER

A Gallup poll of two million employees revealed the value of compassionate managers, finding that most people value having a caring boss higher than money or the fringe benefits they receive. It takes some basic skills to be an effective toxin handler.

- Reading emotional cues of others and themselves
- Keeping people connected and in communication
- Acting to alleviate the suffering of others
- Mobilizing people to deal with their pain and get back to a stable state
- Building a team environment that rewards compassionate action

The impact of using these skills to diminish the emotional pain of even one person in the organization can have a significant positive impact on the whole organization.

USEFUL PRACTICES

Compassionate organizations promote a healthy, productive culture through a set of policies, procedures, and belief systems that produce generative responses from people at all levels of the organization. Useful compassionate practices include:

- Identifying a link between the emotional health of the organization and the bottom line;
- Recognizing and rewarding managers who are good at handling emotional pain;
- Using hiring practices that emphasize attitude as well as technical skill;
- Maintaining fair-minded practices consistent with loyalty, responsibility, and the fostering of community in the workplace;
- Implementing intervention strategies during times of distress and initiating rehab strategies to ensure long-term vitality; and
- Building a culture that values compassion.

Studies reveal a direct correlation between harmony in the workplace (as a result of these compassionate practices) and company profits. For example, there is a 20 percent increase in survival probability for firms that are one standard deviation above the mean as compared to organizations one standard deviation below the mean on the dimension of valuing human resources.

TOXIN HANDLERS

The work of the toxin handler is to respond compassionately to pain in the organization, to reduce its impact, and to enable people to return to constructive behaviors. Toxin handlers have complex profiles. They are caregivers, leaders, social architects, and builders of productive systems of relationships. Their work reflects five major themes:

- **Listening**—providing moments of human compassion by giving attention and consideration to the pain of others;
- **Holding space for healing**—providing support and time needed for healing;
- **Buffering pain**—reframing communications, using political capital, building relationships, displaying personal courage;
- **Extricating others from painful situations**—making the decision to get people out of the situation causing the pain; and
- **Transforming pain**—framing pain in constructive ways by changing the view of painful experiences and coaching.

BURNOUT CAN OCCUR

The potential toll on toxin handlers is, not surprisingly, burnout. Without support and the ability to "decompress," the toxin handler can suffer psychological, physical, and professional setbacks. Often anger and guilt are the first symptoms of problems developing within the toxin handler. It is imperative for a toxin handler to manage negative emotions because the effects of stress last a significant period of time. Stress impairs the immune system and has been shown to influence the brain's neurological pathways.

Paying attention to others more than themselves has its costs, and the potential for becoming addicted to helping others is real. A trap that toxin handlers may frequently fall into is having an agenda for the person being helped. Another particular problem that handlers often face is that they may not know how to handle their own pain. If they over-identify with the role, they may have the incorrect perception that there is no one else they can count on for help. It may be difficult to maintain their perspective or to manage their time when results of this type of work are ambiguous. Adding to the potential for burnout is that all of this work is in addition to the stress and strain of their life experience outside of work.

PROVIDING ASSISTANCE

Healing the handlers is possible when there is a clear personal vision of why they are helping someone, when they are provided with the tools and skills to protect themselves, and when conversations are held that recognize and bring into consciousness the intention to not get overly involved emotionally with the people in pain.

A game plan for self-protection that includes options for action is critical for long-term success. World-class athletes, for example, overcome stress through methods including hydration, physical movement, mental change of channels, balanced eating programs, and emotionally changing channels. It is also necessary to build up one's reserves in advance, and this can be fostered by:

- **Increasing one's physical strength**—keeping fit; getting a massage.
- **Boosting one's emotional capacity**—staying positive; not taking things personally; accepting what you can't change.
- **Regenerating mental capacity**—refocusing the mind; creating personal space; developing mental sanctuaries; learning to say no.
- **Building spiritual capacity**—being clear on values; revering one's life balance.

AIDING AND SUPPORTING TOXIN HANDLERS

What handlers and their organizations can do at the interface between the handler, the organization, and the person in pain is to generate an increased level of organizational understanding, respect, and language for the role and work of toxin handling. This results in the toxin handler's feeling connected and less isolated. There is power in naming this work as a positive, contributing factor in the organization's success. The way in which this work is spoken about is a critical factor in building a compassionate organization. For example, the question "What did you do at work today?" is typically difficult for a toxin handler to answer. A positive way for the toxin handler to answer this question is to acknowledge that there is a lot of pain in the office and to express feeling that progress is being made toward shifting the situation. Other positive actions for the handlers to systematically manage and diffuse the emotional pain in organizational life include:

- Acknowledging the dynamic, by naming the work, giving it legitimacy, and creating a forum to talk about it.
- Offering support, by encouraging toxin handlers to meet with professionals/ experts for assistance.
- Assigning handlers to safe zones, by sending toxin handlers to an outside conference.
- Modeling healthy behavior, by having top leaders demonstrate and reinforce the behaviors.
- Creating a supportive culture, by allowing them to learn from each other.

WHAT DO COMPASSIONATE LEADERS DO?

Leaders sometimes create painful messes by themselves. When this happens, they need a repertoire of personal pain-handling skills. Compassionate leaders:

- Pay attention, because there is always pain in the room.
- Put people first, so as to keep the feelings and the well-being of staff in mind when decisions are made.
- Practice professional intimacy by empathizing without clouded judgment or over-identification.
- Plant seeds, by thinking long term and noticing the power of leadership's compassionate actions.
- Push back, by addressing the toxic sources whether they be people or systems.

Leaders must be willing to place responsibility where it belongs (with whomever is accountable for the toxicity) and then sharpen the practices listed above so that the organization is responsive to pain.

THREE MAJOR STRATEGIES

The compassionate company is more than just the leaders and gifted people who excel at handling toxic situations. The institutional venues and structures necessary to create healthy and productive workplaces can be compared to a biological system. Toxins are natural by-products in a biological system. Using the metaphor, three sets of strategies become apparent for use before, during, and after the toxic situation.

1. *Prevention* can be accomplishing by choosing new people wisely, developing existing staff, being fair minded, and setting a healthful tone.
2. *Intervention* can be implemented by dealing with downturns, dealing with acute trauma, being visible, creating meaning for the pain, and providing a context to talk about the pain.
3. *Restoration and recovery* occurs when managers demonstrate patience and trust, provide guidance, acknowledge pain, and then focus on constructive actions for resolving it.

ORGANIZATIONAL AND INDIVIDUAL CAPACITY FOR HANDLING TOXIC SITUATIONS

The following list of questions can help the organization make an assessment of its organizational capacity and individual capacity for compassionate response(s).

For *organizational* capacity, consider:

What is the breadth of resources that can be provided to the people in need—money, work flexibility, or physical aid as well as others' time and attention?
What is the volume of resources (time and attention) required by the people who are suffering?
How quickly can a response to the suffering be delivered?
How specialized is the need in the organization?

For *individual* capacity, consider:

Can you listen and be aware of grief and maintain awareness of your own and others' response to it?
Do you know how to support initiatives that come from subordinates that may be outside of organizational norms?
Have you expressed sympathy to others in the past and can you imagine doing that in the context of your work life?
Can you deal with fast-moving changes in circumstances that have an emotional focus?

Conclusion

Paying attention to these kinds of questions and pondering how the person or the organization would answer them is an effective initial response. This can lead to a greater acknowledgment of the emotional toxicity and pain, broader self-awareness in the organization, and (hopefully) utilization of the strategies for increasing the capacity for compassionate responses within the organization.

3

AUTHENTIC HAPPINESS

Martin E. P. Seligman

Summary Prepared by Cathy A. Hanson

Cathy A. Hanson is the Director of Human Resources for the City of Azusa, California. She is responsible for all aspects of human resources within a dynamic city environment. A majority of her career has been spent in the human resources departments of Fortune 100 companies (Mars, Disney, and Kraft). Her areas of interest include high-performance work teams (both private and public sector), change management, and team building. She received an M.B.A. from the University of Southern California and a B.A. in Business Administration at the University of Minnesota Duluth.

INTRODUCTION TO POSITIVE EMOTIONS

Most people would like to experience more positive emotion than negative emotion in their (work) lives. However, the focus of modern psychology has been on helping people deal with negative emotions. Little time has been spent on answering questions such as Who experiences a plentiful amount of positive emotions? Who does not? What factors enhance these emotions? and What can individuals (and managers) do to build on and experience more positive emotions?

To begin to address these issues, positive psychology has identified personal strengths that (when used) lead to feelings of happiness, pleasure, and gratification. Three criteria were identified to help define these strengths:

- The strength is valued in almost every culture.
- The strength is not a means to another end.
- The strengths are flexible, adaptable, and moldable.

These criteria were applied to a vast array of research, and six core virtues (and their underlying signature strengths) were identified: wisdom and knowledge, courage, love and humanity, justice, temperance, and spirituality and transcendence. When people identify their own key signature strengths and practice them on a daily basis, this results in greater feelings of happiness, pleasure, and gratification, and therefore they experience more positive emotions.

Martin E. P. Seligman, *Authentic Happiness: Using the New Positive Psychology to Realize Your Potential for Lasting Fulfillment.* New York: Free Press, 2002.

EFFECTS OF POSITIVE EMOTIONS

When it comes to important life decisions, research suggests that people who utilize their signature strengths on a daily basis are smarter (make wiser choices) than people who do not. Other implications of positive emotions include:

- Happy people tend to rely on their positive past experiences when faced with daily challenges, whereas less happy people tend to be more skeptical/doubtful. Based upon their past experiences, happy people tend to assume that their current outcomes will also be positive.
- A positive, optimistic state of mind helps people think in a way that is creative, open minded, and unguarded. A negative, more pessimistic state of mind, however, contributes to a fight-or-flight way of thinking. People in this state of mind tend to focus on what is wrong and how to eliminate it.
- A positive state of mind contributes to a totally different way of thinking and perceiving than a negative state of mind.
- According to direct evidence, positive emotion predicts health and longevity, and consequently helps cushion the downfalls of aging.
- People who experience more positive emotion tend to enjoy higher job satisfaction, earn a higher income, and be more productive in their jobs than their less happy counterparts.
- People characterized by positive emotions tend to endure pain better, and they tend to take additional safety and health precautions.
- When faced with a personal or business challenge, a positive mindset will likely lead to more creative and open-minded solutions.

INCREASING THE LEVEL OF HAPPINESS

Research suggests that happiness and a person's self-set barriers to happiness depend on three factors:

1. *Set range.* This is the general fixed range of happiness and sadness experienced by an individual; it is largely based on heredity and can be wide or narrow. The set range can be influenced by the *Hedonic treadmill,* which is the tendency to adapt to good things that happen by taking them for granted. This necessitates more and more good things in order to experience the same level of happiness again and again. Other than understanding one's inclination to be affected by the treadmill, there is little that can be done to greatly influence a person's set range.
2. *Circumstances.* Some conditions that can raise the level of happiness include:
   - **Money.** Studies have revealed that as purchasing power increases so does average life satisfaction. However, once the Gross National Product reaches $8,000 per person, the correlation disappears. The significance a person places on money influences happiness more than the actual amount of money itself.
   - **Marriage.** Studies have shown that marriage is powerfully related to happiness. However, it is not clear whether happier people get married or whether marriage makes people happier.
   - **Social life.** Studies show that happy people lead more fulfilling social lives. Again, it is not clear whether happy people are more social or whether a social life makes people happier.

- **Negative/positive emotion.** Evidence suggests only a moderate correlation between positive and negative emotion and overall happiness. Therefore, experiencing a lot of positive emotion only moderately protects a person from experiencing negative emotions.
- **Age.** Research shows that life satisfaction increases with age, but the experience of intense emotions, both positive and negative, decreases with age and experience.
- **Health.** When it comes to health, *the biggest impact on happiness is a person's subjective perception of health.* Research has shown that objective measures of good health are only slightly related to happiness.
- **Religion.** The presence of religious beliefs and practices has been shown to increase happiness by instilling hope about the future.

   In simple terms, the level of happiness can presumably be improved by changing one's circumstances. People should get married, develop a fulfilling social life, strive to experience more positive than negative emotions, value their health, and find a religion that provides them with a sense of hope. By contrast, education, climate, race, or gender hasn't been shown to have much of an effect on happiness.

3. *Voluntary variables.* These are intellectual and emotional choices that are made by people. These discretionary changes can be divided into three time frames: past, present, and future.

   - **Past.** According to research, there are three ways to increase happiness about the past: People can let go of the belief that the past (*their* past) predicts the future; they can increase their gratitude about the good things that have happened in the past; and they can learn to forgive (and forget) negative things that have happened in their past.
   - **Present.** Two things have been shown to increase happiness in the present—pleasures and gratifications. *Pleasures* are enjoyable feelings that are fleeting and involve little thinking, but can be nurtured and enhanced. Pleasures can be enhanced in three distinct ways. These include:
     a. *Finding new pleasant experiences to enjoy.* Habituation involves experiencing something that is initially pleasurable, but over time and exposure it loses its ability to elicit the same level of happiness. By contrast, positive people consciously inject as many pleasing events as possible into their work and personal lives and spread these factors out over time, thereby enhancing their feelings of pleasure and avoiding habituation.
     b. *Savoring the positive.* Positive people become aware of the pleasure and then consciously and deliberately focus on the feelings of pleasure. In order to savor the pleasure, people are encouraged to share it with others, or store and revisit pleasurable memories.
     c. *Practicing mindfulness.* Positive people live in the here and now. Meditation is one useful way to increase mindfulness of the present.
   - **Future.** There are two important dimensions that illustrate one's style when contemplating the future—permanence and pervasiveness. *Permanence* is the belief that bad events are unchangeable; this mindset determines how soon a person will give up when faced with adversity. *Pervasiveness* at one extreme is the belief that bad events influence all aspects of one's life; at the other extreme it is the belief that events are confined to the one area that experienced failure. An

optimist will more likely believe that good events are pervasive, while a pessimist is more inclined to believe that good events are caused by specific and temporary factors. A pessimist will believe that bad events are pervasive and permanent. In order to increase happiness about the future and experience hope, negative pessimistic thoughts must be recognized, understood, and logically argued against.

Unlike pleasures, *gratifications* cannot be nurtured and enhanced; they are simply experienced by demonstrating one's personal strengths and virtues. This typically occurs only after much effort, but the result is worthwhile; a positive person will experience a more meaningful life.

USING STRENGTHS TO ACHIEVE VIRTUES

There are six virtues that are endorsed across every major religious and cultural tradition— wisdom and knowledge, courage, love and humanity, justice, temperance, and spirituality and transcendence. However, they are difficult if not impossible to measure. When these six virtues are considered together they capture the notion of good character. The paths to the six virtues and to the resultant good character come through the utilization of a person's *signature strengths*—unique characteristics that are measurable, acquirable, demonstrated across situations, lead a person to feel gratified, are valued by most cultures, and are not a means to another end. In order to achieve the virtues a person must identify and build on their signature strengths in each of the six virtue areas. In order to identify the overall top five signature strengths, 24 components of the six virtues must be explored.

- **Wisdom and knowledge.** There are six routes to display wisdom. These include curiosity and interest in the world, love of learning, judgment/critical thinking/openmindedness, ingenuity/originality/practical intelligence/street smarts, social intelligence/personal intelligence/emotional intelligence, and perspective.
- **Courage.** There are three ways to display courage. These include valor/ bravery, perseverance/industry/diligence, and integrity/genuineness/honesty.
- **Love and humanity.** There are two paths to humanity and love. These include kindness/generosity, plus loving/allowing oneself to be loved.
- **Justice.** There are three routes to display justice. These include citizenship/duty/teamwork/loyalty, fairness/equity, and leadership.
- **Temperance.** There are three routes to display temperance. These include self-control, prudence/discretion/caution, and humility/modesty.
- **Spirituality and transcendence.** There are seven routes to display transcendence. These include appreciation of beauty and excellence, gratitude, hope/optimism/ future-mindedness, spirituality/sense of purpose/faith/religiousness, forgiveness/mercy, playfulness/humor, and zest/passion/enthusiasm.

Once a person has identified which of the 24 components *most* describe who they are, they will have identified their strengths. (Additionally, identifying the 24 components that are *least* like themselves identifies their weaknesses.) From the former list the individual's strengths can be identified. *These signature strengths are the ones that most accurately describe a person's true self.* In order to identify the top five signature strengths, individuals should ask themselves which of these descriptors apply to each of the 24 components:

- a sense of ownership and authenticity
- a feeling of excitement while displaying it
- a rapid learning curve as the strength is first practiced
- continuous learning of new ways to enact the strength
- a sense of yearning to find ways to use it
- a feeling of inevitability in using the strength rather than exhaustion while using it
- the creation and pursuit of personal projects that revolve around it
- joy, zest, enthusiasm (even ecstasy) while using it.

Summary

Organizations and their managers should seek to provide opportunities for employees to experience an increased level of positive emotions at work. In order to enhance positive emotions and thereby create a more meaningful and purposeful life, employees—and their managers—need to recognize their set range, change happiness-influencing circumstances, change voluntary variables in the past, present, and future, and identify and utilize their signature strengths each and every day in all aspects of their lives.

4

PRISONERS OF OUR THOUGHTS

ALEX PATTAKOS

SUMMARY PREPARED BY GARY P. OLSON

Gary P. Olson *is CEO of the Center for Alcohol and Drug Treatment, Duluth, Minnesota. He is responsible for the overall direction of this regional not-for-profit corporation. He received his MBA from the University of Minnesota Duluth.*

INTRODUCTION

How many of us have worked at jobs we didn't really like? Perhaps we were happy to be making a living, but were unfulfilled by the work itself. We found ourselves asking, "Isn't there more to life than this?"

Sometimes we are frustrated when we seem to have little control over our work situation and feel that there is little we can do to change our circumstances. These common experiences often lead us to ask ourselves fundamental questions about the way we live, work, and play.

Viktor Frankl, the world-renowned psychiatrist and Nazi concentration camp survivor, saw these questions as part of a fundamental human drive he called "man's search for meaning." Frankl believed that *the meaning of a person's life can only be determined by your own life, not the circumstances you find yourself in*. Dr. Frankl's theory was put to the test during his incarceration by the Germans during World War II at the Auschwitz and Dachau death camps. He survived these horrific conditions with his humanity intact and the certainty that his ideas had universal application.

The following principles use Dr. Frankl's work to guide our search for meaning no matter what job or situation we are in, and to connect our work with the meaning in other parts of our lives. These principles are:

1. Choose your own attitude.
2. Commit to meaningful values.

Alex Pattakos, *Prisoners of Our Thoughts: Viktor Frankl's Principles at Work*. San Francisco: Berrett-Koehler, 2004.

3. Find meaning in the moment.
4. Don't work against yourself.
5. Practice self-detachment.
6. Use creative distraction.
7. Transcend your personal interests.

MEANINGFUL WORK

The basic principle of Viktor Frankl's work is that *we are entirely free at all times to choose our response to the circumstances of our lives.* Frankl's "logotherapy" was a method by which the therapist helped the client become fully aware of this freedom of choice. Frankl believed in the unconditional meaningfulness of life and the intrinsic dignity of every person. He also believed every person had the capacity to search for meaning under any conditions. In other words, no one is off the hook.

When we search for meaning, we are looking for that which is meaningful for ourselves in relation to our own core values. Situations that may "try our souls" can become opportunities to help us clarify our own values. The way we accept the things we cannot control can lead to a deeper sense of personal meaning.

If we view our jobs as somehow apart from our "real" lives, we shut ourselves off from a large portion of our life experience. This often happens when we fall into the habit of constantly complaining about our work, our bosses, and our co-workers. When we choose to search for meaning and acknowledge our freedom to choose our responses, work becomes a rich opportunity.

CHOOSE YOUR OWN ATTITUDE

The freedom to choose is not always easy to exercise in practice. Our personal ability to cope and adapt are often tested. In order to effectively exercise this freedom, we must be able to look at a situation differently, even if this leads us to choose a path that is at odds with other people's expectations of how someone in our position normally responds.

No one can choose our attitude for us. Everyone knows someone who relentlessly complains about his or her working conditions, but does nothing to change them. It is when we take responsibility for exercising our freedom to choose our attitude that we move from being part of the problem to becoming part of the solution.

When we choose our attitude we:

- can choose to bring a positive attitude to the situation
- adopt a creative approach to imagining what is possible
- unlock the passion or enthusiasm that makes the possible actual

When we abstain from the responsibility for choosing consciously, we are choosing instead to remain locked in habits of thought that may no longer serve our search for meaning. We have the freedom, but we must make a conscious decision to exercise it. Out freedom is limited by conditions, but we *can* take a stand.

COMMIT TO MEANINGFUL VALUES

Frankl described the *will to meaning* as the authentic commitment to meaningful values and goals that only we as individuals can actualize. He believed *the will to meaning is a basic human drive.* Other drives may be more externally apparent, such as the will to power (or superiority) and the will to pleasure. Frankl believed these "drives" were actually efforts to mask a void of meaning that exists in many people's lives.

It is not difficult to find examples of what Frankl meant. It is obvious that no amount of power or pleasure can fill such a void when it exists. If it did, the most powerful and pampered among us should be the most fulfilled and satisfied, but this is not the case. Only the sustained search for meaning can lead to the sense of fulfillment that most of us desire from our work and our lives.

Values that are primarily related to power and pleasure are not those values that lead us to meaning in our lives. The will to power, for example, is always contingent on external conditions. Power relies on a cooperative set of subjects and circumstances to be meaningful at all, and since change is the only constant, power tends to dissipate over time despite our efforts to sustain it. The will to meaning, on the contrary, comes entirely from within us. Only we can discover and realize it.

Some modern, progressive companies attempt to create the illusion of freedom in the workplace, but fail to connect with the emotional, intellectual, and spiritual values of their employees, customers, or communities. Yet business and economics are connected with all aspects of our lives, our communities, and our planet. The inability to honor meaning at the top of any organization often leads to demoralization, dissatisfaction, and, ultimately, decreased productivity.

FIND MEANING IN THE MOMENT

If we could live life over for a second time, would we make different choices? Although meaning may exist in every second, we have to make an effort to find it. Meaningful moments often slip by without notice only to be realized months or even years later. Meaning does not exist within our own minds and it is not created; it is discovered in the world around us. *The search for meaning requires a conscious effort.*

The pace of modern life and work conspires against the search for meaning. Unless we stop to consider why we are doing what we are doing, what our lives and work mean to us, and to examine the reasons we do what we do, we cannot expect to find meaning. This requires time for serious reflection, time without a cell phone to our ear or a list of emails to check. Technology, which is designed to make life easier, can instead become a relentless, demanding set of obligations. It may take a serious effort to disconnect from these tools long enough to find time to reflect.

Finding meaning in our lives and work is our personal responsibility and rests on our ability to achieve a certain level of awareness or mindfulness. To be aware means to stop and consider our situation and discover what life lessons it may hold. When we become aware of the many possibilities open to us, we become open to meaning. We can be creators or complainers, for example, for both of these potentials exist within us. Which potential is realized depends on our decisions, not our external conditions.

DON'T WORK AGAINST YOURSELF

How satisfied can we be if we achieve a lofty goal at the expense of a friendship, loss of respect, or our own health? Meaning exists in appreciation of the moment, the present, or the process—not in a particular outcome!

Sometimes our efforts to create meaning, particularly in our work, can lead us away from meaning. This is because the meaning and value in our work is acquired not simply through our own performance, but in the way our work contributes to society. We do not work in a vacuum. Our bosses, co-workers, and customers have their own agendas that may be at odds with our own. Like the football coach whose plan went awry because the opponent did not follow it, we can't ignore the others on the field.

Our jobs are never just *our* jobs. We work within a fabric of relationships that extends far beyond our immediate workspace. These relationships have meaning individually and collectively. Becoming too focused on ultimate outcomes and results can cause us to overlook the meaning that exists moment to moment. Our anxiety about a successful outcome can actually undermine our ability to "get it right." Instead, we need to focus on the meaning in the process.

Our good intentions can become the cause of failure. This happens when we overlook and neglect the relationships that are integral to the process of accomplishing a larger goal or project. Ignoring the opportunity to experience meaningful moments with others at work undermines the chance for success because business issues and people issues are usually intertwined. Even a desired promotion at work can, in the end, depend more on your relationship with your co-workers than it does on pleasing the boss. Your boss may understand that *your ability to relate in a meaningful and positive way with co-workers is a key indicator of your ability to lead*. Your knowledge of what your co-workers value and care about can be a more important asset in leadership than your job knowledge. The more meaning we experience in the process, the more satisfied we will feel *irrespective* of the outcome.

PRACTICE SELF-DETACHMENT

Humor is an excellent way of distancing ourselves from something—even our own predicament. It can be a form of self-detachment. Our ability to laugh at ourselves can make a serious situation more bearable, not just for us, but for those around us. When we can laugh at mistakes, we can own up to them, learn from them, and move on.

Even in a concentration camp Frankl was able to find humor, and he believed it was an important weapon in the fight for self-preservation. Nevertheless, it is important to distinguish between detachment and denial. *Detachment* is a conscious choice to create psychological distance that opens the door to action, learning, and growth. *Denial* of our experience involves disconnecting from ourselves and others who may share an experience with us. Detachment permits us to acknowledge a mistake, a poor decision, or even fear, but not be paralyzed into inaction.

USE CREATIVE DISTRACTION

Thinking itself can become an obsession, particularly when it is focused on negativity and complaint. Venting frustration can become a habit of blaming and complaining that saps our energy and ultimately leads nowhere. There are times when we need to shift our focus and distract ourselves from something we don't like in order to see the possibilities in a situation. This is the principle of creative distraction.

When we are too focused on something—a demanding boss, a boring task, an unproductive co-worker—we can lose sight of the meaning in our lives. The principle of creative distraction allows us to ignore some aspect of our lives that *should* be ignored. In doing so, we may perceive our situation in an entirely new way. We can then transcend the limits in our condition, avoid becoming self-absorbed, and direct our attention toward discovering new meaning in our lives.

TRANSCEND YOUR PERSONAL INTERESTS

Real success, like happiness, is not a goal or a target. It is a by-product of a dedication to a cause or purpose greater than one's self. When we reach beyond the satisfaction of our own limited needs, we enter the realm of ultimate meaning.

This personal transcendence is for some a religious or spiritual relationship. For others it is our connection with a greater good or with the human spirit. It is sometimes experienced when we are part of a team—doing and being with others. On a team with "team spirit," for example, the greatest reward is being part of the team, part of the process, and not necessarily contingent on the final result of our efforts.

No matter who we are or where we work, the opportunity to go beyond our own interests is almost always present. Companies that can look beyond the bottom line and bring meaning to the business at hand also bring meaning to everyone who works there. It takes more than good intentions to grow meaning in a corporation. For one thing, corporations are not in business to grow meaning! It requires courage and a deep commitment to meaningful personal values on the part of corporate leaders to place meaning before quarterly profits.

LIVING AND WORKING WITH MEANING

The opposite of meaning is despair—a condition brought on by the apparent meaninglessness of life. Each of us has the freedom and responsibility to place ourselves somewhere along a continuum that connects the two. Success or failure in the eyes of others has no bearing at all on where we stand with regard to meaning. A low-profile, low-paying job in a setting filled with meaningful purpose or one where we are able to fully realize our personal values in relationship to our work can fill us with a sense of meaning and purpose. It can truly make life worth living.

When we connect with ourselves, our co-workers, or to the task at hand, we experience meaning. When we continuously adjust our attitudes and reflect on the choices and possibilities open to us, we will be led to discover meaning. No matter what our job or our personal situation is, we can transform it with meaning.

PART XV

EMERGING DIMENSIONS OF ORGANIZATIONAL ENVIRONMENTS

The external environment in which organizations operate has become increasingly complex, adding new challenges and responsibilities for those who manage. The world has moved from international trade to multinationalism to globalization. The global arena is a new domain for many organizations, and it holds key lessons to be learned. The dynamics generated by organizations doing business in the global arena are leading toward the creation of a borderless world. The emergence of the World Trade Organization finds corporations, not nation-states, coming together and playing a significant role in defining the conduct of commerce in this new world.

In addition to an increasingly borderless world, new technologies are having a profound impact upon organizations and the way business is conducted and how work is performed. While the exportation of blue-collar manufacturing jobs has been occurring for some time, with increasing frequency we are now hearing about the exportation of call services, computer information technology/software engineering, architecture, financial services, and accounting jobs. The digital culture is here!

With increasing concerns about global warming, the emergence of the Green party, and the continued lobbying and strength of a variety of environmental groups, an increasing number of organizations are starting to consider ways of integrating environmental concerns into the conduct of their business.

In this section of *The Manager's Bookshelf*, we have chosen to include three readings focused on emerging dimensions of organizations—globalization, the greening of the corporation, and the people skills needed for global business success.

The first reading by Thomas L. Friedman explores globalization, offering the perspective that the world is now (figuratively) flat and "if your map is outdated, it's . . . easy to fall off" (Harvey Mackay). *The World Is Flat* essentially presents us with an update on globalization as the author explores the first few days of the twenty-first century. Y2K, attacks on the World Trade Center and the Pentagon, the Iraq War, and the mobilization of virtually any work that can be digitized—these phenomena present us with a complex world and one that must be understood if we are to adapt and survive. Friedman attempts to demystify this new world that we are confronting, addressing such issues as how the flattening of the world occurred, and what it means to individuals, companies, communities, and countries.

Thomas L. Friedman is the foreign affairs columnist for the *New York Times*. He has won the Pulitzer Prize three times for his outstanding and informed journalism. In addition to his regular editorials in the *New York Times*, Mr. Friedman is the author of three best-selling books: *From Beirut to Jerusalem, The Lexus and Olive Tree: Understanding Globalization,* and *Longitudes and Attitudes: Exploring the World After September 11*.

Peter Robbins, lecturer in sociology in the Institute of Water and Environment at Cranfield University, examines social-environmental corporate cultures and styles of green management. Robbins points out that there are a number of corporations that are beginning to take into consideration the natural environment as a part of their way of doing business—a trend referred to in his book's title as *Greening the Corporation*. As a part of his work, the author examines ARCO Chemical, Ben & Jerry's, Shell, and The Body Shop. Based upon his analysis of these four companies' environmental philosophies and practices, he develops a framework intended to help other organizations deal with the dilemmas of combining traditional business objectives (i.e., earning a profit) with healthy environmental objectives.

The last summary in this section comes from David C. Thomas and Kerr Inkson's book *Cultural Intelligence*. Globalization and the flattening of the world carry with them many different meanings, and one that is of particular importance is that managers need to be prepared to "do business" with people from many different cultures, virtually all at the same time, in the same place, dealing with the same matters. Cultural intelligence (CQ), a relatively new concept, reflects a person's ability to interact effectively across cultures. In *Cultural Intelligence*, the authors present a specific set of techniques that enable managers to increase their CQ and thereby interact effectively in different cultural contexts. Throughout the book the authors present many interesting real-life stories that illuminate good and poor CQ.

David C. Thomas and Kerr Inkson are, respectively, professor of international management at Simon Fraser University in Burnaby, British Columbia, Canada, and professor of management at the Auckland campus of Massey University, New Zealand. Both professors are the authors of other books including *Essentials of International Management: A Cross-Cultural Perspective* (Thomas), *Managing Relationships in Transition Economies* (Thomas), and *Theory K* (Inkson).

THE WORLD IS FLAT

THOMAS L. FRIEDMAN

SUMMARY PREPARED BY STEPHEN RUBENFELD

Stephen Rubenfeld is Professor of Human Resource Management in the Labovitz School of Business and Economics at the University of Minnesota Duluth. He received his doctorate from the University of Wisconsin-Madison, and was previously on the faculty of Texas Tech University. His professional publications and presentations have covered a wide range of human resource and labor relations topics, including workplace accommodations, compensation, human resource policies and practices, job security, and staffing challenges. He has served as a consultant to private and public organizations, and is a member of the Society for Human Resource Management, the Academy of Management, and the Industrial Relations Research Association.

Globalization is revolutionizing the world far more radically and rapidly than industrial development and technological change of the past. As a result, the United States can prosper only if we successfully participate in the world marketplace that encompasses the 95 percent of the world's population that lives beyond our borders. Our standard of living can be sustained only if we accept that we truly are dependent on the rest of the world for access to raw materials, markets, and human expertise. The economic well-being of the United States depends on continuing growth in international trade.

How do we compete on this new and uncharted playing field? The answer is how, not if, to liberalize international trade. But can we spur economic development, both domestically and internationally, while maintaining both our standard of living and quality of life? The answer is yes, but only if we can meet these new competitive realities in a world where national economies are dramatically interconnected and the barriers to world trade have been flattened. Deciphering this conundrum is not a task for the prognosticator or the incrementalist; it will require bold and dramatic actions—now.

The economic flattening of the earth is being stimulated by technology—a permissive technology—that is breaking down barriers that historically inhibited and restricted international trade. This technological revolution and its convergence with economics have severely limited the geographic, cultural, and political abilities of any country to control

Thomas L. Friedman, *The World Is Flat: A Brief History of the Twenty-first Century.* New York: Farrar, Strauss, and Giroux, 2005.

the nature or pace of economic integration. Likewise, it has become almost impossible to fully protect markets and social institutions. In reality, advances in technology and infrastructure have decimated many of the long-term economic advantages enjoyed by western economies. Businesses in the United States and Europe cannot depend on their governments to bail them out. They must stand on their own—they must adapt and find ways to compete effectively.

Technology-driven globalization carries with it both opportunities and challenges. On the one hand, western business organizations must become better at what they do by economizing, innovating, and honing their competitive advantages. But at the same time, these businesses must recognize and respond to the fact that much of the world enjoys an advantage of larger and cheaper labor forces, and in many instances less legal regulation and social overhead. The pressures attributable to the global marketplace, permissive technology, and more assertive consumers are not going to disappear. Major changes are necessary to ensure that the critical elements of competitive success—price, quality, and customer service—are integral to efforts to redefine the traditional business model. The answers ultimately must go far beyond short-term fixes driven by efforts to cut the costs of wages and benefits. Fundamental changes are called for; businesses will adapt or perish.

HOW THE WORLD BECAME FLAT

The globalization of markets has progressed through three stages, culminating in its present-day manifestation, *Globalization 3.0*. Preceding this were *Globalization 1.0* from 1492–1800, initiated by countries through political and sometimes military force, and *Globalization 2.0* from 1800–2000, which was spearheaded by corporations first through rapid and less expensive transportation costs, and subsequently by more effective and lower-cost telecommunications. *Globalization 3.0* is shrinking and flattening the globe, not militarily or through decisions implemented by big businesses, but by the empowerment of a diverse set of individuals and entrepreneurial organizations to act globally. These first two stages of globalization substantially shrank the world and challenged the status quo, but in hindsight, not as dramatically and rapidly as what we are now experiencing.

So what brought us to *Globalization 3.0*? This new socioeconomic environment, replete with completely new social, political, and business models, has been activated primarily by a convergence of *10 forces that have flattened the world*:

Flattener #1 – The fall of the Berlin Wall (11/9/89) not only unleashed forces that liberated captive peoples, but helped to flatten the alternatives to free market capitalism. In conjunction with the emerging user-friendly computer revolution and a common Microsoft-based platform, the hold on access to information that previously sustained totalitarian regimes around the world was now broken.

Flattener #2 – When Netscape went public, the PC-based computing platform was supplanted by an Internet-based platform that drove the widespread use of e-mail and Internet browsing. When combined with a massive investment in fiber optic cable, the opportunity to communicate and interact with peoples of the world was unleashed.

Flattener #3 – The expansion of common standards for Web servers and the associated opportunities for worldwide collaboration created the "genesis moment" for flattening of the world.

Flattener #4 – Open sourcing creates opportunities for *self-organizing collaborative communities* (such as Apache or Wikipedia) to provide free and easy access to knowledge.

Flattener #5 – Stimulated by the time-sensitive demands for Y2K fixes, outsourcing to India and other countries emerged as a central tenet of efficient and effective work and staffing planning.

Flattener #6 – China joined the WTO, jumpstarting a new wave of international trade, and opened the door to large-scale offshore factory relocation.

Flattener #7 – *Supply chaining*, encouraged by Wal-Mart and others, fostered horizontal collaboration and coordination among suppliers, retailers, and customers.

Flattener #8 – Moving beyond the traditional vendor–customer relationship, collaboration emerged that has third parties managing logistics and servicing the supply chain.

Flattener #9 – *In-forming*, with the use of Google, Yahoo!, and MSN search engines, allowed individuals to build and deploy a personal supply chain of information and knowledge from anywhere in the world.

Flattener #10 – The *steroids* or amplifying technologies (such as cell phones, multipurpose devices, digital data, wireless technologies, file sharing, and VoIP) empower and magnify all of the other forms of collaboration.

CONVERGENCE AND SORTING IT OUT

Not all that many years ago, airline travelers purchased tickets through a travel agent *(Globalization 1.0)*. Next, tickets were purchased at an airport-based E-ticket machine *(Globalization 2.0)*. Today, in *Globalization 3.0*, we are our own travel agents working from home—booking flights, selecting seats, and printing boarding passes. This evolution of travelers' roles is illustrative of a *triple convergence* that has taken place.

Convergence I: The evolution of a global, Web-enabled playing field allowed for multiple forms of collaboration in real time, without regard to distance. This has been driven by the combined influence of the 10 flatteners.

Convergence II: The second stage of convergence is an outgrowth of managers, consultants, IT experts, and others developing and using horizontal collaboration and value-creating processes. The move away from top-down models has required new skills and high levels of commitment.

Convergence III: Opening information portals to the three billion people of China, India, Russia, Latin America, and other locales allowed more people to collaborate and compete.

This triple convergence consisted of new players, a new playing field, new processes, and new habits for horizontal collaboration. The world has been flattened; global competition and collaboration are here to stay!

While it is clear that world commerce has been permanently altered, many questions remain. How will companies compete? How will people prepare themselves for economic success? What are the appropriate roles for consumers, employees, shareholders, and governments? Will technology and capital, as postulated by Marx and Engels, remove the barriers and restraints to global commerce? Was Marx correct in *The Communist Manifesto* in speculating that capitalism would give rise to a "universal civilization governed by market imperatives"?

As these radical changes occur, the reality is that economic liberty for one person could result in another person's unemployment. Some questions we must ponder are:

- Who is exploiting whom?
- What does it mean to be a truly global enterprise?
- How will we deal with our multiple roles as consumers, employees, citizens, taxpayers, and shareholders?
- Who owns what?

In a larger sense, we must consider what happens as we move from a "command and control" to a "collaborate and connect" world.

AMERICA AND THE FLAT WORLD

In light of the global shifts and the competitive advantages enjoyed by countries with underutilized labor forces and relatively low costs, should the United States still be advocating free trade objectives? Was Ricardo's nineteenth-century thesis correct—that all countries specialize in areas where they have competitive advantage, and overall income levels in each will rise? The answer to both postulations appears to be "yes!"

Although job loss and economic dislocation are painful to individuals, and despite the populist position that our government should erect walls to protect us and maintain our jobs, the free trade argument remains compelling and essential. Economics is not a zero-sum game, and there remain vast opportunities for unleashing competitive advantage and job creation. It is true that many individuals—particularly those in low-skilled occupations—will suffer, but we cannot succeed by failing to compete. The flattening of the world is, for the most part, unstoppable.

Both for individuals and economies, mediocrity is not a viable route to success. Organizations must strive for competitive flexibility and individuals must enhance their skills. There are some jobs that are specialized, such as surgeons or other knowledge workers whose work is not easily transferred to another location. There are other jobs that may be anchored to a particular location, such as a waitress or plumber. These types of specialized and anchored jobs are largely protected from being outsourced and are therefore considered to be *untouchable*. For all others, adaptability through education and learning is the only real path toward economic security.

Several things about the U.S. system support and nurture individuals to compete effectively in a flat world:

- High-quality U.S. research universities
- Efficient, regulated capital markets
- The openness of American society
- Effective intellectual property protection
- Flexible labor laws
- Political stability
- Large consumer markets
- A tradition as a cultural meeting place

If we encourage the development of a labor force that is knowledgeable, specialized, and constantly adapting, then we (and they) should be well positioned to succeed.

But the United States also has many significant weaknesses that, if left unchanged, will limit its competitive successes. The problem is serious, yet seemingly underappreciated: There is a crisis, a *quiet crisis*, on the horizon. It may be beneath the public's radar, but we are already suffering from three dirty little secrets:

1. A Numbers Gap – insufficient support of science and engineering, both in dollars and educational focus.
2. An Ambition Gap – our youth demonstrate both too little ambition and a work ethic that doesn't compare favorably with their counterparts in other countries.
3. An Education Gap – employees abroad are well-educated and less expensive. As a result, it is likely that jobs will "follow the brains."

These threats are real. Our political leaders must take a stand and respond to the challenge. They must be willing to explain what needs to be done and they must lead and inspire us to rise to the challenge. *We as a country must develop the muscles or competitive abilities of our workforce.*

The tools to advance our competitiveness include:

- Portable pensions and health insurance
- Enhanced opportunities for lifetime learning
- Compassionate programs to offer support and opportunities to those workers who are losers in the global labor contest
- Stock ownership and other ways to give workers a stake in the outcome
- Social activism to transmit values and make the earth more livable
- Improved parenting to ensure that children will be in a position to compete

DEVELOPING COUNTRIES IN THE FLAT WORLD

The challenges and responses for developing countries are different from those of the Western World, but the ultimate goals are not dramatically distinct. Developing countries must critically assess their competencies and their goals. Aside from careful consideration of the role of the central government, broad-based macroeconomic reforms, and infrastructure development, much progress can be made at the microeconomic level to stimulate competitiveness through entrepreneurial development. Likewise, openness to foreign ideas and best practices—*glocalization*—also is critical. While developing countries may have inherent competitive advantages, they must be focused, vigilant, and driven to succeed since their market competitors also are seeking economic success in the flat world.

HOW COMPANIES COPE

These are uncertain times and uncharted waters. Fortunately, there are rules and strategies that can both guide and define competitive success and even survival in the flat world:

Rule 1: Don't try to build walls.
Rule 2: Take full advantage of the tools for collaboration.
Rule 3: Think small—be entrepreneurial.
Rule 4: Collaborate to succeed.

Rule 5: Utilize introspection, focus, and specialization.
Rule 6: Outsource to win, not to save money.
Rule 7: Don't necessarily view outsourcing as evil.

The most successful companies will be those that understand *triple convergence* (the intersection of Web-enabled technologies) and develop strategies for meeting it head-on.

Conclusion: 11/9 Versus 9/11

The flattening of the world is framed by two symbolic dates. The first, 11/9, brought down the Berlin wall and signaled that the windows to the world were now opening. The second, 9/11, revealed the destructive power of a small group of individuals, perhaps brought on in part by a fear of the openness and changes brought on by this flattening. It demonstrated that governments don't have an exclusive monopoly on power—individuals with imagination and goals can use the tools of collaboration and the reduced barriers of the flattened world to achieve their desired ends.

The world continues to flatten, though not at a consistent pace. Some countries and some groups of individuals may be too complacent, too frustrated, too disempowered, too sick, or too comfortable to embrace or pursue the realities of a flattening world. *But ultimately, the greatest danger facing the United States and other countries of the world is a fear of competition and a temptation to rely on protectionist policies to resist the inevitable.*

2

GREENING

THE CORPORATION

PETER THAYER ROBBINS

SUMMARY PREPARED BY ROBERT STINE

Robert Stine is Associate Dean of the College of Natural Resources, University of Minnesota and Leader of the Natural Resources and Environment Capacity Area for the University of Minnesota Extension Service. His interests include leadership, organizational management, and natural resource management and utilization. He received his Ph.D. in Forest Policy from the University of Minnesota, M.S. from Oregon State University, and bachelor's degree from Indiana University.

INTRODUCTION

During the twentieth century, approximately 10 million chemicals were created in laboratories around the world. Most of these chemicals are "building blocks" that are used to manufacture millions of end products, many of which are toxic in nature. Either in the manufacturing process or as part of an end product, these chemicals create environmental challenges for corporations, primarily in the areas of air pollution, toxics, and water pollution. Large agricultural and pharmaceutical corporations must also deal with the issues of biotechnology and biodiversity.

For many years, corporations paid little attention to the environmental impacts of their operations. However, beginning in the 1980s some businesses began to view the environment as a business opportunity. Others began to consider environmental and social issues in their business practices. Collectively, these practices became known as *greening the corporation.*

Peter Thayer Robbins, *Greening the Corporation: Management Strategy and the Environmental Challenge.* London: Earthscan Publications, 2001.

ECOLOGICAL MODERNIZATION

Corporations tend to navigate their way through environmental issues at two levels. The first is at the macro level, where corporations interact with the societies in which they operate. One view on this macro level is the theory of *ecological modernization,* which holds that society (including corporations) can modernize itself out of ecological crises. It does this by integrating economics, natural sciences, corporate management, politics, regulators, and other factors to develop solutions. The ultimate goal is to continue development of modern, industrialized societies that include both economic growth and environmental responsibility.

Ecological modernization has three components, all of which impact a corporation's response to environmental issues. The first component involves institutional learning, or how well corporations respond to critical events and public opinion. Those companies that respond to environmental crises or issues by improving practices and including environmental considerations in their decisions tend over time to become more "green" (i.e., less damaging to the environment).

The second component of ecological modernization deals with how corporations view environmental issues. If they are viewed as "technocratic projects," simply something that needs a technological response to be fixed, then corporations take environmental actions only when they think it benefits their economic interest. In this case, environmental concerns are often considered only after economic objectives have been met. The result is that the environment sometimes wins and—at least in the short term—the corporate bottom line always wins.

The final component of ecological modernizations deals with cultural politics. Democratic, informed debate within a corporation can often lead to changes in how the environment is viewed. So rather than a problem that needs a technological fix, environmental challenges can be viewed as opportunities. Such a mindset is perhaps most often found in small corporations that have a "social-environmental" perspective.

CORPORATE CULTURE AND MANAGEMENT STYLE

Ecological modernization only partially explains the process of corporate responses to environmental issues, because it deals primarily with the macro or social environment in which corporations operate. A fuller explanation, at a more micro level of corporate management, is supplied by looking at corporate culture and management style.

Corporate Culture

Corporate culture refers to the set of norms found in organizations. Two typical corporate cultures are role and power. In a *role culture,* the role or job description is often more important than the individual who currently fills it. Role cultures are characteristic of organizations that operate in stable or noncompetitive markets. A *power culture* is usually found in small, founder led, entrepreneurial organizations. Power cultures tend to have few rules and procedures, little bureaucracy, and control mechanisms that are exercised by the founder(s) mostly through the selection of key people.

Relative to environmental issues, there are subsets of these corporate cultures. For example, a corporation can have a role culture where safety is the highest priority. Such a culture is focused primarily on preventing accidents, and the role everyone in the corporation plays in preventing accidents is highly structured.

Similarly, another corporation could have a role culture where the highest priority is placed on environmental action that builds shareholder value. These corporations might concentrate on pollution prevention, energy conservation, and renewable energy sources—all fairly conservative approaches—as a way of building shareholder value while at some level addressing environmental issues.

Corporations with a power culture, typically led by the founder, have an opportunity to be more proactive relative to environmental issues because the founder can decree it so. For example, Ben & Jerry's, a manufacturer of ice cream and frozen yogurt, has a philosophy of "linked prosperity," which integrates economic, social, and environmental goals. It is a philosophy that comes directly from the founders.

The Body Shop, another founder-led organization, manufactures cosmetics, and has a power culture with a stated philosophy of "profits and principles." While wealth creation is important, the company also actively addresses environmental issues such as energy conservation, waste management, and product life-cycle assessment. The founder has been actively engaged in environmental issues, including fighting the use of animals for product testing, worldwide.

Management Styles

Corporate environmental management styles can be divided into four categories, each more "green" in terms of its environmental progressiveness. The four styles are compliance-oriented management, preventative management, strategic environmental management, and sustainable development management.

Environmental compliance management is the least progressive of the four styles, and reflects a traditional approach to environmental issues. Corporations exhibiting this style respond to environmental issues primarily to comply with legislation or litigation. Any innovative practices are generally directed toward better compliance with environmental laws.

Preventative environmental management goes beyond simply complying with regulations and moves toward pollution prevention and reduced consumption of resources. The majority of companies responding to a United Nations survey fell in this category. They respond to environmental issues in ways that will maintain and protect markets, or in ways that will save them money. Within companies that employ a preventative management style, managers are kept informed of environmental issues with the goal of preventing accidents and liabilities. Audits and assessment of risks and hazards are often used to ensure a preventative approach to operations.

Strategic environmental management incorporates environmental goals into the overall economic strategy of the corporation, often anticipating and pursuing potential green markets. Corporations using this strategy may conduct cradle to grave analyses or environmental research, and they generally respond to environmental issues in a more proactive fashion. This type of environmental management strategy is usually coordinated by the highest level managers within a corporation, and these companies also actively engage in public relations campaigns to reinforce their public image.

Sustainable development management is the most progressive and proactive of the four styles. Relatively few corporations worldwide are practicing this style. One defining characteristic of such organizations is that they strive to take a leadership role in their industries in response to environmental challenges. They typically institute their environmental programs worldwide, including developing countries. Typical of a sustainable development style would be statements such as:

- "We will develop and market products with superior environmental properties that will meet highest efficiency requirements."
- "We will opt for manufacturing processes that have the least possible impact on the environment."
- "We will participate actively in, and conduct research in, the environment field."
- "We will conduct a total review regarding the adverse impact of our products on the environment."
- "We will strive to attain a uniform, worldwide environmental standard for processes and products."

There is some question about whether any corporation can be truly sustainable in the very long term. However, as social expectations change and corporate operations expand into developing countries, *corporations that manage environmental challenges well can reap financial rewards.* If the challenges are mismanaged or ignored, corporations can incur high costs and liabilities.

Conclusion

The interaction between corporations, society, and the environment is still evolving. Corporations are generally reacting to society's concerns about protecting the environment, but in different ways. Some still view environmental issues as simply a problem to be resolved or avoided. Many have a more proactive view and look for ways to incorporate environmental issues into their business practices in a way that helps them create wealth. Finally, there are some corporations that are actively integrating economic, environmental, and social goals in an effort to become fully "green."

3

CULTURAL INTELLIGENCE

DAVID C. THOMAS AND KERR INKSON

SUMMARY PREPARED BY SANJAY GOEL

Sanjay Goel (Ph.D., Arizona State University) is an Associate Professor of Strategic Management and Entrepreneurship at the University of Minnesota Duluth. His current research and teaching interests are primarily in the areas of strategic and international management, management of innovation and technology, entrepreneurship, and governance. His prior work experience includes management consulting in the agribusiness sector, where he was involved in new project appraisals and project monitoring. Currently he assists start-ups in high-tech industries and not-for-profit organizations in the United States and Europe with building strategic and governance expertise.

Globalization is affecting more and more businesses and managers. Globalization of business has been fueled by a myriad of factors in the international business environment, including new international trade agreements, the privatization of state enterprises, the ability to locate business wherever the cost is lowest, the expansion of international migration, the expansion of information and communication technology, etc. Globalization of people has resulted in interacting with people of different cultures in our everyday lives. As a result, there are several ways that intercultural failures can manifest themselves.

These include being unaware of the key features and biases of our own culture, feeling threatened or uneasy when interacting with people who are culturally different, and being unable to understand or explain the behavior of others who are culturally different.

BECOMING CULTURALLY INTELLIGENT

There are three ways to deal with cultural differences. First, we can expect others to adapt to our culture ("Be like me"). However, this is not always a practical and sustainable strategy. Second, we can understand cultural differences. However,

David C. Thomas and Kerr Inkson, *Cultural Intelligence: People Skills for Global Business*. San Francisco: Berrett-Koehler, 2004.

understanding these differences is only a first step toward overcoming cultural differences. There is a powerful third way—becoming culturally intelligent. **Cultural intelligence** means being skilled and flexible about understanding a culture, learning more about it from your ongoing interactions with it, gradually reshaping your thinking to be more sympathetic to the culture, and making your behavior more skilled and appropriate when interacting with others from the culture.

Cultural intelligence has three parts. First, the culturally intelligent manager requires *knowledge* of culture and of the fundamental principles of cross-cultural interactions. Second, the culturally intelligent manager needs to practice mindfulness, which is the ability to pay attention in a reflective and creative way to cues in the cross-cultural contexts. Third, based on knowledge and mindfulness, the culturally intelligent managers develop *behavioral skills* and become competent across a wide range of situations.

What is the extant knowledge about culture? According to Geert Hofstede, culture consists of shared mental programs that condition individuals' responses to their environment. By definition, culture is shared. It is learned and is enduring. It is a powerful influence on behavior. It is systematic and organized. It is largely invisible. It may be "tight" (homogeneous) or "loose" (diverse or heterogeneous).

While nations are often associated with cultures, "nation" and "culture" are not identical. But nations are often formed because of cultural similarities among different population groups. Over time they reinforce their adherence to a national culture by means of shared institutions, including the mass media. Some people also talk about an emerging "global culture," which suggests a convergence of cultures to one culture. However, the evidence for convergence is inconclusive. Even if convergence is taking place, it is taking place at a very slow pace. In addition, in a prescriptive sense, there is increasing recognition worldwide of the value of diversity in human affairs, which would argue for working against convergence of cultures.

DIMENSIONS OF CULTURES

Research on cultures has suggested some general dimensions along which culture can be measured and studied. Geert Hofstede's work (often cited in this regard) initially arrived at four cultural dimensions:

1. *Value orientation,* represented by individualism versus collectivism, is one dimension of culture. In individualistic cultures, people are most concerned about the consequences of action for themselves, not others. In collectivistic cultures, people primarily view themselves as members of groups and collectives rather than as autonomous individuals.
2. *Power distance* refers to the extent to which large differentials of power are expected and tolerated.
3. *Uncertainty avoidance* refers to the extent to which the culture emphasizes ways to reduce uncertainty and create stability.
4. *Masculinity/femininity* refers to the balance between the traditional male goals of ambition and achievement and female orientations toward nurturance and interpersonal harmony.

Shalom Schwartz and his colleagues did a more recent mapping of cultures, and they derived seven different dimensions of culture.

1. Egalitarianism – recognition of people as moral equals
2. Harmony – fitting in smoothly with the environment
3. Embeddedness – people as part of a collective
4. Hierarchy – unequal distribution of power
5. Mastery – exploitation of the natural or social environment
6. Affective autonomy – pursuit of positive experiences
7. Intellectual autonomy – independent pursuit of own ideas

An important aspect of culture is the way we use it to define ourselves. It differentiates us and sets up a boundary that excludes others. It also sets up expectations about the kinds of attitudes and behavior that others can expect from us. This creates potential for bias. Typically, bias is in favor of our own group or culture (the "in-group") and against others (the "out-group") external to our own. We tend to identify everything about the in-group as normal. As a result, actions by a member of an out-group may appear deviant, or wrong.

Cultural problems arise because of the shortcuts that we employ in intercultural contexts; these include

- selective perception (perceiving what the culture conditions us to see),
- social categorization (categorizing people based on limited information),
- stereotyping (perceiving everyone that we believe to be of the same culture to share similar characteristics and behaviors), and
- attribution (attributing behavior of others to what we believe we know about their culture).

In order to prevent automatic processing of information due to these processes, we should exercise mindfulness. **Mindfulness** means simultaneously being aware of one's assumptions, ideas, and emotions (and the shortcuts referred to earlier of selective perception, stereotyping, and attribution), being more aware of the other person's cues and beliefs, viewing the situation from several perspectives, creating new mental maps of others' personalities, complicating the categories by creating new categories, seeking more information, and empathizing with others.

Cultural knowledge and mindfulness are only two of the three aspects required for cultural intelligence. The third aspect is *behavioral skills*—the ability to come up with a culturally appropriate behavior. Learning interpersonal, negotiation, relationship-building, etiquette, influencing, and selling skills are key behavioral skills that contribute to cultural intelligence.

What characteristics help in the development of cultural intelligence?

1. Integrity – having a well-balanced sense of self and understanding how one's own belief system motivates behavior. Understanding oneself is the fundamental base for cultural intelligence.
2. Openness (humility and inquisitiveness) – showing respect and a willingness to learn from others.
3. Hardiness – robustness, courage, intrepidness, and capability of surviving unfavorable conditions.

BECOMING CULTURALLY INTELLIGENT

There are typically five stages in the process of developing one's cultural intelligence:

1. Reactivity to external stimuli. At this stage, there is no recognition of even the existence of other cultures.
2. Recognition of other cultural norms and motivation to learn more about them. At this stage, people are more mindful that there are cultural differences, and they are curious to learn more.
3. Accommodation of other cultural norms and rules in one's own mind. At this stage, a deeper understanding of cultural variation begins to develop.
4. Assimilation of diverse cultural norms into alternative behaviors. At this stage, individuals have developed a repertoire of cultural behaviors from which they can choose with relative ease.
5. Proactivity in cultural behavior based on recognition of changing cues that others do not perceive. At this stage, individuals intuitively know what behaviors are required and how to execute them effectively.

In practical terms, the acquisition of cultural intelligence over time involves learning from social interactions. This requires attention to the situation, retention of the knowledge gained from the situation, reproduction of the behavior skills observed, and finally receiving feedback about the effectiveness of the adapted behavior. Acquisition of cultural intelligence is helped by formal education and training, cross-cultural groups and teams, overseas experience and expatriate assignments, and cross-cultural interactions at home.

APPLICATIONS OF CULTURAL INTELLIGENCE

Developing cultural intelligence helps immensely in managerial decision making. Decision making in western cultures usually follows application of formal logic, giving rise to a rational decision-making model. The **rational model** involves defining a problem, generating a range of potential solutions, testing the solutions against predetermined criteria, and choosing and implementing the best alternative. However, because of incomplete information, biases, and time constraints (among other reasons), in reality managers usually stray away from the strict dictates of the rational decision-making model and simplify the decision context in order to make a decision. Because people in different cultures have different mental programming, the ways in which they simplify the complex process of decision making also differ. The culturally intelligent manager is better able to understand the decision-making methods and criteria used in other cultures.

Cultural intelligence is also useful in improving communication and negotiation processes. In communication, a sender transmits messages to a receiver, who then interprets the message and responds according to that interpretation. Successful communication occurs when the message is accurately perceived and understood. Cultural differences threaten communication because they reduce the availability of codes and conventions that are shared by the sender and receiver of messages. Language codes and conventions are especially difficult to understand and learn, especially in English, which has a vocabulary of over 200,000 words and is spoken in many countries. However, one must be mindful of the different ways in which words in the same language can be interpreted by the receiver of the message. Among conventions, being direct versus indirect with a message, as well as verbosity and silence, varies between cultures. Nonverbal conventions that one needs to be mindful of are physical distance and touching, eye contact between the parties in a communication, body position, gestures, and facial expression of the sender and receiver of messages. When negotiating across cultures, cultural intelligence helps in each phase of the negotiation process—building a relationship, exchanging information, trying to persuade each other, and making concessions and reaching agreement.

Cultural intelligence has great relevance in the context of leadership. Leadership styles vary across countries and regions. For instance, in the Arab world, leadership has strong elements of personal autocracy and conformity to rules and regulations based on respect for those who made the rules rather than for their rationality. Leadership in France is influenced by societal emphasis on hierarchy. The image of leaders in Russia is that of powerful autocrats. Cultural differences can play a role in expectations of followers from their leaders. For instance, in individualist cultures, followers and leaders attempt to involve themselves in the decision making to maximize their individual influence and gain for themselves a good result. Collectivist cultures can rely more on the leader to involve the group, because that will be the shared expectation of both leader and followers. If you wish to be a culturally intelligent leader, you will need to use knowledge and mindfulness to develop a repertoire of behaviors that can be adapted to each specific situation. In cross-cultural situations, it is better not to model your leader behavior after a leader in the follower culture.

Multicultural groups provide another context for employing cultural intelligence. Cultural diversity of a group can be measured by measuring the relative cultural distance. Cultural distance refers to how different each group member feels from each other group member. Culturally diverse groups can also be virtual. Multicultural virtual groups offer additional challenges because of fewer communication cues provided in the message. There are three things that culturally intelligent people can do to reduce or eliminate process losses and to capitalize on diversity. These are to manage the environment of the group, to allow culturally diverse groups to develop, and to foster cultural intelligence in the group.

Finally, cultural intelligence is valuable in managing international careers. While expatriate assignments provide an invaluable opportunity to develop cultural intelligence, they can also be quite challenging, and the process of adjusting to a new culture can be stressful. Typically, expatriates go through periods of honeymoon, culture shock, adjustment, and mastery, which can take more than four years. Repatriates also suffer through a culture shock when they come back home because of changes in themselves and their home country environment. Reflecting on reasons for going abroad, preparing for the transition, and being self-forgiving and patient help in adjusting to the expatriate assignments and the return back home.

XVI

MANAGEMENT FABLES AND LESSONS FOR PERSONAL SUCCESS

Two major interrelated phenomena in business book publishing emerged in the past quarter century. The first was to use the format of a brief "managerial fable" (fabricated storyline) to catch the reader's attention and as a format for presenting a few (usually four to eight) key lessons to readers in a simple, readable, straightforward form. The first book of significance to achieve substantial success with this format was *The One Minute Manager*, followed by dozens of similarly structured books. The second phenomenon involved the explosion in demand (and products provided) for managerial "guidance" books that offered suggestions for personal success. The model of this genre of book in the modern era is unquestionably *The Seven Habits of Highly Effective People*. This last section in *The Manager's Bookshelf* brings you a sampling of both types of books.

Kenneth Blanchard and Spencer Johnson, in the enormously popular book *The One Minute Manager*, build their prescriptions for effective human resource management on two basic principles. First, they suggest that quality time with the subordinate is of utmost importance. Second, they suggest that employees are basically capable of self-management. These two principles provide the basis for their prescriptions on goal setting, praising, and reprimanding as the cornerstones of effective management. *The One Minute Manager* was identified as one of the "seven essential popular business books" by M. L. Jenson (*eBook Crossroads*, December 5, 2005).

Kenneth Blanchard was a professor of management at the University of Massachusetts, and remains active as a writer, management consultant, and co-founder of The Blanchard Companies. Blanchard has also published *The Power of*

Ethical Management, Gung Ho, The One-Minute Apology, Servant Leader, Whale Done, The Heart of a Leader, The Leadership Pill, The Secret, and *Raving Fans*; his books have collectively sold over 17 million copies. Spencer Johnson, the holder of a medical doctorate, is interested in stress and has written the popular books *Who Moved My Cheese?* and *The Present.*

The second book summarized in this section of *The Manager's Bookshelf* has a simple and surprisingly non-business-sounding title: *Fish!* Like several other books (e.g., *The One Minute Manager, Zapp!, Heroz,* and *Who Moved My Cheese?*), which have also sold in large numbers, *Fish!* is short (about 100 pages), easy and quick to read, engaging, and written in the form of a parable. The authors (Lundin, Paul, and Christensen) provide a creative way to convey a central message—that work can (and should be) a joyful experience for all involved. Like any of the books summarized in this edition, we urge you to read the original source in its entirety and then reflect about what you have read. What are the roles of "fun" and "play" at work? Can such an environment be created? Is the conceptual foundation of the authors' message a solid one? Do negative implications as well as positive ones arise from creating a joyful experience at work?

Authors Lundin, Christensen, and Paul and Chart House Learning have also collaborated in the preparation of other products extending the Fish! philosophy and practice. Their follow-up books include *Fish! Tales, Fish! Sticks,* and *Fish! For Life,* and they also have a wide array of videos, calendars, training programs, apparel, and other related products available at their Web site, www.charthouse.com/home.asp. We think you will discover that despite the brevity, simplicity, and creative format of *Fish!,* useful ideas for action and debate can be found in this and almost any type of managerial literature. Like all ideas, of course, they need to be tested for their soundness, validity, and applicability.

Spencer Johnson (co-author of *The One Minute Manager, The Present,* and *"Yes" or "No": The Guide to Better Decisions*) has produced another book selling millions of copies titled *Who Moved My Cheese?* This book catapulted to the top of best-seller lists for *USA Today, Publisher's Weekly,* the *Wall Street Journal,* and *Business Week,* with some companies (e.g., Southwest Airlines and Mercedes-Benz) ordering thousands of copies to distribute to their employees. Written in the form of a fable about two mice and two small people living in a maze, Johnson suggests that change is rampant around us, and thus employees must anticipate, monitor, and adapt to change quickly in order to survive. Unfortunately, fear—and the tendency to cling to the familiar and comfortable past—prevents some people from letting go of old beliefs, attitudes, and paradigms. Readers interested in a critical view of the book should examine Jill Rosenfeld's article, "This Consultant's Whey Is Cheese-y" (*Fast Company,* November 2000, pp. 68–72).

Stephen R. Covey is a well-known speaker, author of several books, and chief executive officer of the Franklin Covey Co. His first book, *The Seven Habits of Highly Effective People,* remains on best-seller lists and has sold over 15 million copies across the world. In it, he offers a series of prescriptions to guide managers as they chart their courses in turbulent times. Drawn from his extensive review of the "success literature," Covey urges people to develop a character ethic based on seven key habits: people being proactive, identifying their values, disciplining themselves to work on high-priority items, seeking win-win solutions, listening with empathy, synergizing with others, and engaging in extensive reading and studying for self-development.

Covey has also published a "Seven Habits" book that adapts the basic principles for families. *First Things First* urges people to manage their time and life well so as to achieve goals consistent with their values. His *Principle-Centered Leadership* book identifies seven human attributes—self-awareness, imagination, willpower, an abundance mentality, courage, creativity, and self-renewal—that, when combined with eight key behaviors (e.g., priority on service, radiating positive energy), help produce effective and principled leaders. His other books include *Living the Seven Habits, Reflections for Highly Effective People*, and *Everyday Greatness*.

The 8th Habit is Stephen R. Covey's latest major publication effort. Driven by the dominance of the Knowledge Worker Age and the pervasiveness of employees who are unappreciated and undervalued, organizations require new leadership and a major change in thinking. *The 8th Habit* urges managers everywhere to create workplaces where employees feel mentally engaged by establishing trust, searching for better alternatives, and developing a shared vision. This begins by leaders finding their own voice as a foundation for inspiring others.

THE ONE MINUTE MANAGER

KENNETH BLANCHARD AND SPENCER JOHNSON

SUMMARY PREPARED BY CHARLES C. MANZ

Charles C. Manz is a Professor of Management at the University of Massachusetts at Amherst. He holds a doctorate in Organizational Behavior from Pennsylvania State University. His professional publications and presentations concern topics such as self-leadership, vicarious learning, self-managed work groups, leadership, power and control, and group processes. He is the author of the book The Art of Self-Leadership *and co-author of* The Leadership Wisdom of Jesus.

The most distinguishing characteristic of *The One Minute Manager* by Kenneth Blanchard and Spencer Johnson is its major philosophical theme: Good management does not take a lot of time. This dominant theme seems to be based on two underlying premises: (1) *Quality* of time spent with subordinates (as with one's children) is more important than quantity; and (2) in the end, people (subordinates) should really be managing themselves.

The book is built around a story that provides an occasion for learning about effective management. The story centers on the quest of "a young man" to find an effective manager. In his search he finds all kinds of managers, but very few that he considers effective. According to the story, the young man finds primarily two kinds of managers. One type is a hard-nosed manager who is concerned with the bottom line (profit) and tends to be directive in style. With this type of manager, the young man believes, the organization tends to win at the expense of the subordinates. The other type of manager is one who is concerned more about the employees than about performance. This "nice" kind of manager seems to allow the employees to win at the expense of the organization. In contrast to these two types of managers, the book suggests, an effective manager (as seen through the eyes of the young man) is one who manages so that both the organization and the people involved benefit (win).

Kenneth Blanchard and Spencer Johnson, *The One Minute Manager*. La Jolla, CA: Blanchard-Johnson Publishers, 1981.

The dilemma that the young man faces is that the few managers who do seem to be effective will not share their secrets. That is only true until he meets the "One Minute Manager." It turns out that this almost legendary manager is not only willing to share the secrets of his effectiveness, but is so available that he is able to meet almost any time the young man wants to meet, except at the time of his weekly two-hour meeting with his subordinates. After an initial meeting with the One Minute Manager, the young man is sent off to talk to his subordinates to learn, directly from those affected, the secrets of One Minute Management. Thus the story begins, and in the remaining pages, the wisdom, experience, and management strategies of the One Minute Manager are revealed as the authors communicate, through him and his subordinates, their view on effective management practice.

In addition to general philosophical management advice (e.g., managers can reap good results from their subordinates without expending much time), the book suggests that effective management means that both the organization and its employees win, and that people will do better work when they feel good about themselves; it also offers some specific prescriptions. These prescriptions center around three primary management techniques that have been addressed in the management literature for years: goal setting, positive reinforcement in the form of praise, and verbal reprimand. The authors suggest that applications of each of the techniques can be accomplished in very little time, in fact in as little as one minute (hence the strategies are labeled "one minute goals," "one minute praisings," and "one minute reprimands"). The suggestions made in the book for effective use of each of these strategies will be summarized in the following sections.

ONE MINUTE GOALS

"One minute goals" clarify responsibilities and the nature of performance standards. Without them, employees will not know what is expected of them, being left instead to grope in the dark for what they ought to be doing. A great deal of research and writing has been done on the importance of goals in reaching a level of performance (c.f., Locke, Shaw, Saari, and Latham, 1981). The advice offered in *The One Minute Manager* regarding effective use of performance goals is quite consistent with the findings of this previous work. Specifically, the authors point out through one of the One Minute Manager's subordinates that effective use of One Minute Goals includes:

- agreement between the manager and subordinate regarding what needs to be done;
- recording of each goal on a single page in no more than 250 words that can be read by almost anyone in less than a minute;
- communication of clear performance standards regarding what is expected of subordinates regarding each goal; and
- continuous review of each goal, current performance, and the difference between the two.

These components are presented with a heavy emphasis on having employees use them to manage themselves. This point is driven home as the employee who shares this part of One Minute Management recalls how the One Minute Manager taught him about One Minute Goals. In the recounted story, the One Minute Manager refuses to take credit for having solved a problem of the subordinate, and is in fact irritated by the very idea of getting credit for it. He insists that the subordinate solved his own problem and orders him to go out and start solving his own future problems without taking up the One Minute Manager's time.

ONE MINUTE PRAISING

The next employee encountered by the young man shares with him the secrets of "one minute praising." Again, the ideas presented regarding this technique pretty well parallel research findings on the use of positive reinforcement (c.f., Luthans and Kreitner, 1986). One basic suggestion for this technique is that managers should spend their time trying to catch subordinates doing something *right* rather than doing something wrong. In order to facilitate this, the One Minute Manager monitors new employees closely at first and has them keep detailed records of their progress (which he reviews). When the manager is able to discover something that the employee is doing right, the occasion is set for One Minute Praising (positive reinforcement). The specific components suggested for applying this technique include:

- letting others know that you are going to let them know how they are doing;
- praising positive performance as soon as possible after it has occurred, letting employees know specifically what they did right and how good you feel about it;
- allowing the message that you really feel good about their performance to sink in for a moment, and encouraging them to do the same; and
- using a handshake or other form of touch when it is appropriate (more on this later).

Again, these steps are described with a significant self-management flavor. The employee points out that after working for a manager like this for a while you start catching yourself doing things right and using self-praise.

ONE MINUTE REPRIMANDS

The final employee that the young man visits tells him about "One Minute Reprimands." This potentially more somber subject is presented in a quite positive tone. In fact, the employee begins by pointing out that she often praises herself and sometimes asks the One Minute Manager for a praising when she has done something well. But she goes on to explain that when she has done something wrong, the One Minute Manager is quick to respond, letting her know exactly what she has done wrong and how he feels about it. After the reprimand is over, he proceeds to tell her how competent he thinks she really is, essentially praising her as a *person* despite rejecting the undesired *behavior*. Specifically, the book points out that One Minute Reprimands should include:

- letting people know that you will, in a frank manner, communicate to them how they are doing;
- reprimand poor performance as soon as possible, telling people exactly what they did wrong and how you feel about it (followed by a pause allowing the message to sink in);

- reaffirm how valuable you feel the employees are, using touch if appropriate, while making it clear that it is their *performance* that is unacceptable in this situation; and
- make sure that when the reprimand episode is over it is over.

OTHER ISSUES AND RELATED MANAGEMENT TECHNIQUES

These three One Minute Management techniques form the primary applied content of the book. Good management does not take a lot of time; it just takes wise application of proven management strategies—One Minute Goals, Praisings, and Reprimands. Beyond this, the book deals with some other issues relevant to these strategies, such as "under what conditions is physical touch appropriate?" The book suggests that the use of appropriate touch can be helpful when you know the person well and wish to help that person succeed. It should be done so that you are giving something to the person such as encouragement or support, not taking something away.

The authors also address the issue of manipulation, suggesting that employees should be informed about, and agree to, the manager's use of One Minute Management. They indicate that the key is to be honest and open in the use of this approach. They also deal briefly with several other issues. For example, the book suggests that it is important to move a subordinate gradually to perform a new desired behavior by reinforcing approximations to the behavior until it is finally successfully performed. The technical term for this is "shaping." A person's behavior is shaped by continuously praising improvements rather than waiting until a person completely performs correctly. If a manager waits until a new employee completely performs correctly, the employee may well give up long before successful performance is achieved because of the absence of reinforcement along the way.

The authors also suggest substituting the strategies for one another when appropriate. With new employees, for instance, they suggest that dealing with low performance should focus on goal setting and then trying to catch them doing something right rather than using reprimand. Since a new employee's lack of experience likely produces an insufficient confidence level, this makes reprimand inappropriate, while goal setting and praise can be quite effective (so the logic goes). The authors also suggest that if a manager is going to be tough on a person, the manager is better off being tough first and then being supportive, rather than the other way around. Issues such as these are briefly addressed through the primary story and the examples described by its primary characters, as supplemental material to the management philosophy and specific management techniques that have been summarized here.

Eventually, at the end of the story, the young man is hired by the One Minute Manager and over time becomes a seasoned One Minute Manager himself. As he looks back over his experiences, the authors summarize some of the benefits of the management approach they advocate—more results in less time, time to think and plan, less stress and better health, similar benefits experienced by subordinates, and reduced absenteeism and turnover.

Conclusion

The bottom-line message of the book is that effective management requires that you care sincerely about people but have definite expectations that are expressed openly about their behavior. Also, one thing that is even more valuable than learning to be a One Minute Manager is having one for a boss, which in the end means you really work for yourself. And finally, as the authors illustrate through the giving attitude of the young man who has now become a One Minute Manager, these management techniques are not a competitive advantage to be hoarded but a gift to be shared with others. This is true because, in the end, the one who shares the gift will be at least as richly rewarded as the one who receives it.

Notes

1. Locke, E., K. Shaw, L. Saari, and G. Latham. "Goal Setting and Task Performance 1969–1980." *Psychological Bulletin,* 90 (1981), 125–152.

2. Luthans, F., and T. Davis. "Behavioral Self-management (BSM): The Missing Link in Managerial Effectiveness." *Organizational Dynamics* 8 (1979), 42–60.

3. Luthans, F., and R. Kreitner. *Organizational Behavior Modification and Beyond.* Glenview, IL: Scott, Foresman and Co., 1986.

4. Manz, C. C. *The Art of Self-Leadership: Strategies for Personal Effectiveness in Your Life and Work.* Upper Saddle River, NJ: Prentice Hall, 1983.

5. Manz, C. C. "Self-Leadership: Toward an Expanded Theory of Self-influence Processes in Organizations." *Academy of Management Review,* 11 (1986), 585–600.

6. Manz, C. C., and H. P. Sims, Jr. "Self-Management as a Substitute for Leadership: A Social Learning Theory Perspective." *Academy of Management Review,* 5 (1980), 361–367.

2 ‖ FISH!

STEPHEN C. LUNDIN, HARRY PAUL, AND JOHN
CHRISTENSEN

Mary Jane Ramirez is a manager who must create an effective team out of a set of employees who have historically been less than helpful to each other and generally unenthusiastic about teamwork. While taking a walk at lunchtime one day, she encounters a strange but compelling sight—the fishmongers of Seattle's Pike Street Fish Market. These employees have created a bustling, fun-filled, joyful work atmosphere both for themselves and for their customers. Through a series of conversations with Lonnie and some deep self-reflectiveness, she gradually uncovers some ideas that will guide her future behavior.

Using the fish market as a metaphor for other organizations, several key premises about employees are identified, and these lead logically to a short series of recommendations for personal effectiveness. The premises (underlying assumptions) include:

- Life is short, and our moments of life are precious. Therefore, it would be tragic for employees to just "pass through" on their way to retirement. Managers and employees both need to *make each moment count.*
- Most people prefer to work in a job environment that is *filled with fun.* When they find this fun or create it, they are much more likely to be energized and release their potential.
- People also like a work environment where they feel they can *make a difference* in the organization's outcomes. They need some capacity to assess their contribution toward those outcomes.
- Almost any job—no matter how simple or automated—has the potential to be performed with *energy and enthusiasm.*
- Employees may not always have the opportunity to choose whether to work or the work to be done itself. However, they will always have some degree of choice about the *way* in which they do their work. At the extreme, each employee can choose to be ordinary or to be world famous. One path is dull; the other is exciting.
- Employees can legitimately act like a bunch of *adult kids* having a good time as long as they do so in a respectful manner (not offending co-workers or customers).

Stephen C. Lundin, Harry Paul, and John Christensen, *Fish!: A Remarkable Way to Boost Morale and Improve Results.* New York: Hyperion, 2000.

When they do act as kids (along with choosing to love the work they do), they can find happiness, meaning, and fulfillment every day.

Based on these premises, four recommendations are offered to employees for their personal effectiveness:

1. Every morning, before you go to work, *choose your attitude* for the day (and make it a positive one).
2. Make an effort to introduce an element of *play* into your work environment; it will benefit you and all those around you.
3. Make a commitment to make someone else's day *special* for them. Do something that will create a memory, engage them in a meaningful interaction, or welcome them to your organization.
4. While you are at work, seek to be *present* with them. Focus your energy on them; listen attentively and caringly; pay attention to the needs of your customers and co-workers.

Following these simple prescriptions will make the work experience joyful for all involved, just as it has for the employees and customers of Seattle's Pike Street Fish Market.

WHO MOVED
MY CHEESE?

SPENCER JOHNSON, M.D.

SUMMARY PREPARED BY GARY STARK

Gary Stark is a faculty member at Northern Michigan University. He earned his Ph.D. in Management from the University of Nebraska, and subsequently taught at the University of Minnesota Duluth and Washburn University. Gary's research interests include recruiting, work-life balance, and the study of how and why people seek feedback on their work performance. Prior to his academic life Gary earned his B.S. and M.B.A. degrees at Kansas State University and worked in Chicago as a tax accountant.

A REUNION

Several former classmates met in Chicago one Sunday, the day after their class reunion. After discussing the difficulties they had been having with the many changes in their lives since high school, one of the classmates, Michael, volunteered a story that had helped him deal with the changes in his life. The name of the story was "Who Moved My Cheese?"

THE STORY

The story revolved around four characters who spent their lives in a maze. The maze was a giant labyrinth with many dead ends and wrong turns. But those who persisted in the maze were rewarded, for many rooms in the maze contained delicious Cheese. Two of the characters in the maze were little people named Hem and Haw. Two were mice named Sniff and Scurry. The characters spent every day at Cheese Station C, a huge storehouse of Cheese. However, the mice and the little people differed in their attitudes about Cheese Station C. These attitudes affected their behaviors. The mice, Sniff and Scurry, woke up early each day and raced to Cheese Station C. When they got there they

---

Spencer Johnson, M.D. *Who Moved My Cheese?: An Amazing Way to Deal with Change in Your Work and in Your Life.* New York: Putman Books, 1998.

took off their running shoes, tied them together, and hung them around their necks so that they would be immediately available should they need to move on from Cheese Station C. And Sniff and Scurry did something else to make sure that they were ready to move on if the need arose. Every day upon arrival at Cheese Station C Sniff and Scurry carefully inspected the Station and noted changes from the previous day.

Indeed, one day Sniff and Scurry arrived at Cheese Station C and found that the Cheese was gone. Sniff and Scurry were not surprised because they had been inspecting the Station every day and had noticed the Cheese supply dwindling. In response to the Cheeselessness, Sniff and Scurry simply did as their instincts told them. *The situation had changed so they changed with it.* Rather than analyze the situation, they put on their running shoes (taken from around their necks) and ran off through the maze in search of new Cheese.

The little people, Hem and Haw, were different. Long ago, when they first found Cheese Station C they had raced to get there every morning. But, as time went on, Hem and Haw got to the Station a little later each day. They became very comfortable in Cheese Station C and, unlike Sniff and Scurry, never bothered to search for changes in the Station. They assumed the Cheese would always be there and even came to regard the Cheese as their own. Unfortunately, unlike Sniff and Scurry, they did not notice that the Cheese was disappearing.

When they arrived on the fateful day and discovered the Cheese had run out in Cheese Station C, Hem and Haw reacted differently than Sniff and Scurry. Instead of immediately searching for new Cheese they complained that it wasn't fair. Finding Cheese was a lot of work in their maze and they did not want to let go of the life they had built around this Cheese. They wanted to know who moved their Cheese.

Hem and Haw returned the next day still hoping to find Cheese. They found none and repeated the behaviors of the day before. Eventually Haw noticed that Sniff and Scurry were gone. Haw suggested to Hem that they do as Sniff and Scurry had and go out into the maze in search of new cheese. Hem rebuffed him.

A similar scenario played out day after day in Cheese Station C. Hem and Haw returned every day hoping to find the Cheese they believed they were entitled to. They became frustrated and angry and began to blame each other for their predicament.

In the meantime, Sniff and Scurry had found new Cheese. It had taken a lot of work and they dealt with much uncertainty, but finally, in a totally unfamiliar part of the maze they found Cheese in Cheese Station N.

Still, day after day, Hem and Haw returned to Cheese Station C in hopes of finding their Cheese. And the same frustrations and claims of entitlement continued. Eventually, however, Haw's mindset began to change. He imagined Sniff and Scurry in pursuit of new Cheese and imagined himself taking part in such an adventure. He imagined finding fresh new Cheese. The more he thought about it the more determined he became to leave. Nevertheless, his friend Hem continued to insist that things would be fine in Cheese Station C. Hem figured that if they simply *worked harder* they would find their Cheese in Cheese Station C. He feared he was too old to look for Cheese and that he would look foolish doing so. Hem's concerns even made Haw doubt himself until finally one day Haw realized that he was doing the same things over and over again and wondering why things didn't improve. Although Haw did not like the idea of going into the maze and the possibility of getting lost, he laughed at how his fear was preventing him from doing those things. His realization inspired him to write a message to himself (and perhaps to Hem) on the wall in front of him. "*What Would You Do If You Weren't Afraid?*" (p. 48), it said. Answering his own question, Haw took a deep breath and headed into the unknown.

Unfortunately, a long interlude without food from Cheese Station C had left Haw somewhat weak. He struggled while searching for new Cheese and he decided that if he ever got another chance he would respond to a change in his environment sooner than he had to the situation in Cheese Station C.

Haw wandered for days and found very little new Cheese. He found the maze confusing, as it had changed a great deal since the last time he had looked for Cheese. Still, he had to admit that it wasn't as dreadful as he had feared. And whenever he got discouraged he reminded himself that however painful the search for new Cheese was, it was better than remaining Cheeseless. The difference was that *he was now in control.* Haw even began to realize, in hindsight, that the Cheese in Cheese Station C had not suddenly disappeared. If he had wanted to notice he would have seen the amount of Cheese decreasing every day, and that what was left at the end was old and not as tasty. Haw realized that maybe Sniff and Scurry had known what they were doing. Haw stopped to rest and wrote another message on the wall. The message read: "*Smell the Cheese Often So You Know When It Is Getting Old*" (p. 52).

Haw was often scared in the maze for he did not know if he would survive. He wondered if Hem had moved on yet or was still frozen by his fears. However, Haw's confidence and enjoyment grew with every day as he realized that the times he had felt best in this journey was when he was moving. He inscribed this discovery on the wall of the maze: "*When You Move Beyond Your Fear, You Feel Free*" (p. 56).

Soon Haw began painting a picture in his mind of himself enjoying all his favorite Cheeses. This image became so vivid that he gained a very strong sense that he would find new Cheese. He stopped to write on the wall: "*Imagining Myself Enjoying New Cheese Even Before I Find It, Leads Me to It*" (p. 58). Outside a new station Haw noticed small bits of Cheese near the entrance. He tried some, found them delicious, and excitedly entered the station. But Haw's heart sank when he found that only a small amount of Cheese remained in what was once a well-stocked station. He realized that if he had set about looking for new Cheese sooner he might have found more Cheese here. He wrote these thoughts on the wall: "*The Quicker You Let Go of Old Cheese, the Sooner You Find New Cheese*" (p. 60).

As Haw left this station he made another important self-discovery. He realized what made him happy wasn't just having Cheese. What made him happy was not being controlled by fear. He did not feel as weak and helpless as when he remained in Cheese Station C. Haw realized that moving beyond his fear was giving him strength and wrote that: "*It Is Safer to Search in the Maze Than Remain in a Cheeseless Situation*" (p. 62). Haw also realized that the fear he had allowed to build up in his mind was worse than the reality. He had been so afraid of the maze that he had dreaded looking for new Cheese. Now he found himself excited about looking for more. Later in his journey he wrote: "*Old Beliefs Do Not Lead You to New Cheese*" (p. 64). Haw knew that his new beliefs had encouraged new behaviors.

Finally it happened. What Haw had started his journey looking for was now in front of his eyes. Cheese Station N was flush with some of the greatest Cheeses Haw had ever seen. Sure enough, his mouse friends Sniff and Scurry were sitting in the Cheese, their bellies stuffed. Haw quickly said hello and dug in.

Haw was a bit envious of his mouse friends. They had kept their lives simple. When the Cheese moved, rather than overanalyze things, Sniff and Scurry moved with it. As Haw reflected on his journey he learned from his mistakes. He realized that what he had written on the walls during his journey was true and was glad he had changed. Haw realized three important things: (1) the biggest thing blocking change is yourself; (2) things don't improve until you change yourself; and (3) there is always new Cheese out there, whether you believe it or not. Indeed he realized running out of Cheese in Cheese Station C had been a blessing in disguise. It had led him to better Cheese and it had led him to discover important and positive things about himself.

Although Haw knew that he had learned a great deal he also realized that it would be easy to fall into a comfort zone with the new store of Cheese. So, every day he inspected the Cheese in Cheese Station N to avoid the same surprise that had occurred in Cheese Station C. And, even though he had a great supply of Cheese in Cheese Station N, every day he went out into the maze to make sure that he was always aware of his choices, that he did not have to remain in Cheese Station N. It was on one of these excursions that he heard the sound of someone moving toward him in the maze. He hoped and prayed that it was his friend Hem, and that Hem had finally learned to . . . "*Move with the Cheese and Enjoy It!*" (p. 76).

BACK AT THE REUNION

After the story the former classmates recounted situations in which they had to face changes in their work and their personal lives and they discussed which maze character they had acted most like. Most resolved to act more like Haw when dealing with changes they would face in the future. All agreed the story was very useful and that they would use the wisdom contained within to guide them.

4

THE SEVEN HABITS
OF HIGHLY EFFECTIVE
PEOPLE

STEPHEN R. COVEY

There are two types of literature on how to succeed. The first type focuses on a *personality ethic.* It claims that you are what you appear to be; appearance is everything. It accents public image, social consciousness, and the ability to interact superficially with others. However, exclusive attention to these factors will eventually provide evidence of a lack of integrity, an absence of depth, a short-term personal success orientation, and basic deficiency in one's own humanness.

The second type of success literature revolves around a *character ethic.* It provides proven pathways to move from dependent relationships to independence, and ultimately to interdependent success with other people. It requires a willingness to subordinate one's short-term needs to more important long-term goals. It requires effort, perseverance, and patience with oneself. One's character is, after all, a composite of habits, which are unconscious patterns of actions.

Habits can be developed through rigorous practice until they become second nature. There are seven key habits that form the basis for character development and build a strong foundation for interpersonal success in life and at work:

1. *Be proactive;* make things happen. Take the initiative and be responsible for your life. Work on areas where you can have an impact and pay less attention to areas outside your area of concern. When you do respond to others, do so on the basis of your principles.
2. *Begin with the end in mind.* Know where you're going; develop a personal mission statement; develop a sense of who you are and what you value. Maintain a long-term focus.
3. *Put first things first.* Distinguish between tasks that are urgent and not so urgent, between activities that are important and not so important; then organize and execute around those priorities. Avoid being in a reactive mode, and pursue

Stephen R. Covey, *The Seven Habits of Highly Effective People: Restoring the Character Ethic.* New York: Simon & Schuster, 1989.

opportunities instead. Ask yourself, "What one thing could I do (today) that would make a tremendous difference in my work or personal life?"

4. *Think "win-win."* Try to avoid competing, and search for ways to develop mutually beneficial relationships instead. Build an "emotional bank account" with others through frequent acts of courtesy, kindness, honesty, and commitment keeping. Develop the traits of integrity, maturity, and an abundance mentality (acting as if there is plenty of everything out there for everybody).

5. *Seek to understand, and then to be understood.* Practice empathetic communications, in which you recognize feelings and emotions in others. Listen carefully to people. Try giving them "psychological air."

6. *Synergize.* Value and exploit the mental, emotional, and psychological differences among people to produce results that demonstrate creative energy superior to what a single person could have accomplished alone.

7. *Sharpen the saw.* Do not allow yourself to get stale in any domain of your life, and don't waste time on activities that do not contribute to one of your goals and values. Seek ways to renew yourself periodically in all four elements of your nature—physical (via exercise, good nutrition, and stress control), mental (through reading, thought, and writing), social (through service to others), and spiritual (through study and meditation). In short, practice continuous learning and self-improvement, and your character will lead you to increased success.

5

THE 8TH HABIT

STEPHEN R. COVEY

SUMMARY PREPARED BY DAVID L. BEAL

David L. Beal is a retired Operations Manager and Vice President of Manufacturing for Lake Superior Paper Industries and Consolidated Papers Inc. in Duluth, Minnesota. Under his leadership, the all-salaried workforce was organized into a totally self-reliant team system using the principles of socio-technical design to create a high-performance system. Dave teaches in the Labovitz School of Business and Economics at the University of Minnesota Duluth, where his areas of interest include designing and leading self-directed team-based organizations, teamwork, and production and operations management. He received his B.S. in Chemical Engineering from the University of Maine in Orono, Maine, with a fifth year in Pulp and Paper Sciences.

INTRODUCTION

The challenges people face in their relationships, families, and professional lives and the complexities of powerful leadership in today's organizations have changed dramatically. Being effective as individuals and leaders in organizational environments is essential for success and goal achievement. While effectiveness drives success, *the higher calling for the future is to move beyond effectiveness to greatness.* Greatness means that we have mastered our human potential in every dimension of our life; the mind, body, heart, and spirit. Within each of us is an inner desire to live a life of greatness and to fulfill our purpose for existence and really make a difference. Greatness is fulfilling, allowing passionate execution and significant contribution for organizations to thrive, excel, and become leaders in today's global society.

The principles presented in *The seven Habits of Highly Effective People* (see pp. 359–360) are enduring and timeless. These character principles affect who and what we are as individuals. The seven habits form the basis for character development and building a strong foundation for interpersonal success. These habits are essential for

Stephen R. Covey, *The 8th Habit: From Effectiveness to Greatness.* New York: Free Press, 2004.

individual effectiveness. *The 8th Habit* moves individuals from effectiveness to greatness by urging them to find their own voice and then subsequently inspiring others to find theirs as well. It moves people from independence to interdependence in a way that develops whole persons to excel in every aspect of their life. This passionate execution and fulfillment of life requires a whole new engrained behavior—the 8th habit.

Because most people feel unappreciated and undervalued at work, they soon become frustrated and victims of the organization and system they work and live in. With little or no sense of voice, they fail to develop their potential or unique contribution to the organization. Humanity's search for its "voice" is the answer to the soul's desire for greatness in life and the organization's need for achieving superior results. Human beings are not physical things that need to be motivated and controlled with an extrinsic approach. People make choices in life, and at work these choices determine how much of themselves they will give to the relationships that make them effective leaders. *Contemporary employees have an intrinsic ability, and hence they desire the freedom to reach full potential and to live in an environment that values and encourages developing all aspects of their life.* This can be accomplished by giving them the knowledge and ability to find their voice and the organizational system for their voice to flourish. This is why the 8th habit is essential for developing trusting relationships, achieving peace of mind, and excelling in all aspects of life.

Most of the inspiration and change in organizations that has sustained prosperity and achievement of overall objectives started with the exceptional leadership of one person, usually the CEO or president. These executives exercised their leadership in profound ways that sustained long-term growth and organizational success. They practiced the 8th habit and learned to identify and understand their voice so as to inspire others to find theirs.

FOUR PATHS TO GREATNESS

The 8th Habit assumes that everyone chooses one of two roads in life. One road is the familiar highway that most people take, while the other is the road to achieve real meaning in life and eventual greatness. How we eventually get there can be as different as black and white. Deep within each of us is an intrinsic desire to achieve greatness in chosen aspects of our life, and in so doing make significant contributions to humankind. To make a significant difference and do what really matters in life, it is essential to:

- Develop the whole person: Explore the mind, body, heart, and spirit.
- Discover your voice: Understand your inherent makeup; have the freedom and ability to choose your direction in life; and develop four capacities of intelligence directly related to the mind, body, heart, and spirit. *When we change our thinking, our life will change.*
- Express your voice: Live a life embodied in the human intelligences of vision, discipline, passion, and conscience and by integrating what you learned into your life.
- Inspire others to find their voice: Choose to expand your influence, increase your contribution, and exercise your leadership in a meaningful and profound way.

FOUR INTELLIGENCES

Corresponding to the four parts of our nature as human beings, the mind, body, heart, and spirit, are four intelligences that everyone possesses. These are the mental, physical, emotional, and spiritual intelligences. *Mental intelligence* enables us to comprehend, reason, solve problems, think, use languages for communication, and visualize the future. Everyone possesses *physical intelligence* that manages all of the complexities of the physical body system, much of it unconscious. *Emotional intelligence* involves knowing one's self in a way that develops compassion, empathy, the ability to translate and successfully communicate with others, and be aware of the impact and influence we have on others. *Spiritual intelligence* is the desire for meaning in life, the fulfillment of our purpose for existence, and the connection with something infinitely greater than ourselves. It is the highest of the four intelligences.

Developing the four intelligences and building capabilities requires knowledge and discipline. Mental intelligence requires disciplined study, learning through education, and having an acute awareness of one's self. Living a balanced life with regular exercise, good nutrition, proper rest, relaxation, and stress management improves physical intelligence. Developing good social and communication skills, self awareness, and a high level of intrinsic motivation develops healthy emotional intelligence. Finally, never compromising one's integrity by being true to the highest level of values and listening to the voice inside while developing meaning in life and practicing a life of service to others for the good of society develop spiritual intelligence.

Possessing a vision for life and seeing what is possible in people is the highest level of mental intelligence. Leading a disciplined life when vision joins with commitment develops physical intelligence. Igniting the fire within is passion and with the desire and strength of conviction for life itself comes the development of emotional intelligence. Finally, listening to the voice inside and following our conscience are the greatest dimension of developing spiritual intelligence. These qualities represent the highest level of expressing our voice.

THE KEY ROLE OF TRUST

Trust is the most difficult value to attain in most organizations. Organizations today find that low trust exists almost everywhere and is chronic in nature. When vision and trust are neglected the result will be a weak culture with no shared vision and value system. Under these conditions, any road will seem like the primrose path, but almost always to the detriment of achieving critical organizational goals. When there is no alignment built into the organizational design, systems, processes, or culture, the organization remains helpless in achieving goals and fulfilling its purpose. When there is no passion for the vision or the achievement of goals and work in the organization there will be a profound disempowerment of the employees. It is for these reasons that the 8th habit is not just developing personal greatness, but just as importantly, it is the process of "Inspiring Others to Find Their Voice" through focus and execution. Focus involves the modeling and pathfinding roles, while execution involves the aligning and empowering roles.

Focus is practicing the modeling and pathfinding roles that inspire others to find their voice. When this happens and it becomes a means for achieving values, the high level of trust and vision that results will create a strong culture and successful organization. Developing the attitude, skill, and knowledge to inspire others to find their voice requires focus and modeling of the following principles:

1. "The Voice of Influence." Finding your own voice and passion to develop others is a first step. You cannot give to others what you fail to possess and put into practice yourself. By being able to expand your influence within your environments and choosing the attitude of initiative, others will be inspired to find their voice and everyone will grow to achieve greatness. It's the fire within each one of us coming together to produce an inferno. Modeling is also the activity of a team, and as teamwork improves organizational goals are achieved.

2. "The Voice of Trustworthiness." Trust comes from trustworthiness, the practice of trusting others first. Trusting relationships do not develop without a belief system that values the trust of others with open and truthful two-way communication. Knowing these principles and putting them into practice will open the path for influencing others and developing trusting relationships.

3. "The Voice and Speed of Trust." Developing strong relationships requires skills that build trust and helps to blend voices, which is literally creating a third alternative for solutions to differences and challenges with others. This rational process is usually a win-win for both parties by finding solutions that are better than either party's position taken alone.

4. "One Voice." The practice of one common voice being heard involves creating a single-minded vision with others about the priorities and values that will achieve critical outcomes.

Execution is the alignment of priorities and values while empowering others to find their voice and use it. The aligning and empowering roles are essential for others in the organization to develop the 8th habit. Execution of the aligning and empowering roles has two requirements:

1. "The Voice of Execution" requires the alignment of goals and systems for results. When the belief systems are untrustworthy, employees are not aligned with the organization's philosophy or values, and untrustworthy systems will dominate. Systems emerge out of necessity for the survival of employees when the behaviors in organizations are not aligned or supportive of the values the organization professes. Trustworthiness is paramount for alignment of values and operational goals within organizations, and when principle-centered alignment occurs, moral authority becomes institutionalized. This moral authority is the capacity to consistently serve the customer and be the supplier of choice with quality products and services, develop trusting relationships in all areas, and achieve organizational goals of efficiency, profitability, speed, and flexibility year after year.

2. "The Empowering Voice" is allowing your leadership abilities and passion for greatness to inspire others and then removing the obstacles that stand in the way for others to achieve their greatness. It's setting others free to grow, getting out of the way by empowering their abilities to achieve positive results no matter how small, and cheerleading their path to greatness.

Greatness Dimensions: Conclusions

The 8th habit is based on three dimensions of greatness: personal, leadership, and organizational. Personal greatness occurs when we put into practice the ability to choose our direction in life, understand and put into practice a principle-based existence, and fulfill the four human intelligences. When the voice within each of us is exercised in a profound and enduring way, others are inspired to find their voice and achieve leadership greatness. Organizational greatness occurs when a critical mass of employees within the organization puts into practice the principles and drivers of execution. There are four disciplines of execution. They are:

1. "Focus on the Wildly Important." The goals and objectives that have serious consequences if not met must be a supreme priority within the organization.
2. "Create a Compelling Scoreboard." The "Wildly Important" priorities promote accomplishment of critical organizational objectives if they are measurable. Without good measures of success, the goal or priority is never understood or achieved.
3. "Translate Lofty Goals into Specific Actions." Align the organization so that everyone on the team knows exactly what they're supposed to do. Teamwork is being creative, identifying better ways of doing things, and improving behaviors and translating goals into tasks that can be accomplished at all levels of the organization.
4. "Hold Each Other Accountable—All of the Time." Accountability ensures that critical organizational goals are accomplished.

When these four disciplines of execution are put into practice, they will enable an organization to achieve breakthrough performance.

Glossary of Terms

Achievement   To take pride in one's accomplishments by doing things that matter and doing them well; to receive recognition for one's accomplishments; to take pride in the organization's accomplishments. (Sirota, Mischkind, and Meltzer)

Acting mindfully   Operating in a manner that allows a manager to better notice the unexpected in the making and halt its development. (Weick and Sutcliffe)

Action orientation   Having a tendency to act, to do something regardless of consequences. (LaFasto and Larson)

Adaptive capacity   The ability to find new skills, new appreciation, a new vision, and new resolve for future encounters based on an experience of change. (Bennis and Thomas)

Adaptive unconscious   The part of one's brain that makes perceptions, impressions, motivations, and decisions very quickly. (Gladwell)

Ambiguity   Inability to characterize important aspects of a decision such as arena of action, objectives, or remedies. (Nutt)

Ambition   The drive for gain and growth. (Bennis and Thomas)

Amygdala   The part of the brain that triggers emotional reactions before the thinking brain has a chance to pick up the signal. (Frost)

Androgyne   To have both male and female characteristics. (Winfeld)

Arena of action   The remedy implied by the concerns and considerations that initiates action. (Nutt)

Asexuals   Those persons who do not become physically and/or emotionally attracted to others, regardless of the other's gender. (Winfeld)

Authentic leadership   Actions by people of high integrity who are committed to building enduring organizations relying on morality and character. (George)

Availability bias   The fallacy of allowing the recency and amount of publicity given to information to be remembered and given more weight than it merits. (Murnighan and Mowen)

Bad followers   Persons who knowingly and deliberately commit themselves to "bad leaders" and who generally mirror bad leaders for a variety of complex reasons. (Kellerman)

Bad leadership   Actions—ineffective or unethical—that are a result of leaders behaving poorly because of who they are, and because of what they want, and acting in ways that do harm (either intentional or as a result of carelessness or neglect). (Kellerman)

Balanced life   Leading a life that recognizes the importance of work, family, friends, faith, and community service, with none of them excluding any of the others. (George)

Balanced path   The approach that harmonizes worker fulfillment with enterprise performance. (Katzenbach)

Big losers   Companies that have demonstrated a persistent lack of competitive advantage through stock market performance significantly poorer than their respective industry average over the period 1992–2002. (Marcus)

Big winners   Companies that have demonstrated sustainable competitive advantage through stock market performance that significantly exceeds their respective industry average over the period 1992–2002. (Marcus)

Bisexuals   Those persons whose capacity for physical and/or emotional attraction extends to either gender. (Winfeld)

Boulder of oppression   Overt and subtle forms of discrimination based on individual, organizational, and societal belief systems that value one social identity group over another (e.g., racism, sexism, ageism, heterosexism). (Miller and Katz)

Burnout　The effects of a mismatch between the needs of an employee and the demands of a job, which can be manifested by an erosion of emotions, frustration, and health symptoms. (Cascio)

Business unit　A unit within an organization that has control over both revenues and costs, and therefore can calculate its own profit or loss over any period of time. (Kaplan and Norton)

Camaraderie　The feeling of having warm, interesting, and cooperative relations with others in the workplace. (Sirota, Mischkind, and Meltzer)

Capabilities　The clearly identifiable and measurable value-adding activities that describe what the organization can do. (Lawler and Worley)

Capitalize　Using an asset, skill, or resource in the most effective and efficient way. (Buckingham)

Cheese　A metaphor for anything that employees are seeking (as rewards for their efforts) or elements of their environment with which they are familiar (that cause confusion if changed). (Johnson)

Choice points　Natural places during a conversation where the course of action can be altered. (Reardon)

Choice-structuring process　A process whose goal is to produce sound strategic choices that lead to successful action. (Argyris)

Circumstance-based categorization　Segmentation of products and services. (Christensen)

Civility　Basing behavior on respect, restraint, and responsibility. (Forni)

Climbers　Companies that lagged their peers in the first period, but achieved performance better than their peers in the second. (Joyce, Nohria, and Roberson)

Coarsening of America　The decline of high-quality social interaction. (Forni)

Collaboration　A coordinated effort among team members to attain an outcome. (LaFasto and Larson); one possible result of conflict resolution in which both sides work together to get what each needs. (Thomas)

Collaborative work system　A form of organization that practices a disciplined system of collaboration and a set of 10 principles to achieve superior results so as to be successful in a rapidly changing environment. (Beyerlein, Freedman, McGee, and Moran)

Commoditization　The process that transforms profitable, differentiated, proprietary products into undifferentiable commodities. (Christensen)

Communication　The process in which a sender transmits messages to a receiver, who then interprets the message and responds according to that interpretation. (Thomas and Inkson)

Compassion　Empathy and caring in action, which enables managers to understand people's wants and needs and feel motivated to act on their feelings. Compassion is the third of three keys for renewal. (Boyatzis and McKee)

Compassionate organization　Organizations that promote a culture of and a set of practices and respectful policies that produce generative responses from their people and link the emotional health of the organization with the bottom line. (Frost)

Compassionate responding　The capacity to listen to grief and to provide sympathy and support in a relatively short time. (Frost)

Competence　The component of integrity that includes expertise in critical leadership skills. (Bennis and Thomas)

Competitive advantage　Structure, human resources, processes, knowledge, culture, and other aspects of the organization that provide a sustainable edge in the marketplace. (Lawler); the edge a firm can gain over its competitors by providing equivalent benefits at a lower price, or greater benefits that compensate for a higher price than competitors charge. (Porter)

Conscious decision making　Processing information on a conscious level to reach a decision. This process is intentional, typically slow, and entails gathering information, employing logic, and coming up with a definitive answer to a problem, before the action can follow the decision. (Gladwell)

Consequence management　A management philosophy that rewards and punishes on the basis of the consequences or results of individual action. (Katzenbach)

Consideration　Imagination on a moral track. (Forni)

Containment　The ability of an organization (derived from resilience and deference to expertise) to recover from unexpected negative events. (Weick and Sutcliffe)

Context　The situational background surrounding a decision. (Nutt)

Controlling insight The best explanation of most events. (Buckingham)

Conversational coherence Knowing when an issue is relevant to an ongoing discussion. (Reardon)

Core competencies Technical areas of organizational expertise that can support the pursuit of strategic objectives and provide the basis for sustained competitive advantage. (Lawler); A combination of technology and production skills that underlie the product lines and services of an organization. (Lawler and Worley)

Core group An interacting set of people that influences the direction of the organization, how decisions are made, and who will be the most influential in making those decisions. (Kleiner)

Critical configuration The effect produced when an organization's strategic intent describes a path that is proximate to both its environment and its identity. (Lawler and Worley)

Cross-dressers People whose gender expression is sometimes at odds with their biological gender and who dress in the clothing of the other gender. (Winfeld)

Cross-selling Selling several products to the same customers as a way to realize revenue synergies. (Kaplan and Norton)

Crucibles Those transforming events or situations that radically change a person's leadership abilities and skills. (Bennis and Thomas)

Cultural distance The degree of difference that each cultural group member feels from each other group member. (Thomas and Inkson)

Culture The way in which the organization brings together large numbers of people and imbues them for a sufficient time with a sufficient similarity of approach, outlook, and priorities to enable it to achieve collective, sustained responses that would be impossible if a group of unorganized individuals were to face the same problem. How things really get done in an organization. (Weick and Sutcliffe); Shared mental programs that condition individuals' responses to their environment. (Thomas and Inkson)

Customer-focused quality A quality measurement that focuses externally on customers and uses customer feedback as the ultimate measurement of quality. (George)

Cycle time The amount of time spent from beginning to completion of a task or project. (Thomas)

Death spiral The opposite of a virtuous spiral, this deteriorating condition flourishes in organizations that mishandle their human capital, in turn causing both individual and organizational performance decline. (Lawler)

Decision myopia Events in the present are valued more than those that will occur in the future, resulting in a tendency for decision makers to overweight present outcomes and underweight future outcomes. (Murnighan and Mowen)

Deliberate strategy Improved understanding of what works and what doesn't based on deliberate, conscious, and analytical decision making. (Christensen)

Differentiation Providing something unique that is valuable to buyers and for which they are willing to pay a price premium. (Porter); Realizing that we are all unique individuals, responsible for our own survival and well-being, while enjoying the expression of our being in action. (Csikszentmihalyi)

Disruption An act of delaying or interrupting the continuity; in the management context, disruption creates an opportunity to examine and evaluate the status quo and improve upon it. (Buckingham)

Disruptive innovations A strategy that targets new, less-demanding customers with products and services that, although not as good as the currently available products, appeal due to simplicity, cost, or convenience. (Christensen)

Dissonance Loss of resonance; out of tune, out of sync; lacking clarity and awareness. (Boyatzis and McKee)

Dissonant leaders Persons who are emotionally volatile and reactive; they are known to drive people too hard for the wrong reasons and in wrong directions, leaving a trail of frustration, fear, and antagonism because they often lack awareness of their emotions and impact on others. (Boyatzis and McKee)

Dissonant leadership The ability to generate discord by being unresponsive to other people's feelings. (Goleman, Boyatzis, and McKee)

Diversity Commitment to the principle that a company's employees and customers reflect the values and the cultures of the community in which it operates. (Batstone)

Diversity in a box model   An organizational belief that differences should be managed, tolerated, or molded to fit the dominant organizational culture. (Miller and Katz)

Downsizing   An intentional, proactive management strategy, which can include reductions in the firm's financial, physical, and human assets. (Cascio)

DPB   Domestic partner benefits. (Winfeld)

Drive to acquire   The innate human need to obtain objects and increase our relative status. (Lawrence and Nohria)

Drive to bond   The innate human need to form reciprocal bonds with others. (Lawrence and Nohria)

Drive to defend   The innate human need to protect ourselves and what we hold dear. (Lawrence and Nohria)

Drive to learn   The innate human need to make sense of ourselves and of our world. (Lawrence and Nohria)

Dynamic alignment   The result created when the strategic intent drives the nature and quality of an organization's competencies, capabilities, and design. (Lawler and Worley)

Ecological modernization   A theory that society can modernize itself out of ecological crises by integrating economics, natural sciences, corporate management, politics, regulators, and other factors to develop solutions that allow both economic growth and environmental responsibility. (Robbins)

Effective managers   Managers who manage themselves and others so that both employees and the organization benefit. (Blanchard and Johnson)

Eighth habit   The passionate execution and fulfillment of life that moves people from effectiveness to greatness through finding their voice and helping others to do the same. (Covey)

Emergent strategy   The cumulative effect of day-to-day prioritizations identifying unanticipated opportunities, problems, and successes. (Christensen)

Emotional fortitude   The ability to be honest with oneself and deal honestly with business realities, based upon the four qualities of authenticity, self-awareness, self-mastery, and humility. (Bossidy and Charan)

Emotional intelligence   A set of competencies distinguishing how people manage feelings and interactions with others. (Goleman)

Empathy   The ability to sense what people are feeling through receiving and interpreting verbal and nonverbal messages. (Goleman); Entering the private perceptual world of another person; being sensitive moment-to-moment to the changing feelings that flow from the other person. (Reardon); The ability to identify with others and, to a certain extent, feel what they feel. (Forni); The process of considering another's needs, feelings, and emotions by aligning one's own feelings with the other person's. (Dean)

Employee enthusiasm   A state of high employee morale that derives from satisfying the three key needs of workers, which results in significant competitive advantages for companies with the strength of leadership and commitment to manage for true long-term results. (Sirota, Mischkind, and Meltzer)

Enlightened management systems   Organizations where employees are assumed to be at the highest levels of the need hierarchy, are capable of self-actualization, and are receptive to management practices that keep people informed, provide clarity of direction, and challenge them to stretch and grow. (Maslow)

Enriched jobs   Jobs that create three psychological conditions: experience of meaningfulness, experience of responsibility, and feedback or knowledge of results. (Lawler)

Environmental compliance management   The organization meets minimal expectations by focusing primarily on complying with environmental laws or litigation. (Robbins)

Equality/equity   The feeling of being treated justly in relation to the basic conditions of employment; the treatment of each individual as important and unique without regard to any other characteristics, such as gender, race, income, or even perceived performance or contribution to the organization. (Sirota, Mischkind, and Meltzer)

Espoused theories   The beliefs and values people hold about how to manage their lives. (Argyris)

Ethics   Value-based positions taken by a decision's stakeholders. (Nutt)

Execution   The disciplined and systematic process of exposing reality (key information) through robust dialogue and acting on it with intensity and rigor. (Bossidy); The alignment of priorities and values while empowering others to find their voice and use it. (Covey)

Executive discipline   The implied rules executives follow to enforce individual accountability and consequence management. (Katzenbach)

External commitment   Commitment that is triggered by management policies and practices that enable employees to accomplish their tasks. (Argyris)

Extrinsic motivation   Anything that can be bestowed upon employees from others to stimulate their motivation and provide satisfaction to them. (Ventrice)

Extrinsic rewards   Rewards that come from external sources, such as money, prestige, and acceptance. (Thomas)

False spiral   A spiral that occurs when an organization or individual believes it has started a virtuous spiral, when in fact it is simply an illusion. (Lawler)

Feedback   Information regarding results of one's efforts (how well one is performing). (Blanchard and Johnson)

Flow   Full involvement with life. (Csikszentmihalyi)

Focal asset   The main product or organizational capability that creates an advantage over the competition, which makes an organization unique and different from competitors. (Buckingham)

Frame   A conceptual window, mindset, or paradigm that illuminates some aspects of a decision and obscures others. (Nutt)

Fraudulent spiral   A spiral that can be easily mistaken for a virtuous one, but is caused by deceitful activities. (Lawler)

Fundamental attribution error   Propensity to place the cause for another person's outcomes on themselves (blame the victim) rather than bad luck or external factors. (Murnighan and Mowen)

Fundamental state of leadership   The condition in which leaders transform themselves from their normal state to become results-centered, internally directed, other-focused, and externally open. (Quinn)

Geeks   Successful leaders under 35 years old who came into maturity during the 1991–2000 decade. (Bennis and Thomas)

Geezers   Highly successful leaders who are now over 70 years old who came into maturity during the period of 1945–1954. (Bennis and Thomas)

Glocalization   Finding ways to be open to, accept, and blend foreign ideas and best practices with a country's values, beliefs, and culture. (Friedman)

Good character   A moral state that is demonstrated when a person utilizes signature strengths and demonstrates a combination of the six virtues. (Seligman)

Good followers   Subordinates who are strong, independent partners with leaders; they think for themselves, self-direct their work, and hold up their end of the bargain. (Kellerman)

Gut feelings   The use of hunches or feelings in guiding one's behavior. (Reardon)

Hedonic treadmill   Ability to adapt to positive experiences that requires more and more of the experience in order to feel the same level of happiness that was experienced initially. (Seligman)

Heterosexuals   Those persons who become physically and/or emotionally attracted to those of the opposite gender. (Winfeld)

High-performance work practices   Management policies and practices (e.g., open communications, information sharing, performance-based pay systems, empowered teams, and extensive training opportunities) that focus on developing and making the most effective use of an organization's human assets. (Cascio)

Highly reliable organizations (HROs)   Organizations that operate under very trying conditions all the time, yet manage to have fewer than their fair share of accidents. Examples include power grid dispatching centers, air traffic control systems, nuclear aircraft carriers, nuclear power plants, hospital emergency departments, and hostage negotiation teams. (Weick and Sutcliffe)

Hindsight bias   Inability to look objectively at a decision's outcome and to have anticipated the consequences of a decision, resulting in decision makers overestimating how well a problem or outcomes from a problem could have been anticipated. (Murnighan and Mowen)

Homosexuals   Those persons who become physically and/or emotionally attracted to those of the same gender. (Winfeld)

Hope   An emotional state accompanied by clear thoughts about what the future can be and how to get there that enables people to believe that their future vision is attainable, and to move toward their visions and goals while inspiring others toward those goals as well. (Boyatzis and McKee)

Hundred-year manager   Manager who leads the business and makes decisions based upon the belief that the company will still be operating one hundred years from now. (Csikszentmihalyi)

Illusion of control   Decision maker acting (reinstate) as thouth he or she can influence purely chance events. (Murnighan and Mowen)

Illusion of correlation   Condition occurring when decision makers focus exclusively on the cell in the matrix that corresponds with a "hit," while ignoring how many times they were wrong. (Murnighan and Mowen)

Illusion of performance   Attributing internal factors (oneself) as the explanation for good outcomes and attributing external factors as the explanation for bad outcomes in greater proportion than merited by the facts. (Murnighan and Mowen)

Illusion of the run   The concept of regression to the mean as the probable outcome, due to the fact that chance is one of the factors in affecting success and failure. (Murnighan and Mowen)

Illusions of causality   Various flawed mental processes that lead the decision maker to inaccurately conclude that causality exists when it does not or that there is no causality when it does exist. (Murnighan and Mowen)

Inclusion breakthrough   When an organization creates a culture in which every individual is valued as a unique and vital component of the organization's success. (Miller and Katz)

Inclusive competencies   Workplace behaviors that encourage communicating across differences, resolving conflict, and valuing every individual as a unique contributor to the organization's mission. (Miller and Katz)

Innovation   The process of transforming discoveries into products, goods, and services. (Drucker)

Inside-out management   Commitment derived from energies internal to human beings that are activated because getting a job done is intrinsically rewarding. (Argyris)

Institutional-building pride   Intrinsic pride that is based on emotional commitment that tends to further collective rather than strictly individual sets of interest. (Katzenbach)

Integration   Creating conditions at work such that individuals can best achieve their own goals by directing their efforts toward the success of the enterprise. (McGregor); Realizing that however unique and independent people are, they are also completely enmeshed in networks of relationships with other human beings. (Csikszentmihalyi)

Integrity   An unwavering adherence to principles on which mutual trust can be based. (Csikszentmihalyi); The ability to do the right thing, which is comprised of three components: ambition, competence, and a moral compass. (Bennis and Thomas)

Intentional change   Deliberate, focused identification of one's personal vision and current reality, and conscious creation of and engaging in a learning agenda. (Boyatzis and McKee)

Interdependence   Mutual dependence that creates a reciprocal relationship between independent entities. (Buckingham)

Intermediary   In the management context, managers act as intermediaries, taking the employee's talents and distributing them to the organization in pursuit of organizational goals. The manager must understand the talents of the employee and the needs of the organization to create a good match. (Buckingham)

Intersexual   A person whose biological sex attributes may be classically male or classically female or a mixture of both, but whose gender identity is fluid and is comfortable and happy with that fluidity. (Winfeld)

Intrinsic motivation   Factors such as job design, meaningful tasks, and feeling trusted that provide an internal source of satisfaction for employees because the reward comes from within. (Ventrice)

Intrinsic rewards   Rewards that come from internal sources, generating positive emotions such as initiative and commitment. (Thomas)

Knowledge workers   Employees with high levels of education, skills, and competencies. (Drucker)

L.E.A.D.E.R.S. Method   A model of leadership that focuses on seven critical leadership skills, including Listen to learn, Empathize with emotions, Attend to aspirations, Diagnose and detail, Engage for good ends, Respond with respectfulness, and Speak with specificity. (Dean)

Leadership capacity   The amount of leadership time and talent available to a group or organization at a specific point in time. (Katzenbach)

Leadership characteristics   A desired combination of heart, purpose, values, relationships, and self-discipline. (George)

Learning   A means to find pitfalls that made a decision fail to meet expectations. (Nutt)

Learning disability   A way of thinking in organizations that keeps managers and others from making necessary changes and adapting to environmental needs. (Senge)

Level 5 leader   A person who builds enduring greatness through a paradoxical combination of personal humility plus professional will and fearlessness. (Collins)

Leveraging diversity   A strategy based on the belief that diversity can be found in all individuals because of each person's unique background, experiences, and perspectives and when acknowledged unleashes the power of human creativity. (Miller and Katz)

LGBT   Lesbian, gay, bisexual, transgender. Sometimes an "S" is added as well (LGBTS), to be inclusive of Straight persons. (Winfeld)

Limbic center   The "emotional center" of the brain that sorts incoming messages based on their relevance to human needs. (Lawrence and Nohria)

Listening to pain   The core competence of the toxin handler that involves listening with compassion and providing a moment of human connection. (Frost)

Logotherapy   A method (developed by Viktor Frankl) by which the therapist helps the client become fully aware of his or her freedom of choice. (Pattakos)

Losers   Companies that lagged peers in both periods. (Joyce, Nohria, and Roberson)

Low-end disruptions   The process of attacking the least profitable and most over-served customers at the low end of the original value network. (Christensen)

Management by objectives (MBO)   A process where employees set goals, justify them, determine resources needed to accomplish them, establish timetables for their completion, and perform accordingly. These goals reflect the overall objectives of the organization. (Drucker)

Management structure   The way managers divide, share, coordinate, and evaluate the work they do in planning and organizing the firm's overall operations. (Drucker)

Manager-led teams   Teams who merely perform the task by carrying out the instructions of their manager or leader. (Hackman)

Mindful anticipation   The useful mindset resulting from a preoccupation with potential failure,

reluctance to simplify interpretations, and sensitivity to operations that enables HROs to respond effectively to unexpected events. (Weick and Sutcliffe)

Mindfulness   The capacity to be fully aware of all that one experiences inside the self—body, mind, heart, spirit—and to pay full attention to what is happening around us—the people, the natural world, our surroundings, and events. (Boyatzis and McKee)

Mind-mapping   A technique for expanding thought and encouraging insight by identifying a number of potential options and omitting ones that seem too risky. (Reardon)

Mission-driven organization   An organization that utilizes its mission statement as an integral part of managing the organization, not merely a plaque that hangs on the CEO's wall. (George)

Mobilization   The process of shaking up, or unfreezing, an organization to make it clear that change is needed. (Kaplan and Norton)

Model I   The management theory that individuals use to protect themselves, while unilaterally treating others in the same (undifferentiated) way. (Argyris)

Model II   The management theory that relies upon valid information, free and informed choice, and internal commitment. (Argyris)

Moral compass   The ability to differentiate good and evil, along with the recognition that leaders do not live their lives alone. (Bennis and Thomas)

Moral competence   The skill of doing the right and moral thing (i.e., the action itself). (Lennick and Kiel)

Moral intelligence   The mental capacity to determine how universal human principles should be applied to our values, goals, and actions. (Lennick and Kiel)

Multi-tracking   The process of taking information from a variety of sources. (Reardon)

Neoteny   The youthful, almost puppy-like quality that attracts others to an individual. It is to have energy, to stimulate and enjoy being stimulated, to be curious, to have a contagious laugh, and to feel alive. (Bennis and Thomas)

New logic organization   A firm with a set of strategies for the pursuit of an organization's objectives that stress product- and customer-focused designs, the effective use of human resources, participatory business involvement, and performance-based compensation systems. (Lawler)

New-design plants   Organization-wide approaches to participative management in which group members participate in selection decisions, the layout facilitates workgroup tasks, job design revolves around teams, and pay systems are egalitarian. (Lawler)

New-market disruptions   The process of creating new value networks and products that are more affordable to own. (Christensen)

Noble purpose   An organization's awareness of its greater purpose, of its destiny, and its understanding of the role it needs to fulfill. (Kleiner)

Openness   Willingness to address issues, speak one's mind, and listen to others' ideas. (LaFasto and Larson)

Optimism   A tendency to expect the best possible outcome or dwell on the most hopeful aspects of a situation. (Buckingham)

Organizational restructuring   Planned changes in a firm's organizational structure that affect its use of people, including the possibility of workforce reductions. (Cascio)

Owning up   Admitting to errors or flaws in a decision-making process. (Nutt)

Partnership relationship   A highly effective method of creating and maintaining high levels of long-term organization performance in which a bond develops among adults working collaboratively toward common, long-term goals and having a genuine concern for each other's interests and needs. (Sirota, Mischkind, and Meltzer)

Peak performers   Any group of employees whose emotional commitment enables them to deliver products or services that constitute a sustainable competitive advantage for their employers. (Katzenbach)

Peer recognition   Formal or informal efforts by co-workers to praise employees for their positive contributions at work. (Ventrice)

Performance-based pay   Compensation systems that reward individuals based on the extent to which their behaviors and outcomes contribute to the achievement of organizational goals. (Lawler)

Play   The introduction of joy, fun, and enthusiasm into a work environment. (Lundin, Paul, and Christensen)

Positive personal style   An attitude and disposition portraying energy, optimism, confidence, and fun. (LaFasto and Larson)

Power culture   An organizational culture that depends on a central source of power, typically the organization's founder, that spreads throughout the organization. (Robbins)

Power curve   Relationship between time and the effects of taking action. (Murnighan and Mowen)

Power stress   A unique brand of leadership stress that stems from choices that are unclear, the incredible complexity of communication and decision making, the need to lead with ambiguous authority, and loneliness at the top. As a result of power stress, leaders may become dispirited, forget their own deeply held values, act out in unhealthy ways, or burn out completely. (Boyatzis and McKee)

Preventative environmental management   An approach that emphasizes pollution prevention and reduced consumption of resources. (Robbins)

Primal leadership   The theory that leadership effectiveness is rooted in the primordial regions of our brain governing our ability to perceive and identify our emotional states. (Goleman, Boyatzis, and McKee)

Principled leadership   Corporate leadership ensures that all of the firm's operations meet or exceed standards developed in accordance with publicly stated principles and values. (Batstone)

Problem   The difference between what is actually happening and what you want to happen. (Blanchard and Johnson)

Process gain   The increment that occurs when the collective efforts of the team exceed what the individual members could have achieved working independently. (Hackman)

Process loss   The deficiency that occurs when a group accomplishes less than it theoretically should, given its resources and member talents. (Hackman)

Processes   The patterns of interaction, coordination, communication, and decision making through which inputs are transformed into outputs. (Christensen)

Productivity   Employee output in terms of the quantity and quality of work completed. (Blanchard and Johnson)

Professional intimacy   Working in a way that honors the integrity of the position, the person, and the organization at a level of connection deeper than normal. (Frost)

Quiet crisis   The steady erosion of America's science and engineering dominance, educational competitive advantage, work ethic, and creativity. The trend line is evident but the consequences for competitiveness are gradual and often not perceived. (Friedman)

Rapid cognition   The act of unconscious decision making, in which situational decision-making clues are gathered quickly by the adaptive unconscious and a decision is made based on limited information. This process is not intentional. (Gladwell)

Rational decision-making model   A decision-making process that involves defining a problem, generating a range of potential solutions, testing the solutions against predetermined criteria, and choosing and implementing the best alternative. (Thomas and Inkson)

Rationality   A way of thinking about a decision that stresses analysis and logic. (Nutt)

Recognition   A personalized acknowledgment of an employee's accomplishments toward organizational goals. (Ventrice)

Reframing   Informally or formally translating communications in the organization in such a way that emotional pain will be reduced or deflected from reaching the intended audience. (Frost)

Renewal   A conscious holistic process (involving body, mind, heart, and spirit) that helps people step out of destructive patterns to renew themselves physically, mentally and emotionally. (Boyatzis and McKee)

Reprimand   Negative verbal feedback provided when undesirable employee behavior and performance occur. (Blanchard and Johnson)

Resonant leaders   Individuals who are awake, aware, and attuned to themselves, to others, and to their world; they chart the path, inspire people, create hope in the face of fear and despair, and move people powerfully, passionately, and purposefully while giving of and caring for themselves so they can sustain resonance over time. (Boyatzis and McKee)

Resonant leadership   The ability to move others in a positive direction by being responsive to their feelings. (Goleman, Boyatzis, and McKee)

Responsible restructuring   An alternative to "slash and burn" workforce reductions, wherein employee' ideas and efforts form the basis of sustained competitive advantage by addressing underlying competitive problems. (Cascio)

Restraint   The art of feeling good later. (Forni)

Risk ratio   A formula used to quantitatively determine where the trigger for decision making should be set, determined by dividing the value of a needless blunder by the sum of the value of a needless blunder + the value of a missed opportunity. (Murnighan and Mowen)

Robust dialogue   The candid exchange of information and feelings, requiring open minds, a desire to hear new information, extensive questioning, critical thinking, and a drive toward closure. (Bossidy)

Role clarity   Clear understanding of one's responsibilities as a team member, both within oneself and by others. (LaFasto and Larson)

Role culture   An organizational culture where the role or job description is more important than the individual who fills it (a typical bureaucracy). (Robbins)

Role of malice   The actions of managers that are designed to degrade others or to undermine the confidence or self-esteem of others. Creating pain may be a source of control to ensure there are no challenges to authority. (Frost)

Root cause analysis   Process used to help accurately determine the underlying cause(s) for a problem while minimizing biases such as the illusion of causality. (Murnighan and Mowen)

Sacrifice syndrome   A trap that leaders may fall into when they sacrifice too much for too long and reap too little, resulting in exhaustion, burning out, or burning up. (Boyatzis and McKee)

Safe zones   Created spaces where toxin handlers are moved out of the stressful situations within the organization for a period of time in order to let them re-energize and rest. (Frost)

Selective adaptation   Choice of a method or action that accommodates identified conditions rather than ignoring or going against those facts. (McGregor)

Self-actualizing employees   Those persons who institute their own ideas, make autonomous decisions, learn from their mistakes, and grow in their capabilities. (Maslow)

Self-designing teams   Teams who perform, self-manage, and also design the team and its organizational context. (Hackman)

Self-detachment   Distancing oneself from something. (Pattakos)

Self-efficacy   A person's belief about their own general competence, their sense of power in affecting outcomes, and control over events. (Boyatzis and McKee)

Self-expression   A balance between self-efface-ment and self-indulgence. (Forni)

Self-governing teams   Teams who perform a task, self-manage, and design themselves as well as establish the overall direction of the team. (Hackman)

Self-managed teams (SMTs)   Teams of workers who, with their supervisors, are delegated vari-ous managerial functions to perform and the authority and resources needed to carry them out. (Sirota, Mischkind, and Meltzer)

Self-managing teams   Teams who perform a task as well as monitor and manage work process and progress. (Hackman)

Self-serving pride   Individualistic pride that comes from drives for power, ego, and materi-alism. (Katzenbach)

Set range   Fixed range of happiness a person experiences that is determined primarily by heredity. (Seligman)

Sexual orientation   The propensity that deter-mines to whom you will become physically and/or emotionally attracted (heterosexual, homosexual, bisexual, asexual). (Winfeld)

Shared vision   The capacity to create and hold a shared picture of the future across a set of individuals. (Senge)

Signature strength   A strength that is measur-able, acquirable, demonstrated across situa-tions, leads a person to feel gratified, is valued by most cultures, and is not a means to another end. (Seligman)

Social loafer   A passive group member who fails to carry one's weight and relies on others for progress and results. (LaFasto and Larson)

Social operating mechanisms   Formal or informal interactions where integrative dialogue occurs such that barriers are broken down and people learn how to work together in constructive debate. (Bossidy)

Social responsibility   The contribution a firm makes to its society. To some, this means mak-ing a profit, while others expect the firm to do more than this by ameliorating social problems. (Drucker)

Soul   The energy a person or organization devotes to purposes beyond itself. (Csikszentmihalyi)

Sour spot   A highly contested market position affording incumbents little opportunity to con-trol the five classic industry forces. (Marcus)

Span of control   The number of subordinates reporting directly to a supervisor. (Thomas)

Stockdale paradox   The capacity by some execu-tives to simultaneously confront the most brutal facts of their current reality while maintaining faith that they will prevail in the end. (Collins)

Strategic environmental management   An approach that incorporates environmental goals into the overall economic strategy of the corporation, often anticipating and pursuing potential green markets. (Robbins)

Strategic intent   The overall guide that an organization uses to decide how it will create value and design itself. (Lawler and Worley)

Strategy map   A logical relationship diagram that specifies the relationship among shareholders, customers, business processes, and an organ-ization's competencies. (Kaplan and Norton)

Summum bonum (chief good)   The belief that whereas people desire other goods (such as money or power) because they believe those things will make them happy, they really want happiness for its own sake. (Csikszentmihalyi)

Supportiveness   A desire and demonstrated willingness to help others succeed. (LaFasto and Larson)

Sustainable development management   An approach that blends economic, social, and environmental goals. An organization sub-scribing to this philosophy often takes environ-mental leadership roles in the industry and typically incorporates environmental pro-grams across the entire organization. (Robbins)

Sustained individual success   Using the talents in work that a person finds rewarding and fulfill-ing over a long period of time. (Buckingham)

Sustaining innovations   A strategy that offers demanding high-end customers better perfor-mance than that which was previously available. (Christensen)

Sweet spot   An attractive market position char-acterized by a lack of direct competition, and presenting incumbents with the opportunity to control the five classic industry forces. (Marcus)

Synergy   Working together, cooperating, com-bining in a cooperative action to yield an out-come that is greater than the sum of its parts, (Covey); Revenue enhancement or cost reduc-tions achieved by increasing markets or shar-ing services across product lines or business units. (Kaplan and Norton)

Team basics The five elements necessary to achieve real team performance: size, purpose and goals, skills, working approach, and mutual accountability. (Katzenbach)

Theories in use The actual rules or master programs that individuals use to achieve control. (Argyris)

Theory X A set of assumptions that explains some human behavior and has influenced conventional principles of management. It assumes that workers want to avoid work and must be controlled and coerced to accept responsibility and exert effort toward organizational objectives. (McGregor)

Theory Y A set of assumptions offered as an alternative to Theory X. Theory Y assumes that work is a natural activity, and given the right conditions, people will seek responsibility and apply their capacities to organizational objectives without coercion. (McGregor)

Thin-slicing The ability of the unconscious mind to find patterns in situations and behavior based on very narrow slices of experience. (Gladwell)

Three factor theory of human motivation A model that asserts that there are three primary sets of goals of people at work—equity, achievement, and camaraderie. (Sirota, Mischkind, and Meltzer)

Time fence Action that would lead to long-term gains is stopped because it also causes short-term negative outcomes (the opposite of a time snare). (Murnighan and Mowen)

Time snare Problem occurring when decision makers let the prospect of short-term positive outcomes cause an action that leads to long-term negative outcomes. (Murnighan and Mowen)

Tipping point A seemingly innocuous event that could be the tripwire that pushes the system over the edge and creates a serious problem; a small change that can result in a large, sudden, and dramatic effect that can multiply geometrically. (Murnighan and Mowen)

Topicality shift Knowing how and when to introduce a new concept into a conversation. (Reardon)

Tough decisions A class of decisions that have ambiguity, uncertainty, and conflict. (Nutt)

Tough love The leadership practice of living in the balance of being both simultaneously compassionate/concerned and assertive/bold. (Quinn)

Toxic tandem A toxic boss who has a toxic handler regularly by his or her side. (Frost)

Toxin handlers Those leaders, managers, and staff that tend to the emotional pain of the people in the organization and work to bring harmony and balance and remove stress and tension. (Frost)

Transgender Umbrella term that includes transsexuals, intersexuals, cross-dressers, transgenderists, and androgynes. (Winfeld)

Transgenderists Transsexual people who choose not to have sex-reassignment surgery. They usually cross-live and take part in hormonal therapy that causes certain sex-characteristic changes. (Winfeld)

Transparency All of the firm's products are honestly presented and its operations are visible to any and all stakeholders. (Batstone)

Transsexuals People whose gender identity does not match their biological gender and are motivated to transition their gender so that it matches their gender identity through sex-reassignment. (Winfeld)

Triple convergence The intersection of web-enabled technologies, workflow software that allowed extensive collaboration with customers, and information access and participation to people of the closed economies, including China, Russia, and India. This is a critical and essential driver of the flattening of the world. (Friedman)

Tumblers Companies who exhibited better-than-peer performance in the first period, followed by underperformance in the second. (Joyce, Nohria, and Roberson)

Uncertainty Doubt about the magnitude of future conditions, such as interest rates. (Nutt)

Undiscussables Topics or processes in decision making that managers believe should be withheld from debate. (Nutt)

Unexpected event The negative surprise that occurs when either expected strategy or performance outcomes fail to materialize or when unexpected impediments to strategy and performance materialize. (Weick and Sutcliffe)

Uniqueness The skills, abilities, personality traits, attitudes, and aptitudes that are present in different amounts and combinations in each person. (Buckingham)

Untouchables People whose jobs cannot easily be outsourced to another country because they are *specialized*, such as surgeons or other knowledge workers whose work is not easily transferred to another location. There are other jobs that may be *anchored* to a particular location, such as a waitress or plumber. (Friedman)

Value chain   The discrete value-producing activities within a firm that are potential sources of competitive advantage. (Porter)

Value network   The context within which a firm establishes a cost structure and operating processes with suppliers and partners. (Christensen)

Values   The standards by which employees make prioritized decisions. (Christensen)

Virtual organizations   Companies that have groups of individuals working on shared tasks while distributed across space, time, and/or organizational boundaries. (Beyerlein, Freedman, McGee, and Moran)

Virtues   The six components (wisdom and knowledge, courage, love and humanity, justice, temperance, spirituality and transcendence) that when taken together describe a person of good character. (Seligman)

Virtuous spiral   The ultimate competitive advantage, it is a win-win relationship that is a source of positive momentum that creates higher and higher levels of individual and organizational performance. (Lawler); A potentially powerful competitive advantage produced when both critical configuration and dynamic alignment exist for long periods of time. (Lawler and Worley)

Vision   A vivid mental image of a potential future for an organization, which can include possible goals, products, customers, etc. (Buckingham)

Warrior spirit   A deep emotional commitment that causes important segments of a workforce to emerge as the enterprise's primary competitive advantage; engendering that spirit demands resurgent sources of emotional energy and clear channels, or management approaches, for aligning that energy. (Katzenbach)

What-if questioning   Examining key assumptions about payoffs to determine the risk in adopting an alternative. (Nutt)

Will to meaning   The authentic commitment to meaningful values and goals (a basic human drive) that only individuals can actualize. (Pattakos)

Winners   Companies outperforming their peers in both periods of examination. (Joyce, Nohria, and Roberson)

Workforce   All of the employees across the baseline of the organization who either make the products, design the services, or deliver the value to the customer. (Katzenbach)

Working group   Any small group collaborating to accomplish a common purpose or goal. (Katzenbach)

Zero-defects   The idea, arising from Total Quality Management principles, that the ultimate goal of continuous improvement is to have absolutely no errors made. (Thomas)

Bibliography of Inclusions

Argyris, Chris (2000). *Flawed Advice and the Management Trap*. New York: Oxford University Press, Inc.

Batstone, David (2003). *Saving the Corporate Soul & (Who Knows?) Maybe Your Own*. San Francisco: Jossey-Bass.

Bennis, Warren G., and Thomas, Robert J. (2002). *Geeks & Geezers: How Era, Values, and Defining Moments Shape Leaders*. Boston: Harvard Business School Press.

Beyerlein, Michael M., Freedman, Sue, McGee, Craig, and Moran, Linda (2003). *Beyond Teams: Building the Collaborative Organization*. San Francisco: Jossey-Bass/Pfeiffer.

Blanchard, Kenneth, and Johnson, Spencer (1981). *The One Minute Manager*. LaJolla, CA: Blanchard-Johnson.

Bossidy, Larry, and Charan, Ram, with Charles Burck (2002). *Execution: The Discipline of Getting Things Done*. New York: Crown Business.

Boyatzis, Richard and McKee, Annie (2005). *Resonant Leadership: Renewing Yourself and Connecting with Others Through Mindfulness, Hope, and Compassion*. Boston: Harvard Business School Press.

Buckingham, Marcus (2005). *The One Thing You Need to Know . . . About Great Managing, Great Leading, and Sustained Individual Success*. New York: Free Press.

Cascio, Wayne F. (2003). *Responsible Restructuring: Creative and Profitable Alternatives to Layoffs*. San Francisco: Berrett-Koehler.

Christensen, Clayton M., Raynor, Michael E., and Anthony, Scott D. (2003). *The Innovator's Solution: Creating and Sustaining Successful Growth*. Boston: Harvard Business School Press.

Collins, James C. (2001). *Good to Great: Why Some Companies Make the Leap . . . And Others Don't*. Cambridge, MA: Harvard Business School Press.

Covey, Stephen R. (1989). *The Seven Habits of Highly Effective People: Restoring the Character Ethic*. New York: Simon and Schuster.

Covey, Stephen R. (2004). *The 8th Habit: From Effectiveness to Greatness*. New York: Free Press.

Csikszentmihalyi, Mihaly (2003). *Good Business: Leadership, Flow, and the Making of Meaning*. New York: Penguin Putnam.

Dean, Peter J. (2006). *Leadership for Everyone: How to Apply the Seven Essential Skills to Become a Great Motivator, Influencer, and Leader*. New York: McGraw-Hill.

Deming, W. Edwards (1986). *Out of the Crisis*. Cambridge, MA: MIT Press.

Drucker, Peter F. (1954). *The Practice of Management*. New York: Harper and Row.

Forni, P. M. (2003). *Choosing Civility: The Twenty-Five Rules of Considerate Conduct*. New York: St. Martin's Press.

Friedman, Thomas (2005). *The World Is Flat: A Brief History of the Twenty-first Century*. New York: Farrar, Strauss, and Giroux.

Frost, Peter J. (2003). *Toxic Emotions at Work: How Compassionate Managers Handle Pain and Conflict*. Boston: Harvard Business School Press.

George, Bill (2003). *Authentic Leadership: Rediscovering the Secrets to Creating Lasting Value*. San Francisco: Jossey-Bass.

Gladwell, Malcolm (2005). *Blink! The Power of Thinking Without Thinking*. New York: Little, Brown.

Goleman, Daniel, Boyatzis, Richard, and McKee, Annie (2002). *Primal Leadership: Realizing the Power of Emotional Intelligence*. Boston: Harvard Business School Press.

Hackman, J. Richard (2002). *Leading Teams: Setting the Stage for Great Performances*. Boston: Harvard Business School Press.

Johnson, Spencer, M.D. (1998). *Who Moved My Cheese? An Amazing Way to Deal with Change in Your Work and Your Life*. New York: Putnam Books.

Joyce, William, Nohria, Nitin, and Roberson, Bruce (2003). *What (Really) Works: The 4 + 2 Formula for Sustained Business Success*. New York: Harper Collins.

Kaplan, Robert S. and Norton, David P. (2001). *The Strategy-Focused Organization: How Balanced Scorecard Companies Thrive in the New Business Environment*. Cambridge, MA: Harvard Business School Press.

Katzenbach, Jon R. (2003). *Why Pride Matters More than Money: The Power of the World's Greatest Motivational Force*. New York: Crown Business.

Kellerman, Barbara (2004). *Bad Leadership: What It Is, How It Happens, Why It Matters*. Boston: Harvard Business School Press.

Kleiner, Art (2003). *Who Really Matters: The Core Group Theory of Power, Privilege, and Success*. New South Wales, Australia: Currency.

LaFasto, Frank and Larson, Carl (2002). *When Teams Work Best: 6,000 Team Members and Leaders Tell What It Takes to Succeed*. Thousand Oaks, CA: Sage Publications.

Lawler, Edward E., III, (2003) *Treat People Right! How Organizations and Individuals Can Propel Each Other into a Virtuous Spiral of Success*. San Francisco: Jossey-Bass.

Lawler, Edward E., III, and Worley, Christopher G. (2003). *Built to Change: How to Achieve Sustained Organizational Effectiveness*. San Francisco: Jossey-Bass.

Lawrence, Paul R. and Nohria, Nitin (2002). *Driven: How Human Nature Shapes Our Choices*. San Francisco: Jossey-Bass.

Lennick, Doug and Kiel, Fred (2005). *Moral Intelligence: Enhancing Business Performance and Leadership Success*. Pennsylvania: Wharton School Publishing.

Lundin, Stephen C., Paul, Harry, and Christensen, John (2000). *Fish! A Remarkable Way to Boost Morale and Improve Results*. New York: Hyperion.

Marcus, Alfred (2005). *Big Winners and Big Losers: The 4 Secrets of Long-Term Business Success and Failure*. Pennsylvania: Wharton School Publishing.

Maslow, Abraham H. (1998). *Maslow on Management*. New York: John Wiley & Sons.

McGregor, Douglas (1960). *The Human Side of Enterprise*. New York: McGraw-Hill.

Miller, Frederick A. and Katz, Judith H. (2002). *The Inclusion Breakthrough: Unleashing the Real Power of Diversity*. San Francisco: Berrett-Koehler.

Murnighan, J. Keith and Mowen, John C. (2002). *The Art of High-Stakes Decision-Making: Tough Calls in a Speed-Driven World*. New York: John Wiley & Sons.

Nutt, Paul C. (2002). *Why Decisions Fail: Avoiding the Blunders and Traps That Lead to Debacles*. San Francisco: Berrett-Koehler.

Pattakos, Alex (2004). *Prisoners of Our Thoughts: Viktor Frankl's Principles at Work*. San Francisco: Berrett-Koehler.

Porter, Michael E. (1985). *Competitive Advantage: Creating and Sustaining Superior Performance*. New York: Free Press.

Quinn, Robert E. (2004). *Building the Bridge as You Walk on It : A Guide for Leading Change*. San Francisco: Jossey-Bass.

Reardon, Kathleen Kelley (2005). *It's All Politics: Winning in a World Where Hard Work and Talent Aren't Enough*. New York: Currency Books.

Robbins, Peter Thayer (2001). *Greening the Corporation: Management Strategy and the Environmental Challenge*. London: Earthscan Publications.

Seligman, Martin E. P. (2002). *Authentic Happiness: Using the New Positive Psychology to Realize Your Potential for Lasting Fulfillment*. New York: Free Press.

Senge, Peter M. (1990). *The Fifth Discipline: The Art and Practice of the Learning Organization.* New York: Doubleday.

Sirota, David, Mischkind, Louis A., and Meltzer, Michael Irwin (2005). *The Enthusiastic Employee: How Companies Profit by Giving Employees What They Want.* Pennsylvania: Wharton School Publishing.

Thomas, David C. and Inkson, Kerr (2004). *Cultural Intelligence: People Skills for Global Business.* San Francisco: Berrett-Koehler.

Thomas, Kenneth W. (2000). *Intrinsic Motivation at Work: Building Energy & Commitment.* San Francisco: Berrett-Koehler.

Ventrice, Cindy (2003). *Make Their Day! Employee Recognition That Works.* San Francisco: Berrett-Koehler.

Weick, Karl E. and Kathleen M. Sutcliffe (2001). *Managing the Unexpected: Assuring High Performance in an Age of Complexity.* San Francisco: Jossey-Bass.

Winfeld, Liz (2005). *Straight Talk About Gays in the Workplace: Creating an Inclusive, Productive Environment for Everyone in Your Organization.* Binghamton, NY: Harrington Park Press.

Index